Rashid's Legacy

Published by Media Prima

Europe Office:
29 Harley Street
London, W1G 9QR
Great Britain
Tel: (+44 207) 6124118
Fax: (+44 207) 1827078

Middle East Office:
PO Box 29997
Dubai, UAE
Tel: (+971 4) 3452020
Fax: (+971 4) 3450707
Email: *administration@mediaprima.ae*

Copyright © Graeme Wilson 2006
First edition: *Father of Dubai* © 1999
Ministry permission number: 242/06/03/06
Editor: Barbara Saunders
Additional Editors: Mike Simon, Susan Wilson,
Roger Thiedeman
Historical review: Dr Fatma Al Sayegh
Research: Elie Moukarzel
Production: Leslie Cox

Extracts from *Arabian Sands* by Wilfred Thesiger
and *Dubai: An Arabian Album* by Ronald Codrai are
reproduced with the permission of Motivate
Publishing, Dubai, UAE

Colour reproduction and printing by
Emirates Printing Press, Dubai, UAE

RASHID'S
LEGACY

The Genesis of the Maktoum Family
and the History of Dubai

by Graeme Wilson

**Media
Prima**

Foreword

HH Sheikh Hamdan bin Rashid Al Maktoum
UAE Minister of Finance and Industry
Deputy Ruler of Dubai

A generation ago my father, the late Sheikh Rashid bin Saeed Al Maktoum, began an odyssey to change the fortunes of his people and nation. He surrounded himself with the best and brightest, and utilised an uncanny instinct for big business and major development initiatives. He ruled Dubai from 1958 to 1990, taking his city-state from a relative backwater and laying foundations for the 21st century.

It was a remarkable testimonial that, on his passing, the United Nations Security Council stood in a minute of silence in his honour. When Sheikh Rashid began his reign, few people in our isolated lands had even heard of the United Nations.

My brothers and I inherited the foundations of modern Dubai. But, just as importantly, we inherited a legacy from him, a blueprint of what it meant to be an enlightened and progressive leader. As I have written before, he was a man who was wise, decisive, compassionate, practical and pragmatic. These were traits that he strove to instill in his sons, family, friends and the citizens of Dubai and the UAE.

On the recent passing of my brother, Sheikh Maktoum bin Rashid Al Maktoum, I was left to reflect on the qualities that he brought to ruling Dubai and the great progress that was made under his leadership. Their imprint remains in everything that myself, Sheikh Mohammed and Sheikh Ahmed do. I speak for them when I say that we will strive to continue to build upon the legacy of Sheikh Rashid and Sheikh Maktoum.

Hamdan bin Rashid Al Maktoum
March 2006

Contents

Camelot

Do not let it be forgot,
That once there was a spot,
For one brief, shining moment that was known as Camelot.
— Anon

Camelot was the most famous castle in the medieval legends of King Arthur Penhaligon. It was where, according to legend, he reigned over Britain before the Saxon conquest. At Camelot, King Arthur established a brilliant court and seated there the greatest and most chivalrous warriors in Europe – the Knights of the Round Table. Camelot was the starting point of the Quest for the Holy Grail and, by the 1200s, it came to symbolise the centre of the Arthurian world. It was a place of culture and the arts. In a backward, medieval world, Camelot was a beacon of human progress and culture.

Then, seven centuries later, Camelot resurfaced in popular, modern culture. This time it was not in Saxon England, but within the glamour and style of the Kennedy White House. JFK surrounded himself with the best and brightest of America's scientists, theologians, literates and thinkers. Then JFK was taken away on that infamous day in Dallas and his legacy dissolved into legend.

Around the same time that Kennedy was reinventing the Camelot concept, in a tiny sheikhdom on the Arabian Peninsula, a Ruler named Sheikh Rashid bin Saeed Al Maktoum was inviting comparisons through his style of leadership. Of course the White House existed in a somewhat different sphere of influence, but nonetheless the analogy held true. Indeed, the Camelot Sheikh Rashid created would go on to have a far greater impact upon Dubai and its future than the Kennedy White House, even allowing for the dream of man walking on the moon that would ultimately be JFK's legacy.

Sheikh Rashid was a man of simple origins. Yet, paradoxically, his responsibilities would require him to bridge an extraordinary era, as he took his sheikhdom from a bankrupt 1930s fishing and pearling village in the 1930s to the modernity of the 1980s.

Sheikh Rashid was a wily and resourceful leader who understood that the tasks he faced were more than any single man could tackle. He drew around him the cream of Dubai society, business leaders and merchants, a hand-picked cadre of young, educated Dubaians, old-school community leaders, artists and poets, and the brightest people he could find, irrespective of nationality. He cared little if some were British or Indians, Arabs or Asians. Everyone sat in the Majlis as an equal, as long as they could contribute toward the progress that he so zealously pursued.

The energy of Sheikh Rashid's Majlis came to be legendary. Dubai's Ruler sat at the heart of a body that bubbled with ideas and concepts. It is something of a cliché, but they really did dare to think the unthinkable. Failure was not an option. Kennedy could dream about placing a man on the moon, but Dubai's Camelot had more fundamental human aims underscoring its existence.

The sheikhdom needed to offer its citizens the hospitals, schools, clean water, electricity, jobs and proper housing, all of which had been denied them for so long under isolationist, de facto colonial rule. Sheikh Rashid fought to overcome the crippling poverty that his people faced in their lives. With limited funds at his disposal he transformed the economy and built an infrastructure that was the envy of the region. His visionary projects were often labelled, even by people within his circle, as White Elephants. Yet without fail they went on to be vital cogs in the wheel of progress.

These projects were part of his legacy to Dubai, a legacy on which Dubai has built its present and future. But the late Ruler did not think only of bricks and mortar, and his plans for the future were not just committed to paper. Sheikh Maktoum, Sheikh Hamdan, Sheikh Mohammed and Sheikh Ahmed were each part of Sheikh Rashid's grand vision. Each was nurtured by his father, groomed with a future place in Dubai's administration in mind. When the Ruler's health faltered, his sons seamlessly carried on from where their father left off.

Sheikh Rashid held his Majlis less frequently following his stroke, but his semi-retirement did not mark the end of the Camelot era. The lessons learned from that heady mix of thinkers and achievers in the Ruler's circle were not lost on this new generation of leaders. All of

Sheikh Rashid's sons drew similar circles around them – the new Camelot generation.

Six years ago, I was privileged to have the opportunity to write a biography of Sheikh Rashid – *Father of Dubai*. It portrayed a remarkable man and his extraordinary life, and was not only the first serious study of Sheikh Rashid, but a vitally important one which redressed the fact that, until then, far too little had been recorded about him. As the members of the Camelot generation which served him grew old, memories became weak and some of those who were part of those dramatic times passed away. We were in danger of losing the essence of this amazing individual.

Since 1999, *Father of Dubai* has been superseded by events. Many people came forward with new information and anecdotes about Sheikh Rashid. And much has changed in the emirate that he left behind. *Rashid's Legacy* is an attempt to marry the plethora of new information with a portrait of the 21st century Dubai, for which Sheikh Rashid laid the foundations, and which his sons have so remarkably developed into one of the most incredible of new millennium cities.

Of course, the tragic passing of Sheikh Maktoum bin Rashid Al Maktoum also presented an opportunity to look back and record his rule, a dramatic period when he and his brothers metamorphasised Dubai. It was a time when the potential that Sheikh Rashid created was realised. History will record Sheikh Maktoum's success — both as a leader and as a man.

Today, the knights of Sheikh Rashid's sons do indeed sit at round tables, but in ultra-modern skyscrapers, a far cry from the mud-walled fort where the dream of a society of well fed, healthy and educated citizens was first nurtured.

Nam et ipsa scientia potestas est

> History will be kind to me, for I intend to write it.
> — *Sir Winston Churchill, statesman*

Inscribed on the wall of the north lobby of The Library of Congress is the Latin phrase *'Nam et ipsa scientia potestas est'*. Sir Francis Bacon said that 'For knowledge itself is power', and it is that search for knowledge of Dubai's history that led to *Rashid's Legacy*. Six years ago, when we launched *Father of Dubai*, this was one of very few books on the history of Dubai and the UAE. Indeed, there were far too few titles on the Arabian Peninsula as a whole. The intervening period has seen an explosion of interest in the region and we have witnessed a limited number of titles grow into a veritable library. A history that was in danger of being lost is now preserved in print.

In Dubai's case, the late Sheikh Rashid bin Saeed Al Maktoum threw himself into a race against time in order to guarantee Dubai's future. He had little interest in the past, or in recording his own endeavours for posterity. Yet he was undoubtedly a genius, and his remarkable life could not be allowed to fade into history without record.

Far greater writers and historians than myself will delve into the history of the emirate and its remarkable family, yet *Rashid's Legacy* will remain a testimonial to the late Ruler of Dubai and his remarkable sons.

I would like to begin *Rashid's Legacy* with reference to some of those who have made this book possible. A publication of this nature and size, some 200,000 words and several hundred photographs in extent, encompassing several years of research and the collective memories of many, would simply not be possible without support.

Sheikh Hamdan bin Rashid Al Maktoum was an inspirational figure in this process, and a clear record of his father and homeland would not have been possible without his support. Also I extend thanks to Sheikh Saqr bin Mohammed Al Qassimi, Sheikh Ahmed bin Rashid Al Maktoum, Sheikh Mansoor bin Zayed Al Nahyan, Sheikh Mohammed bin Khalifa Al Maktoum and Sheikh Ahmed bin Saeed Al Maktoum, for their time and infinite patience.

My work was made possible by Mirza Al Sayegh and this book, in the final analysis, would have been impossible without his vision and personal involvement. We are also indebted to Abdullah Saleh, Hamad bin Sukat, Jamal Huwairib, Sultan bin Sulayem, Maurice Flanagan, Mike Simon, Dr Fatma Al Sayegh, Tawhid Abdullah, George Chapman, William J. Way, Khamis Juma Bu Amim, Shareef Al Halawani and Colm McLoughlin. The Private Office of Queen Elizabeth II and the Royal Photographic Collection at Windsor Castle were most helpful.

During the course of this project we lost a friend in former British Prime Minister Sir Edward Heath. After attending the launch of *Father of Dubai* in 1999, Sir Edward remained in touch regularly and was keenly interested in Dubai and its leadership. He insisted that the narrative of *Father of Dubai* was wrong to end with the death of Sheikh Rashid and that the contemporary success of the emirate was just as anchored in its former Ruler as the achievements recorded during his lifetime. In July 2005, Sir Edward passed away at the age of 89. The project lost a most ardent supporter.

I must also use this opportunity to commend our supporters, for a project of this enormity requires the backing of a cadre of sponsors if it is to succeed. These include the Dubai Petroleum Company, Dubai Duty Free, Emirates, National Bank of Dubai, Damas, Nakheel, Dubai Real Estate Centre and Jebel Ali Racecourse. Without the sense of social responsibility that these organisations have shown, an enterprise such as *Rashid's Legacy* would have been doomed to failure.

It seems far too little just to say thank you. I dedicate my book to those within each of these organisations, with the thought that their support has helped, in some way, to preserve the history of this great emirate and nation for future generations.

Taken from the historic Bayt Al Wakeel house overlooking the Creek. These two photographs are separated by two decades, 1958 to 1978, and show the changing face of the emirate under Sheikh Rashid.

16

Dubai transformed: The Creek is the central artery of the city and its progress has continued to reflect the progress of the emirate as a whole. (inset) A view from the early 1970s. (main photo) Dubai in the 21st Century.

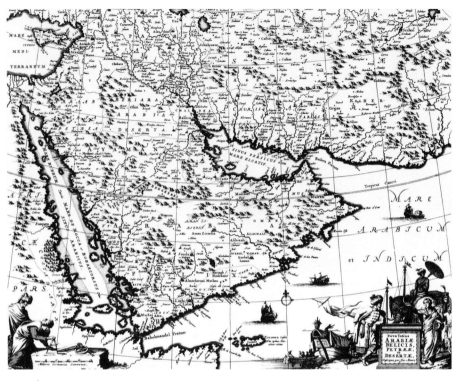

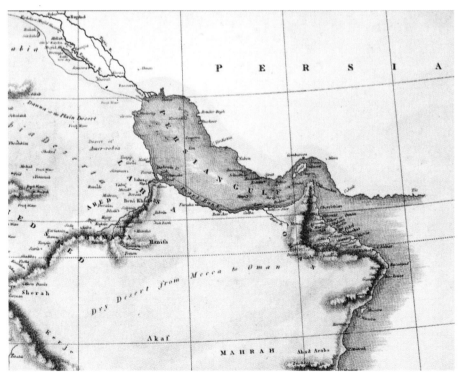

Chapter One

1833

Nine-tenths of wisdom is being wise in time.
- *Theodore Roosevelt, statesman*

Peel back the history of the Arabian Peninsula more than 200 years and one finds largely a blank, a void. For the most part, this is due to the area's lack of strategic importance, not only to the European powers of old but also – surprisingly – to the great Arab cultures, societies that invented modern geography, mathematics and the sciences. Nomadic in nature, little was written of what did happen, leaving much to the imagination as historians try to fill the gaps between the few surviving accounts from travellers and conquerors.

The first traces of human habitation date back nearly to the last Ice Age, in 8,000 BC, while there is abundant evidence that the land mass of the United Arab Emirates (UAE) has been settled since the Late Stone Age when the climate was wetter and more humid than today.

The earliest known inhabitants of the UAE were probably skilled herders, who would have used finely made stone tools. More than likely, they lived along the coasts and on Gulf islands, fishing and shellfish gathering. Remains of many pirogues – canoes made from the trunks of hollowed out trees – have been found.

There is also ample evidence of trade with the outside world, especially with civilisations to the north such as Mesopotamia. Stone tools of the UAE's early inhabitants have been found at dozens of sites from Ghagha' in the west to Khatt in the north. Archaeological investigation in Ras Al Khaimah indicates evidence of human activity at the coastal region of Jazirat Al Hamra. Pottery, beads, net sinkers and flint tools point to a nomadic population living on the coast during the summer months during the Ubaid Period (5,000 to 3,800 BC). This pottery

(opposite page, top) An engraving which appeared in 'A Precise Description of Arabia', published in Holland in 1680. (bottom) An early British map of the peninsula.

shows parallels with Mesopotamia. Also in Ras Al Khaimah are many burial cairns built on high mountain plateaus from the Hafit Period (3,200 to 2,600 BC).

The middle of the third millennium BC saw the rise of the Umm al-Nar Culture (2,600 to 2,000 BC), which was characterised by numerous oasis towns at Hili, Tell Abraq, Bidiya and Kalba, among others, dominated by imposing large, circular fortresses. These agriculturally based settlements were possible because of the domestication of the date palm (Phoenix dactylifera). Some evidence suggests that trade in copper with Mesopotamia and the Indus Valley made the area of the United Arab Emirates wealthy. Excavations on the side of the Juma Valley, near the Dubai enclave of Hatta, have revealed an ancient settlement similar to that at Umm Al Nar.

But it was undoubtedly the domestication of the camel in the late second millennium BC that revolutionised life on the Arabian Peninsula, opening up new possibilities for transport. At the same time, the discovery of the principles of using sub-surface channels to transport water from mountain aquifers to lower lying gardens (falaj) made possible the extensive irrigation of gardens and agricultural plots that resulted in a veritable explosion of settlements. Artifacts point to trade with Mesopotamia, Iran, Baluchistan, and Bactria (Afghanistan). Mesopotamian texts referred to the area as Magan.

The first significant foray into the region by a major power was probably the incursion of Alexander the Great, who dispatched several of his senior generals to scout the Gulf in 325 BC. Although evidence

(opposite page)
Alexander the Great.
(right) Ptolemy.

suggests there were some small settlements – close to the mountains in Ras Al Khaimah and one large base upon Umm Al Nar island in Abu Dhabi – Alexander's interest appears to have faded quickly.

The first cartographic work of the peninsula was the map by the Greek Eratosthenes, produced around 300 BC. This offers little detail other than a rudimentary shape. Around 100 AD Claudius Ptolemaeus (Ptolemy) produced a map, which was at the cutting edge in its detail and accuracy. The Arabian Peninsula is included and in it a region named Icthyophagi, which lies in the area of land now occupied by the United Arab Emirates.

However, along with all subsequent maps produced over the next 1,000 years, this document betrayed a lack of information. Most showed vast rivers that did not exist, while neglecting to portray the Qatari peninsula and Bahrain. None indicated the presence of settlements, although modern archaeological work shows evidence that these existed at various positions on the UAE's coast.

It was the latter half of the second millennium before any serious work was done, and this coincided with the arrival of the European superpowers. First the Portuguese, and later the British and Dutch, entered the Gulf seeking to control the area. Great strides were made in producing the accurate maps these invaders needed.

Many included references to a small village named, among other things, Dubay (or Dubayy) and Dibai. Yet these vague references belie a rich history that is only now fully emerging. Around the eighth century AD, Arabic-speaking Umayyads arrived to spread Islam among the locals, and this seems to have coincided with more permanent settlement in Dubai. Archaeologists have been hard at work in Dubai's Jumeirah district, where evidence suggests a major port and regional trading hub in the ninth century.

"Based on the findings at the Jumeirah site, we have enough reason to believe that this part of Dubai used to be an important trading centre in the region," said Dr Hussein Qandil, the Department of Tourism and Commerce Marketing's head archaeologist.

The Jumeirah site, one of the UAE's largest archaeological sites, was discovered in 1968 and has been preserved for excavation. It was first examined by a team from the American University of Beirut during 1969 and 1970, and then by an Iraqi team in 1975.

Evidence suggests that a town flourished in the ninth and tenth centuries during the Abbasid period in Islamic history. Its era is reflected in its architecture that makes use of arches, towers and carved decorations. Dr Qandil said that his team had found pottery and decorative pieces, indicating they were brought here from as far afield as China, Afghanistan, Mesopotamia and the Far East.

"The pottery's design, decoration and inscriptions indicate that there was good communication and trading between the local residents and the Chinese, Mesopotamians and Afghans," he says. "This area was strategically located when it came to communication between Oman and Mesopotamia. The structure of the houses and the internal settings are very similar. There are traces of geometric and floral designs on the pottery, arches and windows."

Dr Qandil said his team had found two layers of walls in many structures. "I think the buildings were either destroyed or collapsed by the 11th century. Then they rebuilt the new on top of the old," he said.

While this evidence is emerging only now, it can be safely assumed that Dubai's sheltered Creek – actually a tidal basin – had been settled for thousands of years, ever since groups of men first began to fish with nets in communal units. The rich fishing grounds off Dubai are fed by nutritious currents from the Indian Ocean, bringing with them a plethora of fish. This, in addition to the natural harbour, would have made it a good location for families who made their living off the sea.

"Like most Arabian Gulf coastal cities, Dubai was established on land near a creek and fresh water. Creeks provided natural ports for dhows, and the sea was a convenient way of transportation, besides

Some historians contend that Dubai draws its name from a spiney tailed lizard called a Mastigure. Locally, this is called a Dub, or a Dhub.

being a means of providing food and pearl diving," says Rashad M. Bukhash, head of historical buildings section at Dubai Municipality.

Dubai's Creek was well positioned for fishermen, whose boats could shelter there when seas were rough and when strong northerly summer winds, shamals, whipped up sea and sand in violent storms.

The original settlement of Dubai was, in all probability, in Deira and Shindagha, a sand spit at the mouth of the Creek. Al Fahidi Fort is mentioned in government of India dispatches as early as the 1820s. Interestingly, the fort was armed by a handful of Portuguese-made cannons, which remain on display at the restored Dubai Museum to this day. Although they are relics of failed attempts of the Portuguese to dominate the coast, these almost certainly found their way to Dubai at a later date as there were no fortifications built in Dubai at that time.

There is no consensus on how Dubai, or Dibai as it was widely known until relatively recently – and is still known in some quarters – was named. Of two theories widely espoused by historians, the possible favourite is that Dubai is drawn from Dub, or Dhub, the Arabic name for a spiney tailed lizard, known by naturalists as a Mastigure, which was common in the desert of the Lower Gulf, although little known today because they avoid urban areas. Others believe that Dubai is a derivative from an Arabic word meaning 'land devastated by locusts', while some historians believe that the name derives from early descriptions of a place as having "two bays" meaning the Diera and Dubai side of the Creek

"It is impossible to be sure how the name originated," says Sheikh

Mohammed bin Khalifa Al Maktoum. "It can only be conjecture as the true origin of the name is lost in ancient history."

The first written reference to Dubai possibly came from a Venetian jeweller, Gasparo Balbi, who wrote of his travels to Asia in *Viaggio dell'Indie Orientali* (1590). Balbi toured part of the Gulf in order to assess its pearling potential, and his list of place names in the lower Gulf cites Dubai, then a tiny fishing settlement, as 'Dibei'. He travelled from Qatar to Ras Al Khaimah, made reference to the Portuguese fortress at Kalba, and wrote about the Bani Yas in Abu Dhabi. However, it is possible that this reference is to Dibba on the Arabian Sea.

In official Portuguese and British archives there are only passing references to the settlement. It was not until the latter years of the 18th century that the modern sheikhdom started to take shape.

To understand the history of Dubai, its evolution and people, it is important to first understand the fragile political situation that existed throughout much of the second half of the last millennium. The areas that now form the UAE and its desert hinterland were part of what was known as the Coast of Oman, where two major political forces held sway. To the north were lands belonging to the Qawassim. This tribe based itself around the twin ports of Sharjah and Ras Al Khaimah. They were the best of Arab seafarers, plying ancient routes as far afield as the Indian subcontinent and the southern ports of Africa in large wooden boats called dhows. The Qawassim also controlled large swathes of the Persian coast – most notably the thriving port of Lingah, near Bandar Abbas, through which most of the region's trade passed – and many of the strategically important islands between the Persian and Arab coasts.

To the south were the Bani Yas, a federation of tribes merged through blood ties and the need for mutual protection. The ruling families of both Dubai and Abu Dhabi emerged from this federation. The Bani Yas were mostly Bedouin; they were strong in number and experts in desert survival and warfare. Bani Yas territories stretched from the foot of the Qatari peninsula all the way to Dubai – including the Abu Dhabi settlement which had been founded by Bani Yas families in 1761. Their lands also encompassed vast tracts of desert that included the strategically important oasis settlements of Buraimi and Liwa.

With the Qawassim enjoying supremacy on the sea, and the Bani Yas controlling the land, something of a stalemate ensued. Conflicts erupted often, but neither force was able to get the upper hand. As the northernmost coastal point in Bani Yas territory, Dubai was of strategic importance and its residents therefore lived in constant fear of attack and counter-attack. The town and its surrounds were the venue for dozens of battles between the Qawassim and Bani Yas. Although it was primarily a Bani Yas town, it was not unheard of for Qawassim men to occupy the town for short periods, before the Bani Yas could respond and drive the usurpers out.

During the 1600s and 1700s it was probably little more than a collection of huts known as barastis, made of coral blocks and palm fronds. The small fishing community sustained itself through trade, bartering its catch with Bedouin farmers and herdsmen, and with merchants from the outside world for staples such as dates, meat, rice, tea, wheat, fabric for clothing and charcoal for fires. It was a difficult and perilous existence, but the fishing grounds off Dubai are rich. Consistently good catches promoted a settled existence, in contrast to the nomadic life of the Bedouin. In a gradual evolution, families gave up their traditional Bedouin lifestyles to join their cousins in coastal settlements.

The seeds of major change were sown in 1625, when the British and Dutch fleets combined to bloody the noses of the Portuguese in a battle off Bandar Abbas. The Portuguese suffered major losses and retreated to the other side of the Gulf, laying anchor just off Ras Al Khaimah. For a dozen years they attempted unsuccessfully to subjugate the population.

The reason for this emerging international interest in the Gulf was trade. During this period the British were in the thick of intra European fighting as each of the major powers sought to establish its own global empire. The Gulf became of increasing strategic importance in the late 1700s, as its waters allowed a quick and convenient connection between Britain's colony in India and the so called Silk Route. The Silk Route is one of the most significant achievements in the history of world civilisation, a network of caravan ways that crossed Europe and Asia from the Mediterranean coast to China and served as an important means of business relations and cultural exchanges between East and West.

The Gulf passage became a strategic part of Imperial policy, and Britain deployed its military to maintain the Gulf as 'British water' by force. The British proved the most persistent of the foreign powers to 'occupy' the Gulf, largely because India, their enormous colony of tea and spices, lay directly across the Arabian Sea. By the 17th century the East India Company, headquartered in Delhi, had come to rely on the lower Gulf as part of its trading route with Britain. Many slave ships sailed through Gulf waters as well, until a crackdown in the early to mid-19th century.

With their own emphasis on seaborne trade, the Qawassim were soon at loggerheads with the British. The early years of the 1800s were characterised by skirmishes between British warships and Arab seamen in their wooden boats. Despite being woefully outgunned, the sheer number of Arabs sustained the conflict for several generations.

In 1819, the British assembled a task force of large Royal Navy vessels off Bombay under Sir William Grant Kier, a noted naval commander. Kier's orders were simple: To enter the Gulf and subjugate the Qawassim with whatever force was necessary. At his disposal were 3,500 men, along with the 50-gun HMS Coventry, 18-gun HMS Curlew and 26-gun HMS Eden. Oman, a British ally, pledged another 4,000 men to what was the largest armed force ever to have entered the Gulf.

On November 3, 1819 this flotilla sailed from India and, over the ensuing month, fought pitched battles with Qawassim naval units at various points around the Gulf. They landed at several Qawassim ports, on both the Arab and Persian sides of the Gulf, and bombarded others. The campaign culminated in an all-out assault on the Qawassim stronghold of Ras Al Khaimah in December 1819. The British overwhelmed residential districts of the town and, after softening up defences, landed their troops and fought hand-to-hand through the sandy streets.

On December 7, the battle was won and it was then that Kier discovered a flaw in his instructions. No orders were forthcoming from Bombay or London as to how he should ensure that the Arabs would not simply rebuild and regroup at a later date. After signing a peace treaty with the chief of Ras Al Khaimah on December 9, Kier sat on HMS Liverpool awaiting word of his next move. Nearly a month dragged by and no word came. So he developed a broad-ranging treaty, designed to give the British wide powers and to hamper the Arabs in areas where it served British interests to do so.

During this time, Britain made its first official contact with Dubai.

In 1819 the British sent a task force into the Gulf. This successfully destroyed Qawassim naval power, took several Qawassim coastal strongholds and went on to attack Ras Al Khaimah. (opposite page top) The British fleet attacks Lingah. (centre and bottom) The assault on Ras Al Khaimah.

Kier had dispatched boats along the coast, searching for Arab fighting ships that had escaped destruction in Ras Al Khaimah. As the fleet stopped at various coastal hamlets, they forged diplomatic relations with the head of each. In late December 1819, a British vessel laid anchor off Dubai and a scouting party rowed ashore. They found a small town, with a young headman named Mohammed bin Hazza bin Zeyl Al Nahyan.

At the beginning of January, Kier unveiled the 1820 General Treaty of Peace. First to sign was Sheikh Sultan bin Saqr, Ruler of Sharjah, on January 9, 1820. Then Kier summoned eight other rulers from the Coast of Oman – among them Mohammed bin Hazza bin Zeyel of Dubai – to Ras Al Khaimah and asked them to sign the same document. Unwell at the time, the Dubai headman sent an uncle, Zayed bin Saif bin Mohammed, who duly committed Dubai to this landmark 'agreement'.

The 1820 General Treaty of Peace would, in so many ways, change the entire face of life in the area. It altered the political shape of the region in ways that are still causing repercussions. One key area was sovereignty. Up to this point, Rulers had achieved their legitimacy through strength of numbers and the support of their families – the Ruling class. In a world where territorial boundaries were fluid, sheikhdoms were constantly in upheaval. Often a Ruler was only as strong as the result of his last battle, or he was dependent on retaining the support of the Bedouin tribes that roamed the hinterland nearby. Failure or weakness led to being overthrown. Often violently. Often by assassination.

The British treaty legitimised the Rulers who were invited to sign by acknowledging their primacy. More than this, the British gave a tentative legitimacy to the sheikhdoms themselves. Nothing would change overnight. But the treaty sparked an evolution in leadership that would eventually lead to the formation of a more stable system, and a society based around coastal settlements rather than on the prevailing traditional nomadic Bedouin lifestyle.

After the 1820 General Treaty of Peace, Britain took its first hard look at the Coast of Oman. Several reports from the government of India – the region came under the jurisdiction of British India – speak of the Al Fahidi Fort, the only fortification in Dubai at the time. Other than this, Dubai warranted only passing mention. Its people fished and harvested sponges, and the sheikhdom boasted a small pearling fleet –

Dubai remained a tiny backwater but by the 1820s was finally gaining recognition.

pursuits of little interest to the British.

The first thorough description of Dubai was given by the British Lieutenant Cogan in 1822, who recorded that the population then was around 1,200 people, that there was a low wall around the town with three watch-towers, and that the houses were made of mud. Lieutenant Cogan drew the first map of Dubai city and its elevation from the sea.

Only once did a senior official journey there. In 1824, E J Hannus, the British Political Resident in the Gulf, visited Dubai. His records refer to a meeting with Mohammed bin Hazza bin Zeyel. E J Hannus' trip to Dubai was a starting point for the strong political and economic alliance that still exists between Dubai and Britain.

By May 1833, sections of the Al Bu Falasah, one of the major factions of the Bani Yas tribes in Abu Dhabi, began a historic migration that would change the demographics of the Gulf region forever. This was a gradual process over the summer of 1833, during which some 900 people journeyed days across the dunes to make a fresh start in Dubai. At their head was Sheikh Maktoum bin Buti, who ran Al Bu Falasah affairs with the support of his uncle, Sheikh Obaid bin Saeed. Sheikh Obaid, a widely respected intellectual, acted as consort until his death in 1836.

This unusual mass migration changed the face of Dubai. Its population more than doubled, the Al Bu Falasah bringing renewal and growth. Dubai now had a large, skilled and relatively wealthy population, which needed a larger souq, new services, more fishing capacity, merchants, craftsmen and livestock handlers.

Consequently the settlement rose in regional importance.

After the great fire of 1894, rebuilding work led to the arrival of the bastikiyya, or windtower, which became synonymous with Dubai as an architectural feature.

Recognising this, the British quickly began referring to Sheikh Maktoum bin Buti in matters regarding their treaties. His first act in this regard was as a signatory to the Maritime Truce of 1835. This was a hugely significant agreement for the entire Coast of Oman as it sought to prevent the sheikhdoms from waging seaborne conflict during the economically vital pearling season. This truce was found to be so beneficial that it was extended several times. In June 1843, Sheikh Maktoum signed a permanent treaty.

The Maritime Truce was of particular importance to the social and economic development of the region. Stability meant wealth. As the coastal dwellers found their circumstances improving, their way of life became more attractive to the Bedu. Gradually, a significant demographic shift occurred as Bedouin families settled and took up trades such as pearling and fishing. As a result, Dubai's population swelled.

But this new urbanisation did have its problems. In 1841 smallpox broke out on the Bur Dubai side of the Creek, and, consequently, people moved to Deira side and started to build houses and markets. Consequently, Deira became larger than Bur Dubai. In 1894 fire swept through Deira, burning down most dwellings. Richer people began building their houses from coral stone and gypsum which was more fire-resistant. This rebuilding saw a rise of a new style, the windtowers (bastikiyya), which were a somewhat elegant architectural element for their day, as well as acting as conduits for trapped air to be directed to the rooms beneath, a sort of air-conditioning unit. Usually bed and sitting areas were situated directly under the wind-tower to enjoy the cool air coming through. In winter, these wind-towers were boarded up with wooden planks to protect the room from rain.

Newcomers to Dubai were welcomed by Sheikh Maktoum. He encouraged businessmen from up and down the coast to base their fishing and pearling boats in the sheikhdom. The first day of the six-month pearling season was a significant date. It was when Dubai's fleet would strike out for the pearling banks, the boat crews chanting as they rowed. Like most of the townspeople, each year Sheikh Maktoum would stand on the roof of his home near the mouth of the Creek and watch as the bulk of Dubai's menfolk left. It was a time of sadness for many, as husbands and fathers would be missing for half a year. But for Sheikh Maktoum this was also a barometer of Dubai's progress. Each year, he counted a growing number of boats and men. As Dubai's fleet grew, so did its influence, both politically and economically.

This growth in strength can be judged to some degree by Sheikh Maktoum's actions on a regional stage. He was close to Sheikh Zayed bin Khalifa Al Nahyan, a prominent member of the ruling family of Abu Dhabi during the late-1800s. Prior to his accession as leader of Abu Dhabi in 1855, Sheikh Zayed was in personal danger from rivals due to his popularity among the people. Sheikh Maktoum gave him temporary refuge and protection in Dubai. Support for the Al Nahyan noble grew, and in time he claimed the leadership of Abu Dhabi and went on to become one of the greatest Rulers in the history of the sheikhdoms that would eventually make up the United Arab Emirates. Historians have dubbed him 'Zayed the Great'.

Sheikh Maktoum died suddenly in 1852. He had founded the Maktoum dynasty in Dubai and had ruled for 19 years, during which the sheikhdom had grown so quickly that it was barely recognisable from the Dubai of two decades earlier. Sheikh Maktoum had named his eldest son, Sheikh Hasher, as his successor. But Sheikh Hasher was still only a teenager at the time of his father's death and too inexperienced to grapple with the demands of a burgeoning sheikhdom. As an alternative the Maktoum family rallied round Sheikh Saeed bin Buti, brother of the deceased Ruler. It was decided that Sheikh Saeed would groom Sheikh Hasher for future leadership.

The Maktoum family ran its affairs differently, whereby accession was not necessarily decided by birth. A son had the right to succeed his

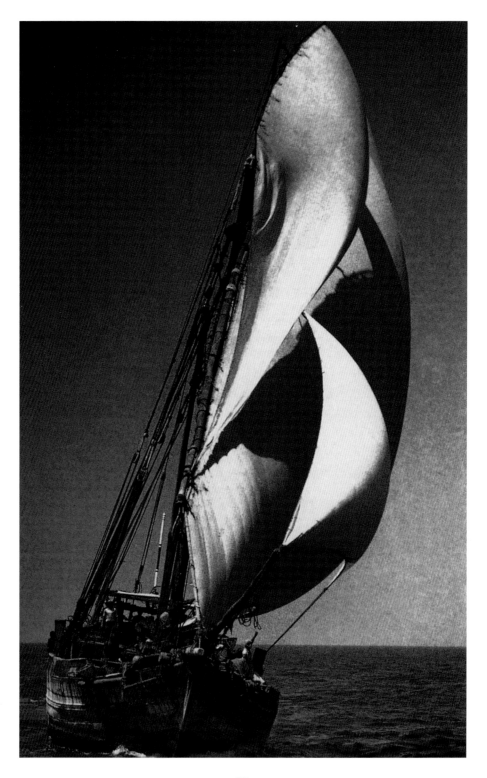

father but, if he was young, a consort would be appointed or an uncle made Ruler. If he was unfit to govern, the family would meet to debate the issue and vote upon a successor. Each Ruler of Dubai found it necessary therefore to rule by consensus, with the family reserving the right to replace him for mismanagement or incompetence.

Sheikh Saeed ruled very much in the mould of his brother. He welcomed to Dubai anyone who wished to live in peace and, unusually for a Gulf Ruler, he kept company with business leaders to encourage their participation in Dubai's economy. However, after only seven years in charge, Sheikh Saeed died in 1859 following a short illness, leaving as his legacy a sheikhdom that continued to prosper.

By this time, his nephew, Sheikh Hasher bin Maktoum, was ready for responsibility. Sheikh Hasher had been schooled in leadership by two Rulers, and he had observed them carefully. He was well-travelled and – by the standards of the day – well-educated. Moreover, he had been guided by his father's teachings along one central theme: trade and commerce were the only way forward, Sheikh Maktoum had said, stressing that without them Dubai would remain small, weak and inevitably vulnerable.

Sheikh Hasher never forgot his father's advice, and he quickly emerged as the most pro-business leader on the Coast of Oman. He ruled for 27 years, during which the population doubled to 4,000 at a time when the entire population on the lower Arabian Peninsula was estimated to be only 100,000. Although his sheikhdom was dwarfed by nearby Sharjah, which had around 12,000 people, Sheikh Hasher saw Dubai's pearling and fishing fleets grow and the souq emerge as one of regional importance.

Compared with elsewhere on the coast, the people of Dubai lived well, secure in the knowledge that their home was unlikely to become embroiled in conflicts and political squabbles, because of its progressive leadership.

Practically the only surviving economic indicator of Sheikh Hasher's era is a survey of large trading vessels registered to each port. This survey was conducted by British officials on behalf of the government of India. Of the 90 large trading vessels registered on the Coast of

Within half a century of the arrival of the Maktoums in Dubai, the tiny sheikhdom had grown into one of the Arabian Peninsula's major trade entrepots and boasted the largest fleet of trading vessels on the coast.

Perhaps the last physical traces of Sheikh Hasher bin Maktoum Al Maktoum's rule are two fortifications that still stand sentry over Hatta.

Oman, 20 emanated from Dubai, 18 from the town of Sharjah, 15 from Ras Al Khaimah and 10 from Abu Dhabi. Important as they were at the time, these vessels provide an economic yardstick by which it can be seen that Dubai's commercial ascendancy was gathering pace as early as the turn of the last century.

With its growing population, Dubai also grew in military stature and, although never willing to be drawn into the ill-judged and inconclusive conflicts that characterised much Arab warfare at the time, the Maktoum family never lost sight of its responsibilities to the Bani Yas federation. In 1891, an appeal for support was received from Sheikh Zayed bin Khalifa Al Nahyan, head of the Bani Yas, Ruler of Abu Dhabi. Sheikh Zayed was assembling an army to defend Buraimi, a strategically important desert oasis region. From among the people in Dubai town and the Bedouin affiliated to the sheikhdom, an army of 300 camelmen and 30 horsemen was raised, a significant force for its day.

Today, Sheikh Hasher's legacy remains visible in Hatta. The enclave's Southern and Northern Towers were built by him in the 1880s in order to protect the town from attack.

But it was the pro-business message that Sheikh Hasher preached, not military prowess, that brought results for Dubai. These were times of change in the Gulf, and Sheikh Hasher had laid the foundation for what was to come. He did not live to see the fruits of his enlightened administration, however, succumbing to malaria in 1886.

Dubai's fourth Maktoum leader was Sheikh Rashid bin Maktoum, Sheikh Hasher's younger brother, who continued the pro-commerce stance. It was during Sheikh Rashid's rule that Dubai's prosperity rocketed.

Across the Gulf, during the 1880s, a nationalist Persian government had come to power. It strongly resented the success of the port of Lingah – the Gulf's major trade hub – under the leadership of the Qawassim, whose power base was Sharjah and Ras Al Khaimah. Gradually, the Persian authorities attempted to exert control over Lingah, hoping to displace its Arab administration. This only served to alienate much of the merchant community based there. Some began to see that their futures lay elsewhere, and started looking for another base of operations.

Lingah's economy was so vast that the trickle of departing merchants was hardly noticeable at the time. Across the Gulf, however, it was significant and people took note. Many merchants opted to relocate to the ports of Ras Al Khaimah and Sharjah, with their familiar Qawassim administrations and good facilities. Ras Al Khaimah was also conveniently located near the Straits of Hormuz. Dubai, with its open policies and liberal leadership, also attracted some Lingah merchants, while a smaller number began operating from Ajman and Umm Al Quwain.

In 1887, the Qawassim were forcibly ejected from Lingah by the Persians, who installed their own administration to run the port. The net result was to increase the exodus of unhappy merchants. In Dubai, Sheikh Rashid welcomed all with open arms and encouraged new businesses to set up in his sheikhdom. These trade refugees from Lingah became a small, but highly significant, section of the community. During his short eight-year rule, Sheikh Rashid saw dozens of major new businesses open in Dubai. When he died in 1894, the town was much larger and more prosperous.

Sheikh Maktoum bin Hasher Al Maktoum succeeded Sheikh Rashid in 1894. A clever man, he had the benefit of a thorough grounding in the wisdom and approach of his father and grandfather. Both had instilled in the young Sheikh Maktoum a need to promote Dubai's trade base. He had learned well and – perhaps more than any other leader on the Coast of Oman – he understood the implications of the historical shift he was seeing in Lingah. He filled his Majlis with merchants who could offer him their personal understanding of market conditions. Using their expertise, he learned what they wanted from a home port and the conditions that would attract more traders to Dubai.

When Sheikh Maktoum became Ruler in 1894, seven years had passed since the Qawassim had been forced out of Lingah. Although the majority of merchants there were reluctant to relocate, a worsening situation forced their hand. The new Persian administration in Lingah was inexperienced; and the Persian government was attempting to squeeze additional revenue out of the souq through higher tariffs and new charges.

News of the growing discord among the most influential members of Lingah's souq reached Dubai's leader. Like many, he assumed that most of them would wish to relocate to the familiar Qawassim-run ports of Ras Al Khaimah and Sharjah, or even the conveniently located Umm Al Quwain or Ajman. Yet it became clear to Sheikh Maktoum that Dubai could be the main beneficiary of Lingah's problems. To achieve this, the sheikhdom would have to overcome both the issue of geography and a marked preference for Qawassim ports.

Sheikh Maktoum set out to make Dubai the most commercially attractive port on the Coast of Oman. In 1901, he began a systematic programme aimed at the most influential merchants in the Gulf. He abolished most tariffs and reduced the few that remained, effectively establishing a free port. On top of this, Sheikh Maktoum sent personal envoys to the most important members of Lingah's merchant community. Dubai offered them free land on which to build, guarantees of tax breaks and a favourable eye from the administration. It was a clever move for, as Sheikh Maktoum fully understood, if the largest merchant operations could be brought to Dubai, then those who traded closely with them, medium and small businesses, would follow. Ensuing years proved Sheikh Maktoum correct. Around 1901, Dubai received the vast majority of merchants relocating from Lingah.

Perhaps surprisingly, Sheikh Maktoum's early successes did not prompt other Rulers in the region to act and compete with Dubai, thereby missing out on this opportunity. The sheikhdom quickly grew into a large and important trade centre. One example of its importance comes from the records of the Bombay and Persia Steam Navigation Company (BPSNC). In the years 1899, 1900 and 1901, Dubai was visited by BPSNC vessels four or five times each year. In 1902, they made 21 visits. One year later a fixed fortnightly service was introduced.

For his vision and success in developing Dubai, Sheikh Maktoum gained special status in the eyes of his contemporaries, including Sheikh

Lord George Curzon,
Viceroy of India.

Zayed bin Khalifa Al Nahyan of Abu Dhabi, who often consulted with his kinsman. It was clear that Sheikh Maktoum and his sheikhdom were interested only in one thing: commerce. As much as possible, Dubai followed a peaceful line. The British, who were still struggling to police the region for their own gains, respected Sheikh Maktoum for this.

In 1903, Lord George Curzon, the Viceroy of India and Queen Victoria's court favourite, visited the Gulf. He was the highest ranking member of the Empire ever to tour the region. His Royal Navy sloop anchored off the coast of Sharjah on November 21, and the senior Rulers of the coast were invited to attend a durbar. Sheikh Maktoum travelled to Sharjah on horseback with his Heir Apparent, Sheikh Buti bin Suhail Al Maktoum, and several senior members of the Maktoum family.

After opening the affair with a general welcome, Lord Curzon went on:

We were here before any other power, in modern times, had shown its face in these waters. We found strife and we have created order. It was our commerce as well as your security that was threatened and called for protection. We saved you from extinction at the hands of your neighbours. We opened these seas to the ships of all nations, and enabled their flags to fly in peace. We have not seized or held your territory, have not destroyed your independence but have preserved it. The peace of these waters must still be maintained. Your independence will continue to be upheld and in this the influence of the British government must remain supreme.

The British government has no desire to interfere, and have never interfered in your internal affairs, provided that the Chiefs govern their territories with justice, and respect the rights of the foreign traders residing therein.

By this time, Dubai was probably the most cosmopolitan town on the Coast of Oman. Its population had expanded to include immigrants from Persia, the Subcontinent and elsewhere in the Gulf. Shortly before the death of Sheikh Maktoum in 1906, a British report estimated that Dubai town had upwards of 2,000 houses, while the 350 trading stalls in Deira souq made it by far the biggest along the coast. During the first decade of the new century, a census counted nearly 7,000 men from Dubai who were directly or indirectly employed in the pearling industry, the highest figure on the coast.

Famed Arabist John Lorimer recorded the statistics of Dubai in 1908 as follows: "There is no customs, the yearly revenue is $51,400 mainly from pearls. In Deira side there are 1600 houses and 350 shops. In Shindagha area there are 250 houses. In (Bur) Dubai there are 200 houses and about 50 shops. There are about 4000 date palm trees in the town, 1650 camels, 45 horses, 380 donkeys, 430 cattle and 960 goats. In the Creek, there are 155 boats for diving and trading and 20 small boats – abras – to take passengers between the two banks of the Creek."

Sheikh Buti bin Suhail Al Maktoum acceded to power in 1906. He was a highly educated individual, a man of letters and a noted poet whose correspondence during his six years as Ruler offers fascinating insights. However, the years of Sheikh Buti's reign were marred by a number of tragedies.

Only in recent decades have the people of the Gulf recorded their history. For a century before that, the foreign powers noted some major events. For the most part, however, the Arabs relied on a tradition of story-telling, passing oral history down from father to son. Such story-telling continues to this day, and around the United Arab Emirates older members of the community still relate the tale of 'the great storm'.

This occurred 'near the end of the pearling season', probably August or September, during the reign of Sheikh Buti. Dubai's pearling fleet – indeed, those of all the sheikhdoms – were still far out at sea at the pearl banks when freak weather hit. The sky turned black, a howling wind swept in, and the normally calm summer sea was whipped up into massive swells. The flotilla of small, wooden pearling boats designed for calm weather were caught in the storm. Battered for hours, the crews of those boats lucky enough to stay afloat tried desperately to reach their friends on other vessels which had sunk or capsized.

After the storm had blown itself out, Dubai's fleet limped back to port. Between 1,500 and 2,000 men had been caught in the storm. More than 200 were drowned. It was a disaster for Dubai, as each of the deceased had been a breadwinner.

In 1910, Sheikh Buti was again a victim of circumstance, caught up in a British armed incursion into Dubai that could have brought the sheikhdom into a state of war with the British. Imperial policy at the time was to keep the Trucial Coast demilitarised, thus preventing threats to internal security and dangers to British shipping. Nevertheless gun-runners did a brisk trade, and at various times the British sent armed sorties into the Gulf to stamp out these operations. In a reference to this illicit trade, Lorimer's *History of the Persian Gulf* reported that the centre of the munitions trade had moved from Ajman to Sharjah and Dubai. Some 120 rifles passed through the latter two ports during September 1902 and a further 200 did so the following month.

In November and December 1910, HMS Hyacinth was heading anti-gun-running operations in the Gulf. During one sweep, HMS Hyacinth picked up a suspicious dhow heading into Dubai under cover of darkness. She tracked the boat and laid anchor off Dubai.

Standard practice at the time was for the commanding officer to contact the sheikh and request permission to search a suspected boat and the property of its owner. On this occasion, however, the captain of HMS Hyacinth chose a different tack. A number of landing vessels were sent to Dubai, carrying a heavily-armed group of Royal Navy marines who were ordered to independently seek out the suspected arms dealers. In all, around 100 men were dispatched.

As dawn broke, townsfolk emerged from their homes to find armed foreigners stalking the sandy streets of Deira. Shots were fired at the British troops and a fire-fight quickly broke out. The marines found themselves pinned down, as dozens of men from all over Dubai reacted to the sounds of gunfire by rushing to the scene with their rifles.

For over an hour the battle raged, during which four British seamen were killed and a further nine injured. An unspecified number of men

from Dubai were also felled by bullets and dozens wounded. Gradually the outnumbered and outgunned British retreated to the shore and held positions near their landing craft. The shooting only ended when Sheikh Buti, braving crossfire himself, emerged from his home and spoke to his people, calling for a cease-fire.

Later that morning, with calm restored, the commander of HMS Hyacinth sent an order that Sheikh Buti pay a fine of Rs. 50,000 in compensation. Among other British demands was the surrender of 400 rifles belonging to his people. Despite being the injured party in this melee, the Dubai Ruler was in no position to negotiate. HMS Hyacinth already had her big guns trained on the town.

After an investigation, on January 3, 1911, the British Foreign Department issued a carefully worded censure to both the British Political Resident and the commander of HMS Hyacinth, saying:

HMS Hyacinth's incursion into Dubai almost brought the tiny sheikhdom to the brink of war.

The government of India is not satisfied with the situation which has arisen in Dubai. From your telegram, they gather that the search of houses took place without the sheikh being present. If this were the case the actions of the Commander were likely to provoke reprisals and were hardly prudent. Some of the conditions imposed on the sheikh they consider onerous.

Sheikh Buti wrote to the British Political Agent, based in Lingah, to retort:

You know full well my attitude of reverence and respect to the British government, also, by the Grace of God, I am not one of those who oppresses others. We experienced such things at the hands of Her Majesty's boat's crew who were there, as we have never experienced before. At (5am) the Captain of the Man-O-War landed with his troop of about 100 sailors. The moment they arrived they began slaughtering and killing my men...it was afterwards that I found out that 37 of my men were killed.

Sheikh Buti died in 1912 after having ruled for six years. His successor, Sheikh Saeed bin Maktoum Al Maktoum, inherited a booming trade hub that had come to dominate all others on the Trucial Coast. One visitor to the town wrote:

...its souqs, or markets, on either side of its broad Creek are the most picturesque I have ever seen in the Middle East and take one back to the time of the Arabian Nights. In the narrow lanes, roofed with matting, where the gloom is flecked by spots of sunlight, Arabs, Persians and Baluchis display their multifarious and many coloured wares. Wild eyed tribesmen with their camel canes and daggers, haggle with shopkeepers and the wealthier Persian merchants, with their long flowing robes and gold brocaded headdresses, pass to and fro, intent on their business...

Graceful dhows glide into the Creek, lower their sails and cast anchor, while the whole day small craft are busy ferrying shoppers from one bank to another.

The rectangular houses of the sheikhs and merchants, with their tall wind-towers, cast white reflections on the water. Conditions are no doubt primitive, but there is an air of bustle and prosperity about the place that gives it a peculiar charm.

It was Sheikh Saeed's father, Sheikh Maktoum, who had laid the foundations for this growth and prosperity. The town was a centre for the economically vital pearling trade, while a vast majority of imports and exports from the Trucial Coast passed though its souq. Once a backwater, over the course of just 15 years Dubai had metamorphosed into the best-developed town in the area.

At its centre from 1912, Sheikh Saeed was a man who understood the souq and its workings well. Before he became Ruler, he had dabbled successfully in business himself, becoming wealthy as a fishing and pearling boat owner. As such Sheikh Saeed was respected by the merchant community in Dubai. This was something that he would come to rely on.

Sheikh Saeed's administration was something of an anomaly in comparison to others in that much influence fell to the Ruler's wife, Sheikha Hassa bint Al Mur Umm Rashid. Sheikha Hassa was a powerful woman, almost without parallel in that era. While respecting the norms of the day in terms of a woman's modesty and reserve, she was also successful in business. She often conducted business meetings, speaking with her partners and customers from behind a heavy black curtain.

Sheikha Hassa was also unusual in that she had an influential voice in politics. Indeed, her strength was very important. Sheikh Saeed was a placid character given to ruling with simple Bedouin diplomacy. With a long, greyish beard and round spectacles, he looked and acted anything but the part that he had inherited. At every opportunity he would head for Dubai's desert hinterland to hunt with his falcons, an escape from the pressures of leadership. When at his large house in Shindagha, he doted on his sons, Sheikh Rashid who was born in 1906, and Sheikh Khalifa, in 1912.

One story that is still recounted among those close to the Dubai ruling family illustrates the softness of Sheikh Saeed's style. One morning Sheikh Saeed rose early, even before the guards of his modest palace, to discover one of his retainers stealing an expensive Iranian carpet from his Majlis. "Put it back," Sheikh Saeed advised the thief, "the guards will certainly catch you."

The would-be thief took Sheikh Saeed's advice, and continued his employment in the Maktoum household for many years as though nothing had happened.

Another recollection is told by Sheikh Mohammed bin Khalifa Al Maktoum, his grandson, who says: "People would call on Sheikh Saeed asking for help. Times were hard. He would listen to their story and write instructions on a chit, which would then be taken to his clerk. It was normal for a deserving case to receive Rs. 6, which sounds only a small amount today, but in those days could feed a family for several months.

"One day Sheikh Saeed's clerk asked to see him immediately. The

Pearling, so long the economic lifeline that supported the region's economy, was about to become its downfall.

Ruler had, by accident, written an order for someone to be given Rs. 60, which would keep a family well for years! Sheikh Saeed realised his mistake, but was unwilling to upset the person who had received this gift, so he ordered that Rs. 60 was paid. It was a king's ransom, but Sheikh Saeed was adamant that it was his mistake and that the person concerned should not be disappointed at having his good fortune rescinded. That was the sort of man he was."

For a time Sheikh Saeed could afford such benevolence. The early years of Sheikh Saeed's reign were marked by a smooth continuation of the policies that so encouraged economic growth in Dubai. Sheikh Saeed – supported all the while by the amazing Sheikha Hassa – ruled effectively and wisely. It seemed that Dubai's rise to prominence would continue indefinitely. However, unforeseen events being played out in Japan, however, would soon have grave repercussions for the Gulf.

The gains of the previous two decades in Dubai had been hard won, but they would be swept away almost overnight. Sheikh Saeed would need all his political ability and the support of his close family to steer Dubai through its greatest crisis.

Two unique photographs believed from around 1920, showing Sheikh Saeed visiting Persia with his sons. (top) Sheikh Saeed is centre, with Sheikh Rashid standing behind him and Sheikh Khalifa front. (bottom) Sheikh Saeed flanked by Sheikh Rashid and Sheikh Khalifa. Behind Sheikh Rashid, partially hidden, is Sheikh Juma.

Chapter Two

Pearl Harbour

Pearl fishing is the premier industry of the Persian Gulf…Were the supply of pearls to fail….the ports of Trucial Oman, which have no other resources, would practically cease to exist.
— *John Gordon Lorimer, Arabist*

It is safe to assume that few people in the Gulf, or indeed the rest of the world, are familiar with the names Kokichi Mikimoto, Tokichi Nishikawa or Tatsuhei Mise. Yet these three men inadvertently ruined the economy of the Gulf, threw tens of thousands into abstract poverty and were the root cause of many residents of the Arabian Peninsula dying of starvation.

The people of the region, particularly those from Bahrain and Qatar in the north, to Abu Dhabi, Dubai and the Qawassim sheikhdoms of the lower coast, had built their lives and economies around just one export – pearls – until the discovery of oil much later, the only major foreign currency generator in the region.

The unique lustre of pearls depends upon the reflection and refraction of light from the translucent layers, and is finer in proportion as the layers become thinner and more numerous. Natural pearls were so rare and expensive that they were reserved almost exclusively for the noble and very rich. A jewellery item that today's women might take for granted, a 16-inch strand of perhaps 50 cultured pearls, often cost between $500 and $5,000. At the height of the Roman Empire, when pearl fever reached its peak, the historian Suetonius wrote that the Roman Emperor Aulus Vitellius financed an entire military campaign by selling just one of his mother's pearl earrings.

No one will ever know who were the earliest people to collect and wear pearls. George Frederick Kunz, who is considered by many to be America's first gemologist, in his 1908 masterpiece *The Book of the Pearl* states his belief that an ancient fish-eating tribe, perhaps along the coast of India, initially appreciated the shape and lustre of saltwater pearls, which they discovered while opening oysters for food.

No matter the origin, a reverence for pearls spread throughout the world over the ensuing millennia. India's sacred books and epic tales abound with pearl references. One legend has the Hindu god Krishna discovering pearls when he plucks the first one from the sea and presents it to his daughter Pandaia on her wedding day. China's long recorded history also provides ample evidence of the importance of pearls. In the Shu King, a 23rd century BC book, the scribe sniffs that as tribute, a lesser king sent 'strings of pearls not quite round.'

In Egypt, decorative mother-of-pearl was used at least as far back as 4200 BC, but the use of pearls themselves seems to have been later, perhaps related to the Persian conquest in the fifth century BC.

Rome's pearl craze reached its zenith during the first century BC. Roman women upholstered couches with pearls and sewed so many into their gowns that they actually walked on their pearl-encrusted hems. Caligula, having made his horse a consul, decorated it with a pearl necklace.

Pearls, in fact, played the pivotal role at the most celebrated banquet in literature. To convince Rome that Egypt possessed a heritage and wealth that put it above conquest, Cleopatra wagered Marc Antony she could give the most expensive dinner in history. The Roman reclined as the queen sat with an empty plate and a goblet of wine (or vinegar). She crushed one large pearl from a pair of earrings, dissolved it in the liquid, then drank it down. Astonished, Antony declined his dinner – the matching pearl – and admitted she had won. Roman writer Pliny the Elder, the world's first gemologist, writes in his famous *Natural History* that the two pearls were worth an estimated 60 million sesterces, or 1,875,000 ounces of fine silver ($9,375,000 with silver at $5/ounce).

The Arabs have shown the greatest love for pearls. The oldest known Gulf Pearl, found in Kuwait by archaeologists, is 7,000 years old, has a drill hole and was thus probably part of a necklace. The depth of their affection for pearls is enshrined in the *Koran*, especially within its description of Paradise, which says: 'The stones are pearls and jacinths; the fruits of the trees are pearls and emeralds; and each person admitted to the delights of the celestial kingdom is provided with a tent of pearls, jacinths, and emeralds; is crowned with pearls of incomparable lustre, and is attended by beautiful maidens resembling hidden pearls.'

Even the *Bible* makes reference to pearls as being 'so precious that a man would give all his life possessions for just one pearl.'

During the long history of pearls, the principal oyster beds lay in the Arabian Gulf, along the coasts of India and Ceylon (now Sri Lanka), and in the Red Sea. Chinese pearls came mainly from freshwater rivers and ponds. Nearly all the pearls in commerce originated from those few sources. Divers manually pulled oysters from ocean floors and river bottoms and checked them individually for pearls. Not all natural oysters produce pearls however. In fact, in a haul of three tonnes, only three or four oysters will produce perfect pearls.

Kokichi Mikimoto, the son of a noodle maker, had a dream and a hard working wife, Ume. Together they set about to do what no one else had done – entice oysters to produce round pearls on demand. Mikimoto did not know that government biologist Tokichi Nishikawa and carpenter Tatsuhei Mise had each independently discovered the secret of pearl culturing: inserting a piece of oyster epithelial membrane (the lip of mantle tissue) with a nucleus of shell or metal into an oyster's body or mantle to cause the tissue to form a pearl sack. That sack then secretes nacre to coat the nucleus, thus creating a pearl.

Between them Mikimoto Nishikawa and Mise had achieved the impossible and brought an economic boom to Japan. Yet this spelt disaster for everyone associated with the natural pearl industry.

The natural pearl had, unbeknown to all, reached the zenith of its popularity around 1900. In the period 1830 to 1900, output was worth an average of $1,750,000 a year, rising to nearly $4,000,000 in the first decade of the 20th century. With increasing wealth and a demand for rich, rather than gaudy or showy jewellery such as diamonds, no gem commanded better market prices than the pearl. In 1917, Cartier acquired its New York premises when the company sold a double row of natural pearls, then valued at over $1 million, to a woman who paid with her town house. This house is today the main Cartier premises in New York.

With prices for natural pearls spiralling throughout the early 1900s, the Gulf experienced an unprecedented boom. The start of the pearling season saw an ever greater number of boats leaving their home ports for the pearling banks. Bahrain had 900 pearling dhows, Kuwait 600, and the Trucial States 1,200 (of which 335 were from Dubai).

On each boat the captain's knowledge of the different pearl banks was as important as the dangerous work of the divers. The pearl banks

Pearling was the backbone of the Gulf economy and, by the early years of the century, accounted for an estimated 95% of economic activity. The importance of the industry was quite apparent, as were the sacrifices made by pearl divers as they plied their dangerous trade, visible from the emaciated bodies of these fishermen.

were generally some distance from the coast lying at depths of 46 to 120 feet. An experienced captain attempted to avoid areas visited in the previous season to prevent over fishing. When a good site was selected, the boats were moored and, when the harvest of oysters diminished there, the captain would choose a new location. Navigation was limited to the stars, a simple compass and the captain's knowledge and experience of the pearl banks.

Each boat carried a crew of between 15 to 80 sailors. The men slept and worked on dhows as little as 15 metres long. Conditions were unbearable with the humid heat, lack of space or privacy, and no place to escape the constant wet, slimy and foul-smelling decks, covered in rotting oysters. Refreshment during the day was limited to a little coffee. An evening meal of dates, rice and fish was often their only nourishment.

Each year more foreign pearl merchants arrived in the Gulf, competing to buy up the best pearls of the year's harvest. Prices rose steadily throughout this period and the coastal towns grew increasingly prosperous on the back of this industry. By the early 20th century the pearl industry in the Gulf was at its height and accounted for up to 95% of national income. As urban life improved, more of the region's Bedu turned their backs on the traditional ways of life, becoming part of a widespread pattern of greater urbanisation. In Dubai – the most flourishing of the sheikhdoms – whole new neighbourhoods of barasti houses sprang up.

Local pearl merchants were borrowing money to buy more boats and employing more men to collect more pearls. Many boat owners from other ports visited Dubai to recruit their crews. The bulk of the pearling labour market on the Trucial Coast was found in the town. In every way, Dubai was a regional hub of this booming industry.

The boom years of pearling were a strain for a Ruler used to managing the affairs of a small, relatively peaceful town. Sheikh Saeed was an old-fashioned leader, and in the past his close-knit village community had been easy to control. Now, with thousands of outsiders flocking into the town each year, Sheikh Saeed was trying to manage the affairs of an urban community of such a size that it needed all his attention. This was not his forte. He was a simple man who relied more on gentle diplomacy than heavy-handed authority to maintain his rule.

On one occasion, in order to gauge the feelings of his people, Sheikh

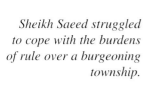

*Sheikh Saeed struggled
to cope with the burdens
of rule over a burgeoning
township.*

Saeed famously went incognito into the town. In Islam, humility is rewarded, and no more so in the symbolic act of humility when a man helps draw water that is used in cleansing the hands and feet of others before prayer.

The Ruler, of course, would find this impossible as he would be mobbed in the street by well-wishers. But Sheikh Saeed disguised himself in rags in order to visit a public mosque, draw water from a well, and carry this to the mosque. Unrecognised, he milled around with the people for a time after prayers, asking questions and taking the opinions of ordinary people about the state of the sheikhdom. Only when he was spotted did the Dubai Ruler make a hasty retreat to his home in Shindagha.

He was an old-school Ruler, unequipped for the pressures and demands of administering a flourishing town. As these demands grew, he leaned more and more on those around him. This included his wife, Sheikha Hassa, a formidable woman decades ahead of her time. While ensuring that she preserved the modesty that her gender and her status demanded, Sheikha Hassa was very much a power within both political and economic sectors in Dubai.

"My grandmother was a strong character, who played an unusually forthright role in society," says Sheikh Hamdan bin Rashid Al Maktoum. "She was highly educated and turned her intelligence to business. She involved herself in the pearling industry and also in the souq."

Society's norms dictated that the wife of the Ruler was not seen in public. Despite these confines her business interests thrived. In the political arena she also enjoyed a voice. Her husband, Sheikh Saeed, was struggling with his responsibilities and, increasingly, with an unsettled Majlis. She emerged as an advisor and sounding board for the Ruler, a source of good advice.

The eldest son of Sheikh Saeed and Sheikha Hassa was 16 years old in 1928. Sheikh Rashid had been brought up within Dubai's ruling household. In many ways he already bridged the gap between two eras, a period when the people of the peninsula were predominantly nomadic and the pearl-driven period when urbanisation was transforming society. Sheikh Rashid was raised through both eras and understood both.

Already he had been noted as a wily and effective operator. He had been a regular in his father's Majlis from his early teens, had learned much from Sheikh Saeed and Sheikha Hassa, and was considered a natural leader of men. While Sheikh Saeed administered at arms-length from his home in Shindagha and Al Fahidi Fort, Sheikh Rashid was a man of action.

He was fully aware, from his hours in the Majlis, of the economic realities of the day and of the problems which his family and his state were facing, even before the collapse of pearling. Life was tough for the people and their challenges many.

Sheikh Rashid was fiercely committed to the future of Dubai. He gathered around him those who thought along similar lines and, even in his late teens, his Majlis came to rival those of his parents in importance. He attracted a great deal of support due to his status as an imposing figure who got things done – perhaps more so than his father. Taller than the Ruler, more opinionated and decisive, Sheikh Rashid decided what he wanted and then concentrated on achieving his aims. He was also a persuasive character and would use this to cajole others into taking his position. This ability to get things moving attracted the bulk of the city's 'young Turks' to his side; gradually Sheikh Rashid won over the more conservative city elders as well so that he enjoyed a wide base of popular support.

"He was a dynamo. There was always so much to be done around Sheikh Rashid," says Rashid Abbas. "I recall him surrounded by older men, the merchants, extolling a vision of a proper town. He could not see the point of coasting along with the status quo. He wanted to build something.

"That is not to say he was too opinionated though. He listened to the thoughts and absorbed the experiences of those who knew better than him, the merchants who had travelled extensively around the region, to India, Britain even. He was learning all the time."

It was learning on the job, and throughout his late teens the young prince, unofficially Heir Apparent as Ruler of Dubai, built his support base and began to exert his forward-thinking personality upon Dubai. Sheikh Saeed certainly recognised his eldest son's dynamism.

"Sheikh Rashid once told me that Sheikh Saeed insisted that he attend his Majlis every day. In that way he both immersed his son in the business of affairs of state, learning the politics of the sheikhdom, and the Ruler also had beside him an astute and wily advisor," says Abbas. "No-one crossed Sheikh Rashid. Even then his intellect was sharp and his maturity way beyond his years. He did not tolerate people who were trying to take liberties with the government or Ruler."

Sheikh Rashid stood shoulder-to-shoulder with his father in major policy matters, and he was a particularly outspoken proponent of retaining the commerce-friendly course which had paved the way for Dubai's souqs to be the biggest on the coast. As a businessman himself, he always kept a close eye on the markets. He invested in pearling and trading dhows, and held the valuable rights for taxi services between Dubai and Sharjah, running these businesses personally and using them to hone his commercial skills.

Young Sheikh Rashid was immersed in public and commercial life by the late 1920s. He was a character upon whom his father could lean and devolve powers to. It was just as well, for the world was about to come crashing down on the people of the Arabian Peninsula.

By the early 1920s the Japanese had taken the discoveries of Mikimoto, Nishikawa and Mise to another level. Cultured pearl farms had sprung up. By the latter part of the decade a cheap alternative to natural pearls had begun to pour onto international markets.

During the summer of 1928, Dubai's pearling fleet was at sea. Just fewer than 400 boats were in the fleet that year, employing around 4,000 men. But while the divers were busying themselves on the sea floor, thousands of miles away the market for their produce was rapidly drying up. The extent of this can be seen from the fate of those aforementioned 'Cartier' pearls. In 1957, half a century after they had traded at $1 million, they were auctioned for just $170,000.

During 1928, in the fashion capitals of the world, the market for

natural pearls crashed dramatically. In November 1928, Dubai again resounded to the rhythmic chanting of the pearlers as they rowed home following a long six-month season at sea. The last day of the pearling season was traditionally a day of joy. It was a day when the town rejoiced at the safe return of its menfolk. On this occasion, however, a gloom hung over Dubai. The foreign pearl merchants had, almost without exception, failed to arrive for the end-of-season buying period. The few who had come were themselves reeling from a sharp dip in demand on the international markets. They were seeking only to purchase limited stock at shockingly low prices.

The effect was catastrophic and immediate, not only for local pearling merchants, but for the entire community. This was an industry built on borrowing. Boat owners bought their vessels on credit. Their crews, who would be away for six months, were paid half their salaries on departure – borrowed from moneylenders at a high rate of interest – and half on return. The final instalment came out of the revenues from that season's catch. With no sales there was no money to pay these men. The boat owners themselves were immediately made bankrupt.

Almost overnight, the majority of families on the Trucial Coast – those whose menfolk worked in the pearling industry – were reduced to destitution. The souq, from which the community bought its provisions, was almost as hard hit.

"It was a disaster, of unimaginable proportions," says Abdulmagied Seddiqi. "In days, towns that had existed for generations were thrown into a crisis from which there was no obvious answer."

Dubai's pearl fishermen had returned to land facing an uncertain future and immediate economic destitution as a large section of the fleet never set sail again.

Naturally enough, the people looked to their leaders for a solution. Yet losing around 75% of liquidity from the market was a disaster from which there was none.

For Sheikh Saeed the crisis was all too much to deal with alone. He was besieged in his Shindagah home by citizens seeking relief, perhaps a little money to buy food, a job from the Ruler, even just a word that their leader had a plan. To make matters worse, a new British-brokered agreement made the Trucial Rulers personally responsible for the return of absconding debtors. If they failed, the Rulers would be held responsible for the debt. In times of relative economic buoyancy, the idea of accountability might have been a good one, but not when so many people were unable to pay bills. This situation soon sank into chaos as there was so much debt and so many debtors.

Sheikh Saeed turned to the only individual around him with the dynamism and vision to step into the breach. His son had ideas as to how Dubai could undertake an urgent retrenchment of its economy. He also enjoyed the confidence of the people. Sheikh Rashid believed that fishing was the only clear solution at this juncture.

Dr Abdullah Al Taboor, a writer and researcher in heritage, says: "The people of the UAE have lived on the sea for ages. They have faced a lot of its dangers in their effort to make a living. The rough and strong sea current of the Gulf bears clear testimony to the dangers our fathers and ancestors faced in their quest for a decent means of livelihood at a time when other means rarely existed. A situation which gave them no other option than going to sea to make a living."

Locally referred to as 'Al Samaamik', Dubai's fishermen could boast vast knowledge and experience, knew the types of fish available each season, and the best way, time and spot to fish for them. Sheikh Rashid knew personally many Al Samaamik. Although he had never been involved in the fishing industry until this point, this was his answer to the puzzle. Fishing would employ men, bring valuable food for Dubai's people and provide a product for export.

Many pearl fishermen, during the off-season, worked on fishing boats. Others worked on boats and ships carrying goods from Dubai and back between other Gulf ports and the costal towns and cities of India and the Eastern costal towns of Africa, particularly Zanzibar.

"In summer, the weather becomes very hot, forcing the fish to go deep into the sea, which makes fishing very difficult and unprofitable," says Isa Humaid, a veteran fisherman.

But the summer was not, now, a consideration. Dubai needed food, jobs and exports. There are nearly 336 fish species in the Gulf. All represented a little respite from the economic calamity that had beset the town.

With Sheikh Rashid advising him, Sheikh Saeed put as many men as he could afford back out to sea. The Ruler invested his precious state coffers in new fishing vessels. In a practice that he would later make his signature, Sheikh Rashid used his relationships with wealthy merchants all along the peninsula to borrow money, invest in boats and employ people. Later he would return these loans with the profits made from fishing.

It was some little comfort that Dubai was already in a relatively better position than some sheikhdoms in that it boasted a significant trade base and was not fully reliant on pearling. This helped somewhat, and the people of Dubai were thankful for their lot when, due to the crisis befalling them, there were reports of malnutrition and starvation elsewhere.

The following May, the beginning of the 1929 pearling season, around 60 boats of Dubai's fleet stayed at home. The remainder sailed more in hope than with certainty. The community prayed that demand for pearls would pick up. It never did.

Over successive years the Gulf pearling industry sank into oblivion. In the early 1920s, Sir Percy Cox, the British Political Agent, estimated that the pearling industry generated some £3 million for the Gulf. By

In the face of the crash of pearling Dubai's administration invested heavily in fishing in order to both feed the people, create jobs and produce a cash export.

1946, one credible estimate put the industry's value as low as $250,000.

This was a time of belt-tightening for Sheikh Saeed's administration. For the first time in decades, and only after Sheikh Rashid had consulted with the merchant community, Dubai imposed tariffs for imports and exports. Yet the income this generated was not enough to allow the investment necessary to keep Dubai from entering a prolonged recession.

Thanks to the foresight and energy of its Heir Apparent, Dubai survived the pearling crisis and its people would not starve. But, having overcome this telling moment in the history of the sheikhdom, Sheikh Saeed's administration would find itself facing even greater challenges – this time from within.

Chapter Three

The Crisis Years

We can let circumstances rule us, or we can take
charge and rule our lives from within.
— Earl Nightingale, media personality

As the sheikhdoms of the Lower Arabian Peninsula struggled with the collapse of their economies, circumstances – many of them manmade – worked against them. For the Ruler of Dubai and his energetic eldest son this was especially true, as Dubai found itself squeezed by political problems from outside and difficulties within its own ruling family. For the Trucial Coast, the early decades of the century were blighted by problems.

Despite a biting recession, however, Dubai continued to enjoy an enviable stability in comparison with other states along the coast. To the west, in Abu Dhabi, it was only the arrival of Sheikh Shakhbut in 1928 that brought peace from internal political strife, while in the other direction, Sharjah was in the hands of Sheikh Sultan bin Saqr Al Qassimi. As Dubai boomed, Sheikh Sultan was facing the eclipse of his sheikhdom as the trading capital of the Trucial Coast, which was a big financial and political blow. Relations between the two sheikhdoms were difficult, and were to get far worse over the next decade.

Most worrying, however, were the events unfolding elsewhere on the Arabian Peninsula where the warrior king, Abdul Aziz ibn Saud, had emerged as a major power.

In 1901, at the age of 22, Ibn Saud succeeded his father as the leader of the Saud dynasty. He then set out to reconquer his family lands. In 1902, together with a party of relatives and servants, he recaptured Riyadh with only 20 men. Many former supporters of the House of Saud once again rallied to its cause. In the two years following his dramatic capture of Riyadh, Ibn Saud captured almost half of Nejd, and finally

Dubai Ruler Sheikh Saeed bin Maktoum Al Maktoum.

consolidated control over the Nejd in 1912. He was proclaimed King of the Hejaz in 1926 and King of Saudi Arabia in 1932.

Due to the commitments of the Trucial sheikhdoms with Britain, the empire of Ibn Saud seems to have had little direct contact with its neighbours. The future King believed that, in time, the sheikhdoms of the coast would come to him, without any need for him to challenge the British and their treaties directly.

In fact, what diplomatic contact there was, was extremely positive. Most of the Trucial sheikhs maintained warm, if low key, relationships with their powerful neighbour. Ibn Saud himself was widely respected as an individual. He adhered strictly to Islamic Shariah law and was essentially a kind man who cared for the welfare of his people.

Elsewhere, the Wahhabi empire dominated the Arab hinterland and was certainly in the market for a principality which boasted a major port, while across the Gulf, the Iranians were both a political and military force to be respected.

For much of the time, Dubai's Rulers kept their own counsel in inter-state and inter-tribe affairs, maintaining agreements with several major tribes that each would stay out of third-party conflicts. One of these tribes was the Duru, which based itself in the Tunum area of the desert. It was a powerful group who could raise a large number of armed men when necessary. On one occasion in 1922, a conflict between the sons of Zayed bin Khalifa, the great leader of Abu Dhabi, spilled over into a war which eventually enveloped most of the major tribes and settlements which fell under the Bani Yas Federation.

The 1922 death of Sheikh Hamdan bin Zayed, an ally of Ibn Saud, had brought Sheikh Sultan bin Zayed to power, and the conflict which followed was fought out between the tribes. Loyal to the new Ruler were the dominant and well armed Manasir, while rival tribes such as the Awamir, Duru, and the Bani Qitab formed an alliance against him.

By August of that year, the situation was so serious that Sheikh Sultan, grandfather of current UAE President Sheikh Khalifa bin Zayed Al Nahyan, appealed to Sheikh Saeed of Dubai for military help.

Dubai was unwilling to refuse a legitimate and fully recognised Ruler of Abu Dhabi and, in the weeks that followed, Sheikh Rashid put together an armed force, which he placed under the control of the embattled Sheikh. This force from Dubai was part of a 500-strong army which was involved in a bloody attack on Al-Falayah, a Bani Qitab settlement not far from Ras Al Khaimah, in mid-September 1922. The affair is included in a report filed by the British Residency Agent of the day, who also recorded a counter-attack against Buraimi oasis – part of Abu Dhabi – some days later. Sheikh Sultan retaliated almost immediately with an offensive against the Duru, his forces once again including men seconded from Dubai. During the attack, the warriors burned several buildings and stole the Durus' largest herd of some 50 valuable female camels. The raid was in direct contravention of a non-aggression arrangement between Sheikh Saeed and the leaders of the Duru, a fact the tribesmen could not ignore. Little more than a week later, a party of Duru camelmen attacked the outskirts of Dubai town during the early hours of the morning. Before the armed retainers at Sheikh Saeed's house and guards at Al Fahidi Fort even had time to respond, several townspeople were shot dead and the Duru made off with around a dozen camels.

This was, by and large, the limit of Dubai's involvement in this dispute, although Sheikh Saeed and Sheikh Rashid subsequently organised meetings with other Trucial Sheikhs to establish an alliance in case further action should be needed. It is doubtful whether Dubai would have become further involved, because Sheikh Rashid's priority was always the economic benefit of his own sheikhdom, and any conflict, especially one which interrupted a pearling season already crippled by recession, would certainly not have been good for business.

At any rate there was no escalation of hostilities. When the Duru and Awamir – the former previously affiliated with Dubai – subsequently announced that they had agreed in future to align themselves with Ibn Jaluwi, the governor of the Hasa province, an uneasy calm settled.

Politically though, the defection of the two tribes to Wahhabi control was a blow to the Trucial Coast, being certain evidence of Ibn Saud's encroaching power. Over the months which followed, the two tribes were behind several guerrilla attacks, mainly against Abu Dhabi property, which caused concern all along the coast.

Even Isa bin Salih, the powerful Imam of Oman, was unwillingly drawn into the problem when attacked. In July 1925 Sheikh Saeed quietly sent his cousins, Saeed bin Buti and Suhayl bin Buti, to broker an alliance between Dubai, Abu Dhabi and Oman. All agreed to fight together should any aggressive power take further steps to encroach on their territory.

There was also concern over the emergence of a strong Iranian government. General Reza Shah Pahlavi staged a coup d'état. General Reza seized key parts of the capital city almost without opposition and forced the government to resign.

During Reza Shah's 16 years of rule, major roads and the Trans-Iranian Railway were built, modern education was introduced and the University of Tehran was established. On March 21, 1935, he formally requested that the international community stop using the name Persia, which had been in use in the West since ancient times, and to henceforth use Iran as the official name.

His achievements were great, but by the mid-1930s Reza Shah's dictatorial style and rabid nationalism had caused intense dissatisfaction both throughout Iran and among his neighbours. No more was this the case than in the Trucial States, where Reza Shah made it clear that he wished to reassert territorial claims over several islands in the Gulf and made little show of hiding his ambition to absorb some of the defenceless Arabian Peninsula into his state. Several of the islands were of strategic importance, while others potentially held mineral wealth.

In 1928 Persian forces arrived on the island of Henjam. The Arabs of Henjam could trace their arrival there to a migration in 1856. In that year, Sheikh Obaid bin Juma Al Maktoum had quarrelled with his cousin and brother-in-law, Sheikh Hasher bin Maktoum Al Maktoum, Dubai's Ruler. Sheikh Obaid had taken his own and 14 other families, with 13 pearling boats, into self-imposed exile. They lived for a couple of years on Greater Tunb, but a water shortage on the island forced another move and they had taken refuge on Henjam.

In 1927, the Persians hastily constructed a customs office and several officials were installed, much to the fury of the local residents; over subsequent months the growing hostility led to bloodshed. In May 1928 the then Ruler of the island, Sheikh Ahmed bin Obaid bin Juma Al Maktoum, Sheikh Saeed's father-in-law, was forcibly expelled, taking up residence in Dubai where there was plenty of support for him in government and sympathy from the population at large, many of whom had relatives living on the islands.

A month later relations between both sides of the water deteriorated still further when Persian troops landed on another island which had been settled for generations by Arabs, and established another customs post. Matters came to a head when a passenger boat from the Trucial

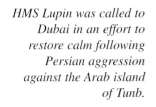

HMS Lupin was called to Dubai in an effort to restore calm following Persian aggression against the Arab island of Tunb.

Coast, which was heading for Tunb en route from Dubai, was intercepted by a Persian navy motor launch. The Royal Navy's Senior Naval Officer in the Gulf was informed of the incident almost immediately, urgently cabling the British Admiralty to request instructions. It is his subsequent report which gives the clearest account of what happened.

The Dubai-registered vessel was transporting mainly women and children, all of whom were taken by the Persians to Lingah, where they were placed in custody and the women stripped of their jewellery, before being imprisoned.

News travelled fast and along the Trucial Coast several merchants with links to the Persian authorities had their buildings attacked, reflecting the widespread anger of the population at large. In Dubai, especially, there was outrage in the streets. Several Persians were attacked by a mob and the British Residency Agent, Isa bin Abd Abdulatif, was called in to help restore calm.

Several of the Rulers sent urgent messages to each other discussing the possibility of sending a joint fleet to retaliate. At the Majlis, too, there were angry scenes. At one point Abdulatif was forced to call in the gunboat HMS Lupin in an effort to restore calm and guarantee the safety of Persians in the city, particularly from relatives of the women and children who were still being held hostage in Lingah.

It was at this crucial moment that the British failed Dubai once again. Sheikh Saeed and Sheikh Rashid were aware that any military response from Dubai would inevitably bring the might of the Persians bearing

British Prime Minister Winston Churchill led the charge to find reliable oil deposits, while Saudi Arabia's King Abdul Aziz ibn Saud was dismissive.

down on the tiny city, but were nonetheless under great pressure to respond forcefully. They were promised by the Political Agent that British forces would ensure that the Persians ended this affair with a bloodied nose. Both leaders accepted this, publicly placing great store in British assurances, and for a while at least, a measure of calm returned to the streets.

For a time the British authorities considered intervening with a gunboat, but when diplomatic pressure worked in winning a release for the prisoners, they decided to leave the matter well alone, even though the Persian charges of smuggling seemed to be completely false. According to a telegram sent by the British Charge d'Affaires in Iran, who visited Lingah, the Persians claimed to have found 400 pounds of sugar and two tons of rice on board the boat they had seized, which belonged to Badr bin Mohammed, a prominent Arab businessman in Dubai. Therefore, Persian customs on Tunb claimed, the boat was actively smuggling. The locally-based British Political Resident had been on the quayside when the boat arrived in Lingah, and could report seeing only two bags of sugar.

The Imperial authorities eventually tried to make up for their weakness with hard cash: a few months later, the government of India handed over compensation of Rs. 5,000 to the families of those who had been unlawfully held. Sheikh Saeed and Sheikh Rashid were both present to see this implicit admission of failure, but if it was an attempt to placate dissent, it was too little, too late. The Ruler's prestige had been at stake during this crisis. He had trusted his Imperial allies, and had personally guaranteed, both to his own family and to angry factions in the community, that retribution against Persia would be swift and tangible. The loss of face and the impression of weakness that followed when the British failed to live up to their promises to him would, ultimately, be one catalyst for nearly a decade of trouble in Dubai.

The one bright spot was oil, although this too was to become an issue that divided rather than united those in power in Dubai. Even before the First World War, the Western world had begun to consider the implications of an increasingly mechanised and oil-hungry economy. On July 13, 1913, Winston Churchill had told Britain's House of Commons: "On no one quality, on no one process, on no one country, on no one route and no one field must we be dependent. Safety and certainty in oil lie in variety and variety alone."

Britain's oilmen first extracted Middle Eastern oil in April 1927, from Kirkuk, an area of present-day Iraq. Earlier, on December 2, 1925, the Ruler of Bahrain entered into a contract with the Anglo-Persian Oil Company. At the time, many Arab leaders did not fully grasp the implications of oil. The Ruler of Bahrain agreed on Anglo-Persian searching for oil on his territory only if they first found water. Ibn Saud, the founder of modern Saudi Arabia, stated in his Majlis: "What use is oil? You cannot drink it..."

Discovering commercial quantities of crude reserves in Bahrain took time. Situated below Jebel Dukhan, the *Mountain of Smoke,* and 'spudded' on October 16, 1931, Oil Well No.1 finally began to blow heads of oil on the morning of June 2, 1932, to much celebration on the part of those involved in the project. Life on the island would be changed forever.

Following the discoveries in Kirkuk and Jebel Dukhan, the British intensified their search for oil through the Anglo-Persian Oil Company – later renamed the Anglo-Iranian Oil Company and then Petroleum Development (Trucial States) – and its subsidiaries. In May 1937, Sheikh Saeed was the first Trucial Ruler to sign a commercial agreement with Petroleum Concessions Ltd. (PCL), a subsidiary of the Anglo-Iranian Oil Co. formed to explore and exploit Arab Gulf states' hydrocarbon reserves. He was followed by the Ruler of Sharjah in September of the same year, and then Sheikh Shakhbut signed for Abu Dhabi in 1939, with others following: Ras Al Khaimah (1945); Umm Al Quwain (1945); Ajman (1951); and Fujairah (1953).

Dubai was to receive a small annual fee and a meagre Rs. 3 for every ton of crude oil barrelled during exploratory drilling. Oil exploration was, therefore, viewed as a potential contributor to Dubai's coffers nearly three decades before exports left the emirate proper. However, during this period, fees from exploration were low in comparison to revenues generated when the pearling industry was at its most robust.

"Sheikh Saeed had to cut his cloth accordingly, look for savings and invest whatever precious income there was in supporting the economy," says Saif Ahmed Al Ghurair. "Sheikh Rashid was actively investing and managing the sort of business that employed men and made a reliable return on government investment. He was a canny operator and hundreds of men from the old pearling fleets had found a living to feed their families through his enterprise. Really it was he who had been the saviour of Dubai during the dark days of the collapse of pearling."

Sheikh Saeed undertook a round of belt-tightening. Reducing the

The search for mineral wealth changed the demographics of the desert.

expenses of his own household was not enough. Somewhat reluctantly, Sheikh Saeed made deep cuts into the annual gifts that Dubai made to its Bedouin allies – a traditional gesture in all the sheikhdoms. With a population of 18,000 at this point, Dubai was the largest town on the Trucial Coast, and Sheikh Saeed made it clear to all in his Majlis that he had a responsibility to the entire population, not just to the self-serving interests of a few influential voices. Wealth needed to be shared more evenly. No-one, especially those who were already relatively rich, could expect favours.

As a result of this even-handed policy dissent grew. Yet there was no other course. It was Sheikh Buti bin Suhail, Ruler between 1906 and 1912, who had unknowingly reintroduced the elements of discord within the Majlis that would break out into the open during the late

1930s. He had accepted the return to Dubai of Buti and Saeed, the parties who had been exiled to Sharjah in 1894 for opposition to Sheikh Maktoum bin Hasher. The two had then settled in Deira, appearing to lead quiet lives. But the Tunb incident was an opportunity. A case was made that the British had let Dubai down badly and that the Ruler had been weak.

In 1929 a small section of the Majlis felt sufficiently powerful to seek a larger role in government. One individual even went to the British Political Resident claiming to be the popular choice to lead, but his effort to usurp the Ruler found only a sharp response from the British. Sheikh Saeed was reaffirmed as the legitimate and incontrovertible Ruler.

The situation settled somewhat after this, but two years later, on May 5, 1931, there was further trouble following an incident at the mouth of the Creek. A boat belonging to an official of the British India Steam Navigation Company collided with one owned by Said bin Buti. There was only minor damage to the boats, but several crew members of the British vessel were attacked and beaten up, apparently with the knowledge and approval of the owner. When the British owner of the vessel was himself threatened with physical violence, what had been a minor, if embarrassing incident, began to take on far wider implications.

Within days, the Dubai Ruler had been asked to intervene by the British. But despite the mild-mannered Sheikh Saeed's admonishment of those involved, his order for an apology was pointedly ignored for some three months, and the guilty parties even refused demands that they visit the Majlis to discuss the matter. This was a slap in the face and yet another challenge to his authority.

By the early 1930s Dubai's population was approaching 18,000. Oil had been discovered in Bahrain in 1932, and the search was on in much of the Gulf region. Only the Second World War would interrupt the exploration effort and delay the inevitable entry of the Trucial States into the boom. The expansion of the petroleum industry put an even greater premium on the maintenance of economic and political stability and, as the major controlling power in the area, the British were anxious to discourage any distractions to the discovery and development process.

Both Sheikh Saeed and Sheikh Rashid had long been regarded as the most forward thinking leaders along the Trucial Coast. Dubai was the major trading entrepot on the Arabian Peninsula, and despite the recession, its diverse souq retained a level of wealth that was the envy of neighbouring sheikhdoms. Even so, at what was still a time of economic crisis, Sheikh Saeed continued to feel pressure from discontented groups within the community, all of whom were acting out of self-interest.

One particularly thorny issue, according to British records of the period, was law and order. With a growing, multi-national and multi-ethnic population, Dubai's demographics were changing. Sheikh Saeed was often characterised within the Majlis as being too lenient and, late in 1930, he gave in to demands that justice and punishment be placed in the hands of a more formal body, a committee comprising several Majlis dissenters and a number of more radical community leaders.

Within weeks this brought the problems that the Ruler and his heir had feared. An Arab national named Salim bin Fairuz was convicted of a relatively minor theft in the souq, a crime which demanded he have one hand cut off. Sheikh Saeed routinely reduced such sentences, for minor crimes, to imprisonments coupled with banishments. But the new body sought to show its strength and its independence from the line that Dubai's Ruler took. This grizzly punishment was summarily carried out, bringing a stinging rebuke from the British authorities for Sheikh Saeed and creating a diplomatic embarrassment for his administration. Sheikh Rashid – who was quite capable of being a strongman when Dubai's strategic need required – abhorred such violent state sanctioned punishments for petty crimes. He let it be known that be believed such actions to be irremissible.

Increasingly vocal opposition in the Majlis was to cause another difficulty: In 1931 Sheikh Saeed was forced to pull out of an agreement to establish a small Royal Air Force (RAF) fuel dump and allow flying boats to land on the Creek. Despite being a potential money-spinner for government coffers, several prominent dissenters claimed this would be an unacceptable infringement of Dubai's sovereignty.

It was an issue that festered, not because Sheikh Saeed was particularly fond of British intrusion, but because of the financial windfall that the fuel dump and landing rights would have provided. In the midst of recession, the sheikhdom could simply not afford to turn its back on hard cash. Two years later Sheikh Rashid had had enough of the Majlis troublemakers. He demanded openly a reversal of that decision and, in 1933, Sheikh Saeed entered into a six-year agreement with the British.

The first aeroplane to land in Dubai touched down in January 1937, while the first commercial flight to Dubai began months later, in October 1937. It was an Imperial Airways flying boat service, calling on several major conurbations in the Middle East, including Alexandria, Basra and Bahrain, and terminating in Karachi (then part of British India).

This was a shrewd commercial decision by the Ruler, which not only boosted trade links with the outside world but also brought in more than Rs. 5,000 of landing fees during the first year of the agreement alone. Yet even that was not enough to recommend it to some in the community. This income went the same way of the oil money – back into a meagre infrastructure improvement scheme and also invested in many of Sheikh Rashid's economic projects. Some demanded a cut for their personal use.

"Sheikh Saeed and Sheikh Rashid held firm," says Rashid Al

The 1937 arrival of an Imperial Airways Short C-class flying plane service brought the prospect of a new era - but was instead a source of instability.

Muhairi. "They had skillfully avoided the destitution that had afflicted many coastal towns and certainly some of the interior. Dubai was still afloat in economic terms. Its people had food. The souq was doing relatively well. It was not the time to begin lining the pockets of a few."

This was a view shared by historian Jim Thomas who would write later in his 1979 paper, *Dubai and its Ruling Family*:

> *The Ruler and his immediate family put all of their assets at the disposal of the state. There is evidence that Sheikh Saeed, as was common for a Trucial Ruler, had personal assets abroad, in India for example. These were sold for re-investment in Dubai. The family, again as was common, held the rights to some lucrative trades and items of commerce. For example taxi services between*

Dubai and Sharjah. In more prosperous times these were considered a perk, not unlike Civil List payments made by the taxpayer in Britain to the Royal Family...In these dark times for Dubai, Sheikh Saeed and his immediate family made it known that profits from these businesses were going into state coffers. This was not unlike if Queen Elizabeth offered to forego her Civil List payments should Britain enter a bad recession."

Despite the evident belt-tightening by Sheikh Saeed and much of his family, others wished to continue living in the lifestyle to which they had become accustomed. By the height of summer in 1934, Sheikh Saeed was worried by reports filtering to him regarding the intentions of individuals in the city. The British Political Agent reported of Sheikh Saeed on October 23:

As his friendship and valuable assistance in Trucial States negotiations have brought about the present trouble, we have a moral obligation to assist him now. I consider that the only way to prevent bloodshed is that we should inform them [the leaders of the opposition] of the circumstances, that their intrigues are known and that they will be personally held responsible for any trouble that may arise.

Officially, though, Curzon's policy statement of 1903 still held true for the British, who were determined not to involve themselves in internal politics, despite the fact that most of Sheikh Saeed's difficulties had been caused by the British. The Political Agent in Bushire seemed to advise caution. However, he must have known that the action he recommended to his superiors would have a profound effect on the situation.

"Involving us [is not] the considered policy of His Majesty's government," he wrote on October 24. "I am asking the Senior Naval Officer to go as soon as possible in a sloop to stand off Dubai, with the Residency Agent aboard. The Residency Agent will convey a message to the sheikh. The presence of a sloop should have a steadying effect on the situation, safeguard our nationals' lives and property, and also afford some moral backing to the sheikh."

Throughout the summer, the young Sheikh Rashid worked tirelessly to maintain loyalty to his father. He had learned his diplomacy well at the Majlis and among the Sheikh's friends. He now moved easily between ally and foe alike. From negotiating with Maktoum family elders to travelling into the desert interior for meetings with the Bedu who were affiliated to Dubai, he now proved himself an adept negotiator. As well as among ordinary people, Sheikh Saeed's support base held among the sheikhdom's powerbrokers.

The British Political Agent in Bahrain was insisting on a supportive, but passive, approach, as recommended by his superior in Bushire. The overwhelming military strength of the British at the time was, he understood, highly effective even from a distance. Naval guns did not need to be fired to have their effect. At the end of October, a British Naval vessel, HMS Lupin, took the Assistant Residency Agent to Dubai, ostensibly to deliver a message to Sheikh Saeed about the safety and protection of British subjects in the city. Its delivery sent quite a powerful message to the population at large. The British were signalling, in theory at least, that they were there to support the legitimate head of state.

Behind the scenes, cautiously and deniably, the British were preparing to break their own long-standing policy of non-interference. The Political Agent in Bushire had made no mention in his dispatches to the Foreign Office of any plans to do more than offer a message of support – but through the Commanding Officer of the HMS Lupin, his proposals went further than those he had cleared with his government.

On the afternoon of October 27, the Commander received the following telegram: "Please inform the Sheikh of Dubai that I shall probably be able to send him some rifles and ammunition shortly, should he require them. You should let this message be known in town..."

It was a forceful gesture. The arrival of HMS Lupin, anchored just off the entrance to the Creek, had already been seen as a mark of British support by the population at large. The initiative was now firmly with Sheikh Saeed and his son, and they seized their opportunity.

At the instigation of Sheikh Rashid, the Ruler moved quickly to call a Majlis on the very evening that the British vessel arrived off his coast, with invitations extended to all the major political factions in Dubai. His son at his side, Sheikh Saeed demanded an oath of allegiance from all present, which he duly received. In a clever twist, the earlier diplomacy of Sheikh Rashid was called into play as a steady stream of Bedu tribal leaders, affiliated to Dubai, visited Sheikh Saeed to pay their respects. Sheikh Rashid's meetings with the tribesmen were paying dividends, as this was an impressive show of support for the Ruler and his family. Sheikh Saeed invited the most prominent of his Bedu allies to join Maktoum family elders in pledging their support for his continued rule. A contingent reported to comprise 800 armed tribesmen were camping just on the outskirts of the city: Sheikh Saeed's position was virtually unassailable – and there was more to come.

A few days later, the Political Agent in Bushire moved again behind the scenes to show the strength of support. On October 29, a handful of Westland Wapiti biplane fighter aircraft of RAF 84 Squadron were due to arrive at Sharjah Aerodrome on a two-day visit. In a telegram to his counterpart in Bahrain, the Political Agent suggested innocently that "a flight over Dubai would not go amiss."

The idea was conveyed to the RAF Gulf Headquarters in Baghdad, and the same day, Flight Commander Evans, head of 84 Squadron, was instructed to "mount a number of flights over Dubai each day" during their stay at Sharjah.

Over ensuing days a steady stream of tribal heads and Dubai community leaders made the pilgrimage to the Ruler's Shindagha house to swear their allegiance. During the same period 2,000 rounds of ammunition, along with fifteen 30-bore Mauser rifles, were dispatched to Dubai. There was no secrecy about the delivery; on the contrary, after consultation with Sheikh Saeed, the launch carrying the armaments arrived in the middle of the morning, when Dubai souq was at its busiest. They were packed in open wooden boxes which left little to the imagination.

Apart from the policy of backing the existing Ruler in the interests of stability, there was genuine personal regard among the British officials who came into contact with Sheikh Saeed and Sheikh Rashid. Captain T Hickinbotham, the Acting Political Agent in Bahrain for much of 1937, was prompted to report to his superiors that Dubai's Ruler was "one of the pleasantest persons on the Coast with whom to have dealings, as he always behaves like a gentleman."

Much of the political instability with which Sheikh Saeed had to contend can be blamed on the economic troubles of the day. Several of those most prominent in the opposition had seen their financial fortunes dwindle, and their motives in taking advantage of the political

The RAF's 84 Squadron flew a number of Wapiti sorties over Dubai in order to emphasise Britain's support for Sheikh Saeed's legitimate rule.

antagonism to the Ruler could well be assumed to be at least as much personal as political.

British policy in the Gulf was, at this same juncture, adding to the difficulties of every Ruler along the coast. The British were demanding that all the sheikhdoms under their control actively discourage the slavery and arms trades. Although Dubai was probably a relative backwater for these industries, many merchants had profitable ties into both. The British intelligence network was keen to spot traders trying to flood the peninsula with arms, stirring up trouble in the interior. One such individual, a Kuwaiti named Khalaf El Ali El Zamami, was caught in December 1937 attempting to import a massive consignment of cartridges and 15 revolvers into Dubai. The arms, which El Zamami was importing under the cover of his date shop in the Deira souq, had been tracked from their purchase in Hamburg all the way through their shipment to Dubai by steamer from London.

The dealer had already been caught smuggling arms elsewhere on the Trucial Coast and, during a meeting in the Dubai Ruler's Majlis on February 27, 1938, the Political Agent requested that El Zamami be expelled from the city.

In his reply, the Ruler seemed to temporise. "I write to ask you to inform the Political Agent about Khalaf El Zamami. When I parted with you, the time was up for prayers and I had to go," he wrote to the Agent's office. "When I returned from prayers I sent Rashid Bin Yulaiyil [one of the Maktoums' most trusted lieutenants] to El Zamami with instructions that he should leave by today's steamer. He went with him and took his bedding to the ferry, but the ship left before he was able to go on board. If God is willing, he will leave for his home on the coming Sunday night."

During 1937 London was reinvigorating its anti-slavery policy along the whole Trucial Coast, with new regulations, which Dubai had accepted, now declaring an outright ban on the import of slaves. Those who were already in service could seek British help in organising repatriation to their own countries, a process known as manumission. These provisions caused a great deal of unease throughout the region.

Few slaves had taken the manumission option prior to the economic depression, but as more of their fellows had been freed by households which were now unable to support large numbers of servants, the benefits of living independently were becoming abundantly clear. The number of manumission requests grew, and so did resentment among many families.

The British were also squeezing the most influential gun-runners on the coast, with the Ministry of Defence ordering ever-increasing vigilance as the prospect of war with Adolf Hitler's Germany became greater. The Gulf – with its hidden promise of oil wealth – would be a great prize for the Nazis. Despite an apparent commitment to this sort of effective peace-keeping, Sheikh Saeed was not universally praised for his stance.

On a local level, the political scene was as muddied as it was in Europe. In the Ruler's Majlis there were anxious discussions over how to lessen the instability of the recent troubles and the ongoing depression, as this was affecting the markets badly. Sheikh Rashid advised his father to take the bull by the horns and bring one of the most discontented malcontents, Said bin Buti, into the fold. Bin Buti was appointed Wali of the Deira quarter of Dubai, a localised mayoral post, and took up his position with some enthusiasm. He made every householder responsible for cleaning the frontage of his home, using tax revenues to employ street cleaners.

Once brought into the very heart of the mainstream political system with the status and dignity of office, Said bin Buti himself evolved into an ardent loyalist – but his initial success brought jealousy from those who also wanted a greater stake in power.

The young Sheikh Rashid (right) and his uncle, Sheikh Juma bin Maktoum Al Maktoum, both played a key role in the Ruler's administration and were visible in political circles fighting attempts to divide the sheikhdom.

For much of 1938, several issues festered within the Majlis. As usual, Sheikh Saeed relied heavily on Sheikh Rashid, whose instincts had already carried his father through many problems. This year, though, was to see many issues come to a head.

October 1938 saw formation of an elected Majlis, presided over by Sheikh Saeed, whom the British consistently declared to be the only legitimate Ruler of Dubai. Sheikh Saeed was dubious and reluctant to devolve powers to a body that was dominated by those who had been so keen to get their hands on state money for personal use. But this elected Majlis was seen by many as a compromise, and at a time when Dubai needed coherent government it was hoped that this would, finally, put an end to the bickering.

The new body took on tax-raising powers and elected ministers and, for a time, enjoyed tremendous popularity among the people of Dubai. A report by the British Political Resident noted that the body was the "popular party" in local politics at this time.

In fact, this apparent revolutionary approach to government was not without its precedent elsewhere in the Gulf, the leaders of Kuwait having devolved power to an elected Majlis in 1938. The similar system in Dubai got off to a purposeful start. The chief Majlis spokesman coined the term 'wajibat wataniyyah', the concept of individual responsibility to the state as a whole. It was a brave theory, but did not survive long.

The Majlis sought to develop several basic infrastructure projects and set up new public services, which brought it initial popularity. But those entrusted with power found consensus increasingly difficult to achieve. Self-interest brought member into conflict with member. Soon, those who had rallied around the concept of wajibat wataniyyah had taken advantage of their powers to vote themselves generous salaries.

Pork barrel politics is a derogatory term describing government spending that is intended to benefit constituents of a politician in return for their political support, either in the form of campaign contributions or votes. Typically it involves funding for government programmes where economic or service benefits are concentrated in a particular area but where costs are spread among all taxpayers. Members of the Dubai Majlis were particularly adept at pork barrel politics. One of the more extraordinary decisions during the short life of this body was to give pensions to elders from certain areas in Dubai and not others.

The body soon became paralysed by allegations of bribery and the perceived domination of government departments by a small handful of lawmakers; abuses like this rapidly turned the initial support for the reformed Majlis into open derision. Sheikh Saeed removed himself from meetings and, after a time, refused outright to attend. Sheikh Rashid was scornful of Dubai's costly excrescence.

By the beginning of 1939, Sheikh Saeed returned to make a personal intervention. Yet he was unable to prevent the work of the Majlis from grinding to a tense halt. None of the lofty plans for Dubai had been achieved, but the ineffectual talking-shop continued to gobble up much-needed customs revenues through member salaries and pork barrel spending. After a brief period of belief in the new concept, Dubai's population was disillusioned by the whole idea, and Sheikh Saeed faced increasing demands to freeze all funding to the body.

For the sake of his family, for the sake of his sheikhdom, Sheikh Rashid had to step into the breach.

Chapter Four

Checkmate

Whether a man is burdened by power or enjoys power;
whether he is trapped by responsibility or made free by it; whether
he is moved by other people and outer forces
or moves them - this is the essence of leadership.
— *Theodore White, political historian*

In late December 1938, it was announced that Dubai's Crown Prince, Sheikh Rashid, was to marry Sheikha Latifa bint Hamdan Al Nahyan. The sheikha had lived in Dubai since childhood, when her family had fled Abu Dhabi after the murder of her father, Sheikh Hamdan bin Zayed Al Nahyan, Ruler of Abu Dhabi, in 1922. The whole community celebrated on March 29, 1939. Sheikh Rashid's status ensured that dignitaries from all along the coast attended. Hundreds of armed men from Bedouin tribes loyal to Dubai packed the town, shooting their rifles into the air in celebration. Dubai's people thronged the streets and joined in great feasts laid on by the Maktoum family.

The main festivities were to be held in Deira, near the home of Sheikha Latifa, and an area in which the power players of the 'Elected Majlis' retained much of their dwindling support base. From the Deira side of the Creek, there had been rumblings that these discredited leaders would launch a bid for secession, to split the city-state in two.

Something of a stalemate had developed between the legitimate Ruler and these usurpers. Indeed, taxes were being collected there that had nothing to do with the Dubai government or Sheikh Saeed. A dangerous situation had evolved. For one day, March 29, 1939, the tensions that bubbled under the surface were due to be set aside. This was a royal wedding, a day of widespread jubilation when differences were traditionally forgotten and the population celebrated. That afternoon the Maktoum family staged several feasts around the town. All were invited. In addition to town-dwellers, the streets were now

Sheikh Rashid changed the course of Dubai's history on March 29, 1939.

thronged with hundreds of Bedu tribesmen, singing, dancing and letting off gunfire into the air.

Yet the festivities were underscored by Sheikh Rashid's determination to unite his town again and bring an end to the instability. This opportunity would be possibly the only chance to end to the crisis without open warfare on the streets of the town. It was a chance that he was determined to grasp. During the build up to his wedding, Sheikh Rashid had met with his allies in the community and leaders of loyal Bedouin tribes in order to plan a definitive end to the crisis.

On the day itself, Dubai was a place of celebration. The sandy streets were full of revellers. It was quite normal, given the circumstances, for Deira to be thronged with heavily-armed Bedu. No-one suspected what was afoot. Sheikh Rashid and his allies caught his opponents unaware. In the early afternoon, without warning, the Bedu and Sheikh Saeed's retainers suddenly took control of Deira Customs House and several other strategic buildings. Elsewhere Sheikh Rashid and his supporters were able to capture the majority of the dissenting Majlis members. Most others surrendered later that day. Hardly a shot was fired. Aside from a few casualties during the course of the operation there was no ongoing fighting. One rebel barricaded himself in his home, but after a short stand-off surrendered.

Indeed, within several hours, having dealt with the imprisonment of his captives and ensuring his men were in total control, Sheikh Rashid appeared that evening at the main feast in his honour. It was an event that, according to oral history, was remarkable for its atmosphere.

Sheikh Saeed, as host of the reception, had laid on thousands of servings of Mensaf, a traditional Bedouin meal consisting of rice covered with beef or lamb, cooked with yoghurt and flavoured with pine nuts. Perhaps tonnes of Khobz and Fateer – Bedouin bread and cookies – had been baked, and guests were served the traditional strong, scented coffee and dates that underscore Arab hospitality. The event was symbolic in more ways than the wedding of the anointed future Ruler of the sheikhdom. It was an event of unity. People from both sides of the Creek, somewhat separated for months by the actions of a few irresponsible politicians, flooded the area for a celebration that united them once again. The Bedu, so much a part of the day's events, but also a key part of the very fabric of society even in these times of increased urbanisation, were also there in numbers. For hours, into a night lit only

The sandy streets of Dubai resounded with the rhythmic chanting of the Al Ardha as the people celebrated both the wedding of Sheikh Rashid and the end of nearly a decade of political instability.

by the stars and torchlight, the two sides of Dubai and the two sections of Dubai society joined together to celebrate a remarkable and defining day in the history of the sheikhdom. In their gallebeyahs and thobes, the Bedu danced a tahtib, a mock battle set to music where men strut and posture, showing off their strength, then attack and parry in time with the music. Then came the one-string rababa violin and dalouka (big drums), beaten rhythmically as they perform the Al Ardha (war dance), armed with swords and whips. The Al Ardha is the most typical of the dances of the Gulf Arabs. In the Emirates, the local version is called the Iyala – with formations of several hundred men facing each other, taking turns reciting stirring poetry while brandishing swords. To this day the dramatic performances of the Iyala preserve poems which originated in the Nejd.

There were also renditions of dances such as the Harbiya, punctuated by the enthusiastic performance provided by rifles, the Haban, also known as the Khamiri, or the Khayali, and the Mated. And, no celebration was possible without the Liwa, where a large number of male participants arrange themselves into a circle, anchored by drum players.

Into the night the dancing and feasting continued. At the centre of it all was Sheikh Rashid, looking relaxed and happy. His work was done. It was time to look forward, both to married life and to a professional life that, it was hoped, would not be marked by such internal strife. In a single day – the day of his own wedding – Sheikh Rashid had seized the initiative and strengthened the legitimate rule of his father.

Now it was time to concentrate on progress.

Chapter Five

Beginnings of Progress

All progress occurs because people dare to be different.
— Harry Millner, author

The events of 1939 put an end to the era of instability that was born out of the death of pearling and continued for nearly a decade. But that was not the end of the story. For most observers the matter put the seal on a growing reputation for the Crown Prince. At a stroke, he had ended the struggle that was crippling Dubai's business community. Sheikh Rashid had usually been seen to be offering his father wise counsel, and when the two decided to act, more often than not Sheikh Rashid had taken the lead. The round-up of the Majlis troublemakers was the culmination of years of shrewd politics and diplomacy on the part of the young sheikh.

After the military victory, however, Sheikh Saeed needed to lay the matter to rest. Typically for a Ruler who governed with a degree of mercy, Sheikh Saeed did not seek to punish malcontents with the same severity as those now in custody showed when they took on the powers for dispensing justice. The problem came about over the question of where the ill-fated Majlis leader and his entourage and supporters were to go.

Most of those who had served in the Majlis who had not been captured on March 29, 1939, had fled to Sharjah. Intelligence reports indicated that they were growing increasingly belligerent and anxious either to have another attempt at taking power in Dubai, or perhaps creating a power-base elsewhere. Fearing these ambitions, Abu Dhabi flatly refused to entertain British ideas of taking any Dubai exiles there. Ras Al Khaimah had been suggested as a possible choice. Inevitably, the intrigue and hostility that followed them saw more doors close. By July,

From his palace in Shindagha, Sheikh Saeed's directives were concerned with making economic progress after a decade lost to political infighting.

Sheikh Sultan bin Salim, Ruler of Ras Al Khaimah, was refusing to allow them to settle anywhere within his lands.

The situation was getting out of hand, and Sheikh Shakhbut of Abu Dhabi sent his brother, Sheikh Hazza, to look into it. He was met halfway by Sheikh Rashid and the pair made their way to Dubai together for extensive talks. A few days later, the Political Agent also spent three hours closeted with Sheikh Rashid.

The situation rumbled on into 1940, when on January 26 it suddenly exploded. That morning Sheikh Rashid and a number of his retainers were camping three miles from the outskirts of the Deira quarter of Dubai when 50 well-armed rebels swooped down on them. For an hour the two sides exchanged a withering fire; one of Sheikh Rashid's men was killed and several of their opponents shot dead or injured, before the raiders retreated into the desert.

A week later the head of the Dubai exiles and 200 armed Bedu occupied a building on the coast of Sharjah, in an area four miles southwest of Sharjah City called Khan, the closest conurbation to Dubai. A standoff followed as Sheikh Rashid and his men took up their positions at the nearest point to Khan in Dubai territory. Sheikh Juma bin Maktoum and additional men took up their posts at one side, guarding Sheikh Rashid's flank.

It was a curiously haphazard battle, which lasted for several days. Both sides opened up with their cannon, but rounds were at such a premium that they were literally exchanging shots – as the enemy cannonballs landed, they were gathered up, loaded into the guns, and fired straight back where they had come from. Sometimes, when supplies were low, 'retrievers' were sent out under cover of darkness to reclaim shots that had fallen in no-man's land.

Hostilities continued with greater or lesser intensity for some months, although the British occasionally flexed their muscles to ensure that a cease-fire was adhered to when their own civil or military aircraft might be endangered. In his book, *This Strange Eventful History*, long-term UAE resident Edward Henderson described the scene:

> *Imperial Airways, the forerunner to BOAC, would still refuel its flying-boats on Dubai Creek and send passengers over to the fort in Sharjah by bus for lunch. During this operation the war was suspended by mutual agreement between the belligerents, and*

A rare shot of Dubai from the air, taken around 1935.

passengers would pass through the lines without, in most cases, realising anything unusual was afoot, since the air crews, who knew about it, had no wish to alarm them by explaining it...

Three Trucial Rulers, Sheikh Ahmed bin Rashid Al Moalla of Umm Al Quwain, Sheikh Rashid bin Humaid Al Nuaimi of Ajman and Sheikh Sultan bin Salim Al Qassimi of Ras Al Khaimah, were invited to mediate by Sheikh Saeed, who still lived up to his reputation as a man of peace. It was probably only their intervention that prevented the whole situation from escalating even more dangerously. An uneasy peace crystallised as the two sides faced each other. On March 29 the Ruler of Ras Al Khaimah met Sheikh Rashid at his campsite to request that the exiles be granted an allowance, drawn in part from their confiscated assets in Dubai. Agreement to this proposal calmed the situation considerably.

The 1930s had been an uncomfortable time in Dubai, and as stability returned, Dubai's Ruler was happy to take more and more of a back seat. Although Sheikh Rashid was not to succeed his father officially for nearly two decades, from the beginning of the 1940s it was plain to see that it was Sheikh Rashid who was making the decisions. The spring of 1940 marked the beginning of a gradual retirement for Sheikh Saeed, who dropped further and further into the background. He was happy to slip out from Dubai and indulge his main passion, hunting. Over the course of the next decade, more and more responsibilities fell to Sheikh Rashid.

By 1945, Sheikh Saeed had all but ceased to hold a Majlis, an indicator that leadership of Dubai was effectively in the hands of Sheikh Rashid at this time. This period of gradual retirement also coincided with the Second World War, a conflict so removed from the impoverished Trucial States that one could reasonably assume that it never bothered the people of the area. However, this was not the case.

On the outbreak of war, the Shah of Iran, Reza Shah Pahlavi, gave increasing indications that he planned to side with Hitler's Germany. This was a frightening prospect for the Allies, who quickly embarked on a programme of trade sanctions. Britain and the Soviet Union occupied Iran and installed Mohammad Reza, the eldest son of Reza Shah Pahlavi, as Shah. The new, ardently pro-Western Shah replaced his father on the Peacock Throne on September 16, 1941. Swiss-educated, he became the self-styled His Imperial Majesty Shahanshah Aryamehr (Light of the Aryans), and was the last reigning Shah of Iran. It was hoped that the younger man would be more open to influence, and while this was the case during the war, after it the Shah proved an unreliable partner for the Western powers, nationalising the oil industry. His nationalist tendencies would later have profound repercussions for the territorial integrity of the United Arab Emirates.

Throughout the war years, much of the Iranian population, resentful of occupation and foreign meddling in the departure of Reza Shah Pahlavi, supported Nazi Germany. In order to weaken the state, Britain and the Allies maintained a trade embargo against Iran. Unfortunately, the people of the Trucial Coast were caught in the economic crossfire, as their economies were dominated by commerce with Iran. The region had hardly emerged from recession following the collapse of the pearling industry. Times were desperately hard even without an Allied embargo targeting Iran. The British blockaded Iranian ports and, as a further measure, Whitehall imposed restrictions on most basic foodstuffs entering the Gulf. Each of the sheikhdoms was allotted quotas of staple foods such as wheat, rice, sugar and tea. Each week, these were delivered to the Ruler, who was responsible for distribution to his people.

This was a tough policy that both reduced markedly the amount of food available to the people of the Trucial Coast, and decimated trade links with the community's biggest export market, Iran. This was a double blow that many would not survive. The biggest flaw in this scheme was that supply quotas were decided by bureaucrats in Britain and India according to the estimated population of each sheikhdom. Population figures were little more than guesstimates, inaccurate and almost completely ignoring the Bedu, who made up a substantial segment of the population. Because of this anomaly, the Bedu were predictably the first to suffer. The British made little or no food available to them. Local historians relate that many Bedu in the desert interior suffered from chronic malnutrition, leading to a huge increase in sickness and infant mortality. In the towns, the Rulers struggled to ensure that their people were taken care of, but many still went hungry.

Britain's warm relationship with the Maktoum family now paid dividends for Dubai. Sheikh Rashid always cooperated with the British where their demands did not go against Dubai's interests. He had allowed a post office to be opened in Dubai in 1941, and earlier defied the critics of the administration to grant landing rights to British aircraft on the Creek. Because of this enlightened approach, British officials in the Gulf studiously maintained friendly personal relations with Sheikh Saeed and Sheikh Rashid. The British were now keen to support Sheikh Rashid when he claimed rationing would destabilise his administration at a time when greater stability was needed to revive Dubai following its year of political impasse. After some discussion with his superiors in Whitehall, the British Political Resident in Bahrain agreed to entrust the sheikh with personal responsibility for rationing Dubai.

Sheikh Rashid was not doing this just for his own prestige, however. He agreed to revised supply quotas of wheat, rice, sugar and tea, ensuring that the people of Dubai were adequately fed. The renegotiated quotas, in some cases, far outstripped basic demand in the town. This surplus was then quietly passed on to some of Dubai's merchants, who either sold it on to other sheikhdoms or often – at inflated prices – to others willing to risk the wrath of the British to illegally supply the Iranians.

This was risky for Dubai as the British were always suspicious and watchful. But the benefits outweighed the risks for Sheikh Rashid. He not only saw to it that his people did not starve, but used the residue to counter the effects of a recession that lasted throughout the Second World War.

At the cessation of hostilities in Europe, sanctions against Iran were eased and trading conditions throughout the Gulf improved considerably. Dubai boomed once again, under a leader who encouraged commerce and was keen to use his revenues to boost the sheikhdom's infrastructure further. One of the great British travellers and explorers, Wilfred Thesiger, visited the town in the spring of 1949. He was a seasoned traveller, known as 'Mubarak bin London' by the Bedu, who had accepted him as one of their own. He recorded his impressions in the best-selling memoir of his experiences, *Arabian Sands*:

> *...the creek which divided the town, the largest on the Trucial Coast with about twenty-five thousand inhabitants. Many native craft were anchored in the creek or were careened on the mud along the waterfront. There were booms from Kuwait, sambuks from Sur, jaulbauts, and even a large stately baghila.*

> *Naked children romped in the shallows and rowing boats patrolled the creek to pick up passengers from the mouths of alleys between the high coral houses, surmounted with square wind turrets and pleasingly decorated with plaster moulding. Behind the diversity of houses which lined the waterfront were the suqs, covered passageways, where merchants sat in the gloom, cross-legged in narrow alcoves among their piled merchandise.*

> *The souqs were crowded with many races – pallid Arab townsmen, armed Bedu, quick-eyed and imperious, Negro slaves, Baluchis, Persians and Indians. Among them I noticed a group of Kashgai tribesmen in their distinctive felt caps, and some Somalis off a sambuk from Aden.*

> *Here life moved in time with the past. These people still valued leisure and courtesy and conversation. They did not live their lives at second hand, dependent on cinemas and wireless. I would willingly have consorted with them, but I now wore European clothes. As I wandered through the town I knew that they regarded me as an intruder. I myself felt that I was little better than a tourist.*

Another account is offered by Ronald Codrai who, as an oil company representative, lived in Dubai and travelled extensively on the Trucial Coast for several years at mid-century. In his 1992 book, *An Arabian Album*, Codrai published an extract from his diary from April 15, 1948, a rare first-hand account from a Westerner during this period:

> *Met for the first time the Ruler of Dubai and his son Rashid when I called on them to thank them for the camels and escort they had provided for my trip from Dubai to the Dhaid area.*
>
> *Gray-haired and walking with the aid of a stick, Sheikh Saeed must be over sixty, although he is of slight build and is a good-looking man with very clear eyes. Sheikh Rashid is in his thirties, with black hair, very large, flashing eyes and quick movements. They were very friendly, patient with my attempts at Arabic and amused at its Egyptian/Lebanese mix. They were further amused when I said I was Codrai bin Codrai, for to have the same name for son and father is to indicate not knowing one's father!*
>
> *They served refreshments consisting of dates, vermicelli sprinkled with sugar, and tinned peach slices. Chasing and trying to grasp the peaches with the fingers calls for special skill. After coffee, a container of burning frankincense was passed round the Majlis, but had been over-fueled and gave off clouds of smoke which filled the room and caused some of the large assembly to cough. On the Ruler's instructions it was placed outside the door. When I left, a camel squatting near the door was bellowing furiously, either at the smoke or because it was being branded.*
>
> *The Ruler's house is practical for receiving the many townees and Bedu who seem to call on him, and the only furnishings in the Majlis are carpets.*

During this era Sheikh Rashid had to overcome an almost crippling lack of funds to embark upon a campaign of modernisation and new projects. One advisor from this juncture told a local newspaper: "The activity was non-stop. For every Rs. 50,000 from customs dues he would start another project costing six million."

But Sheikh Rashid was never wasteful. He invested in either public service necessities, or in projects that would generate more income. His mother, Sheikha Hassa, herself a successful businesswoman, had told her eldest son: "Never sow seeds which don't bear fruit," and this came to be a guiding ethos throughout his life.

Sheikh Rashid invested heavily in schools and attracted teaching support from the governments of Kuwait and Egypt. In 1949 he opened

*The Trucial Coast desperately
needed a modern medical facility.
Al Maktoum Hospital opened in
1949. (top) Sheikh Rashid and
other Trucial Rulers at the
opening ceremony. (centre) The
first ward and ambulance
(left) A mobile vaccination unit.*

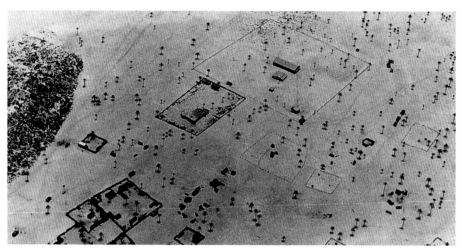

(top) Al Maktoum Hospital sat within its own compound, the adjacent building being the home of the Trucial States Medical Officer, Dr Donald McCaulley. (centre) A unique shot of the labour team that worked on the hospital. (right) British engineer Bill Smith, who was charged with building the hospital.

Al Maktoum Hospital, the first modern medical facility on the Trucial Coast. Later he expanded it with financial support from the Trucial States Development Fund (through the Trucial States Council, the British-led administrative committee comprising the political agent and the Rulers of the sheikhdoms, which first sat in March 1952).

The opening of a hospital was a major breakthrough for both Dubai and the region. Year after year Al Maktoum Hospital dealt with a growing number of patients. Sheikh Rashid funded an almost annual expansion of services and construction of new wards.

When his own finances did not allow, he was never too proud to seek help. In 1958, for instance, he pre-empted private sector involvement in the western world's medical system when seeking sponsorship for Al Maktoum Hospital. That year he secured support from British Petroleum, now BP, which paid for generators that supplied electricity to two new wards.

Sheikh Rashid's best-known project from this era was the development of Dubai's Creek. His sheikhdom had, by the 1950s, eclipsed Sharjah as the main trade hub on the Trucial Coast. In 1950, a British report stated that 110 ships called on Dubai, compared with 31 in Sharjah. Another document the same year, produced by the Residency Agent, reviewed three main export areas. In September 1950, £26,000 was attributed to shells, dried fish and bird guano, £5,000 to red oxide and Rs. 1.5 million to pearls. The same document estimated that up to 85% of imports were re-exported, mostly to Iran.

Yet despite these impressive figures, Dubai's port was crude and inefficient. Large vessels had to weigh anchor a mile offshore and unload onto smaller tenders that were able to navigate the Creek's shallow waters. Gradual silting meant that even fishing boats were finding the Creek difficult to navigate. By 1954, the Creek was as shallow as two feet in some places.

Consultants Sir William Halcrow and Partners were contracted to survey the Creek and reported back with plans for dredging that would cost around £600,000. This was a massive amount for a tiny sheikhdom, yet Sheikh Rashid told those in his Majlis: "We must. Everything depends on our finding a way."

He reformed Dubai Customs during the 1950s, agreed a new tax with the merchant community that would help fund the scheme, and took a major loan from the Kuwaiti government. The project eventually began in 1959 and transformed Dubai town forever.

"After the Creek's dredging was completed, more ships called in at Dubai to unload their cargo," observed one of the most influential figures in this administration. "The need for warehouses and other port facilities became very urgent because shipping lines had decided to use Dubai as their main port in the Gulf...the customs duties on imported goods were then used for building other facilities."

This new infrastructure was a boon to shipping and cargo handling in Dubai and was the key to winning the sheikhdom's battle to become the key trade entrepot on the coast. One British trade report, for the last quarter of 1960, stated: "During October, November and December, a total of 79 ships called at Dubai, of which 51 were British. A total of 25,486 tons of cargo was discharged and 245 tons were loaded. No ship called at Sharjah during the period under review. Sharjah cargo was relayed through the port of Dubai."

An annual Trucial States summary for the same year reported: "Dubai, still the commercial capital of the Trucial States and likely to remain so throughout, at least, the 1960s in spite of developing oil wealth in Abu Dhabi, has enjoyed another prosperous year. Trading activity has shown a considerable upward trend, with the value of imports at over £6 million, showing an increase of over 20% in 1959."

Sheikh Rashid had effectively taken control of his father's administration after 1939 and emerged as the most enlightened leader among the seven Trucial States – indeed, the entire Gulf. It was two decades before he became Ruler in his own right on the death of Sheikh Saeed. During that time his innovative thinking ensured that Dubai would have the necessary infrastructure to overcome recession and consolidate its position as the Lower Arabian Peninsula's leading trade hub. From this point onwards the sheikhdom would continue to grow and prosper. But Sheikh Rashid was not finished.

His grand scheme needed more big projects, and he needed help...

Chapter Six

Unusual man… with an unusual vision

There is a boundary to men's passions when they act from feelings;
but none when they are under the influence of imagination.
— *Edmund Burke, statesman*

The Suez Crisis hit the Middle East in 1956. It pitted Egypt against an alliance of France, Britain and Israel, the European nations seeking to protect their economic and trading interests in the Suez Canal, while Israel wanted to open the canal for its shipping. When the USSR threatened to intervene on behalf of Egypt, the United States feared a larger war, and forced the British and French to withdraw.

Along with the Cuban Missile Crisis, this was perhaps one of the closest moments during the Cold War when the prospect of conflict between east and west was most real. In Britain, the crisis resulted in the resignation of the Prime Minister, Anthony Eden.

One of those in the ruling Conservative Party to avoid any sort of blame was a young newcomer to the Commons, Edward (Ted) Heath. The son of a builder, Heath had been elected Member of Parliament for Bexley only in 1950. He was swiftly appointed as Government Whip and, because of the convention that Whips do not speak in Parliament, had managed to keep out of the controversy over Suez.

Heath was a newcomer to the Commons, but he was adept at politics and had long since allied himself to Eden's eventual successor, Harold MacMillan – nicknamed 'Supermac' and 'Mac the Knife' – who was Prime Minister from 1957 to 1963.

For Heath it was the beginning of a career in which he rarely put a foot wrong. An intellectual giant, he won the leadership election in 1965, and became the youngest leader in the party's history. The success of his party in the general election of 1970, and his personal elevation to Prime Minister, surprised almost all contemporary commentators and

The first colour photograph ever taken of Sheikh Rashid, around 1964.

was seen as a personal triumph.

Ted Heath may have avoided the fallout from Suez, but the crisis was to prove an awakening for the future Prime Minister. He read vociferously on the Middle East, and while his contemporaries focused totally on the likes of Egypt, Syria and Iraq, Heath enjoyed delving into the modern political histories of lesser-known states. The Trucial States, amid whispers of unheralded oil supplies and their apparent backwardness, fascinated him.

"The Trucial States were very, very interesting and I read a great deal on them even in the mid-1950s," Heath told the author. "I still recall coming across one briefing paper in the Commons Library that mentioned a coastal town called Dubai and its rather unconventional Crown Prince."

Heath, still at the beginning of his political career at that time, could not possibly have imagined that he would later meet that same Crown Prince on nearly a dozen occasions and that they would, in different ways, have a profound impact on the history of the Lower Arabian Peninsula.

"A few times during this period, from various different sources, I came across a passing reference to Dubai and sometimes also this fellow, an unusual man... with an unusual vision, who had taken on the challenge of bringing his town out of the dark ages," said Heath. "I got the impression that he was respected for his brains, and his effort, but among British officials there was something of an attitude that he would eventually fail as, without oil, there was nothing he could achieve."

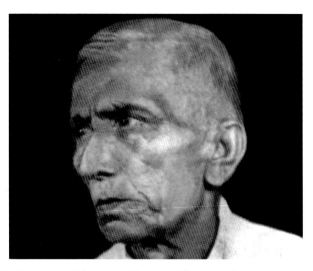

Future British Prime Minister Edward Heath and Sri Lankan watchman Mohi Eldin Pakeerali encountered Sheikh Rashid in different ways, but formed high opinions of the future Dubai Ruler.

With a chuckle Heath shrugged his shoulders as if to say how wrong could they be. How wrong they were would become personally evident to Heath later in his career. The future British Prime Minister and the future Prime Minister of the United Arab Emirates and Ruler of Dubai would encounter each other personally a few years later, when, as Heath put it, he saw "just what a remarkable man we were dealing with".

Even from his late teens, Sheikh Rashid's daily schedule was rigorous. He rose before six and attended morning prayers; most of the city was usually still asleep when he left the family home in Shindagha. By horse or occasionally camel, and later in his life by car, he would tour Dubai, to see for himself the projects and public works that were underway.

Although his informal morning tours were no secret, meeting the Ruler so casually, often without his guards and attendants, could be quite a shock for the unprepared.

"I arrived in Dubai on a steamer from India in 1948 to work for a construction company," says now-retired Sri Lankan businessman Mohi Eldin Pakeerali, who later went on to be part of the team that built Dubai International Airport. "Of course, in those days I was little more than a hired hand and was often left behind as night watchman. One morning I was at a site in Deira, near Al Nasr Square, if I recollect rightly one of the first three-storey buildings. It must have been winter as there was a heavy mist. It was late in my shift when I suddenly saw this figure on the other side of the site, when I was the only one who should have been there. There was a problem at the time with people stealing bags of cement. I shouted at this person, perhaps even cursed a little, and made my way over. Only when I was almost there did I see it was Sheikh Rashid. He was alone and had arrived to inspect the site.

"I thought he would throw me into jail. As I was apologising profusely he just chuckled. I think my horror at what I had done tickled his sense of humour."

Encounters with errant watchmen aside, Sheikh Rashid would travel the city largely incognito, given that it was so early in the morning. He mostly made these tours alone, his only concession to muggy or chill weather being a paletot.

By eight in the morning, he would return to his home for a light breakfast before making his way to Customs House, the office of the Ruler, by nine, a starting time which he observed strictly. It was a modest affair overlooking the Creek, his own single room quite lacking the grandeur or the trappings of office that might normally be associated with his position. He sat on a plain wooden chair behind a small desk, normally strewn untidily with papers, while his guests perched on similarly humble seating or a nearby suite. So unassuming was the Ruler's personal office that Sheikh Rashid himself was once mistaken for a clerk by newcomers, something that entertained him. It was here that he was at his most comfortable and relaxed. He had a firm open-door policy, rarely turning anyone away.

"Sheikh Rashid would often find it difficult to work as so many people wished to see him. But he would sit back from his papers and listen intently," says Saif Ahmed Al Ghurair, who would call on him regularly. "I rarely saw or heard of him losing his temper with anyone. He would occasionally light his pipe as he listened, and when replying, would pause at the end of a sentence to choose his words carefully. His response was always measured. He was never hasty."

By one in the afternoon, Sheikh Rashid would leave his office and return to his house, where he would eat lunch, usually consisting of fish, before taking a short afternoon nap. After being woken at around four, he would again leave his home to tour the projects and works with which he was most concerned.

During his early years, before he had even thought of owning a motor vehicle, Sheikh Rashid would go through this arduous ritual in the afternoon heat alone on foot, or in the saddle, constantly stopping to confer with whomever he encountered – merchants, traders, or simply a passing member of the public.

He was particularly fond of riding in the afternoon. The Maktoum family maintained a stable of up to 20 horses next to Al Fahidi Fort, today the Dubai Museum, and in their private gardens in Ras Al Khaimah where, as a youngster, Sheikh Rashid had first learned to manage a horse. He was especially active in the saddle during the late 1930s and 1940s, even after acquiring his first car. This was the period during which he and his versatile Arabian horse, 'Al Sqalawi', became something of a local sensation.

A big bay-coloured stallion, the animal formed a firm attachment to his owner. When Sheikh Rashid dismounted to speak with someone or to walk, the horse would follow, never allowing him out of sight. Sheikh Rashid loved horses, and his horsemanship showed it. He and Al Sqalawi sometimes put on impromptu shows, a few tricks, which were "actually quite good," recalls Hamad bin Sukat. "He was attached to Al Sqalawi. When the horse died Sheikh Rashid continued to ride, but not quite as much."

For a man who was not known for over sentimentality his reaction was extreme – he never replaced Al Sqalawi and thereafter mostly used a car for his tours. The Ruler's first car had been purchased in 1932, but had often remained idle during the Al Sqalawi era. It was only after the death of his horse that Sheikh Rashid began increasingly to take his morning and afternoon tours of Dubai by vehicle. It was the second automobile to arrive in the Trucial States, the first having appeared two years previously, owned by the Khansaheb family. In 1934, Sheikh Rashid took delivery of a brand-new Ford which was brought to Dubai by boat, having been purchased through the Bahrain-based Kanoo Company.

After returning home in the evening, it was time to take on more official business in the traditional evening Majlis, an occasion where the Ruler gives his people the opportunity to meet him and share problems or grievances. This duty was one that Sheikh Rashid took very seriously, but however long-suffering he was, his open-door policy could sometimes try the patience of friends and confidantes.

"You expect complaints in a Majlis, but some individuals took a liberty in complaining to Sheikh Rashid almost every day. This said, he would sit and hear their problems with boundless patience," recalls Zakariah Doleh, a Dubai property developer. "One evening Sheikh Rashid was deep in thought when a known trouble-maker entered, a man who came to the Majlis nearly every evening to moan. He started shouting in Sheikh Rashid's direction, and was rounded on by some of the Majlis heavyweights, notably Humaid bin Drai, who demanded he leave Rashid in peace for once."

Bin Drai himself takes up the story: "I told this man to be quiet, but Sheikh Rashid intervened, quite upset, and insisted that he wished to hear these minor grievances. That was his personality. He momentarily forgot the pressing problems of the state to deal with an individual. He cared for his people."

Official business settled, usually by nine in the evening, Sheikh Rashid would turn the Majlis into a debating chamber. Surrounded by those whose views he respected, and who had shown themselves capable of achieving the tasks he set – almost a prerequisite for those whom he called his friends – he found himself free to share his dreams and aspirations for Dubai.

"Sheikh Rashid was in the habit of opening the floor to discussion. When he had an idea or a scheme, he would ask those assembled, his confidantes and those whose opinions he trusted, their thoughts," recalls Saif Ahmed Al Ghurair, the prominent local businessman and head of a family which has been well-established in the city for more than a century. "Sheikh Rashid would sit back and listen intently, watching as the debate was passed around the room. Often there would be friendly argument and a whole range of opinions surfaced.

"Eventually, he would sit forward and add his voice to the proceedings. But his opinion would not necessarily stifle talk and the voicing of contrary opinion. In the Majlis he loved to join in the debate. It was usually quite lively."

This process seemed to work, and over the years Sheikh Rashid drew around him a growing number of men who in his view represented the brightest of the local community. They were encouraged to think the unthinkable, and when projects emerged many of those within the favoured grouping found themselves charged with the planning and execution of Dubai's bravest schemes.

Donald Hawley, a former British Political Resident, told his colleagues in the Arabian Department of the Foreign Office that Dubai's Majlis was "an Arabian Camelot," with Sheikh Rashid presiding over it like the legendary King Arthur. Hawley was a fluent Arabic speaker, and no stranger to the Majlis; during the early years of Sheikh Rashid's rule, he was one of the most trusted foreigners in Dubai.

The Ruler's opinions were crystal clear: "Although undoubtedly a strongman within his own sphere of influence, Sheikh Rashid is something of a democrat in some ways," he wrote. "He respects talented individuals and will include them in discussions on policy and Dubai's projects. The Ruler's internal political position continues to grow stronger...most people are very content when they compare themselves with their neighbours."

Dubai's progressive Majlis system was an important factor in encouraging the city's development – but although Sheikh Rashid could be unforgiving if he were let down, his casual generosity to his inner circle of confidantes sometimes caused anxiety. In 1961, the Political Agent reported: "I have been trying to persuade Sheikh Rashid for some time not to give away his land, which is a valuable asset in a relatively poor state, and to auction it. But he still gives it away to people who could afford to pay, and the other day gave a large plot...shown as a municipal reserve on his own town plan!"

Sheikh Mohammed bin Khalifa Al Maktoum, the Ruler's nephew, was a trusted part of the vibrant Majlis scene. Today the chairman of Dubai's Lands Department, he recalls the melting point of ideas which was the sheikhdom's think tank: "An idea would be thrown into the discussion. While concepts would be passed around, torn apart and put back together, Sheikh Rashid would sit back and say nothing. It might take a few days of solid discussion to reach a conclusion, but this inevitably proved the right way. Sheikh Rashid would listen and form his own views. This method of doing things was never a failure. You only have to look at the progress achieved to see that."

It is a view echoed by Hamad bin Sukat, one of the closest of confidantes and an inseparable friend of Sheikh Rashid during the last 50 years of his life: "Sheikh Rashid did not want to be surrounded by people who agreed with him all the time. He was very down to earth. From every foreign trip he made, he brought back ideas to Dubai and considered their application. Often these debates went on late into the night. Later, Sheikh Rashid would formulate his plans. If someone made a valid point that contradicted his own view, he would be happy to take this on board. In that sense he was very democratic."

Sheikh Rashid considered the Majlis to effectively be the parliamentary chamber of Arab democracy. Although he was a supreme authority, he

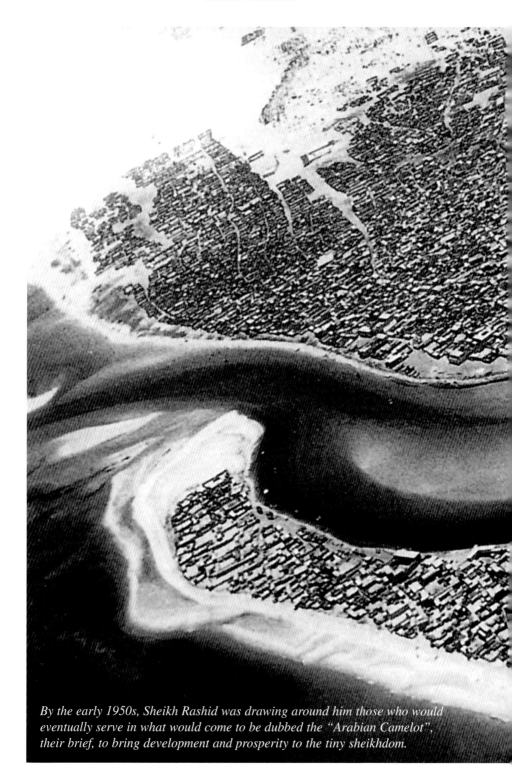

By the early 1950s, Sheikh Rashid was drawing around him those who would eventually serve in what would come to be dubbed the "Arabian Camelot", their brief, to bring development and prosperity to the tiny sheikhdom.

conducted his Majlis with adherence to free speech. People could speak their minds without fear of punishment. On another occasion several Majlis stalwarts were disgusted by the tone of one man who complained bitterly and somewhat disrespectfully to the Ruler. Sheikh Rashid sat calmly through the encounter and, when questioned later about his lenience, he told prominent businessman Khalaf Al Habtoor: "I will not use my power against those who are less powerful than I."

Certainly there seems to have been nothing autocratic about his behaviour. He often amended his plans at the end of a Majlis debate to take into consideration what he had heard. It was undoubtedly from these lively exchanges that the formulae for many of the Dubai government's most original projects came. It was a closed group, numbering on occasions from 20 to 50 people, who were privy to the innermost aspirations of their Ruler. Their lively discussions went on until a conclusion was reached, or until Sheikh Rashid himself tired after a long and strenuous day. Only when the evening Majlis was completed would he take his evening meal, usually beef. First-time guests to these gatherings were warned that when he called ahead by telephone to Za'abeel Palace to order a meal prepared for his arrival, it was time to take their leave, unless they had been invited to join him.

On one occasion, however, this simple routine fell apart, recalls Zakariah Doleh: "The palace cooks knew that Sheikh Rashid was returning only when he called the gatehouse. The same group of people usually were on guard there, so they knew Sheikh Rashid's voice. Once though, a new man was on duty and told the Ruler of Dubai, in no uncertain terms, to stop bothering the palace and find himself a restaurant. Sheikh Rashid was momentarily speechless and then broke into fits of laughter. Even when he explained who he was, the guard thought the call was a prank. Luckily for him, Sheikh Rashid was a man who revelled in humour and repeated this story for visitors to his Majlis for many months to come."

After a light evening meal Sheikh Rashid would end his day after midnight, barely five hours before he was to rise the following morning. But despite these 18 to 19 hour days, those in the inner circle whom he invited to visit Za'abeel Palace for dinner would find him unable to switch off mentally. He would often continue discussions on projects and development well into the night and therefore sleep for only three or four hours.

Throughout his 78 years, Sheikh Rashid was often to draw on the influence of his mother in his measured decision-making. He was undoubtedly ambitious and, surrounded as he was by like-minded modernisers, the mood in the Majlis was often one of unbridled optimism.

On the morning after a good session in the Majlis, he would often have finalised plans mentally and would send for those he needed, either to meet informally before breakfast at the palace or in his office. It mattered little that Sheikh Rashid spoke only Arabic; his way of getting around the language barrier in dealing with employees who spoke other languages was simplicity itself. Kamal Hamza, first head of Dubai Municipality, remembers the Dubai Ruler's elementary approach to the problems of communication:

"Sheikh Rashid used to draw every project on the sand with a camel stick before asking engineers to prepare designs for them. He used to tell us to have a road there, or a building there. The designers used to follow his markings on the sand," he recalls.

From the minds of those serving in Sheikh Rashid's Camelot, to the sand, where Sheikh Rashid often etched his plans, the beginnings of a new Dubai were now being forged. The sheikhdom was about to enter the most dramatic period of development in its history.

Chapter Seven

Foundations

You can't build a reputation on what you're going to do.
— Henry Ford, industrialist

After 1940, as the Ruler, Sheikh Saeed was content to recede further into the background and leave the business of running Dubai to his son. Sheikh Rashid effectively taking on the powers of the Ruler. With political stability regained, and the levers of power within his grasp, Sheikh Rashid was now free to pursue the development that he so desperately wanted.

One problem was money – and, for a change, not the lack of it. In 1946, one year after the end of the Second World War, a report produced for the Imperial Bank of Iran – a forerunner to the British Bank of the Middle East – commented that the merchant community of the Trucial States was now almost entirely centred on Dubai. But despite this status as a trading hub, old habits continued, particularly with regard to money. Many people kept their savings buried in the sand under their homes, while the richer merchant classes normally used a small personal safe or even chose to hide small fortunes around their business premises. Sheikh Rashid knew that a modern banking system would strengthen the trading community in the city, and he sought to bring a reliable depository to the sheikhdom, although this was to take nearly a decade.

On January 5, 1954, an agreement was signed with the Imperial Bank of Iran. Negotiations had not gone completely smoothly, with the bank holding out for an exclusivity clause that would give it a monopoly for a quarter of a century, while Sheikh Rashid, drawing on the experiences of Bahrain further up the Gulf, had pressed for a 15-year agreement. The two parties settled on 20 years, with Sheikh Rashid gaining an article in the agreement providing for the employment of Dubai nationals as

Having taken on most of his father's powers, Sheikh Rashid now began a quest to bring development to his city-state.

clerical and junior staff whenever possible.

Dubai's souqs, which had grown during the Second World War, bucking a recessionary trend that had been evident all along the Trucial Coast, exploded into further growth with the end of the conflict. New businesses began to arrive in large numbers, the Gulf economy was booming and in Dubai there was a government that was stable, set low taxes and could even be said to be disinterested in unwieldy administration.

By 1952, Sri Lanka-born Mohi Eldin Pakeerali had risen through the ranks at his construction company to become a foreman when, while on a job, he saw an opportunity to purchase some building equipment from a defunct contractor.

"The government just wanted commerce to grow. With a friend who was a Dubai national, we bought the equipment and employed a few men. After my partner made some representations directly to Sheikh Rashid, we tendered for several government jobs and were given work," said Ali. "The government paid on time and was accommodating, but I always remember Sheikh Rashid's instructions to my partner."

"Get it right, deliver on time and on budget," Dubai's Prince Regent instructed them. There were countless instances of people failing to do so, something that he would not tolerate.

In 1954, attracted by negligible customs duties and an absence of red tape, the Imperial Trading Corporation (ITC) of Karachi set up its regional office in Dubai. G B Choithram Jethwani, who arrived in the sheikhdom with ITC and who still works in Dubai as GeeBee Trading Company, remembers the simplicity of Sheikh Rashid's pro-business administration: "I had lived in Hong Kong and Singapore, and had been warned that Dubai would be basic in its amenities. There was no air-conditioning so I simply bought two fans, installed them each side of the seat in my office, and ran them off car batteries. I also brought in a kerosene fuelled fridge freezer. There were no licensing requirements in 1954. You just began trading and pretty soon you would inevitably get to know Sheikh Rashid, as he encouraged people to go to the Majlis and talk to him."

Dubai was well known for its open-door policy, but Choithram points out that the administration was tolerant only up to a point. "Our company first came to Dubai in 1950 in the pursuit of a large debt

Sheikh Rashid, his brother Sheikh Khalifa (second right) and Easa Saleh Al Gurg (left), during a visit to the home of prominent Indian businessman G B Choithram to mark the festival of Diwali.

from a Persian merchant in the souq. Sheikh Rashid knew that Dubai needed a good reputation and did not allow the merchant class to be irresponsible and get themselves into debt. Once we had proven our case he jailed the merchant. Ultimately we got paid."

Several years later Choithram, by then an established senior figure within the Indian community in Dubai, was seconded into a debt inquiry by Sheikh Rashid. One of the top Persian merchants faced ruin after a shipload of sugar had failed to arrive from Holland. After weeks of awaiting the overdue boat, Lloyds of London eventually confirmed that the vessel, which the suppliers had said was transporting the consignment, did not even exist. Sheikh Rashid checked the Persian merchant's invoices for himself and then, convinced that a swindle was being perpetrated, dispatched the head of the Customs Department, along with Choithram, to investigate.

"I was called to the Ruler's Office and given a couple of hours' notice that we were going to Europe," Choithram recalls. "The Dubai government paid and made all the arrangements for an investigation which took us to Holland, Germany and London. We eventually resolved the matter. This was typical of Sheikh Rashid's no-nonsense approach."

While Dubai was performing relatively well, the immediate post-war years saw no great improvement in the economic health of the Trucial Coast as a whole, with the biggest casualty being the general welfare of the population. Between the wars the first real strides in the fields of medical care and basic education had been made, but now the development

113

Dubai in the early 1950s. There was still little tangible development or much sign of prosperity, although the town was by now the most prosperous on the Trucial Coast.

of these basic amenities was virtually suspended. By 1947 Sheikh Rashid was acutely aware that for Dubai's population of 25,000 to grow any further, the sheikhdom had to improve on its extremely basic services. Up until the end of the war any serious injuries or illnesses on the Trucial Coast were still being treated as far afield as Bombay in India, while relatively minor ailments were either treated with locally produced potions, or not at all.

For several years the British had been attempting to improve cooperation between the sheikhdoms of the coast, and after Sheikh Rashid had repeatedly brought up the subject of health care with British representatives, improvements in medical services began. As early as 1939 Dr Habib Al Redha, the town's first qualified doctor, opened a pharmacy in the Bur Dubai souq area. While the new development was welcomed by expatriates, who suffered their ailments in silence, took a long journey to a Western-run facility in Muscat or Bahrain, or trusted the doubtful locally-produced cure-all potions. Western medicines were still looked on with great suspicion by the local community.

The attitude of the ruling family in Dubai helped, Sheikh Saeed and Sheikh Rashid both having visited and employed the care of medical centres in India and Iran. But breaking down barriers among the Arab population was clearly going to take time. The opening of the Al Redha Pharmacy coincided with the appointment of a British Medical Officer to the Trucial Coast, jointly financed by the government of India and the British Foreign Office. The officer travelled through the sheikhdoms every few weeks, but while his services were in demand from expatriates, others in the community were not convinced.

For hundreds of years people with illnesses had taken their troubles to the mutawwa (religious man) whose response was an act of faith. Alternatively, some communities had what could be loosely described as a medicine man or woman who relied, like healers of the Middle Ages, on local herbal potions. While they had their successes, both the mutawwa and practitioners of traditional medicines also had extremely high mortality rates among their patients. Phlebotomy, or blood-letting, was common.

"Sheikh Rashid knew that these Western treatments were, in most cases, going to be better for the people. To break down the barriers, he encouraged everyone in the Ruler's household to go to the visiting doctor. Sheikh Rashid also made it known to everyone in the Majlis that he believed they and their families should utilise him when they were ill," says Hamad bin Sukat. "He also made a point of visiting the doctor himself, not necessarily for treatment, but as a show of support – a confidence-building measure."

With many prominent Arab members of Dubai society and their families seen to be using these new medicines and strange techniques, gradually suspicion gave way to a reluctant acceptance. The visit of the British doctor became an event in the town's diary, and even the Bedu, always most suspicious of any Western influence, could often be seen sporting crisp white bandages, a striking contrast to their worn brown kandoras, as they passed through the souq.

By 1950, a report on the dispensary indicated that 6,685 people used the facility in one year. Malaria continued to be the most common affliction needing treatment, along with heat stroke and sunburn. Among other common ailments were diseases of the digestive system, eye problems, and ulcers.

Until the opening of Al Maktoum Hospital in Dubai, there was not a single modern hospital in the whole of the 32,000 square miles of the Trucial States. This first modern, fully-equipped medical facility opened in Deira in 1949, funded broadly by Dubai with some limited British aid. There was also some financial input from neighbouring sheikhdoms in return for access to emergency care. In 1951, for instance, Sheikh Rashid paid Rs. 40,000 towards a Rs. 70,000 annual budget for the running of the hospital. After the British government and the other Trucial Rulers had contributed there was still a shortfall, which was eventually made up by an appeal to the larger companies trading in Dubai, who raised Rs. 7,000. The following year, there was an even larger shortfall in the budget, and a second surgeon was badly needed to cope with growing demand. That year the annual appeal brought a poor result, so the British government agreed an additional £2,000 payment and requested help from the Red Cross with provision of some medicines. Initially, with only 38 beds, Al Maktoum Hospital was extremely limited in its emergency care. But out-patient facilities developed rapidly, and it was soon attracting residents from all along the coast, in addition to many of the Bedu tribes from the interior who flocked into Dubai.

The seven Trucial Rulers all had seats on the hospital's executive committee. Also sitting on this body were Easa Saleh Al Gurg of the British Bank of the Middle East – today the UAE Ambassador to Great

Britain – Bill Duff of the Customs Department, and the British Political Agent. Al Maktoum Hospital is viewed by many historians as Sheikh Rashid's first pet project. Sitting alongside his father in several Trucial States Council meetings throughout the 1950s, Sheikh Rashid often spoke of the need to add further facilities. With its ad hoc system of finance, which left it constantly short of cash, Al Maktoum Hospital was only just able to function, and further development was impossible. Within a decade the 16 men's beds and 12 women's beds were clearly insufficient to serve a community of 100,000 among the seven Trucial States. The hospital's Annual Report for 1959 said that in-patient figures had risen from 143 in 1954 to 416 in 1958. It was a massive improvement but, the report said, still inadequate. Between 1956 and 1958, out-patient care had risen from 10,522 to 19,045.

Despite a general lack of funds, Sheikh Rashid continued to channel what additional cash he could toward the hospital. While the British authorities grappled with an overall problem in the region, Sheikh Rashid personally ordered and paid for a new Labour Room and Female Waiting Room. He also funded a women's health information programme. The 1959 Annual Report said that of the 142 babies delivered at Al Maktoum Hospital during 1958, 104 were normal births – "which is very encouraging" – and indicated that "the dangerous local custom of using salt after confinement is decreasing as new knowledge filters through. The use of salt after confinement is often the cause of prolonged labour and in some cases it makes it a mechanical impossibility for the child to be born."

By the middle of the century, Britain's policy of non-interference in the internal affairs of the Trucial Coast had, at last, been replaced with a more positive approach. In the face of an oil rush involving several other international powers elsewhere in the region, London and Bombay had decided to take a more active role. This included material support in the form of expertise and limited financial aid, much of which was channeled into the friendly entrepot of Dubai, supporting Sheikh Rashid's own initiatives.

From early in the 1950s, an attempt had also been made to add a more formal touch to the occasional meetings between the Rulers of the coast. The British proposed the formation of a Trucial States Council, and March 1952 saw its first meeting. Subcommittees covering education, public health (centred on Al Maktoum Hospital) and

Pictured with a British advisor, Abu Dhabi Ruler Sheikh Shakhbut remained on the fringes of the Trucial States Council.

agriculture were formed to report to the wider Council.

From the beginning this informal grouping, sitting only twice a year, became hostage to the individual personalities within it. Sheikh Shakhbut of Abu Dhabi attended only infrequently, while others occasionally boycotted meetings to protest at British decisions or score points against fellow Rulers. On the whole, though, the Council seems to have been successful in its limited spheres of interest. Examination of a typical session, held at Sharjah on November 17, 1953, shows that among the issues discussed were oil revenues, road traffic regulations, travel documents, Al Maktoum Hospital, slave traffic (the 1926 Slavery Convention adopted concrete rules and articles, and slavery and slave trade were banned, but the practice took decades to be completely stamped out), and water resources. Both Sheikh Saeed and Sheikh Rashid were present.

In the late 1950s, before the Trucial States Development Fund was set up, the British Foreign Office gave the Council a hefty £10,000 annual 'development budget,' with an eye to encouraging further cooperation between the seven sheikhdoms. In 1959 the Rulers agreed unanimously to use this to purchase a Caterpillar road grader and, the following year, to establish a small medical unit in Ras Al Khaimah.

As the seeds of limited progress were being sown elsewhere on the peninsula, Sheikh Rashid was paying attention to his own sheikhdom. The town could only grow so far without basic amenities. A town plan was in place, and basic roads were replacing sand tracks through the heart of the town. Medical facilities were now available. All brought a better life and greater prosperity. Yet for Dubai nationals to prosper within this newly affluent trading environment, Sheikh Rashid also understood that they needed to be equipped to capitalise on the opportunities that were present. That meant education.

Even half a century ago, education in the region was in a shocking state. A few children from rich families would be shipped abroad. Throughout the sheikhdoms, a merchant or two was philanthropic enough to fund a school, limited places meaning that even then only a tiny percentage of children would learn to read or write. However, the recession in the pearling trade, coupled with a wartime embargo, had financially crippled many within the upper classes, including the larger merchants, who had been forced to curtail such philanthropic spending.

In Dubai, the 1930s had seen the closure of Al Falah, Al Saada and Al Salmeia Schools, leaving only Muhammad bin Ahmad bin Dalmuk's Al Ahmadiya as a source of proper education in the town. Indeed, while Al Ahmadiya was important, its syllabus centred on Arabic and Koran studies, and therefore did not add tremendous value to a pretty dismal situation.

Apart from the education offered by Al Ahmadiya, some boys and girls were instructed in the Koran through a Kuttab (religious school), although the mutawwas who ran these showed little interest in the three Rs.

"Both Sheikh Saeed and Sheikh Rashid were aware that education was important if society in Dubai was to be developed," recalls Dubai academic Abdullah bin Jassim Al Muthairy. "Sheikh Rashid had himself been one of the few who had benefited from the opportunity of a basic education. Those he drew around him in the Majlis as his acolytes were all the most able in local society, most of them from families which were keen to ensure their early education. Therefore Sheikh Rashid knew well the value of a proper schooling."

Education seemed a seed that would eventually bear fruit for the whole community. Al Muthairy himself had benefited from Sheikh Rashid's predisposition in favour of schooling. When he was a young teenager his father, Jassim Al Muthairy, had died prematurely, leaving a large family.

"I went to Sheikh Rashid in his Majlis to ask for help. He responded by giving me a letter to gain entry into a local school and then paying for my education fees, enabling me to later get a good job and support the family," says Al Muthairy.

Such off-the-cuff scholarships were not uncommon. In 1952 Ahmed Al Ahli, a father of five, died when the fishing boat he was serving on capsized 10 kilometres off the coast. His family was destitute.

"I was the eldest son, at 11," says Mohammed Al Ahli. "At the time, I was a runner, doing odd jobs in a food shop in the souq. I earned a couple of rupees, but that was it. My family had nothing when my father died."

Mohammed and his mother visited Sheikh Rashid at his office to plead their case for help.

"I remember him sitting back in his chair as we spoke. His face was full of sorrow as he heard our problems," recalls Al Ahli. "When my mother had finished, he ordered his staff to give us some coffee and explained what he could do."

Sheikh Rashid gave the young boy a far higher-paid menial job in his office and found him a place with a private tutor who ran small classes in written and spoken Arabic and English. He also gave a small grant to the family, promising that when Mohammed could take on the duties of a better-educated employee his salary would rise. True to his word, a little more than a year later Mohammed joined one of the small government departments that Sheikh Rashid was opening to serve his thriving entrepot.

One of the most educated men in Dubai just before the war was Sheikh Mana bin Rashid Al Maktoum. Sheikh Mana was a major participant in the Ruler's Majlis and played an important part in Dubai's fledgling education system in the 1930s. Considered something of an intellectual, Sheikh Mana was informally given the portfolio of education. As Minister of Education, he used his office to develop the schooling system by cajoling local individuals and enterprises into offering the same sort of financial assistance that had been seen before the Great Depression.

In 1945, Dubai teacher Hassan Mirza Al Sayegh established Al Madrasah Al Ahlia. Al Sayegh had not intended to become a teacher and was involved in commerce, but in the early 1940s he had been crossing the Arabian Gulf in a dhow that sank during a storm. Unable to swim, he saved himself by clinging to a piece of flotsam. It was a stroke of unbelievable luck that Al Sayegh was picked up by a current and, after days adrift, found himself washed up on shore.

Al Sayegh's miraculous escape was tempered by his condition. The piece of wood that carried him to safety had a rusty nail embedded in it. This had repeatedly been battered by the waves into his pelvis. The youngster was shipped by his family to India, where he required surgery that would make him lame for the remainder of his life.

India, however, was to change the course of his life. Over a slow and painful recovery period the youngster had nothing to do and could only sit. His family decided to give him an education and he was sent to a majoos, a Zoroastrian school for the Farsi community.

Zoroastrianism, which was founded in Persia by the prophet Zarathustra in the sixth or seventh century BC, is therefore one of the oldest religions in the world. The adherents of Zoroastrianism are known as Parsis because they originally fled to India to escape persecution in Persia.

There are not many Parsi communities left in India – with the majority concentrated in Mumbai (Bombay) – and their number there is gradually declining, but at the time of Al Sayegh's ensconcement within a Parsi school the education offered was of an extremely high standard. Around the time of the end of the Second World War, in 1945, Al Sayegh returned to Dubai. He was much changed. He could speak English, Persian, Farsi (a language derived from Persian), and had an excellent grounding in mathematics, making him one of the most educated men in Dubai. He set school fees at a very reasonable Rs. 2 per term, and Al Madrasah Al Ahlia was consequently packed with students drawn from the ruling family, as well as the merchant and middle classes. Because of its comprehensive syllabus (all other schools taught only Arabic and Koranic studies) the school was arguably the best to be found in the Trucial States at the time and, such being its reputation, Sheikh Rashid enrolled his second son, Sheikh Hamdan bin Rashid Al Maktoum, for his early schooling. The Dubai Ruler wished his son to speak English.

Classes of between 12 and 16 pupils began at 8 am and were completed just before noon prayers. Al Madrasah Al Ahlia would grow and eventually have a hand in the early education of many members of the generation that would surround Sheikh Rashid in the 1960s and 1970s. Many pupils were drawn from families that are prominent in Dubai and the UAE today, such as Al Rostamani, Al Futtaim, Al Ghurair, Al Habtoor, Al Dowais and Al Fardan.

A class at Al Madrasah Al Alia with Hassan Mirza Al Sayegh (in suit), Sheikh Hamdan bin Rashid Al Maktoum on his right. (inset) Al Sayegh in later years.

Both Sheikh Rashid and Sheikh Mana were active in seeking further support for education from richer Gulf States and from Great Britain. Soon after Al Madrasah Al Ahlia was opened, the British began funding a small fee-paying institute near the present day Clock Tower, while Egypt, Qatar, Saudi Arabia and Kuwait gave varying degrees of assistance. The latter was particularly keen, and for many years such was Kuwaiti encouragement that Dubai's whole education system was modelled on that of Kuwait. During the early 1950s the Kuwaiti government built and largely funded several schools, while in November 1958 Qatar, in addition to sending Arabic text books and teachers, donated two school buses to Dubai.

The education system was beginning to boom. A new primary school named Al Saeedia was opened near Customs House, overlooking the Creek. This school became the most important in Dubai, but was not without its problems. The first headmaster, Hashim Abu Emara, arrived and was doing a good job. But he was a controversial figure, a fervent Arab nationalist who was not afraid to speak his mind. Abu Emara soon attracted the wrath of the British, who generally stayed out of internal affairs unless anything – or anyone – threatened their position. The British had contributed little to society, but took exception to the headmaster of one of the Trucial Coast's few schools speaking out.

Abu Emara was replaced by the famous Zuhdi Al Khateeb, a venerable and non-political headmaster who took Al Saeedia through its golden period. He was so well liked and, indeed, considered so scholarly that he maintained a close relationship with Sheikh Rashid. Al Saeedia grew quickly causing Al Madrasah Al Ahlia to lose its pupils and, eventually, Hassan Mirza Al Sayegh would close his establishment and join Al Saeedia as a teacher.

Students graduating from Al Saeedia mostly moved on to Al Shaab, and then to Dubai Secondary School. The latter also acted as a base for the Dubai troop of the Boy Scout movement, of which Sheikh Rashid was chief patron. Throughout the Gulf States, however, education was seen as a breeding ground for dissent, perhaps even a battle ground for the hearts and minds of youngsters. The cause was Arab nationalism and, whatever his own personal sympathies, Sheikh Rashid was keen that the modern Dubai he was creating remained on a firmly neutral course. As the education system in Dubai was to develop, this was an issue to which he would return often in the future.

Dubai had long since overtaken Sharjah in the race to be the foremost town on the Trucial Coast. As early as the beginning of the Second World War, the population was double that of Abu Dhabi, and four times that of Sharjah. In trade terms, Dubai was far and away the leader.

Sheikh Rashid was quick to use his influence with the colonial power, along with his history of friendship, to bring material benefits to the emirate, Al Maktoum Hospital being a prime example of this. But while Dubai could certainly claim to be the trading capital of the coast, much to his chagrin, Sharjah was still Britain's seat of political power in the Lower Gulf.

An understanding of the emerging importance of the area led the Foreign Office to upgrade the post in Sharjah from Residency Agent to Political Agent in May 1953. Clearly, however, Sheikh Rashid had a case when he called for Britain's representative to be based in his town. He repeated the point in many consultations with the Political Agent during these years, and was rewarded for his perseverance in 1954 when the Agent finally moved to Dubai.

It was a highly positive development. The Political Agent took key roles in the Trucial States Council, initially as its chairman; he was Commander-in-Chief of the Trucial Oman Levies (later Trucial Scouts); and was judge and adjudicator in the majority of inter-sheikhdom disputes. He was also at the centre of all Britain's development projects along the Trucial Coast, charged with their planning and overall supervision. This was done on a case-by-case basis until 1956, when the Political Agent in Dubai was given a £450,000 annual budget as part of the Trucial States Development Fund. In many ways this was the final acknowledgement that Dubai had completed its journey of half a century, from a little-known backwater to being the effective capital of the Trucial Coast.

Chapter Eight

What's good for the merchants...

*Far better it is to dare mighty things, to win glorious triumphs,
even though checkered by failure, than to take rank with those poor
spirits who neither enjoy much nor suffer much, because they live
in the gray twilight that knows not victory nor defeat.*
— *Theodore Roosevelt, statesman*

Sheikh Rashid was a man of action, not words, yet one statement he made during his life has continued to be repeated and remains a summary of the thinking that underpinned his extraordinary drive. "What is good for the merchants, is good for Dubai," said Sheikh Rashid to his Majlis.

By the early 1950s, under a leadership that was effectively spearheaded by Sheikh Rashid, Dubai was regaining its buoyancy, its well-appointed Creek, the artery through which most of the city's trade flowed, at the centre of the biggest town on the Trucial Coast. With limited wharfage available, larger dhows, the traditional wooden vessels that plied the trading routes of the Gulf and surrounding oceans, were forced to moor three abreast.

"Even medium sized vessels were forced to anchor offshore and were unloaded using barges. Today 2,000 tonnes can be unloaded in half an hour. In 1951 that same amount took days," says George Chapman, who arrived as Gray Mackenzie and Co's 'man' in Dubai at the beginning of the decade

This made the task of Gray Mackenzie and Co, the licensed shipping agents in Dubai since 1891, altogether more difficult. Sheikh Rashid also believed that the resulting confusion was also creating loopholes in the collection of some of his much-needed tax revenues.

As early as 1952 Sheikh Rashid had noted in the Majlis that to boost

Sheikh Saeed and Sheikh Rashid with a number of nobles. Dubai's leadership was preparing to embark upon a period of unprecedented development.

the economy's capacity, facilities in the Creek needed expansion. Even then there were warnings that the nine-mile stretch of water was silting dangerously. For a period of months, Sheikh Rashid changed his rigid schedule to include, as often as possible, around half an hour standing near the tip of the entrance to the Creek, near his Shindagha home. He would watch the tides, occasionally stopping a fisherman or dhow captain to consult them. Dubai had often relied on its fishing fleet for its very existence since the 1700s, and Sheikh Rashid was to discover that the same ocean swells that were responsible for the area's rich fishing grounds were those which were slowly choking the Creek.

From late-September to mid-April, roughly 200 kilometres of Trucial States coastline is fed by a cool, plankton-rich stream of water from the Indian Ocean. This body of water provided a source of nutrition for local fish stocks, while bringing with it schools of non-indigenous tuna, mackerel and anchovy. This additional source of nutrition was vital to a region that relied on the sea for much of its food.

As late as 1969, the Trucial States Development Council reported that upwards of 30,000 nationals relied on the fishing industry for their income, far more than during the 1950s when fishing was a less well-organised industry. Older fishermen can still recall disastrous years when the Indian Ocean failed to feed the Gulf as normal. Fish stocks were affected badly, with devastating economic effect. Dried fish, for human and animal consumption, was one of few sources of protein in the desert hinterland, and was also a major export. The Trucial States Council reported that on an average annual catch of 10,000 tonnes during the early 1960s, as much as 6,000 tonnes found their way on to international markets, generating much-needed income.

Among the elders of the city there were several fishing merchants – boat-owners and heavyweights in the fish souq. As was appropriate when dealing with some of Dubai's major tax payers and employers, Sheikh Rashid ensured good relations with each.

The big fishing merchants owned large sail boats which held up to 30 people and set nets sometimes hundreds of metres long, parallel with the shore. It remains one of the most romantic of sights in the Arab world to see the crew pulling both ends of the net ashore a few hours later, chanting rhythmically throughout, before emptying the catch on the beach to be dried and sorted.

Of all the Trucial States Rulers, Sheikh Rashid was perhaps the most vocal in his support of the fishing community. He was also respected for his understanding of the industry, having on a number of occasions sailed with them. Up to the 1940s the seas around Abu Dhabi, and to a lesser extent Dubai, also boasted a large population of dugongs, or sea cows, believed to be the animal from which seafarers' stories of mermaids had arisen. Solitary and rarely-seen creatures, the occasional dugong did find itself caught in fish nets and would be killed and eaten. This would happen perhaps only a couple of times a year in Dubai and it became normal that the merchant owning the boat presented this animal to Sheikh Saeed or Sheikh Rashid, as a mark of respect.

During the 1950s, parts of the Creek silted up so suddenly that fishermen, some of whom utilised the Creek daily, were caught out and found themselves running aground. One fisherman, Rashid bin Dafous, recalls a long afternoon attempting to free his boat – and livelihood – from a sandbank.

"Once a boat was stuck it had to be dragged ashore. On this occasion myself and my crew were attempting to dislodge the boat, when we were spotted by Sheikh Rashid," says bin Dafous, who later served as chairman of the Dubai Fishermen's Cooperative Association. "He came over to us and told me everything would soon be put right."

The clamour for action grew that year, with the trading community making several representations requesting action. But for Sheikh Rashid, simply retaining the status quo seemed an anomaly. Instead he was formulating plans on a much grander scale. By 1954, shipping lanes into and out of the Creek were reduced by the build-up of silt, in some places the depth of the water becoming as shallow as two feet.

"In winter, the silt build up would cause the mouth of the creek to move 600 or 700 yards. The Creek was Dubai's lifeline, but boats were capsizing and sinking. It was a major headache," says Chapman.

Sheikh Rashid had tackled this growing threat to Dubai's prosperity by commissioning the consultants Sir William Halcrow and Partners to survey the Creek and urgently report back with plans to permanently open up the waterway. Halcrow eventually presented Sheikh Rashid with a massive redevelopment plan which, predictably, Sheikh Rashid wished to understand intimately before giving the go-ahead. Engineer Neville Allen, one of the top brains working for Halcrow in Dubai at the time, recalls: "It was a difficult job, but he was interested in learning as much as he could about any form of development. It was not enough to

say we are doing this or we will do that. He wanted to know why. And with his very lively mind he could understand our reasons."

Despite the limitations of his education, Sheikh Rashid was soon discussing with engineers the relative merits of training walls, steel piling and explosives. Allen recalls making what was expected to be a short final presentation to him, with drawings, on the final day of his initial survey.

"Sheikh Rashid made me stay with him for a number of hours to explain this drawing, and we had to keep the 'plane in Sharjah waiting," says Allen. "He wanted to learn the whole idea of the planning, the elevations and cross-sections, whatever was in the drawing."

The whole project would cost around £600,000, an impossible investment for the government of the day with its restricted revenues.

"We must," Sheikh Rashid told his Majlis, when those he trusted gave up in dismay at the price tag. "Everything depends it."

Dubai's commercial artery, its Creek, was silting up badly and this was having a major impact upon economic activity. The people turned to Sheikh Rashid to do something.

Seemingly undaunted at the prospect of spending, on one project, a figure which amounted to several years' Gross National Product for his city, Sheikh Rashid approached the task of financing in three ways, in advance of a proposed 1958 starting date on the scheme. Having long suspected the Customs Department of being inefficient, he countered this through the appointment of two new officials. At Sheikh Rashid's request the Emir of Bahrain seconded to Dubai Mahdi Al Tajir, one of his most effective officials, as Head of Customs, while Dubai national Ahmed bin Sulayem, a favourite of the Majlis, returned from a stint in Bombay, as number two in the department. Mahdi Al Tajir, who was to become one of Sheikh Rashid's most trusted lieutenants, remembers the scenario: "When Sheikh Rashid was asked by businessmen and merchants to widen and deepen the Creek, he immediately told them that he had to find the money for the project. The businessmen proposed that the government impose customs fees on imported goods."

The government set a base rate of Rs. 4 on every Rs. 100 of imported goods, a rate of 4% which, according to Al Tajir, realised around Rs. 60,000 annually, most of which was gobbled up by the Creek project.

In Sheikh Saeed's days 'government' was a relative overstatement; all along the coast there was little in terms of infrastructure and social service. Aside from the Ruler – the highest authority, decision-maker and arbitrator in disputes – there was little or no formal administration.

Taxes had long been collected on a system called Iqta, or 'tax farming'. Historically most prevalent in Egypt, Rome, Great Britain, France and the Middle East, it was the principle of giving the responsibility of tax collection to citizens or groups, rather than the government. The system was considered very effective for tax revenue collection. Any surplus in yearly revenues remained with the nominee as profit, and this was why the method was weak, because the tax-farmers often abused the taxpayers for tax collection in order to maximise their returns.

In Dubai, Sheikh Saeed had divided the town among either the leading merchant or local head man in each area. The last man to hold a Tax Farming Agreement with the government was a Mohammed bin Ahmed in 1954.

This system ensured that at least some cash was entering the Ruler's coffers. But the lack of sufficient up-to-date economic information often meant the Ruler set a low figure on some areas, ensuring his administration received less than it might, while some farming representatives retained a small fortune.

Within a year this new broom of Al Tajir and bin Sulayem had swept away much of the previous inefficiency and the collection of duties was up. This increased figure was gobbled up by what was the most ambitious development project ever undertaken along the Trucial Coast, although even then tax revenues would be only a drop in the ocean.

Dubai undoubtedly needed a healthy Creek for its very existence, and Sheikh Rashid also understood that the merchants relied on the Creek for their own prosperity. It was to them he turned next when seeking further funding for the dredging. He introduced so-called 'Creek Bonds', ensuring some of the major users of the Creek had a personal investment in the project. The uptake on these was extremely high, an indication of his support on the ground. Even following this initiative, however, there was a projected deficit in funding of some half a million pounds and the Dubai government, with the support of the British authorities, completed a loan arrangement from the Emir of Kuwait.

The 'Dubai Creek Dredging Fund' eventually raised £200,000 through improved tax collection, 'Creek Bond' sales, loans, and small donations from businessmen and some of the banks in Dubai. With this in place, Sheikh Rashid could get to work.

By 1959 the project began in earnest, the heavy dredgers, mechanical diggers and modern lifting gear being in complete contrast to the sleepy wind-tower houses which bordered much of the Creek. Initially, the project aimed to create a canal 4,000 feet long and six feet deep and in a second stage sheet piling of 1,200 feet and 11,700 feet was laid on both sides of the creek. As a result, shipping movement would increase and vessels of up to 500 tonnes were able to enter the Creek.

"Dubai was propelled into the modern age with the dredging of the old Creek," says Hashim Al Dabal. "Dredging of the Creek allowed bigger ships to come into the city thus bringing trade and prosperity with them. Dubai, building its infrastructure side-by-side the growth in commerce, soon became globally acknowledged as the regional trade hub with its outreach extending from India to the eastern coasts of Africa and all across the Gulf – a reputation that successive series of conflicts in the Gulf have not been able to diminish.

"The Creek is a dearly loved symbol of Dubai. It has been our lifeline and has served our city well."

Despite the project's obvious benefit to all, the interruption to normality along the Creek was a constant source of problems for Sheikh Rashid, who was often called on to arbitrate on disputes between engineers and dhow-owners. This minor conflict of interest was nothing by comparison, though, to the disturbance caused by engineers' widening of the Creek using dynamite. Sometimes homes adjacent to the blasting were damaged, or walls collapsed.

Sheikh Rashid visited the workings on the Creek several times each day, often finding himself being called upon to order an obstinate boat-owner to move on, or placate a resident whose home had fallen victim to shockwaves from the blasting. Over the course of the project he was to pay, sometimes from his own funds, to rebuild several walls and out-buildings.

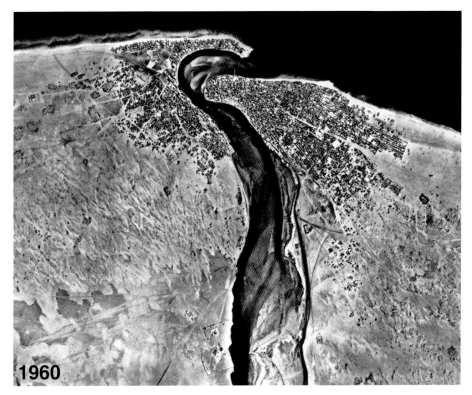

These extraordinary photographs show how Sheikh Rashid's Dubai Creek Development Scheme transformed the Creek itself over just a 16 year period, while the city grew to an almost inconceivable degree.

Government coffers were given a small boost soon into the project after Sheikh Rashid ordered that excavated rocks and silt be dumped in low-lying areas along the Creek, in particular a strip of muddy sand fronting the Deira side. This created new land above the water level, in a prime location in the centre of the city. Within months he was selling off tracts of reclaimed property to those who were in a position to build and create jobs. This revenue, in turn, helped offset costs.

Despite the inconvenience to householders, merchants and fishermen, by and large those whose living was being made through the Creek were only too aware that Dubai's expansion would put them on a par with the thriving entrepots of Bahrain and Kuwait further up the Gulf. To allow work to continue, larger dhows were often called upon to weigh anchor off the Creek for hours, or even days, waiting for wharf space. All this was a major inconvenience, but despite disruptions to the pattern of life Sheikh Rashid had a great deal of support for his effort.

"He knew that Dubai was better positioned geographically than other ports in the Gulf, but needed to accommodate the new-generation larger vessels. When it came to development of the Creek he was very single-minded," says Hamad bin Sukat. "He told me that Dubai had in the past been built around the Creek, but the time had come to build the Creek around Dubai's future."

By the end of 1960 Halcrow had virtually completed the Dubai Creek Development Scheme. Dredging and sheet piling had made the Creek viable for vessels with an eight-foot draft. The expected immediate increase in traffic along the artery meant the government had to extend the Customs House Jetty and provide additional landing points.

"After the Creek's dredging was completed, more ships called in Dubai to unload their cargo," observes Al Tajir. "The need for warehouses and other port facilities became very urgent because shipping lines had decided to use Dubai as their main port in the Gulf...the customs duties on imported goods were then used for building other facilities."

The Creek scheme was such a success, and tax earnings grew to such an extent, that Sheikh Rashid was keen to pay back Dubai's loan from the Emir of Kuwait early, thus freeing his hands to finance other public works. A confidential report by the British Political Agent indicates that Sheikh Rashid made an additional payment of £150,000 to Kuwait in May 1960 which enabled the whole sum of the loan to be paid back far earlier than originally agreed. Hardly surprising, then, that none of the richer regional governments with whom Sheikh Rashid enjoyed close relations ever denied a request for a development loan. After Dubai had paid back two-thirds of its Creek loan in just a fraction of the agreed time, the Emir of Kuwait, Sheikh Abdullah al-Salim al-Sabah, wrote personally to Sheikh Rashid saying that his government "would listen sympathetically to any future requests for assistance you might make."

During this same period the Iranian government was also offering massive loans to the Dubai Ruler for development work. This was, perhaps, partly because of Sheikh Rashid's mainly neutral stance to his neighbours across the Gulf, when many on the Arabian Peninsula were hostile to what was viewed as an imperialist regime. At a time when Dubai still needed funds to fuel the Ruler's ambitious projects, Sheikh Rashid was asked about his intentions by the British Political Agent – who was well aware the Iranian funds could cause tension among all the administrations along the coast.

"He had no intention of accepting Iranian assistance because he considered that this would upset the Kuwaitis, of whom he had great hopes," stated Walmsley in a confidential report.

Sheikh Rashid's intentions underlined the ease with which he slipped between the roles of pragmatic and ambitious Dubai Ruler and that of what could be described as something of a spokesman on behalf of his fellow Rulers.

"He has heard that the Kuwaitis were thinking of giving more help to the Trucial Coast and he intends to pay Kuwait a visit," commented the same report. "He intended not to ask for further assistance for Dubai, which is now managing quite nicely, but for the coast as a whole, as far away as Fujairah and Dibba. He was not thinking of specific projects so much as sounding out Kuwaiti opinion generally and persuading them to send some of their own people to see what needed doing. He would keep us [the British] closely informed at every stage but considered that we should keep in the background and let him make the running.

"The approach Sheikh Rashid proposes to make to Kuwait, if successful, will undoubtedly enhance his local paramountcy vis-a-vis all the other Trucial States Rulers..."

In his Annual Review of the Trucial States for 1960, filed to the Foreign Office in London, the British Political Agent based in Dubai gave his customary summary of the affairs of each state:

"The development of Dubai...proceeded vigorously. The Ruler took great personal interest in it and, with more limited resources than his neighbour in Abu Dhabi, he achieved much...many of the local Arabs took an increased interest in trade and the Ruler's 'open door' policy led to an influx of Indian and Pakistani traders, pushing up tax revenues. New shops and residential areas sprung up in accordance – in the main – within the development plan."

When Dubai embarked upon its ambitious Creek Development Scheme, Sheikh Rashid had seemingly arrived. The project was, by far, the biggest single development project ever considered on the Trucial Coast, and had been achieved in the face of general cynicism. Few outside of Dubai had believed Sheikh Rashid's vague plans were achievable. Now there was a realisation that here, at last, was someone who could get something done.

"Sheikh Rashid was determined, and everyone around him, in his office and the Majlis, did everything to support him. He would convince and motivate everyone around him," recalls Hamad bin Sukat, who was often present in the Majlis during brainstorming sessions.

Sheikh Rashid thought on his feet, making decisions almost immediately after informally sounding out the opinions of those whose judgment he trusted. He was sometimes so informal that social events would become policy-making sessions.

"He encouraged people with good ideas about their jobs, or the country's future, to speak out," says Sultan Ali Al Owais, then a young national who caught the Ruler's eye and later among the UAE's leading business leaders.

The Majlis was an unusual mix of nationals, Arabs, Indians and Europeans, all of whom were included in a haphazard, but seemingly effective, decision-making process. It was here that Dubai's multinational business leaders agreed to a tax for the Creek project, while Sheikh Rashid also used his Majlis to check the pulse of the commercial community toward subsequent increases to fund the formation of a municipality, a police force and a schools department.

Perhaps his effectiveness in the Majlis, and as a diplomat, was due to his easy manner with the people who came before him. With none of the airs and graces often associated with leaders, Dubai's Ruler left a deep impression.

A unique photograph from the 1950s. Flanked by armed retainers, Sheikh Rashid and an oil company representative use a pile of stones to mark the position of a successful oil strike. But Dubai still had decades to wait until it could begin reaping the benefits of its mineral resources.

"The thing that struck me most about His Highness was his eyes. Even when he was smiling, his eyes were deep and penetrating," says Sergio Magnaldi, who much later would greet Sheikh Rashid as the manager of the Hatta Fort Hotel. "The magnetism which people associated with Sheikh Rashid came from his eyes. He could hold you there with his eyes. If he met you once, he remembered everything about you, your family, how many children you had. It was amazing because you would not expect Sheikh Rashid to remember such things."

On one occasion in 1960, Sheikh Rashid and several members of his entourage, including bin Sukat, paid a courtesy call on his sick brother-in-law, Sheikh Hamdan bin Hamdan Al Nahyan, in his Deira-based Majlis. During the course of the evening someone suggested that the further integration of Deira and Bur Dubai could be achieved if access was made easier. As late as this, the two sides were linked by abra (water taxi) or a journey by motor vehicle of up to an hour, to traverse the head of the Creek, some six miles inland. A pedestrian bridge also ran from Bur Dubai to Shindagha. That night Sheikh Rashid returned to his palace with bridge-building firmly on his agenda. The following year work began on the two lane Al Maktoum Bridge. This was in part financed through a £190,000 loan from Sheikh Ahmed bin Ali Al Thani, the Ruler of Qatar, who was a close friend and ally of Sheikh Rashid and whose son later married Sheikha Mariam, Sheikh Rashid's eldest daughter. In 1962, Sheikh Rashid inaugurated the bridge, opening a new chapter in the commercial life of the city and firmly ending the 'two sides' mentally which had often led to political problems in the past.

Al Maktoum Bridge joined together a population said to be approaching 50,000 during the early 1960s, and doubling during the years between 1955 and 1967. Dubai was still to wait years for its entry into the oil-exporting era and consequently services for the community were poor. As the effective master of the Dubai government since as early as the end of the Second World War, Sheikh Rashid appears to have been fully aware of the condition of his state's infrastructure. Relatively well-travelled compared with most people in the Trucial States, he made up for any deficiencies of education with what some feel was a photographic memory.

He had, therefore, an understanding that before any ongoing development work could be undertaken, a measure of responsibility must be taken for planning. In 1954 he formed a formal Municipality charged with basic regulation, evolving a city plan and adding further cohesion to the raft of major developments which were soon to be launched on Dubai. A formal city plan was the municipal authority's most pressing problem in 1954, for several reasons. The economic and social boom of the time was transforming Dubai, land prices were rocketing and legal ownership of valuable swathes of sand within the limits of the town was largely unknown. It was also understood that without cohesive administration of development at large, the town was set to become a messy collage of residential, commercial and industrial buildings.

By 1965 a comprehensive plan was produced for, and approved by, the Dubai Ruler, superceding a rough lands plan formulated during the late 1950s and itself subsequently amended in 1971 to account for the growth of the city. In addition to local officials, the plan was formulated with the help of British consultants Doxiades Associates and a group of experts from the United Nations Development Programme (UNDP). Sheikh Rashid, though, still confounded those around him by giving away tracts of the sheikhdom in acts of almost reckless generosity. This was most true when, as he saw it, nationals were able and willing to develop land which was not being utilised.

The 1965 Town Plan, however, was to instill a proper perspective on the future of Dubai and, in at least small part, helped to cap the excesses of the Ruler's generosity. Many sovereign functions of the Trucial Sheikhdoms were still in the hands of the British administration at this juncture. This included the judicial system which, locally, was feudal and antiquated. By agreement with the Rulers, the British Political

Agent had taken on some powers by the late 1940s as Justice of HM's Court.

There was, however, no formal police force on the Trucial Coast and the sheikhdoms themselves had no regular armed forces either, aside from the Rulers' armed retainers. This left them vulnerable, especially during an era when land – all of it potentially rich in oil reserves – was rising in value. As early as 1950 the British had helped finance the Trucial Oman Levies, a small garrison of which was stationed in most of the coast's towns and key positions. Armed and funded by the British, the Trucial Oman Levies had begun in 1950 under the command of a British officer from the Jordanian army, a handful of Arab officers and around 50 non-commissioned officers and ranks. Initially they were centred in Sharjah, but grew to include men stationed in all the seven sheikhdoms, from where most of the Levies' strength was drawn.

The arrival of the Levies was pivotal in the history of the area. Their patrols, mounted in Land-Rovers and Bedford Personnel Units, came to be respected both on the Coast and among the tribes of the interior, and a trust in their impartiality meant that they were fine arbitrators. A first Levy base was opened in Dubai in 1952, on land and in buildings donated by the Ruler. The Levies, later the Trucial Oman Scouts, provided security. In Dubai they were able to work hand-in-hand with what was at the time the first internal police force along the coast. Sheikh Rashid instigated moves toward establishing the Dubai Police in 1956 – under a Western expatriate commander and officers – and partly funded this by levying an increase on import tax of just two annas (one-fiftieth of one rupee). An initial annual budget of £15,000 was shared equally between the British and Dubai governments, with the latter providing buildings to the fledgling service. As the force expanded the British offered more funds toward operating costs, and by 1958 the working budget had risen to £21,832, with £14,332 of this channeled through the Foreign Office in London.

Sheikh Rashid encouraged Dubai nationals to enter the service. The Majlis in Shindagha was never a place for handouts, Sheikh Rashid usually responding to requests for help by arranging jobs, places in education or training – self help. And for a time, any healthy, young or middle-aged national who asked his help in finding a job was dispatched to police headquarters with a letter from the Majlis nominating him into a training programme. Within months there was the nucleus of a professional force capable of replacing an age-old system of part-time 'night watchmen' circulating the town, a force of nearly 80 by the beginning of 1957. Three years later, in 1960, the city boasted 106 qualified policemen. A 1961 report put the annual clothing budget at £808, which included the purchase of 90 pairs of sandals, pullovers and 90 lengths of cord on which Dubai's police were to hang their whistles.

During the mid-1960s Sheikh Rashid bought two dozen new Land-Rovers for the force, a considerable investment for the government at the time. The vehicles arrived by boat when the Ruler was away on a hunting trip in Pakistan. No-one had been informed as to whom they were allocated. In the days before Sheikh Rashid returned, all were given to leaders among Dubai's Bedu tribes and disappeared into the desert with their new owners, only to be recalled when Sheikh Rashid found out what had become of the new police vehicles. All made it back to the city when Sheikh Rashid sent word, but could only be prised from the Bedu when replacements were promised. The police recieved their Land-Rovers, and the dealer obtained another large order.

Despite a growing number of police recruits and better infrastructure, Dubai's boom was already placing great strain on the limited service, a fact acknowledged by a report from the Political Agent to the Foreign Office in April 1961. The Dubai Police, it stated, were finding themselves stretched impossibly to cope with a burgeoning population, comprising in large part Asian labourers who had in some cases brought with them the crime and social problems from their homelands. The Dubai Police were further charged with supporting the efforts of the equally stretched Customs and Immigration Departments. The same document also paints a worrisome internal picture of the other sheikhdoms where there was no formal police force. The remaining sheikhdoms relied on the old system of paid retainers and guards, along with a judicial system revolving around the respective Ruler himself. One step in the right direction had been the Trucial Oman Scouts; however the same document raised serious doubts as to the direction in which this organisation was heading. The Political Agent conceded that the Scouts were doing a reasonable job, but indicated that their British sponsorship and British hierarchy meant that they were "more like a UK military unit" than a police force for the Trucial States. By 1967 the complement of Dubai Police officers had risen to a reported 430, and stood at 1,500 in 1975, when Sheikh Rashid appointed his third son, Sheikh Mohammed, to head internal security.

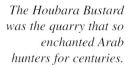

The Houbara Bustard was the quarry that so enchanted Arab hunters for centuries.

Since the end of the reform movement crisis, Sheikh Rashid had effectively led Dubai, as Sheikh Saeed went into virtual retirement.

"He was a very quiet, gentle man," says Chapman. "He did not show a great deal of interest in the day-to-day running of Dubai by this time. But he was fully aware of how astute Sheikh Rashid was and was therefore content to leave this to his son."

And while Sheikh Saeed became less visible, in his son's aggressively modernising Majlis, traditional respect ensured that when it came to major decisions, Sheikh Saeed was always fully briefed and consulted by his son. During the latter years of his life, during the 1950s, Sheikh Saeed held court informally from a group of wooden benches arranged just outside his Shindagha home, where he would still receive citizens until just months before his death. Sheikh Rashid visited daily as circumstances would allow, taking the opportunity to ensure his father's broad acceptance of the major enterprises of the day.

Although frail, Sheikh Saeed continued his passion for hunting, and often headed for Iran with Sheikh Rashid. The houbara (a species of bustard) was still plentiful and there were larger mammals to chase as well. For Sheikh Rashid, consumed through most of the year by the desire to drive his projects forward and develop Dubai, hunting provided an escape throughout his life, a few weeks when he could switch off from being a leader and become one of the group.

Until the second half of the 20th century, the desert of the Arabian Peninsula was well stocked with game, and sufficiently remote to provide local hunting opportunities. However, the encroachment of a

143

larger population and growing number of active hunters gradually eroded the levels of game in the Dubai desert. The shy houbara for instance, will fly up to 500 kilometres at a time in the search of a quiet area to feed, and once falcons or humans had hunted a colony, the birds would move on. Sheikh Saeed taught both Sheikh Rashid and Sheikh Khalifa hunting skills, a prerequisite for any Arab of noble blood. The three went falconing and shooting together for many years, and following the death of Sheikh Saeed, his sons often hunted together.

The remote countryside of Iran became a favourite spot for wealthier hunters, particularly the ruling families of the Trucial States, while at times the wilds of Pakistan, Morocco and more recently the Asian former-Soviet republics have also been the scene of this oldest of Arab sports. Each year Sheikh Rashid would take two trips abroad for hunting, the first of around 20 days, before the summer, and the second, his annual December expedition, generally to Iran.

"It is a common misconception that the houbara is all which is hunted," explains Sheikh Mohammed bin Khalifa Al Maktoum, himself something of an expert in falconry. "Sheikh Rashid and my father also hunted grouse, rabbit and gazelle."

On occasion the Ruler's party flew to their destination, but Sheikh Rashid preferred taking his launch, the Zaabil, which took half a day to reach the Iranian port of Bandar Abbas. From there they would take four-wheel-drive cars into the interior and set up a tented village.

"Like Sheikh Saeed before them, Sheikh Rashid and Sheikh Khalifa were crack shots with a rifle. Sheikh Rashid was renowned for his accuracy," recalls Sheikh Mohammed bin Khalifa. "On one occasion the party was travelling by car across a mountain range, when in the valley below a herd of gazelle was spotted. The herd was already running from the noise of the vehicles and was far off. Sheikh Rashid threw himself from the car and, standing, he shot, with open sights, six gazelle with six shots. It was remarkable marksmanship from such a distance – on a moving target, without the benefit of sights – and this story was recalled around camp fires for many years."

To be invited to accompany Sheikh Rashid on a trip was a great honour – one which fell on more than one occasion to Zakariah Doleh.

"From a base camp in the desert we would depart early in the morning in a number of Land-Rovers, stopping only to meet for lunch. All the vehicles went their own way to areas which they knew were good for houbara, the best of which were a closely guarded secret," says Doleh. "Sheikh Rashid knew several, deep in the desert outside Dubai. There were five of us and a driver in his Land-Rover, and it was noticeable that in this environment he wanted just to be part of the group, not the leader."

Doleh admits to panicking when, after a full day in the field, night-time settled over the area with his party still far in the desert.

"Sheikh Rashid negotiated our way back to a pre-arranged meeting point by navigating with the stars. It was pitch black," he says.

The evening meal consisted of a traditional Arab dish, harise, a meat dish with wheat which is buried in a pit to cook over charcoal.

"Sheikh Rashid took charge," says Doleh. "He was laughing and joking, even stirring and adding ingredients to a stew, something which would have been unthinkable back in the city. I'd never seen him enjoying himself and so very informal. Away from his responsibilities and the constraints of office, Sheikh Rashid was one of the boys."

But these moments of freedom were only fleeting. The longest Sheikh Rashid allowed himself to be away was a few weeks, although he would occasionally mix business with pleasure by finding time to hunt while on an official visit. On one occasion, however, it was the other way round: politics encroached into hunting on one of Sheikh Rashid's earlier visits to a fledgling Pakistan. After a week away in Peshawar, he was staying in Karachi before flying home, when the then Pakistani leader Zulfikar Ali Bhutto heard that he was there.

"I've travelled through the Gulf and Middle East," he told Sheikh Rashid when arriving unexpectedly at the hotel that evening. "Wherever I have gone they have told me that I should meet Rashid." After an extended four hours of informal discussion Bhutto left, and subsequently became a close friend of Sheikh Rashid's until his execution after falling from power some years later.

At home, Sheikh Rashid was still grappling with the task of developing his country with severely restricted revenues. Around him Saudi Arabia, Bahrain and Kuwait were already enjoying the fruits of what would become a trillion-dollar boom, but despite continual positive geological reports, there was still no commercial flow of oil to transform Dubai.

But Sheikh Rashid's shrewdness was making the best of the situation. The Dubai government had first agreed a concession to drill for oil in its territory in 1937, five years after oil had been struck in Bahrain and the island had been thrust into an unprecedented boom. Among neighbouring

The Middle East's first oil production came through this well in Kirkuk, in present day Iraq. (opposite page) Dubai would have to wait a generation before it would see the fruits of the oil boom.

states there was an understandable desire to join the new prosperity, but for many membership of this exclusive club was to prove elusive, if not impossible. Frustration was felt along the Trucial Coast where only a little economic activity had remained following the death of pearling.

The Ruler of Ras Al Khaimah, Sheikh Sultan bin Salim Al Qassimi, was the first of the Trucial Coast leaders to seek the help of geologists in preparing a preliminary survey of his lands, in 1935. For Dubai meanwhile, the oil business was to prove a small but significant income generator through a fixed annual fee and a provision for Petroleum Concessions Limited (PCL) to pay Rs. 3 for every ton of crude collected during the exploratory drilling.

At Sheikh Rashid's insistence, Sheikh Saeed had also won a provision for the employment of Dubai nationals in the programme. Unlike the same clause in the contract later brokered with the Imperial Bank of Iran, the potential for huge profit if commercial deposits were discovered had also allowed Sheikh Rashid to hold out for a basic training package. This enabled Dubai nationals to take on higher-paid positions within PCL, and would eventually make local labour financially attractive to similar organisations in the Gulf, who were used to the expense of bringing in expatriates.

The Second World War had interrupted the process of oil discovery, and further delayed Dubai's entry into this enticing boom. As demand in the Western markets spiralled after 1945, so the clamour for concessions grew – at exactly the time when the contracts on Dubai's drilling concessions were due for renewal. By this time, Sheikh Rashid was

leading negotiations on behalf of his father. He was not impressed by the deals his neighbours had struck: in some of them, as little as 20% of the profits would go to the state.

Early geographical surveys had indicated that Dubai had the potential for massive crude deposits, and Sheikh Rashid entered negotiations at something of an advantage. In 1937 PCL had been the sole bidder for rights and therefore in the stronger position. This time, Sheikh Rashid and his advisors met with the Anglo-Iranian Oil Company, with the negotiators knowing there were several other offers in hand. Using this advantage Sheikh Rashid broke the mould of agreements along the coast. He demanded an unparalleled equal split of revenue between his government and the Anglo-Iranian Oil Company and, to the surprise of most within the industry, succeeded in getting just that. In many ways Sheikh Rashid's deal was remarkable and had a profound effect on the oil exploration industry within the Gulf and elsewhere around the world. Dubai had set a precedent, and from now on, concessions were generally granted on very much the same financial basis.

The foundations of prosperity were now in place and things were changing for the better in Dubai. Yet Sheikh Saeed would not live to see the fruits of his and Sheikh Rashid's labours.

Chapter Nine

End of an Era

O soul, in rest and satisfaction. Come back to thy Lord…
Enter thou, then, among My devotees.
Yea, enter thou My Heaven.
— *Holy Koran*

By 1958, Sheikh Saeed was in steadily declining health, weakened by age – he was 76. He had never quite recovered his physical presence after a near fatal bout of malaria in 1931, but this was something different. Now he appeared less and less in public and rarely took his informal Majlis outside the doors of his home. When he did appear, those who saw him were often shocked by how frail he had become. On good days he walked with a stick, and when his spirits were high he loved nothing more than to spend time with his grandchildren.

"He loved to take us into the desert and organised impromptu shooting competitions among his grandchildren," says Sheikh Mohammed bin Khalifa. "He was really happy when he was surrounded by family."

But at other times, he required one or two attendants to help him move around. Around Dubai, news of the Ruler's gradual weakening attracted a steady stream of senior figures, visiting his Majlis to pay their respects whenever he was able to spend an evening there. Sheikh Rashid spent more time, as did his sons, while the British Political Resident also called regularly. From neighbouring states both Sheikh Shakhbut bin Sultan Al Nahyan, Ruler of Abu Dhabi, and Sheikh Saqr bin Sultan Al Qassimi, Ruler of Sharjah, travelled to Dubai to see Sheikh Saeed.

During the summer of 1958, Sheikh Saeed was almost bedridden in Shindagha, surrounded by his family. Sheikh Rashid had accompanied

By the summer of 1958, Sheikh Saeed was ailing and the Maktoum family prepared for the worst.

149

his father to Hatta, Dubai's mountainous enclave, for a spell in August. It was cooler there than on the coast, where humidity was often 100% and temperatures hovered around 50 degrees Celsius. Hatta had always acted as a tonic to the aged Ruler. Indeed, family members recall that Sheikh Saeed rallied briefly in the soothing climate, but his strength waned and the party returned to Dubai.

During the first week of September, the Senior Medical Officer for the Trucial States, Lieutenant Colonel Dr Donald McCaully, attended the Ruler often. He was called urgently to his bedside on the afternoon of September 9. Over the preceding few days, Sheikh Saeed had repeatedly slipped into unconsciousness and, as was the custom, had been attended by his close family around the clock. Dr McCaully, who enjoyed the absolute trust of the Maktoum family, did his best to make him comfortable, but had reported privately to the British Political Agent that there was little he could do. Sheikh Saeed, he said, was simply weakening through old age.

By September 9 he had faded near to death, only rousing to speak briefly, quietly, with his eldest son and heir apparent, Sheikh Rashid, and then also to Sheikh Khalifa.

Mostly, however, he simply lay in his bed, growing weaker. Just before seven in the morning, he passed away.

At sunrise of the morning of September 10, 1958, Dubai's population woke, having suffered another humid, uncomfortable late-summer night. Temperatures were already in the 80s (Fahrenheit) as first light broke, and would rise well above 100 degrees before lunchtime, making all activity on its busy waterfront and in its souqs an effort. But something else was in the air this particular morning. There had been much activity around the Ruler's Shindagha home in preceding days. The British doctor had been seen coming and going. It was no secret that the old leader was ailing.

Just after 7.30, the cries of the muezzins rang out from the minarets of the city's mosques. Instead of calling the faithful to prayer, this morning they were conveying sad news. Dubai's Ruler of half a century was dead. The sad, haunting sound of Koranic verse hung over Dubai like a cloud. In the absence of newspapers, televisions or radios to bring them the news, it was left to the mosques to confirm what most had been expecting.

Within minutes of the Ruler's passing, news of the death had spread.

Dr McCaully hurried to inform British Political Agent James Hawley, who wrote a detailed account of the events that followed. By the time he was dressed and en route to Shindagha, up to 1,000 people, by his estimate, had assembled for the funeral. He wrote of "crowds of white-clothed people waiting silently, sitting where they could in the shade of the walls…there were a few rough wooden benches in the shade, too, and the more important citizens were sitting on these…there seemed to be a good deal of coming and going by white-clad figures in cars and on foot, but most people were just waiting, reflecting no doubt on the death of a generally benevolent and well-loved old man."

In traditional Islamic manner, Sheikh Saeed's body was prepared immediately for burial; as this was taking place inside the house, on the streets outside there was an outpouring of grief the like of which had perhaps never been witnessed in Dubai. Sheikh Saeed's uninterrupted rule had been unusually long by Gulf standards: most of his people had known no other Ruler. As the news spread across the city, citizens began to converge mutely on the Ruler's house to pay their respects.

A short while later, from within the Maktoum's Shindagha home, a high-pitched wail from a woman signaled that the funeral procession was about to start. The gates opened and eight men appeared carrying a wooden bier containing the body of Dubai's Ruler wrapped tightly in a red-chequered cloth. The procession moved off towards Dubai proper with Sheikh Rashid and Sheikh Khalifa heading a cortège numbering perhaps 2,000 people as others fell in behind. Both were dressed in plain white. As a mark of respect, they had discarded the customary black robe, or waber al jamal, which the ruling family would normally wear over their shoulders in public.

Immediately behind the body walked 15-year-old Sheikh Maktoum and 13-year-old Sheikh Hamdan. At 9, Sheikh Mohammed was considered too young to accompany them and he stayed at home with grieving family members, along with his youngest brother, Sheikh Ahmed.

Along the route, thousands more citizens paid their respects. Today, contemporary estimates from those present state that between 10 and 15 thousand people, nearly half of Dubai's total population, were part of, or witnessed, the funeral procession.

As the bier swayed towards its destination, a crowd of young Dubaians jostled to walk near it, competing for the honour of acting as a pall-bearer, even for a few precious seconds. While most in the main procession were male, the women of the city showed their own respect by lining the street crying. "Their wailing was terrible," recalled one foreign national who was there. "It was a piercing shrieking which eerily followed the body throughout the course of the journey to its final resting place. Those women who were not able to journey outdoors made their pain felt through shrieks from inside their homes."

The procession passed the home of Sheikha Moza, Sheikh Saeed's favourite daughter and Sheikh Rashid's eldest sister. Every few minutes the mourners would be brought to a halt and the wailing of the women, many of whom had fallen in to march beside the bier, would peter out into silence. Sheikh Mohammed Noor, a Dubaian who was a senior Qahdi in Saudi Arabia, recited passages from the Holy Koran. He had been quietly recalled to the city some days before, in anticipation of the almost inevitable passing of the Ruler.

For much of the way, Sheikh Mohammed Noor marched at the head of the procession, immediately behind the body of the Ruler. It was a mile and a half from Shindagha to Dubai's main graveyard, a journey which took over an hour through the heat and rising humidity of the September morning.

The bier was then handed to a group of senior mourners, who had been ceremonially washed in a cleansing ritual, and Sheikh Saeed's body was quickly placed in his grave. Sheikh Mohammed Noor and a Dubai-based Qahdi both recited Koranic verses, and the massed people of Dubai, both nationals and expatriates, fell into silence.

There were perhaps 15 minutes of prayers. Then, relatives and citizens moved deliberately forward in order of seniority to pay their final respects, and toss a handful of soil into the grave of their Ruler. Sheikh Rashid, weakened by several days attending his father's bedside, along with the emotion of the occasion, is said to have passed out at one stage during the ceremony. However, he recovered sufficiently to spend nearly two hours at the grave of his father, as his people filed past to offer him their condolences. Sheikh Rashid "was disheveled and wild-eyed after the sleeplessness and emotion of the preceding two days," recalled one eyewitness. "In the Trucial States the death of the Ruler is regarded as a personal loss and it is the custom to use the phrase 'May God give you consolation', which is usually addressed to relations or very close friends."

In a report to Selwyn Lloyd, Britain's Secretary of State in 1958, Political Agent Hawley wrote:

The ceremony had in many ways been a moving one: the jostling round the bier, the dusty crowd trampling behind it, the women's grief, the orderly rows of men praying by the body and the greetings exchanged between the bereaved ruling family and the people, all contributed to make it so; but the chief impression which I was left with was the complete lack of pomp and circumstance, despite the solemnity and unique nature of the occasion.

Sheikh Saeed, grandfather of the present day Ruler of Dubai, Sheikh Mohammed bin Rashid Al Maktoum, had ruled over the development of Dubai as a busy trading post of some 30,000 people – an emirate whose population had tripled during his years in power. In later years, aided by his skilful and wily son, he had overseen Dubai's survival and subsequent return to prosperity through the political minefields of two World Wars, the collapse of the pearling industry and a failed experiment with an elected Majlis, all defining points in the history of the sheikhdom.

The grief shown by the thousands of mourners was indeed genuine: the late Ruler had been deeply loved and respected by his people. In their emotional state, the people scarcely noticed the handover of power to the next generation. Often difficult in the Arab world, it was, on this occasion, a process of seamless continuity. For perhaps as long as two decades before the death of his father, Sheikh Rashid had been increasingly taking on the affairs of state as Crown Prince. Though he deferred to his father on important matters, he had been left to rule Dubai. It was hardly from the shadows, therefore, that Sheikh Rashid took centre stage as Ruler of Dubai, the ninth member of the Maktoum family to shoulder the burden of leadership of tribe and state.

The day after his father's death Sheikh Rashid presented the British Political Resident with a letter that stated:

Now that my father's days have ended, I have officially assumed government of the state as his successor. Cordial relations and strong and permanent friendship existed between Her Majesty's government and him, built on foundations of sincere dealings and loyalty. I consider that these relations continue as

before, without any change whatsoever. I ask Almighty God to enable us to cooperate successfully for good and to bring about progress. Will you kindly convey this to Her Majesty's government.

His accession marked a first for the region when, on October 4, 1958, the first ever formal inauguration ceremony for a Ruler was staged. Dubai was bedecked with bunting, and Dubai's distinctive red-and-white flag was flying everywhere, on boats and buildings. Dressed in their khaki uniforms and red and white gutras, the Dubai Police formed a guard of honour.

At 10 am, the British Political Resident and Political Agent arrived aboard HMS Loch Insh to participate in a ceremony at Al Fahidi Fort. Most of the Trucial Rulers were present, along with the Maktoum family and Dubai's major merchants. Burrows, the Political Resident, who spoke Arabic well, stood before a microphone and delivered a

HMS Loch Insh arrived in Dubai to participate in the official inauguration of the new Ruler.

short speech on behalf of the British government:

We are here for two purposes. One is to commemorate Sheikh Saeed bin Maktoum, who ruled Dubai for more than 30 years. We mourn his death and remember gratefully the good works that he did for his country and his people, and his friendship with the British government. Our second purpose is to welcome Sheikh Rashid who is now recognised as the Ruler of Dubai, and to wish him success and prosperity. He is already experienced in the difficulties and responsibilities of government while acting for his late father. We have seen during these years how Dubai has grown and prospered under his wise guidance. The administration has been much improved by the foundation of the Municipality. Public security has been provided by the Police Force, economic prosperity has been greatly increased by the building of the new customs premises and work will soon begin on deepening and improving the Creek and harbour.

The British government is pleased to see the states of the Gulf advance in this way. It is ready to give such help and advice as may be required and is within their resources. But it is better when the greater part of this work can be done by the efforts of the inhabitants themselves, through the cooperation of the Ruler and the merchants and all the classes and races of the community. We have also been pleased to note how, during recent years, relations between the different states of the Trucial Coast have become better. Until recently it was a question of preventing wars between these states. Now that is inconceivable and the problem is to find new ways of building mutually useful cooperation and association between them, in the common interest of all.

I will end in conveying renewed congratulations to Sheikh Rashid on his recognition as Ruler both on behalf of the British government and of myself.

As the Political Resident handed Sheikh Rashid a formal letter of friendship, the marines aboard HMS Loch Insh fired their cannons in a five-gun salute. After several other speeches – including young Sheikh Maktoum's first public address – Dubai celebrated. Banquets were held in various locations around the town. Bedouin tribesmen thronged the town, chanting their support and firing their guns in the air.

Afterwards Sheikh Rashid went to the shore to see off the British officials and then returned to his Shindagha home. That evening, much of the family arrived for a private banquet within the walled confines of their home. Outside noisy celebrations went on for much of the night.

"I felt that this was a happy occasion, extremely well organised by the local people," wrote Hawley later. "Genuine goodwill appeared to be felt by the people of all communities towards Sheikh Rashid and the ruling family and throughout we [British government representatives] were treated with great courtesy and friendship."

Indeed, October 4, 1958 was a red-letter day for Dubai. Its new Ruler was ready to unveil a raft of new initiatives that would transform the public face of the sheikhdom. It was ironic that Sheikh Saeed should

*Dubai Camel Souk,
pictured towards the late
1950s. A great deal of
work needed to be done
if the sheikhdom was to
make any progress.*

have died just as Sheikh Rashid was preparing the biggest series of developments ever witnessed along the coast. He was only months away from announcing a raft of projects that, he believed, would transform the sheikhdom in preparation for an impending oil boom. But first, Sheikh Rashid was called upon to observe the traditional 40 days of mourning for his father. He kept up the pace of his everyday work in private, but in public he was seen less on the streets of Dubai, maintaining a respectful low profile.

Sheikh Rashid had effectively ruled Dubai for two decades already, so the nominal changeover of power hardly registered in the day-to-day workings of the sheikhdom. What mattered was that the wheels of progress had been in motion for some time.

Dubai was about to start a new chapter in its history.

Chapter Ten

A New Generation

*Of all nature's gifts to the human race, what is sweeter to
a man than his children?*
— *Marcus Tullius Cicero, Roman statesman and orator*

October 4, 1958 had been a moment of celebration for Dubai. It had
also been a highly significant day in the history of the sheikhdom. Not
only did leadership move between generations, from Sheikh Saeed to
his son, but the day also saw the first step in the emergence of a new
generation. The day was punctuated by many speeches – but none as
significant as that made by the new Ruler's eldest son, his first in public.
On the day that his father became Ruler, Sheikh Maktoum stepped out
into the spotlight, his first step on a road that would later see him serve
as Crown Prince, become Prime Minister of his country and, slightly
over four decades later, himself become Ruler of Dubai.

Sheikh Rashid had waited less than one year before he was rewarded
with his first child following his marriage to Sheikha Latifa bint
Hamdan Al Nahyan in 1939. Mariam was born before the end of that
year.

In 1943, Sheikha Latifa gave birth to a son who was named
Maktoum, in honour of Sheikh Rashid's grandfather, Sheikh Maktoum
bin Hasher, whose enlightened policies around the turn of the century
had attracted merchants abandoning Lingah and so transformed Dubai.

On December 25, 1945, Sheikha Latifa bore a second son. He was
named Hamdan, honouring Sheikha Latifa's late father who had ruled
Abu Dhabi between 1912 and 1922.

A daughter, Hessa, named after her grandmother, followed. Sheikh
Rashid, a devout Muslim, decreed that his third son should be named to
honour the family's faith. At the time of his birth, in 1949, he was

*Sheikh Rashid and two of his four sons, Sheikh Hamdan (left)
and Sheikh Mohammed*

named Mohammed, after the Prophet. A year later, in 1950, Sheikh Rashid's fourth son, Sheikh Ahmed, was born, taking the given name of the Prophet Mohammed, while Maitha, Sheikha and Fatima would later be born to the couple, making nine children.

The late 1940s and early 1950s were boom times in Dubai, largely as a result of Sheikh Rashid's legendary foresight and hard work. Estimates put the population of the town as high as 30,000 in the early 1950s. With stability and a strong economy, his people were happy and settled.

In this environment, the children of Sheikh Rashid and Sheikha Latifa enjoyed a happy and carefree early childhood in the Maktoum family's Shindagha home. They were doted upon by their parents. Sheikh Saeed, according to reports, chose to spend time with his grandchildren to the exclusion of other activities.

On the birth of Sheikh Ahmed, his brothers, Sheikh Maktoum, Sheikh Hamdan and Sheikh Mohammed were aged 7 years, 5 and 1, respectively. All found their natural play companions among their cousins and the children of the major trading families in Dubai, the sheikhdom's aristocracy. The family home – today known as Sheikh Saeed House, a museum – was dominated by children.

As they grew, even as toddlers, they liked nothing better than to kick a ball around the enclosed sandy courtyard. There were also many traditional games that were practiced in all households, such as Luhol and Huwaim, known elsewhere as tag and hopscotch, respectively. Another favourite was called Al Karabi. In this game each player has to hop, holding one foot behind the body, while attempting to knock over an opponent with the torso or one free limb. On many temperate winter afternoons, Sheikh Saeed and Sheikh Rashid would sit on a bench in the courtyard at Shindagha and roar with laughter as they watched the children and their friends play Al Karabi, a game which both had enjoyed as youngsters. It was a casual and relaxed atmosphere completely free of airs and graces.

Family friend Hamad bin Sukat remembers Sheikh Mohammed as an active youngster. "He was forever on the move, playing games and exploring. He was inquisitive and wanted to know what was going on around him. Sheikh Maktoum and Sheikh Hamdan watched over their younger brother. As they were older they moved around the town more, and Sheikh Mohammed always went along when he could."

Of Sheikh Ahmed he recalls: "He was the youngest of the four, but you would not have known it. Sheikh Ahmed was in the centre of everything going on. Sheikh Saeed was very, very fond of him."

When in Dubai, Sheikh Saeed held a Majlis on wooden benches near the entrance to his Shindagha home. Sheikh Rashid's sons could often be found there, sitting beside Sheikh Saeed or on his knee.

"I was only eight when my grandfather passed away, but I can distinctly recall my brothers and I with him," says Sheikh Ahmed bin Rashid Al Maktoum. "Of course, I was too young to know that he was the Ruler. To me he was just a very soft, kind old man who was never without a smile for us."

Perhaps the highlights of the year for the family were its hunting trips.

"When responsibilities become heavy, hunting is an ideal method of relaxation as it is both a change of pace for your body and for its mental intensity," says Sheikh Ahmed bin Saeed Al Maktoum. "Sheikh Rashid was truly dedicated to his work. He was highly disciplined. Perhaps his only outlet for relaxation was hunting. The houbara is a challenging prey. One needs to be a keen thinker and adept with a falcon to be a successful falconer. It is a sport that demands total concentration."

Sheikh Rashid's sons were introduced to the sport at around the age of six. As was the norm, they began their education simply by following the action, from the rear of Sheikh Rashid's Land-Rover. At home, Sheikh Rashid and several attendants taught them the skills involved in handling and caring for falcons. One of the family's senior falconers, Humaid bin Amhai, worked with them almost daily in order to hone their skills.

The falcon has been trapped in the Middle East region for centuries. Bedouin tribes of the past used the bird for hunting game that formed a nutritionally important part of their diet. By the 1950s this had changed somewhat, with imported meat providing better nutrition, yet this traditional pastime had come to be seen by nobility as a sport. The falcon remained – and does to this day – an integral part of the Arab's lifestyle and tradition because falconry is an important sporting activity.

Falcons are trapped in the autumn, used for hunting in the winter, and released back into the wild in spring, and – just as he had been a generation earlier – Sheikh Rashid instilled in his sons the skills that were necessary to train a wild falcon. The royal aviary included the saker falcon (Falco chernig), peregrine falcon (Falco cherrug perigrinus) and gyr falcon (Falco rusticolus). Each was different and demanded that the boys learn separate handling and hunting techniques.

It was only when the brothers had a firm grounding in the art of falconry, and a growing knowledge of what went on during a hunt, that they would graduate, one year later, to join in with a bird of prey on their arm, accompanying their grandfather, father and brothers into the Dubai desert as fully-fledged members of a hunting party. It was something of a coming of age, a right of passage. Although not men in a physical sense yet, joining in this ritual as part of the group was an important step in their growth toward manhood.

From the late 1950s as they grew from children and into young men, all frequently accompanied their father on his annual spring hunting trip to the interior of Iran. Hunting was an exhilarating feeling, a buzz that has persisted throughout the life of all four. All were drawn to the 'adrenalin' and continued to participate in the sport until the present day, finding the intensity of the sport, returning to their Arab roots and the opportunity to distance themselves from the modern world, a most attractive combination.

Hamad bin Sukat, who accompanied Sheikh Rashid during many of his hunting expeditions, recalls; "They were all quite individual personalities, yet when it came to hunting they were the same. Like their father, they adored hunting and enjoyed the freedom that leaving life behind in the city afforded them.

"Don't forget also, Sheikh Rashid worked very hard. Hunting trips were one of the few times when he switched off from his official duties completely. Hunting brought him closer to his sons."

In addition to hunting there was another skill that was a prerequisite for a young man of noble birth. The Arabian horse was an icon of Arab culture. The animal had played a key role in the history of Islam and the Arabs. After the death of the Prophet Mohammed in 632 AD, the Islamic armies – mounted on Arabian horses that were faster, hardier and that had more stamina than all others – swept all before them to conquer Egypt, Palestine and Syria. The Islamic armies defeated the Kingdom of Sassanides in one battle, and charged forward through Persia, Afghanistan, India, Tibet and Turkestan.

But the Arabian horse was much more than a war horse. On the

Arabian Peninsula the horse meant survival, and for the pure nobility of the animal he was often considered a part of the family unit in a way that camels and falcons could never match. From memory a Bedu could relate as many as five generations of the breeding pedigree of his horse. Selective breeding and natural selection, along with existing in the harshest of environments, meant the Arabian's strengths were enhanced with each passing generation.

Being so highly regarded in Islam, it was inevitable that the Arabian would also become a potent symbol. In a time before roads and cars, poor men relied on camels or donkeys for transportation. Noblemen owned Arabian horses. A long, desert journey would always be made on the back of a camel, but for short journeys and travelling close to home a man of status would always take his Arabian horse.

"I recall my grandfather, Sheikh Saeed bin Maktoum Al Maktoum, talking fondly of his adventures on horseback and recalling the part that horses played in our history, including some of the great battles that shaped the Arabian Peninsula," says Sheikh Hamdan. "My father was himself a noted horseman and personally instructed my brothers and I as we learned to ride.

"He often told us that horses were the most beautiful, loyal and intelligent creatures in the animal kingdom, and this is something that I have never had cause to question."

For reasons historical, cultural and religious, coupled with his own affinity for the horse, Sheikh Rashid took it upon himself to instill in his sons the same passion that he had enjoyed throughout his youth. As soon as they were steady on their feet, Sheikh Maktoum, Sheikh Hamdan, Sheikh Mohammed and Sheikh Ahmed were placed on a horse and taught the rudiments of horsemanship, often riding bareback. Despite the fact that by the mid-1950s the pressures of governing a burgeoning Dubai with a population of around 40,000 people left Sheikh Rashid with less time for family matters, he would sometimes interrupt a normally rigid working schedule to oversee his boys' riding lessons. It was not something that even a Ruler left to retainers or servants, as tradition dictated that riding was a skill passed down from father to son.

The brothers and their close friends rode nearly every day. After school finished they would dash from their homes in Shindagha, then to the stable at Al Fahidi Fort. They rode in the vicinity of Dubai town and, as grandsons of the Ruler, they were normally accompanied by one or more retainers. The terrain offered plenty of scope for amusement and development. They quickly graduated from hacking around the area to racing with his friends on the vast, flat sands of the beach at Jumeirah. To fishermen and their families, who lived in small communities in the area, the sight of Sheikh Rashid's sons on horseback became almost a regular afternoon occurrence.

"After school we would rush as quickly as we could to Sheikh Rashid's stables, saddle up, ride across Sheikh Zayed Road, which I recall was just one lane in those days and not terribly busy," says Sheikh Ahmed bin Saeed Al Maktoum. "Then we would ride along the beach in Jumeirah, usually in the area which is today in the area of Mercato shopping mall."

"By early afternoon, Dubai's fishing fleet had returned to shore and most people were sitting mending their nets, or repairing their vessels, ready for the following day's fishing," said Rashid Al Daouk. "A thunder of hooves in the distance would be the first indication that the Maktoums and their friends were on their way. Moments later they would flash by. After making sure they were out of the way, most people would stop what they were doing and wave or cheer the boys on."

Hunting and horseback riding may have been shared passions, but Sheikh Rashid also took the preparation of his sons as future leaders very seriously. Traditionally, those within the ruling families would grow in two directions. A small number, those likely to accede to power, took positions serving the current Ruler, while the majority went into business and served in the Majlis.

Things were changing, however. Dubai was by far the biggest town on the Trucial Coast and the old system, with power almost exclusively in the hands of one man, was becoming inadequate to meet the demands of development and the needs of the population. Sheikh Rashid recognised this, and the need to ensure that his sons would later deliver rule that was homogeneous with his own. During the 1950s especially, Sheikh Rashid had devolved secondary powers into a fledgling government and a growing army of officials. Sheikh Rashid believed that in subsequent years his sons would form the backbone of a larger administration. As the eldest son, Sheikh Maktoum was his anointed successor, yet Sheikh Hamdan, Sheikh Mohammed and Sheikh Ahmed also needed the skills to be effective in their future positions.

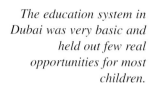

The education system in Dubai was very basic and held out few real opportunities for most children.

From around the age of four, all began their studies, privately tutored in the Arabic language, while a mutawwa (religious man) from the local Kuttab gave religious instruction. Soon after, basic mathematics was added to their studies. By the age of six all were also introduced to English, learning from a number of expatriates living in the sheikhdom, one of whom was the portly British head of Al Maktoum Hospital, Dr Donald McCaully, who was close to Sheikh Rashid.

Sheikh Maktoum joined Al Ahmadiya School, a small primary school in the Deira quarter of the town. The establishment taught Arabic grammar, English, mathematics, geography and history. He would be followed there by his brothers.

The Kuwaiti government built and funded two schools in Dubai during the 1950s, while Qatar donated school books and funded teachers for others, but Al Ahmadiya School remained the best institution for primary students.

Later all moved to a new and modern facility in Shindagha, Al Shaab School – financed by members of the merchant community and constructed on land donated by the Dubai government – Dubai Secondary School or passed through Al Madrasah Al Ahlia, established under Hassan Mirza Al Sayegh.

Away from school, the boys' days were spent in Dubai. Even as late as 1959 a British report on the subject indicated that the ruling family enjoyed privileges still afforded only to a minority. That year only 105 pupils were enrolled in four intermediate level schools, while seven primary schools had 410. The Kuwaiti government was providing four

Al Ahmadiya School, in the Deira quarter of Dubai. Among the pupils who studied there was Sheikh Maktoum, eldest son of the Ruler and himself future Ruler of Dubai.

teachers and the Qataris a further three, along with a changeable quota from the United Arab Republic. The best academic units, in the opinion of the Political Agent, were the Saadiya Boys School in Dubai and Khansa Primary School in Deira, while for girls there was Khowla Bint El Azwer in Dubai and Khansa Primary in Deira.

When the school day finished the brothers and their closest friends would make for Al Fahidi Fort to ride, or head for a small, roughly marked football (soccer) pitch in Shindagha.

As the Trucial States had gradually opened up to the outside world, almost inevitably some of the culture had followed and alongside games such as Luhol, Huwaim and Al Karabi, football had appeared. Sheikh Mohammed was the keenest of the sons of Sheikh Rashid, but all played at various times.

In 1961 Sheikh Mohammed was instrumental in persuading Sheikh Rashid and some of Dubai's merchants to contribute toward a football 'strip' for an informal Dubai team. The team usually played on flat sand below the tidemark near Shindagha, clad in red and white, the colours of Dubai's flag. The team was a select side, mostly locals with a few expatriates. Despite his youth, Sheikh Mohammed occasionally played for Dubai. Sheikh Rashid, who was normally far too preoccupied with the affairs of state to concern himself with sports, sometimes watched from the touchline during an important game, although he was careful to remain neutral when their opposition was foreign.

The quality of Dubai's opposition varied from teams of expatriates representing oil companies to select sides from other sheikhdoms.

During the early 1960s, it also became the norm for visiting naval vessels to challenge Dubai. They did so with varying degrees of success. For example, the American sailors aboard USS Valcour, which called at Dubai in May 1962, were largely ignorant of 'soccer' and suffered a 14-0 drubbing at the hands of the local side. Sheikh Mohammed scored a goal in this encounter. By contrast, later the same year, a side from Britain's HMS Loch Lomond defeated Dubai 1-0.

On quieter days, the boys would return home and sit with their grandfather, Sheikh Saeed, at his Majlis, listening to the stories and anecdotes of the ageing Ruler and those close to him. This was the traditional oral way of retaining the history of the Arabian Peninsula, passing it on from generation to generation.

"Sheikh Saeed was an excellent storyteller. What may have been crusty historical tales were full of passion and life when he told them," says Hamad bin Sukat. "Even we, from the older generation, were fascinated and these stories stayed with us."

"They would sometimes sit for hours and listen to Sheikh Saeed's stories. They were very close," says Mohammed Al Naboodah, a friend and local businessman. "In this informal Majlis, Sheikh Saeed was surrounded by elderly members of the Maktoum family and members of senior Arab families based in the town. Here they learned about the past and heard first-hand accounts of the major events that had shaped the region."

Sheikh Rashid encouraged his sons to spend time around Sheikh Saeed, not only because he was their grandfather, but because the sagely Dubai Ruler was still holding an informal Majlis and continuing to take decisions. This period was their introduction to the business of ruling Dubai.

When Sheikh Maktoum made his public speaking debut at the inauguration of his father, it was the symbolic beginning of the preparation of all the brothers for their future roles within government. Sheikh Rashid had his eye firmly on the future.

Chapter Eleven

The New Ruler

We are what we repeatedly do.
Excellence, then, is not an act, but a habit.
— *Aristotle, Athenian philosopher*

The death of Sheikh Saeed in 1958 came at a critical juncture when his regent was preparing to unveil a radical new agenda of development projects for Dubai. Sheikh Rashid seems to have reached a point when his frustration over a lack of finance – the major stumbling block to many of his dreams of development – came to a head. The new Ruler was relatively well-travelled and knew of the living conditions to be found elsewhere in the world, which were, by and large, lacking in his own state.

Within months of assuming power – and maintaining a studied low profile for 40 days in traditional manner, out of respect for his father – the Ruler's Office had posted decrees concerning the establishment of an electricity company, while work was to begin, with immediate effect, to establish an airport capable of opening Dubai to international aviation. He had also succeeded in persuading the United Nations Technical Assistance Office to finance and administer an exhaustive survey into water resources, at the same time that the British financed Trucial States Development Office was managing an agricultural survey around Dubai.

Significantly, the period when Sheikh Rashid was laying the foundations for modern Dubai's infrastructure occurred in the same year when one of the men who would later play a major role in Dubai's global evolution was born. Sheikh Saeed had married again during his last years, and fathered a son, Sheikh Ahmed bin Saeed Al Maktoum. Born in the year of his father's death, Sheikh Ahmed was brought up like a

Sheikh Rashid at his desk in Customs House. As he acceded as Ruler of Dubai he launched a raft of initiatives to modernise the sheikhdom.

son by his half-brother Sheikh Rashid, who wanted only the best for him. After ensuring a good overseas education, he always desired that Sheikh Ahmed return to Dubai and take a leading role in furthering the development of the city.

He was not to be disappointed. Sheikh Ahmed completed his senior schooling in America and returned during the 1980s to play a part in shaping modern Dubai, his responsibilities including Dubai's Department of Civil Aviation, Department of Tourism and Commerce Marketing and Emirates airline. The latter, Sheikh Ahmed innovatively turned from a $10 million start-up carrier into a multi-billion airline that has had a major impact upon the more recent history of the emirate. All evidence suggests that Sheikh Ahmed shared his eldest brother's wily and dynamic approach to life.

Sheikh Rashid had been in power barely six months when, in May 1959, the well respected Al Maktoum Hospital head physician Dr Donald McCaully was called to his home. The Ruler was complaining of chest pains and, although the doctor could find nothing to indicate serious illness, he referred the new Ruler to Dr J B Harman of St Thomas's Hospital in London, who also had a private practice in Harley Street.

In July 1959, Sheikh Rashid, who was 47, flew to London where he underwent extensive tests and a barrage of x-rays. Dr Harman evidently found nothing more serious than a "touch of arthritis" and, on July 3, the Foreign Office in London reported to the Political Agent in Dubai, quoting the physician as saying he was "in remarkably good health for his age." After a week of rest in Geneva, Sheikh Rashid returned to Dubai.

By this time, Dubai's population had risen to slightly under 30,000 people, a large number of those expatriates. For the vast majority, with their homes powered by privately owned generators, a supply of clean, fresh water was still some years away. In addition to the provision of electricity, Sheikh Rashid made it a priority of his government to have water in every home within five years. He personally had seen the effects of drinking dirty water when Sheikh Saeed became severely ill for some weeks in 1931, probably with cholera.

Cholera is an acute, diarrhoeal illness caused by infection of the

Most people took their water from brakish wells that were alive with diseases. This photograph from the early 1950s shows two women drawing water from a well.

intestine with the bacterium Vibrio cholerae. The infection is often mild or without symptoms, but sometimes it can be severe. A rapid loss of body fluids leads to dehydration and shock. Without treatment, death can occur within hours. A person may get cholera by drinking water or eating food contaminated with the cholera bacterium. In an epidemic, the source of the contamination is usually the faeces of an infected person. The disease can spread rapidly in areas with inadequate treatment of sewage and drinking water. The cholera bacterium may also live in the environment in brackish rivers and coastal waters. Shellfish eaten raw have been a source of cholera.

Dubai's residents, along with all those living throughout the Trucial States, were also being exposed to a frightening array of other water-borne diseases besides cholera, such as Botulism, Hepatitis A, Dysentery, Cryptosporidiosis and Polio. The latter was particularly horrific. Poliomyelitis (polio) is a highly infectious disease that invades the nervous system, and can cause total paralysis in a matter of hours. It can strike at any age, but mainly affects children under three.

"Generations of children in the Trucial States had seen their playmates afflicted by these horrific diseases. Sheikh Rashid knew people whose life had been taken. He was aware of those who suffered in the community, and saw for himself those who had required treatment in Al Maktoum Hospital," says Dr Rashid Al Amri. "As Dubai grew in size and affluence, he saw an opportunity and an urgent need to do something."

"Sheikh Rashid was well aware that for the city to grow much further in the future, more expatriate labour would be needed. And for more people to be attracted, particularly at senior levels, Dubai had to provide water and electricity," reports Hamad bin Sukat. "The government was still struggling financially, so Sheikh Rashid was taking every avenue to secure finance. He told me that Dubai had to have an infrastructure in place to maintain its status as the trading capital of the region, which was particularly tough when the oil boom was already underway elsewhere. He was also adamant that if a basic infrastructure was there, we would be able to benefit quicker when commercially viable oil deposits were discovered in Dubai."

Sheikh Rashid was dismayed, on his early morning tours of Dubai, to witness the primitive level at which some residents in his city lived. One major source of water in Dubai was a large natural pool in the area which is today Karama, replenished during winter rains and often little more than a muddy hole in the ground during the following summer. Many business-minded residents of the city found a niche through the supply to householders of cans and tins of water from the Karama pool. Alternatively, several merchants owned former army tankers, which toured residential districts offering water for a small charge.

Elsewhere in the town one could find several sweet water wells, the busiest being one close to Al Fahidi Fort, while in Deira another was to be found at the site of the Hamarain shopping centre. There was a small well near Dubai Hospital, plus several in Jumeirah. These were utilised by thousands of residents from each area, who queued to fill their bottles and jerry cans. At the other end of the scale, some of the wealthier residents had small battery-operated pumps which fed portable tanks.

Cholera and these other illnesses were still prevalent at certain times of the year. Certainly at the end of summer, residents found their water supplies susceptible to viruses, a situation which was only partly eased when instant water purification tablets became widely available in 1956.

Shockingly, it is only in recent years that the international community has viewed the provision of clean water as a human right. This was enshrined in the United Nations General Assembly's Committee on Economic, Social and Cultural Rights on the right to water in November 2002, and in the UN Millennium Development Goals. Both stated that water is a fundamental human right, and asserted that access to water can mean the difference between sickness and health, cyclical poverty and economic development. By the dawn of the current millennium the UN estimated that more than a billion of the world's inhabitants lack adequate access to safe drinking water. Dubai is not a part of this gruesome statistic, but nevertheless its population had suffered until far too late in their history.

In 1959 the Dubai government entered into an agreement with Qatar, the latter providing some finance and seconding expert manpower to oversee a major drilling project as a part of the newly created Dubai Water Department.

There certainly were strong fresh water sources in Dubai. The Bedu knew that. They had long used a pure drinking well in the Al Awir area, some 15 miles to the south of the town, a place which Sheikh Rashid also knew well.

Early in 1959 the arrival of chief engineer Eric Tullock opened the

Sheikh Rashid attacked the water problem in Dubai, tapping into fresh water resources outside the town. Here he is photographed with Dubai Municipality head Kamal Hamza (right) at Al Wahoosh.

way for a series of geological surveys to ascertain the suitability of Al Awir to supply the whole of Dubai with its water requirements. With samples having to be sent to either Qatar or Britain, the process was very slow and it took just over 18 months for a comprehensive result. A 120-foot well in Al Awir produced excellent water and was proven to be capable of providing a supply that would quench the thirst of a town the size of Dubai. Indeed the news was better than expected. From the days of drawing water from a stagnant pool on the outskirts of the town, Dubai's new supply contained aluminium, fluoride, iron and silica in amounts recommended by the World Health Organisation. In addition, Bedu wells at Al Wahoosh and Habab were found to be equally suitable and included in the next phase of the project. Within months of this positive result, cement piping was being laid apace.

"The more densely populated areas of Dubai were going to be slow to supply," says Hamad bin Sukat. "So Sheikh Rashid looked at underdeveloped areas on the fringes of the town, consulting the Majlis as to which areas were the best to develop. We needed more housing and business premises anyway to cope with existing growth."

For a couple of years, Sheikh Rashid had been aware of the financial difficulty suffered by many families in Dubai as property rents escalated due to increasing demand. A trickle of complainants at his office had grown into a flow, as apartment rents almost doubled to between Rs. 8,000 and Rs. 16,000.

"He knew that the only way Dubai was to attract the right kind of people was to ensure they were able to earn a good living," says

L R Lulla. "Rents were growing alarmingly, far faster than salaries. But he believed in a free market and found himself only able to exert minimum pressure on property owners to keep rents low."

General consensus among planners was that Satwa and Karama were perfectly situated for development, both being relatively clear of buildings aside from the occasional shanty house.

"Once it had been decided to create Karama and Satwa, Sheikh Rashid decreed that much of the development would be given over to low cost housing. He was dynamic in pursuing this. Whoever would agree to build, he would give them valuable tracts of land, insisting that construction work began as soon as possible," says Zakariah Doleh, who was one of those in a position to fulfill Sheikh Rashid's requirements. "If you promised to build though, you had to ensure you did. Sheikh Rashid would follow the progress on each and every plot he gave away. There were people who did not bother to work on land they had been given, and although Sheikh Rashid would never take back what he had given, you would be sure that they never felt his generosity again."

In typical fashion, within months of his decision Sheikh Rashid had either begun building himself or cajoled his favoured developers into immediate action. His aim was to create a colony where rents stayed at between Rs. 5,000 and Rs. 10,000. Across Satwa, Karama, and to a lesser extent Al Ghusais, there were many dozens of projects under way. The three areas were transformed into massive building sites that, combined with other work going on in the late 1960s around the city, caused a crisis within the construction sector.

At one point, in a matter of weeks, the price of a sack of cement went from Rs. 5 to Rs. 17 as supplies dried up. This excessive jump in price caused many sites to suspend work as basic costs spiralled out of control. As work on individual buildings, most half-finished, began to stop, Sheikh Rashid again took a practical step. He dispatched several of his closest lieutenants to Bombay on a mission to buy up some 3,000 tonnes of cement. The arrival of this consignment around three weeks later restored the price to its original level, and work on the idle building sites resumed at full pace. Sheikh Rashid never let supplies drop low again.

In addition to running water, the city's new suburbs were also the first to be properly supplied with electricity. At the turn of the decade, residents of the city fell into two groups: those who relied on candles or kerosene lamps for night time lighting; or the minority whose buildings had generators. The latter, of course, were not only afforded lighting but enjoyed the benefits of air-conditioning and, for the very few, fridges (refrigerators). Television was still more than a decade away.

With the establishment of the Dubai Electricity Company (DEC) in 1959, Sheikh Rashid had decreed DEC should urgently develop a reliable supply for both domestic and industrial purposes, providing the organisation with a starting capital of Rs. 3 million. The company set up its first office in a rented house near Al Nasr Square.

Dubai's first power station saw four 360 kilowatt, eight-cylinder supercharged diesel engines installed. A further spur was purchased to supply Dubai International Airport. DEC built its first generator in Deira, one of six during the initial stage, on a site adjacent to today's Sheraton Hotel. This went on line in July 1961 and provided power for most of Deira side. Within six months DEC had connected hundreds of homes and businesses. At the end of the first quarter 770 consumers were connected, and by the summer of 1962 there were nearly 2,500 consumers and another 50 to 100 under connection every week. At this point DEC was generating some 21,000 kilowatts per week.

Behind all this work was Sheikh Rashid, who ensured that he kept abreast of every development. All projects were followed closely by a nominated member of the Ruler's inner circle, and each evening in his Jumeirah Majlis he would sit to hear a progress report.

"Sheikh Rashid would grasp even the most technical points very quickly," recalls Mohammed Rafie Al Mulla. "Above everything he wanted you to get the job done well and then move on to something else in the same field."

A man renowned for his cool-headedness, Sheikh Rashid preferred to deal with problems in a calm and reasonable manner, never being seen to become angry in public. One morning he was joined by property developer Zakariah Doleh for an early morning trip around construction works in Satwa, when Sheikh Rashid saw something amiss.

"We all thought Sheikh Rashid had an almost photographic memory and on one occasion he showed me his incredible attention to detail," says the former Kuwait-based businessman. "He came across one plot on which building work was going on, which he clearly thought had been retained as government land, and ordered the foreman on the site to stop work until checks could be made.

Sheikh Rashid and Sheikh Hamdan preside over a board meeting of Dubai Electricity Company. To Sheikh Rashid's left is Bill Duff.

"The following morning I was with him again when he discovered that work had continued unabated, without any checks being done. He was furious and called everyone concerned from their beds, there and then, to settle the matter. It turned out that Sheikh Rashid was correct, the national who claimed the site had recently moved a date palm onto the plot. For centuries date palms, which were passed on from generation to generation of a family, were used as markers to signify ownership of land. In this case, someone was trying to take land, in the hope that Sheikh Rashid would not know what was going on. How wrong he was."

As development of large tracts of Satwa and Karama continued, the first major water project in the emirate of Dubai was completed in July 1961, a central pipeline from Al Awir to Ras Al Khor, from where individual areas were later to be connected to the central supply. From the mid-1960s Satwa and Karama were the first in Dubai to boast running water into each home, before work began to bring the service into existing built-up areas. Initially, during the early years when reliability was being established, water was provided free to all households. By the middle of the 1960s more than a million gallons of water per day were being pumped into the thirsty city.

Elsewhere in Dubai, plans for an airport had long been of primary interest to Sheikh Rashid, who in pioneering the effort to broaden the capacity of the Creek had displayed an understanding that trade links could only be maintained and expanded through the provision of necessary infrastructure.

"An airport will bring us within hours of places which it has taken us days or weeks to reach. We have already lost one opportunity to Sharjah," Sheikh Rashid told his Majlis during the latter half of the 1950s, referring to the occasion some 20 years earlier when his father had been forced by internal opponents to pass up the chance to have Britain build an aerodrome in the sheikhdom.

"Dubai must lead, not be led," he added.

Commencing in the late 1930s, Dubai's air links to the world were provided by commercial flying boat services. But for nearby Sharjah, the air age had already begun in June 1932, when Imperial Airways inaugurated landplane services to and from the sheikhdom with large four-engine Handley Page H.P.42 Hannibal-class biplanes.

Earlier still, since late 1918, Royal Air Force (RAF) flights to India had stopped at Cairo, Baghdad and Shaibah (near Basra), before continuing along the Persian/Iranian (or northern) coast of the Gulf via Bushire, Bandar Abbas and Jask to Gwadar in Baluchistan, before reaching their destination in Karachi (then part of pre-Partition British India). But the rise of a strong Imperial government in Iran, which made matters difficult for the British aviation authorities, soon rendered the Trucial Coast as a more viable alternative.

With active support from the British government, Imperial Airways (the forerunner of BOAC and, later, British Airways) had also been seeking a base along the Trucial Coast. Sheikh Saeed and Sheikh Rashid were initially keen on this when approached in December 1931, but the internal opposition they were facing presented a firm barrier to the concept.

Dubai's sole entry into the civil aviation industry was an Imperial Airways flying boat that ran services into Dubai Creek (left). The Trucial States' civil aviation hub was Sharjah Aerodrome (right).

With Umm Al Quwain already eliminated from contention because of its Ruler's hostility to the idea, Sheikh Sultan bin Saqr Al Qassimi of Sharjah stepped in personally to secure the airport for his sheikhdom, correctly guessing that the resulting commercial spin-off would help his emirate in times of economic downturn. And Sheikh Sultan had other motives, demanding as part of the agreement that the British re-route their fortnightly mail steamer from its traditional call in Dubai. Against a background of protest from Dubai, the British acquiesced.

Separately, 'Bahrain, off Arabia' was initially chosen as the main landing base by the RAF, with a support station in Muscat and a refuelling depot in Ras Al Khaimah, the latter established under threat from the British authorities with the intervention of Sheikh Saeed as an arbitrator.

Having missed the chance to have a proper aerodrome built in Dubai at the expense of the British, Sheikh Saeed and Sheikh Rashid were in no mood to be left out of Imperial Airways' scheduled flying boat route to India (later extended to parts farther east). To persuade Imperial Airways of the validity of including Dubai as a stop, Sheikh Saeed had guaranteed a fixed number of seats on each flight, using his own funds.

The first Imperial Airways flight alighted on Dubai Creek in October 1937. Service frequency, between Southampton and Karachi, was once a week. The flights were operated by four-engine Short S.23 C-class Empire flying boats, capable of transporting 24 passengers at a maximum speed of 200 miles per hour over a range of 760 miles. Aside from Sheikh Saeed's guarantee, Imperial Airways paid Rs. 440 (Indian currency was the legal tender in Dubai in those days) for traffic rights, while the fee levied for each landing and takeoff was a mere Rs. 5. This brought the government significant revenues for many years, but hardly comparable to those enjoyed by neighbouring Sharjah following the establishment of its land-based facility.

Two decades later, Sheikh Rashid was well aware of the growth of air traffic internationally and its impact on world markets. For the international visitor, a journey to Dubai usually meant a flight into Bahrain, followed by an uncomfortable boat ride or infrequent flying boat connection into the Creek.

"For years Sheikh Rashid had toyed with the idea of establishing an airport in Dubai, making Dubai a regional hub," says Mohidin bin Hendi, former director-general of the Dubai Department of Civil Aviation. "Even during the mid-1950s it was becoming clear that during the second half of the century most forms of commerce would be utilising air transportation. Sheikh Rashid was well briefed and understood the implications. He knew that an open skies policy would establish Dubai as the regional centre of aviation."

At the time the nearest airport, Sharjah, was serviced by Gulf Aviation (then a BOAC-controlled company, which later became Gulf Air) with 15-seat de Havilland Herons and 8-seat de Havilland Doves flying routes along the coast. Later these routes would be serviced by 22-seat Douglas DC-3 Dakotas and, later still, the larger four-engine Vickers Viscount turboprops. The most important of these was the three-times weekly flight to Bahrain, whereby international visitors could connect with intercontinental flights to Europe and the Far East. Each flight worked on a general quota system. Typically on a Heron, two or three seats were reserved for passengers from Dubai, four from Sharjah, while the oil companies and other Trucial Sheikhdoms had smaller allowances. By the 1950s, these Gulf services were almost always fully subscribed. For Dubai especially, with its growing merchant community and development programme, this was a source of friction with Gulf Aviation on a number of occasions. Sheikh Rashid – to his great embarrassment – often found his VIP guests unable to join flights as promised. On one occasion, when two British businessmen, guests of the Dubai Ruler, had found themselves left on the tarmac, one of those closest to the heart of the Majlis told the head of Sharjah Airport: "Perhaps it is time Dubai had its own airport."

This was no throw-away comment. Sheikh Rashid was nothing if not ambitious.

Well before his accession as Ruler, Sheikh Rashid had brought up the subject of a new airport in his regular meetings with British officials, supporters of a variety of development projects in the region. Sheikh Rashid had requested financial and technical aid in order to build Dubai's own facility. In one 1959 communication the Political Agent confirmed to the Foreign Office:

> *Sheikh Rashid is under pressure from the merchant community to build an airport, even if it meant that these facilities could only be afforded by passing a higher cost on to them. Sheikh Rashid had even told me that when on his travels he is embarrassed when people ask him if Dubai has its own airport. He believed that Dubai must have an airport to enhance its own name.*

In 1958, soon after he had become Ruler, Sheikh Rashid one evening announced to the Majlis that he wished to proceed, as soon as possible, with the development of an airport. Just months later, a flat area at Al Ghusais and another near Jebel Ali had been short-listed as possible sites for such an undertaking. In February 1959, a senior inspector from the British Air Ministry in London was seconded temporarily to Dubai to assess plans. Much of his work centred on the favoured Jebel Ali site. There he worked on plans for a 7,000-foot runway, capable of taking Dakotas, Herons and Doves. He estimated a bill to the sheikhdom of £459,000 for developing the site, and running costs of around £50,000 per annum.

For some time it seemed that the proposed airport would eventually go to Jebel Ali. However, the logistics of building a facility even farther from Dubai city than Sharjah Airport eventually saw efforts concentrate in the Al Ghusais area, where studies into the soil structure pronounced it just as suitable. The following month, with typical Sheikh Rashid decisiveness, work began on the initial phase of the airport, a 5,905-foot compacted sand runway.

By May 19 preliminary work was far enough ahead for the first actual tests of the runway, with a Dove aircraft from Middle East Airlines (MEA) seconded for the task. It was the first time an aircraft had landed and taken off from Dubai soil. This historic occasion was

On September 30, 1960, Sheikh Rashid inaugurated Dubai International Airport. (top) The first terminal building. (down) A Gulf Aviation Heron on the apron. (inset) The emergency crew.

witnessed, at a safe distance, by the Ruler and some 200 dignitaries. Later, Sheikh Rashid himself went aloft on one of the Dive's five test flights that day. These test flights allowed engineers from MEA to assess the landing strip, and that afternoon they declared Dubai's airport suitable for MEA aircraft, which would begin a service when the facility opened formally

The issue of active British support was passed between officials in London and the Gulf for several years – with a suggestion surfacing that Dubai and Sharjah pool resources to build a joint airport – before a firm decision was made. Sheikh Rashid was finally informed of a negative decision, when Winchester, the Political Agent, visited the Majlis.

"I appreciate your frank reply," he stated, after hearing the long list of reasons why his allies felt unable to provide assistance. "I shall be just as frank with you. Dubai shall have its own airport."

If he was unhappy at Britain's lack of assistance on the project, Sheikh Rashid did not show it. He later gave the Political Agent a letter informing Her Majesty's government that Royal Air Force (RAF) aircraft would be welcome at the new facility. The following month the British agreed to "assume responsibility for civil aviation under the International Civil Aviation Agreement of Chicago."

For a year the airport project proved a boon for the local community in terms of jobs, the terminal and attendant buildings employing a large number of carpenters and craftsmen. Indeed, such was the scale of the venture that there was a dearth of labour. Prisoners from Naif jail were employed to put up a barbed-wire perimeter fence. They were collected each morning in a contractor's van and watched over by a solitary policeman. To ensure enough staff could be found, Sheikh Rashid paid high salaries, but in return he asked a great deal. His timetable for completion was tight. The project's work-force, most of whom resided in central Bur Dubai and Deira, would walk en masse to the site each morning, and often would only finish work when daylight faded.

At this time the number of labourers required for all of Dubai's public and private works meant a massive influx of workers, mainly from Pakistan and India. One of Sheikh Rashid's closest confidantes in the public works projects, engineer Abdul Ghaffar Hashim Al Maimani, recalls his almost paternal concern for those employed in his country. "Sheikh Rashid would shake hands with the workers and talk to them as he toured a worksite. He would distribute gifts among the labourers and would ensure the supply of food was good to sites which were remote," recalls Al Maimani. "He would himself supervise labour welfare activities. On occasion, when there was an accident, he would personally arrange to take an injured worker to the hospital, sometimes in his own car."

As was his style, Sheikh Rashid was never far from the centre of the project. "Although several of the men he trusted most were always overseeing work at the airport site, the final decisions on most matters were usually made by Sheikh Rashid himself. That was how he liked it," recalls Saif Ahmed Al Ghurair. "Only several weeks into work on the airport, he found himself torn between his evening Majlis and the need to be at the airport approving contracts and following the work as it progressed. Of all his many projects, the airport was the one which seemed most dear to him."

This conflict of responsibilities was resolved with typical practicality. Sheikh Rashid utilised a contractor's hut adjacent to the rapidly evolving runway. Whenever necessary, an impromptu Majlis was held there, on what was to become the concourse of his ground-breaking airport.

On September 30, 1960, Sheikh Rashid officially inaugurated Dubai International Airport, complete with a small terminal and control tower, encompassing the Trucial Coast's first two duty free shops, both owned by nationals. Much to the amazement of many, he also ordered a car park with capacity for 500 vehicles. At the time this was virtually unused, but within a decade the car park required expansion. With the opening of the airport, Dubai entered a new era of travel, residents finding themselves within reasonable flying distance of destinations which previously took weeks to access by boat or land. Initially, Gulf Aviation operated two routes, Dubai–Muscat and Dubai–Abu Dhabi–Bahrain. Kuwait Airways flew a weekly Dubai–Kuwait City service.

Sheikh Rashid wanted more, making strong representations to British Overseas Airways Corporation (BOAC) that it should operate its larger Vickers (BAC) VC10 four-engine jetliners through Dubai. BOAC turned down the offer, claiming Dubai would be a wholly unprofitable stop. But Dubai's leader was certain there was a demand and, recalling his success with Imperial Airways some 20 years before, set out to ensure the VC10 paid a regular call to his new airport. Over the coming weeks his staff made representations to all the major firms based in Dubai, with expatriate staff, requesting advance bookings. This filled well over a third of a VC10, leaving the Dubai government to guarantee seats to the 60% break-even threshold that BOAC had set. One year after the opening of the airport, BOAC added a second scheduled weekly VC10 flight out of Dubai.

While air services were improving, Sheikh Rashid was also turning his attention to accommodating people visiting his city. As late as 1957 there was no hotel. Those visiting Dubai in connection with the oil industry stayed in spare bedrooms of colleagues permanently resident in the sheikhdom. For those on political or commercial business, the nearest available beds were at Sharjah Fort, or the newly created Gulf Hotel in Bahrain, neither of which were convenient for people working in Dubai. In 1957 Sheikh Rashid leased to the oil companies a three-bedroom flat above his government garage in Shindagha. It cost Rs. 30 a day for each individual in the guest house, with two, three or sometimes even four men occasionally forced to share a bedroom. The guest house was basic, with no running water and electricity provided by a generator, the reliability of which was often questionable.

The guest house was superseded, in 1959, by the Airlines Hotel, an eight-room, two-storey complex in Bur Dubai, which was comparatively luxurious, with a constantly restocked water tank and lighting by kerosene lamps. As traffic into Dubai increased, the Airlines Hotel was extended until it boasted 35 rooms.

Both were managed by L R Lulla, an Indian executive who had known Sheikh Rashid when he worked at Sharjah Airport, and later still when he joined Dubai Airport. He had managed both the guest house and the Airlines Hotel.

"Sheikh Rashid always asked how his visitors found Dubai and had heard good reports about the Airlines Hotel. One day he sent for me and asked if I would like to run a bigger and better hotel," says Lulla. "He was fully aware that as Dubai expanded and became more modern, the city would need hotels capable of hosting a greater number of people."

Much later, in 1968, Sheikh Rashid built the 45-room Ambassador Hotel in Bur Dubai, while private concerns added the 85-bedroom Carlton Towers Hotel in Deira. He later gave the Ambassador to Lulla, a favourite hotelier, and as the city expanded over the next few years the Ambassador was to host many of the most famous visitors to Dubai. Sheikh Rashid was often to use the hotel – in the design of which he had played a major part – for the majority of his official banquets until the early 1980s.

At the beginning of the 1960s, Dubai was still some years from its entry into the oil boom, but its far-sighted Ruler had steered his city on a course to becoming a thriving entrepot. With a population approaching 35,000, an international airport, thriving seaport and growing infrastructure, the sheikhdom was enjoying a relative boom period, made all the more remarkable by the shoestring on which it was financed and managed.

Despite a growing position as a political heavyweight within the Gulf, Sheikh Rashid continued to maintain the common touch which had made him such a popular figure for close to four decades. By 1960 he was 54, but still maintaining a rigorous schedule: he continued to tour Dubai soon after dawn and seldom finished his evening Majlis before midnight.

He also took pains to maintain links outside his immediate circle, at the Ruler's Office and his tight-knit Majlis. Through the years, Sheikh Rashid maintained close links with the British and he also understood that many of the Indian merchants in his city were important conduits in the process of development, playing an active part in their community.

"During Diwali, Sheikh Rashid came and lunched with my father and ate moong, rice, puri and sira. He also loved curd," recalls Indian businessman Vijay Bhatia whose father was a confidante of Dubai's Ruler and one of the most important members of the Indian community during the middle part of the century. "During Eid, or weddings in the Ruling family, knowing my father was a vegetarian, special food was prepared separately for him."

Sheikh Rashid also had time for the Christian community in his midst. In 1966 he donated land to the Roman Catholic Mission in Dubai, laying the foundation stone for what was to become St Mary's Church. Four years later he gave land to the Protestant community and inaugurated work on Holy Trinity Church.

It was this tolerance which filtered down from the Majlis to produce a society at peace with itself. Elsewhere in the Gulf, the influx of foreign cultures and religions was seen to be causing problems within the local community, creating friction and open instability. In Dubai, Sheikh Rashid was adamant that the same mistakes – especially secular intolerance – would not be repeated. But while his benevolent side was well known, Sheikh Rashid had not been adverse to dealing firmly with a situation when more conservative management was needed.

"We are too small to get involved," he would say, when attempts were made to drag Dubai into external problems. And he also made it completely clear that foreign conflicts and political problems were to remain foreign. Following partition of India, and the subsequent hostility between India and Pakistan, the large communities from each country based in Dubai occasionally reacted to their political problems at home. This was intolerable to Sheikh Rashid who, on a number of occasions, called leaders of the two communities before him.

"Forget your nationalities. Dubai is home for both Pakistanis and Indians," he stated during a meeting at his Jumeirah guest house – today called Union House – which was attended by top businessmen and community leaders from each nation. "I want you to consider yourselves esteemed guests of Dubai. But I have to warn you categorically that we will not allow foreign politics to be played out in the streets of this city. At least here, solve your differences."

Religious and cultural conflicts were an anomaly to him and he worked to ensure that the communities living in his lands existed peacefully. More than granting religious freedom he showed genuine respect to other faiths, visiting friends during the major festivals.

"I recall Sheikh Rashid coming to the house at Christmas," says George Chapman, whose residence was Bayt Al Wakeel, a two storey building overlooking the Creek.

Throughout his life, Sheikh Rashid showed an infallible belief in Islam. He prayed five times each day, ruled with the Shariah laws as his guideline, and never became tainted by the money and power which were to come his way in ever-greater amounts throughout his long life. When hunting in the deserts, Sheikh Rashid would carry a compass and bring the hunt to an abrupt end when it was time for him and his associates to pray. Leading by example, Sheikh Rashid observed the constraints of Ramadan to the letter. Ramadan is the ninth month of the Islamic year. Siyam ('fasting') is the fourth of the Five Pillars of Islam, and requires fasting every day during the month of Ramadan. Muslims fast during the daylight hours and in the evening eat small meals and visit with friends and family.

It is a time of worship and contemplation. A time to strengthen family and community ties. It was Sheikh Rashid who first ordered the cannons at Dubai's Al Fahidi Fort to be fired each evening during Ramadan to mark the end of fasting.

Sheikh Rashid's attitude of social and religious tolerance was well known and became imbibed in Dubai's culture and ethics. The Ruler donated land to both the Anglican and Protestant communities so that they could build churches.

In the days before Eid Al Fitr he was also extremely active in the cattle souq. Eid Al Fitr marks the end of Ramadan, and is a joyous occasion with important religious significance. Happiness is observed at attaining spiritual uplift after a month of fasting.

"Sheikh Rashid would go into the souq to see the cattle, sheep and goats which were on sale," says Humaid bin Drai. "He would send animals to everyone he could think of, especially those who served him at some point who were not so well off. Eid was very special for him, an excuse to let generosity get the better of him."

Eid was a time of responsibilities, when the foreign powers, such as Britain and the United States, jostled to show the most courtesy and took up the Ruler's time with shows of friendship. Although hospitable to all governments, Sheikh Rashid remained singularly unimpressed by extravagant gestures and words.

This was underlined in one of the regular communications to the Foreign Office by the British Political Resident in Dubai in 1961, who enjoyed a warm relationship with Dubai's Ruler, in which he reported on a visit to Dubai by a US Navy vessel and the subsequent guided tour for Sheikh Rashid at which he was also present. During the course of the inspection, the ship's captain tried too hard to impress; some of his statements made Sheikh Rashid visibly cringe, the British representative reported. In a quiet moment Sheikh Rashid displayed his own typical dry humour in a comment to the Political Resident, when he noted that superior wealth did not necessarily bring with it superior intelligence...

Chapter Twelve

Maktoum United

The goal of education is the advancement of knowledge and
the dissemination of truth.
— *John Fitzgerald Kennedy, statesman*

During the latter part of the 1950s and into the 1960s, Sheikh Rashid
had begun to emerge as a dynamic leader, while his reforms and
mammoth new projects were beginning to have a profound effect on
Dubai. The Creek development project had renewed and enhanced
Dubai's status as the major trade hub of the lower Gulf. Living
standards were improving through electricity and water ventures, and
activity surrounded a variety of infrastructure works, including a new
airport.

In the town there was a feeling of optimism. Sheikh Rashid – not that
he cared much about such things – was riding the crest of popular
support. On a regional level he was well respected by fellow Rulers,
both for what he was achieving at home and the peaceful course upon
which he had set his state.

Throughout the region, it was a period of renewed confidence and
peace, the souqs and bazaars teeming with merchandise and busy with
trade. Although many problems persisted, it seemed that the Coast of
Oman was at last coming to terms with the death of the pearling industry.

Just around the corner, however, was the first major crisis with which
the new Ruler had to deal. On April 7, 1961, the London registered
British Steam Navigation Company vessel MV Dara had weighed
anchor just off the entrance to Dubai Creek, as she did every fortnight.
The vessel had sailed from Bombay on May 23 on a round trip to Basra,
calling at intermediate ports.

One of the larger vessels to ply the Gulf waterways, the 5,000 tonne

*The gateway to the Bell School of Languages in Cambridge, England, a facility
that would educate a generation of Maktoum family members.*

The MV Dara disaster was particularly hard on Dubai. 212 passengers and 24 crew perished. (left) The MV Dara in flames. (right) In happier times the arrival of the vessel was a key link to the outside world.

MV Dara carried passengers and cargo and was usually employed on the route between Bombay and Kuwait, calling at Dubai. She had accommodation for 20 First Class, 54 Second Class and 1,377 deck passengers. The MV Dara was both part of a central artery used by Dubaians and expatriates to reach the outside world, and a key trade link into the sheikhdom.

Late that afternoon, the wind quite suddenly picked up, reaching Force Seven gale strength. Unusual in its intensity, the wind prevented boarding and unloading to continue. After suspending both for a time, the MV Dara fell behind schedule. This was enough to persuade the captain to continue his journey southward, despite the fact that operations into Dubai had not been completed. Indeed, the MV Dara made such a speedy exit that Dubai Immigration Department Officer Belal Fairooz found himself suddenly heading off on an unexpected excursion. Also stuck on board were relatives and friends seeing off the passengers, hawkers, cargo labourers and shipping officials.

The MV Dara set sail with 819 passengers and crew aboard. Around 80 of these were booked from Kuwait to Dubai but had been unable to leave the vessel and were promised tickets on the steamer which was due to make the return journey, some days later. In Dubai itself there were as many as 60 disappointed ticket holders who had been unable to get aboard the vessel, and would thus be forced to either wait one week for her return or make other arrangements.

The sky remained dark and winds whipped up the sea for much of the evening, hampering the ship's progress. She was still visible from the

coast of Sharjah when darkness fell.

At 4.43 am the following morning, an explosion ripped through the boat, destroying many Second Class cabins, while a fire began to take hold of a larger part of the passenger areas. Within minutes the captain sounded the call to abandon ship and sent out Mayday messages, which were first heard at exactly 5 am. The vessel was reported as being off Umm Al Quwain.

The explosion and fire had claimed a great many lives, but the disaster was compounded by an outbreak of panic among crew and passengers, with many perishing by jumping into the sea or throwing themselves into already crowded lifeboats, which then capsized.

Then a second explosion, seen by several people in Umm Al Quwain, ripped through the stricken vessel. Only a raging fire illuminated the horrific scene as lifeboats struggled to get clear of the MV Dara in heavy seas and pick up the few survivors who had thrown themselves into the water.

The British Steam Navigation Company office in Dubai was notified and, as was usual in times of disaster, the 'bush telegraph' quickly ensured that Dubai's population soon knew there had been a disaster. Sheikh Rashid was woken at his Shindagha home and notified of the MV Dara's plight. He immediately consulted with the British Political Agent. The wind had abated slightly and he dispatched his personal launch, Al Hamar (The Red), and ordered other government and Maktoum family-owned vessels to head immediately for the burning wreck in search of survivors. Along with several British, German,

Japanese and Norwegian ships that were close at hand, and some civil shipping from Sharjah, Ajman, Umm Al Quwain and Ras Al Khaimah, the Dubai fleet found a burning wreck several miles off the coast. The few passengers able to swim were picked up and by late morning all survivors were brought ashore, many on the passing steamer Empire Guillemot, which by mid-morning arrived in Dubai carrying 340 survivors, 10 with serious injuries.

Sheikh Rashid had personally taken charge of the scene when he was informed that the survivors were coming into Dubai. A nearly completed hotel was hastily commandeered for a reception centre, manned by the Dubai Police, Royal Air Force (RAF) personnel from Sharjah, Trucial Oman Scouts, staff from the Ruler's household and many civilian volunteers.

From a total of 819 on board at the time of the explosion, the disaster's death toll reached 212 passengers and 24 crew. Of those who made it to Dubai, several were suffering from third-degree burns, while others had head wounds and the great majority were suffering from exposure. Some had been badly wounded by shards of metal when the first explosion ripped through the ill-fated vessel.

All through the day Al Maktoum Hospital was at full stretch treating the worst injured, while impromptu field stations, including one in Sheikh Rashid's Customs House office block, sprung up for those less affected. This sheer mass of patients placed great strain on Dubai's limited medical facilities, which were backed up later by the arrival of a British medical team. Consequently, the Dubai Ruler spent all day coordinating the various agencies in their efforts.

For Dubai, especially, the MV Dara brought great losses. Several Dubaians perished in the disaster, leaving behind families, while the expatriate community was particularly hard hit as dozens perished. In the aftermath, Sheikh Rashid supported many families financially for some time and paid to help bereaved expatriates return to their native countries.

Meanwhile, three British frigates and a US destroyer sent parties on board MV Dara and were able to get the fire under control. What was left of the hulk was then taken in tow by the Glasgow salvage vessel Ocean Salvor, but sank on the morning of April 10.

The MV Dara disaster aside, this period was notable for its progress, and this reflected on the reputation of the Ruler. It was undoubtedly

Sheikh Rashid's straightforward approach – apparently the exception in a region where intrigue and political infighting were commonplace – which now propelled him into the role of diplomat. Although hailing from a tiny state which, during his early years, did not enjoy the benefits of oil wealth, he was accorded something of a special status. A clear neutrality existed in Dubai's foreign policy, and as such, its Ruler was widely respected. Unusually for an Arab Gulf leader, he was cordial with the Iranian government, enjoying a warmer relationship with the Shah than most. At the same time, Dubai acted as a peacemaker for the northern Trucial States, had closer political ties with the superpowers than most, and even managed to tread the fine line between supporting and marginalising Arab nationalism.

Sheikh Rashid's skills were an undoubted advantage in pursuing one of the thorniest issues in regional politics. The tiny sheikhdoms of the Trucial Coast, including Bahrain and Qatar, were dwarfed by their powerful neighbours. At some point in their history most had been subject to territorial claims by the regional powers. With the discovery of oil, each state had the added potential of holding billions, or even trillions, of dollars of oil reserves, making them an even more enticing target. Considering this, plus a need to cooperate for mutual development, Sheikh Rashid was keen to expand relations among the smaller states.

On January 13, 1961, future British Prime Minister Edward (Ted) Heath, then the Lord Privy Seal, visited Dubai on a short trip to the Gulf. Heath was well-read in Gulf affairs, yet well-read on the subject, and was only scheduled for a short face-to-face meeting with Sheikh Rashid. Their discussion, however, went on for upwards of two hours. Only slightly over two years into his rule, Sheikh Rashid was relaxed in his position, readied no doubt by decades of effectively leading Dubai. He was noted as a "modernist, regional leader" and wasted no time in bringing up the concept of federation with Heath, sounding out British feelings on the oft-touted subject. Heath was also keen that dialogue should begin, the British long-term view being that a larger entity, certainly one encompassing the poorer states, would be more likely to succeed as an independent nation. After conferring with the Dubai Ruler, Heath offered to continue the dialogue and invited Sheikh Rashid to meet him in London that summer.

"He was so bright. Such a wonderful character," Heath said. "There was something about him, a charisma, even when you did not agree with what he was saying you could not help but warm to him.

"I recall that I arrived in Dubai and was scheduled to see Sheikh Rashid for maybe half an hour. But we warmed to each other and after official business was completed, over Arabic coffee, our discussion went on. He delighted in telling me about his grand plans for the future. He was very ambitious and some of what he was saying would have sounded like fiction, but if you knew about Sheikh Rashid – and I did – you knew that he was serious and capable of achieving just about everything he set his mind to.

"A few years later I returned to Dubai – and he had."

Evidence of Sheikh Rashid's preoccupation with Trucial unity is carried in British communications to and from the Political Agent's office in Dubai throughout the first half of that year. And, at Heath's request, Sheikh Rashid began making arrangements to visit Great Britain later in 1961. As is standard procedure when political decision-makers are set to meet, the Political Agent in Dubai was instructed to report to the Foreign Office on Sheikh Rashid's thinking, therefore enabling the Lord Privy Seal to be in a position to develop the theme further during their talks.

What becomes clear, particularly from a conversation in the Dubai Majlis between Sheikh Rashid and the visiting head of the Foreign Office Arabian Department, is that at this stage few envisaged Abu Dhabi as part of the process. Sheikh Shakhbut, the Ruler of Abu Dhabi, was a perennial absentee from meetings of the Trucial States Council. If Sheikh Shakhbut was not interested in even the Council, a body aimed at promoting cooperation in development projects, most thought that Abu Dhabi would follow an independent course.

"The Ruler considered that a federation of some sort would be perfectly possible between himself and all the states to the east, including Sharjah. He intended to talk to the Ruler of Sharjah about this. It was however important that Her Majesty's government should tell the Rulers the approximate lines of such a federation," state minutes from the aforementioned meeting. "The Ruler said that he [Sheikh Rashid] would like to use Sheikh Zayed as an intermediary in breaching the subject with Sheikh Shakhbut, the Ruler of Abu Dhabi. He doubted

The new Ruler found himself engaged in efforts on two levels,
both in Dubai and on a pan-Trucial States basis.

however whether Abu Dhabi could be brought in, since Shakhbut showed every sign of wanting to go his own way."

Indeed, the minutes of a meeting of the Trucial States Council of May 16, 1959, one of the few Sheikh Shakhbut attended, indicate that of the Rulers present he was by far the least enthusiastic to even vague mention of federation. He also spoke against a watered down suggestion that the Council itself be put on a more formal footing.

Heath was informed in a confidential report commissioned ahead of these talks with Sheikh Rashid (and Sheikh Saqr bin Sultan Al Qassimi, Ruler of Sharjah, who was in London at the same time) that "it is not easy to see how a federation could have much life without more idea of how this would be financed. Dubai is by far the most developed of the northern sheikhdoms, but even then would not be able to afford to bankroll a federal structure, while Abu Dhabi looked unlikely to participate."

Sir William Luce, the influential Bahrain-based British Political Arabist, gave a similar assessment. Luce, whose opinions on the Arabian Peninsula were viewed by the Foreign Office as perhaps the most credible of any, stated: "I have serious doubts whether a federation of Trucial States, less Abu Dhabi, is a desirable aim of policy. It would mean creating a federal entity with a population of about 65,000, some of which is likely to move to Abu Dhabi as opportunities of employment increase there."

Noting the disastrous and costly Aden federation in which Britain had participated, he went on: "We should be creating all the complicated paraphernalia of a federal constitution for, and entering into a new treaty with, an entity which in absence of oil could never hope to be tangible."

The views of Luce were to have strong bearing on the British stance to the process for some time to come and, indeed, this evolved position must certainly have led to the eventual elevation of Sheikh Zayed as Ruler of Abu Dhabi. For a great many years Sheikh Rashid was never slow to portray Sheikh Zayed as one of the most forward-thinking politicians to be found among the Trucial States.

In July 1961 Sheikh Rashid made his second visit to Britain as Ruler of Dubai, the political highlight of the visit being a second face-to-face meeting with Heath. Sheikh Rashid appears, from British communications, to have been offered a full diplomatic visit, surrounded by a great deal of pomp and ceremony. But, like the previous year, he had instead opted for a low-key stay while taking pains not to be lured into impromptu 'summits' with other Gulf leaders, most of whom were regulars in the British capital throughout the summer. Indeed, the previous year Sheikh Rashid had asked to be informed of the dates during which Sheikh Saqr bin Sultan of Sharjah and Sheikh Ahmed bin Ali of Qatar were in London, so that he could select alternatives.

Keeping a low profile also meant that Sheikh Rashid was free to pursue his own plans. He had followed a hectic work schedule since his inauguration in 1958, relaxing only when taking short hunting trips. The winter of 1960-61 had been trying, particularly in the aftermath of the MV Dara disaster, and Sheikh Rashid was determined to make the most of his trip to Britain.

Along with a party of eight, including close advisors and friends Easa Saleh Al Gurg and Mahdi Al Tajir, Sheikh Rashid flew to Beirut on June 10 to join the cruise ship Azonia for a 10-day trip which took in Alexandria and Venice. They subsequently visited Austria, Germany and Denmark, before making their way to Britain.

In London he was also invited to attend a garden party at Buckingham Palace, where he met Queen Elizabeth for the first time, and spent 20 minutes in friendly chat with her. The party also attended the International Horse Show, before visiting Wembley Stadium – along with King Hussein of Jordan – to see England and France contest a football (soccer) international. At Wembley, Sheikh Rashid was joined by two of his sons, Sheikh Hamdan and Sheikh Mohammed. Sheikh Rashid even found time to try his hand at golf, staying at the Gleneagles Hotel on July 23, after travelling to Scotland aboard the Flying Scotsman train.

Scotland was a place that was featuring heavily in Sheikh Rashid's plans at the time, for it was here that his eldest son, Sheikh Maktoum, had continued his studies.

The Dubai Ruler had long underscored his interest in education through the development of the scholastic system in Dubai. He wanted his sons to have a broad education, the sort that had not been available to him as a youngster. Sheikh Maktoum had left Dubai for Britain in September 1960. There, he studied English language and literature at an institute in Cambridge and later completed his education at the prestigious Gordonstoun boarding school in the north of Scotland.

The elite Gordonstoun School in Scotland was to host Sheikh Maktoum as a student.

Gordonstoun is a private school located in a 17th century house near Elgin, Moray, in Scotland, that was founded as an international school in 1934 by Dr Kurt Hahn. It boasted a tough régime. Dr Hahn placed great emphasis on militaristic discipline and physical education, particularly outdoor activities such as sailing and hill-walking. He developed a routine founded on belief in an egalitarian society, with firm principles of human conduct: the strong must be courteous to the weak, and service to others is more important than self-service. The school gained a reputation for harsh conditions, with its cold showers being particularly cited as a problem.

Among a distinguished list of alumnae are Prince Philip – now Duke of Edinburgh – William Boyd, Charles Kennedy the economist, Roy Williamson and Crown Prince Alexander of Yugoslavia.

At Gordonstoun, Sheikh Maktoum mixed with the sons of leaders and political and economic heavyweights from all over the world. It might have been a difficult adjustment, culturally and climatically, for an Arabian prince, but Sheikh Maktoum graduated well.

"I recall Sheikh Maktoum as a shy young man, but when he got used to people he had a warm and very generous personality," says Richard Blandy MBE, who left Gordonstoun in 1965. Another pupil studying there at the time was Prince Charles, now the Prince of Wales, who joined the school on May 1, 1962.

Sheikh Maktoum would graduate from Gordonstoun and return to Dubai where he would play an ever-increasing role within his father's administration.

Leaving Scotland in 1960, the Dubai party returned to London where Sheikh Rashid got back to affairs of state. The text of his meeting with Heath is recorded in Foreign Office files, and offers a unique insight into the thinking of the British government and the Dubai Ruler at that juncture. During the meeting, Sheikh Rashid is quoted as saying:

"It is very important to decide how best to approach Sheikh Shakhbut. The best thing to do would be for the British government to draw up a plan for the federal union and to explain it to the Rulers."

Heath asked: "Would it be better for the British government to do this, or for the Rulers to work out a plan of their own?"

"There would be no difficulty from the eastern Rulers. It is important that the Political Agent should personally get in touch with each Ruler individually. It is no use discussing the project in the Trucial Council," replied Sheikh Rashid, who responded to questioning on Qatar's intentions towards the federal project with an accurate judgement of what was to happen nearly a decade later. "Qatar will never get on with Abu Dhabi, nor with Bahrain," he said.

Sheikh Rashid appears to have liked London, but officials charged with organising this and subsequent visits to the British capital found him quite a handful.

"Sheikh Rashid likes to go where the mood takes him, when in London," one Political Agent reported, when providing a brief to the Foreign Office for a trip to the city in 1963. Indeed, often the Dubai Ruler would confound his hosts with requests to see off-beat sites. For example, while on a visit in 1961 he asked for a guided tour of the London Underground as he was bemused by tales of subterranean trains. And often daily programmes prepared well in advance were altered, or even postponed, around requests to go elsewhere.

In July 1963, for instance, the national tabloid *Daily Mirror* reported that Sheikh Rashid had unexpectedly turned up at Battersea Fun Fair, in London. The *Mirror* reporter asked what he thought of the fair, to which he got the unexpectedly frank reply: "I love the place. We don't have anything like this in the Gulf." Sheikh Rashid's growing importance within the political hierarchy of the Arabian Peninsula, plus the favourable impression he created, led Foreign Office officials to search for something special as a gift to him from the state to mark his 1961 semi-official visit. On the last full day of the trip, Sheikh Rashid was presented with a pair of rare Greenland Falcons, purchased at great expense.

Back in the Middle East, Sheikh Rashid continued his diplomatic offensive. That autumn he was seen in Kuwait and Qatar, in addition to visiting and receiving several of his fellow Trucial Rulers. On August 5 he visited Cairo, and on August 12 Damascus – both political centres of the ultimately unsuccessful United Arab Republic – for consultation. This important trip was followed by a two-week official visit to Iran, where Sheikh Rashid continued his ongoing process of discussion with the Shah and other senior officials.

Welcomed in capitals throughout the region, Sheikh Rashid was unable to make headway in the capital closest to home: Sharjah. The continuing strains between Dubai and Sharjah led to the Dubai Ruler and Sheikh Saqr bin Sultan Al Qassimi failing to sit for private discussions in either London, where they were scheduled to meet, or on home soil.

It should also be noted that, although Bahrain was largely antagonistic towards the union movement of the time, Sheikh Rashid had long maintained a good personal relationship with the emir, Sheikh Salman bin Hamad Al Khalifa. The two were arguably the Rulers most friendly toward Britain on the Peninsula, and Sheikh Rashid had kept in contact during Sheikh Salman's last years, as he struggled with the effects of diabetes and general ill-health. He was one of the first foreign leaders to be informed when Sheikh Salman suffered a severe heart attack – from which he recovered – in June 1959.

"Sheikh Rashid often talked of Sheikh Salman with respect," recalls Hamad bin Sukat. "He liked what the Bahraini leader had achieved in his country and I think you can see that both leaders were thinking very much on the same lines. Both had developed their seaports and air facilities at roughly the same time, opening their states to a greater degree of prosperity."

On November 2, 1961, Sheikh Salman passed away in his palace at Safra, in Bahrain. Three days later Sheikh Rashid travelled with a large entourage to Bahrain where he was one of the first to pay his condolences to Sheikh Isa bin Salman Al Khalifa, the new Ruler. Sheikh Isa also had strong views on the union he was being persuaded to consider, although standing on opposing sides of this most important of issues did not prevent the two having the warmest of relations. Sheikh Isa visited Dubai often.

An all-consuming public life left Sheikh Rashid with little time for himself and his family. However, those who knew him were well aware of his deep affection for his wife, Sheikha Latifa. For her part, Sheikha Latifa was devoted to her husband. The union had been a traditional arranged marriage and, despite beginning with a wedding which was the centre-piece of the deciding chapter of Dubai's decade of uncertainty, husband and wife were the warmest of companions when opportunity allowed. Sheikha Latifa remained in the background, unseen by most. While she was happy to assume a more traditional role than her gregarious mother-in-law, Sheikha Hessa, she played a major part in the life of Sheikh Rashid.

Born into the Abu Dhabi ruling family, which made her a distant relative of the Maktoums in Dubai, Sheikha Latifa was the daughter of Sheikh Hamdan bin Zayed Al Nahyan, Ruler of Abu Dhabi between 1912 and 1922. Following her 1939 wedding to Sheikh Rashid, Sheikha Latifa again found herself in a position of influence. Over subsequent years following Sheikh Rashid's accession as Ruler, Sheikha Latifa took on a little highlighted role in the community.

"She was a very kind woman, very gentle, and she doted on her children," says Sheikh Ahmed bin Saeed Al Maktoum. "I know of countless occasions when she reached out to people in the community."

She was distressed by the effects of poverty, often giving money to women in need, and occasionally stepping in to help a family with its long-term hardships.

"Sheikha Latifa appreciated her position and recognised what her husband was trying to achieve," says one of those who benefited from her generosity. This elderly national woman, who still lives close to Za'abeel Palace, recalls several of her friends who felt the kindness of the Ruler's wife:

"A neighbouring family had been suffering since the man of the house, involved in the pearling industry, had lost his job during the troubles. Used to life as a seafarer, he had found jobs hard to come by since and the family had fallen on hard times. Sheikha Latifa knew that just giving money was not always the answer to alleviating problems. When she heard this story, she asked Sheikh Rashid to find employment for the man. He did this, and changed everything for that family. She was loved by all across the city."

"She was devoted to her children," says bin Sukat, recalling that when her sons travelled abroad to study, their mother was deeply upset.

"Her sons were always destined for positions of responsibility within the state and even as youngsters were taught to maintain a correct level of decorum in public, but in private Sheikha Latifa would dote on them and spoil them at every opportunity."

After the departure of Sheikh Maktoum to Gordonstoun, Sheikha Latifa was set to lose more of her sons to further education. During the early 1960s, change was also taking place within the Maktoum family. Sheikh Rashid had long underscored his interest in education through the development of the scholastic system in Dubai. He wanted his sons to have a broad education, the sort that had not been available to him as a youngster.

Sheikh Maktoum's brothers were completing their secondary education at home. For Sheikh Hamdan and Sheikh Mohammed, this meant the Dubai Secondary School, while Sheikh Ahmed attended Al Shaab School. They studied diligently when required, and as demanded by Sheikh Rashid, but, in common with most children around the world were consumed more by hobbies. While the three Rs (reading, writing and 'rithmetic) were required, the two Hs – horses and hunting – had much stronger appeal.

Lessons for Sheikh Hamdan and Sheikh Mohammed at Dubai Secondary School began at 8 am and followed the pattern of hour-long class periods, punctuated by short breaks when pupils would spill into a sandy playground. Football was a favourite during this time, while a game known locally as Gaba, best described as tag using balls thrown to catch an opponent, was also popular.

"There were several sheikhs studying at the time," says Sheikh Mohammed bin Khalifa Al Maktoum, an older nephew whom Sheikh Rashid brought up as his son. "Each had a group of friends, perhaps 20, who followed them."

The school day ended at 2 pm, and by 2.30 the young sheikhs would head for Al Fahidi Fort and their horses. During the winter they would often go into the nearby desert with their falcons. At other times, the princes and their friends would take on other groups in games of football on the beach in Shindagha. As more expatriates swelled the population, the sport grew considerably.

Despite the popularity of football, friends recall that hunting and shooting remained the passions that fuelled the boys' free time. "Although he was only young, Sheikh Mohammed learned quickly and

*An early photograph
of Sheikh Mohammed
in the saddle.*

developed a real affection for hunting. He became an authority on the houbara and his skills were well known," said Mohammed Mirhashim, a long time personal friend. "It would be fair to say that he was one of the best hunters in the UAE."

The sheikhs and their friends would try to get as far into the desert as possible so they could find wildlife that was not disturbed by the presence of man. Although the houbara (a game bird of the bustard species) naturally avoid peopled areas, small mammals such as rabbits and desert hares, as well as small birds, were found in the city's environs. These made excellent substitutes, and the experience gained in their pursuit laid the foundations for future battles of wit with the houbara.

For some time Sheikh Rashid had been considering his sons' futures. Sheikh Maktoum was at Gordonstoun and positioned as his father's successor. Sheikh Hamdan was showing business acumen and already spending a great deal of his time in the Ruler's Office, and Sheikh Rashid saw a future for him in guiding Dubai's expanding commercial activities. Sheikh Mohammed had unmistakable direction. "Sheikh Mohammed was a leader. There was no question about it," says bin Sukat, a friend of Sheikh Rashid. "In every aspect of his life you could see that people followed him."

Just as he plotted the future of his sheikhdom in terms of bricks and mortar, Sheikh Rashid was active in defining the training and development of his sons for the responsibilities that would later be theirs.

Sheikh Mohammed was to follow his elder brother to Cambridge. In August 1966, he flew from Dubai to Bahrain, and then on to London accompanied by his cousin, Sheikh Mohammed bin Khalifa Al Maktoum. The pair were enrolled in the Bell School of Languages in Cambridge, one of Europe's premier schools for the study of both English language and literature. Although both young men had travelled abroad before, this was to be the first time that they were away from Dubai for an extended period. Sheikh Mohammed bin Khalifa – five years the elder – was a link with home, but Britain in the mid-1960s was still a sharp contrast to Dubai. It was the Britain of Harold Wilson, who a year earlier had led the Labour Party to victory in one of the most divisive elections ever seen in Britain. Race and colour had played a big part in the election, especially in the Midlands. But if either of the two sheikhs expected problems, as foreigners, they were in for a surprise. In Cambridge, and travelling around Britain, they discovered a warm, welcoming nation. Sheikh Mohammed bin Khalifa relates today: "We were accepted everywhere and found the British people very open and charming – more so than today even."

Seeking a family environment for his son and nephew while they were in the United Kingdom, at the suggestion of the British authorities Sheikh Rashid enrolled them in a homing programme organised through the school. The two Dubai sheikhs were lodged with Mrs Jo Summers, famous in Cambridge student circles for her many years of taking in students and giving them the best of care. A large, happy woman, Jo Summers lived with her husband and two children, a son and a daughter, in a six-bedroom house not far from the Bell School of Languages, on the outskirts of Cambridge. This was to be the young sheikhs' home from home.

It must have been with a mixture of exhaustion and trepidation that the boys, escorted by British government officials, drove from the railway station in Cambridge to their new home. They had been travelling for the better part of 15 hours. Had they been worried, they soon found their concerns groundless. Jo Summers and her household had a deserved reputation.

For years youngsters had made temporary homes there. Mrs Summers treated them all like her own children, and many continued to visit and stay in touch with her long after they had left Cambridge.

Sheikh Mohammed bin Khalifa recalls: "She was very nice to us.

The Summers family home at 15 Brookside in Cambridge.

A lovely lady. Being around Mrs Summers felt like being with family. It was easier to be so far from Dubai, when we were in such a warm environment."

Jo Summers devoted an extraordinary amount of time to her newcomers from Dubai. On their first morning, the two sheikhs descended the stairs to discover the kitchen table laden with eggs, beans and a small mountain of fresh toast.

From this good start, the cousins set about exploring the town. Although British poet Rupert Brooke wrote: "For Cambridge people rarely smile, being urban, squat, and packed with guile...". They found a very different place, one that fascinated and charmed them.

Cambridge was – and remains – a culturally diverse town, filled with foreign students and British intellectuals. For those willing to experiment with new experiences, there were a myriad of things to do and see. From his father, Sheikh Mohammed had developed a love of poetry. He had absorbed the works of the great Arab poets, such as Al Mutanabi, considered the Shakespeare of the Arab world for his genius with language. Now, in Cambridge, Sheikh Mohammed was surrounded by students who thrived on poetry.

He immersed himself in evening poetry readings at local cafés and – ambitious for a boy who was studying the language properly for the first time – dabbled at writing in English himself. His teachers at the time recall that his studies were helped immeasurably by his fascination with poetry and voracious appetite for literature.

Sheikh Mohammed became a regular visitor to university bookshops for heavier material, and the local Woolworths for the best-sellers of the day. It was 1965, and some of the great writers of the century were at their peak. Robert Lowell's *For The Union Dead*, a collection of American poems, and Ernest Hemingway's posthumous *A Moveable Feast* were popular student reads. Both found their way into the young sheikh's small library at 15 Brookside.

Sheikh Mohammed bin Khalifa also remembers this as a time of exploration. The pair used weekends to visit London and to savour Britain's countryside and towns. During longer holidays, half-term breaks and Bank Holiday weekends, they ventured farther afield, often driving to the coast and taking a ferry to France. Then they had mainland Europe to explore. They loved France, Belgium and Switzerland, and adored the anonymity of being away from Cambridge and Dubai.

Sheikh Rashid had wanted the two young men to live like regular students and to experience life as normal people. They received a weekly allowance and were obliged to save up for extras such as travelling to the Continent. Sheikh Mohammed integrated himself fully into student life. As well as poetry, sports held a great interest for him, and in particular, rowing. It was natural that the sporty Sheikh Mohammed would try his hand, and within weeks of arriving in Britain he took lessons at the Queens' College Boat Club.

"There was much to do, especially in the summer," says Sheikh Mohammed bin Khalifa. "We played football, went bowling, rowing and horse riding. We got to know much of the area."

There were also opportunities for an Arabian sheikh to pursue more traditional pastimes, albeit in a Western setting. Sheikh Rashid had many friends in Britain and his son found himself with more than enough invitations to large estates for hunting and shooting. He learned to stalk red deer instead of Arabian gazelle and rode out in some of the most beautiful scenery imaginable. Only once, however, did he accept an invitation to join a foxhunt. He never returned to what he considered an ugly sport in which the odds are grossly stacked in favour of the hunter. "I like to ride horses fast and jump fences. But one fox chased by 40 hounds and 20 horses? That is not fun for me," he said.

Back in Cambridge, teachers at the Bell School of Languages were recording leaps and bounds in Sheikh Mohammed's progress. One teacher's report card notes that "Mohammed has a natural aptitude for language and learns quickly...he has taken upon himself to help some of the other Arab boys in his classes...he generally leads discussions ...some of Mohammed's efforts in poetry show aptitude..."

The experience at Bell School of Languages was positive, and although Sheikh Rashid was loath to spare another of his sons, soon afterward Sheikh Hamdan joined his brother. He too moved in at the home of Mrs Summers, a lady whom Sheikh Hamdan still remembers with a great deal of warmth and affection.

With its international reputation, the Bell School of Languages attracted a wide range of nationalities. In Sheikh Hamdan's and Sheikh Mohammed's classes there were many Chinese and Japanese students, a large number of Spaniards and others from North and South America, Australia and Africa. Also in the Bell School for a period was Sheikh Hamad bin Khalifa Al Thani, today Emir of Qatar, and his brother

Sheikh Maktoum   Sheikh Hamdan   Sheikh Mohammed.

A school photograph from the Bell School of Languages Easter Term 1966.
In the photograph are Sheikh Maktoum, Sheikh Hamdan and Sheikh
Mohammed.

Issam Al Khayat, teacher and Arab student liaison at the Bell School of Langauges. (opposite page) Several Maktoums made the school football team.

Sheikh Abdulaziz bin Khalifa Al Thani.

It was an intriguing melting pot of nationalities and cultures. Indeed, the school took advantage of this to brighten classes by encouraging interaction as part of the syllabus. Both Dubai sheikhs also used the opportunity to learn about many of their classmates, their backgrounds and countries in a one-on-one situation.

Tutors at the school during this period, among them Issam Al Khayat, the only Arabic speaker on staff, remember a couple of bright pupils.

"Hamdan was a serious young man, who obviously had a purpose. He was thinking of the future and the school was simply a stepping stone toward the responsibilities that would be his," says Al Khayat. "He was very personable and a good student."

Of Sheikh Mohammed, Al Khayat recalls: "Mohammed was very gregarious and sociable. People liked him. He was very down to earth."

One of their most endearing traits, recalled by several long-standing members of staff, is that between lessons and during lunch break, the brothers habitually sat and talked at length with fellow classmates, almost grilling them for information on their histories, cultures, politics and aspirations.

So happy was Sheikh Rashid with the success of the education offered at Bell School of Languages that other young sheikhs followed, among them many cousins. At one point, there were so many Dubai sheikhs studying there that a Maktoum United football team was formed to play against the school team.

"Maktoum United were a committed side, I think their forte being

their fitness," says Al Khayat. "The school team had their hands full as they were talented, but the boys from Dubai were very fit and could run rings around them on the park."

A generation of the Maktoum family would pass through the doors of the Bell School of Languages, later returning to their homeland to help shape the destiny of the nation.

Le Monde

SUPPLÉMENT
LE MONDE ÉCONOMIE
L'Europe des Vingt-Cinq
en quête de croissance
EMPLOI

FONDATEUR : HUBERT BEUVE-MÉRY - DIRECTEUR : JEAN-MARIE COLOMBANI

MARDI 3 JANVIER 2006

CE MÉTROPOLITAINE

...u zéro, dans le village ukrainien de Boyarka, dimanche 1er janvier. GLEB GARANICH/REUTERS

...a Russie interrompt ...rniture à l'Ukraine

...ses de pression en Europe. La France se dit à l'abri

...manche 1er jan-
...ion, nous avons
...r l'opération de
...stème de gazo-
...é Serguei Kou-
...Moscou et Kiev
...scussions pour
...sur le gaz expor-
...est pas à propre-
« Concernant le
...nule est simple :
...aine », a précisé

...tions prises au
...bénéficiait jus-

qu'ici d'un prix de 50 dollars les 1000 m³,
inférieur d'environ quatre fois à celui prati-
qué sur le marché mondial. A l'occasion de
la renégociation des contrats, Gazprom a
exigé brutalement une hausse des tarifs à
220 dollars pour la même quantité, l'Ukrai-
ne se disant de son côté disposée à payer
son gaz « au prix du marché » à condition
que l'augmentation soit graduelle.

Cette décision de la Russie a été jugée
« irresponsable et déstabilisatrice » par les
Ukrainiens. Aux Etats-Unis, le porte-paro-
le du département d'Etat estime que cette
démarche « crée une insécurité et pose la
question difficile du recours à l'énergie pour
exercer une pression politique ».

Le gouvernement français affiche
quant à lui sa sérénité. « Il n'y a pas de ris-
que pour l'approvisionnement de la France », a ainsi déclaré M. François Loos,
ministre délégué à l'industrie, réagis-
sant à la crise russo-ukrainienne. A tra-
vers les installations de Gazprom, la Russie fournit 21 % du gaz consommé en
France. En cas de baisse d'approvisionnement, Gaz de France a prévu de se tour-
ner vers ses deux autres principaux four-
nisseurs, la Norvège et les Pays-Bas.
Déjà très élevés fin 2005 en raison de
risques de pénurie, les prix pourraient
encore grimper. ∎

LIRE PAGE 4 ET NOTRE ÉDITORIAL PAGE 2

LIRE PAGE 4 ET NOTRE ÉDITORIAL PAGE 2

Dix ans après sa mort, François Mitterrand revisité

Janvier 1996-janvier 2006 : dix ans
après sa mort, François Mitterrand
continue à exercer sur les Français
une étonnante fascination. En ce
début d'année, publications en tout
genre, avalanche de docu-
mentaires télévisés en
témoignent, qui retracent
inlassablement la saga mit-
terrandienne. Entre l'im-
muable statue du général
de Gaulle et la photo incer-
taine de Jacques Chirac,
son successeur, il apparaît
comme le dernier monar-
que, « le dernier des grands
présidents », selon le mot
qui lui fut prêté.

Son exceptionnelle longévité politique
y aura été pour beaucoup, comme son
talent à écrire le roman de sa propre vie.
Depuis Jarnac jusqu'à l'Elysée, depuis sa
première élection dans la Nièvre en 1946
jusqu'à la fin de règne crépusculaire un
demi-siècle plus tard, depuis cette « jeu-
nesse française » et maréchaliste jusqu'au
triomphe de mai 1981, à la tête d'un Parti
socialiste conquérant et dominateur,
depuis l'espoir levé, alors, par cette victoi-
re et ses réformes jusqu'aux désillusions,
deux septennats plus tard, d'une gauche
déboussolée par les « affaires » et le chô-

mage, François Mitterrand aura épousé
son siècle, le vingtième, et son temps.

Au-delà de la mémoire – entre chromo
et sépia – soigneusement entretenue par
ses proches et ses thurifé-
raires, au-delà de l'attache-
ment des Français à cet
homme qui les incarnait
jusque dans ses ambivalen-
ces, la place est désormais
aux historiens. Il leur
revient de faire sereine-
ment la part des choses,
des œuvres et des ombres,
des transformations d...
pays qu'il a voulues, comme des mutations qu'il a
subies, à commencer pa...
cette fracture sociale que son successeu...
pas plus que lui-même, n'est parvenu ...
réduire. ∎

GÉRARD COURTO...

Portrait. Mazarine Pingeot, la « peopl...
de la famille » ▸ P. 18
Débats. Tilo Schabert : « Quand
Helmut Kohl instruit à charge ».
Paul Quilès : « La volonté
et la méthode » ▸ P. 19
Focus. Que reste-t-il des années
Mitterrand ? ▸ P. 20-21
Enquête. Hôtel du Vieux Morvan,
chambre 15. ▸ P. 22-23

Les pressions s'accentuent pour différer les élections en Palestine

C'est mardi 3 janvier que doit débuter
officiellement la campagne pour les
élections législatives en Palestine.
Mais les troubles qui se multiplient sur le
terrain, en particulier dans la bande de
Gaza, font douter que le scrutin puisse se
dérouler dans des conditions de régularité
satisfaisante.

Au cours des dix derniers jours, trois kid-
nappings ont été commis par des milices
proches du Fatah, le parti au pouvoir, dont
certaines, comme les Martyrs d'Al-Aqsa,
sont ouvertement hostiles à la tenue d'élections. A Gaza, le Beach Club, un bar géré
par les Nations unies, a été plastiqué. Ces
attaques s'ajoutent à d'autres actions

menées auparavant contre des bâti...
publics ou des bureaux de la comm...
électorale.

Malgré ce chaos, le président p...
nien, Mahmoud Abbas, a rejeté l'éve...
té de différer les élections, d'autant...
récent sondage accorde à son par...
43 % des intentions de vote, une net...
ce sur le Hamas (25 %). Il reste que...
gne au sein de certains courants d...
ajoutée aux entraves posées par Isra...
ganisation du vote à Jérusalem-Es...
thèque, en plus de l'anarchie r...
dans la bande de Gaza, les chance...
se dérouler un scrutin calme et final

LI...

Affaire Vincent Humbert : non-lieu général requis

Procureur de Boulogne-sur-
Mer (Pas-de-Calais), Gérald
Lesigne devait transmettre
au parquet général de Douai, lun-
di 2 janvier, ses réquisitions dans
l'affaire Vincent Humbert. La
mort de ce jeune tétraplégique, le
26 septembre 2003, avait relancé
le débat sur l'euthanasie. Le
magistrat réclame un non-lieu
général pour Marie Humbert, sa
mère, et pour le docteur Frédéric
Chaussoy, l'anesthésiste-réani-
mateur, qui étaient respective-
ment poursuivis pour le délit
d'« administration de substances
toxiques » et pour le crime
d'« empoisonnement avec prémédi-
...». Le docteur Chaussoy

« La Version de Browning », mise en scène par Didier Bezace
(à droite) temps fort de la Commune en 2005. PASCAL VICTOR/MAXPPP

Edwy Plenel Procès

Chapter Thirteen

Nation Building

Whether a man is burdened by power or enjoys power;
whether he is trapped by responsibility or made free by it;
whether he is moved by other people and outer forces or
moves them – this is of the essence of leadership.
— *Theodore White, historian and novelist*

Back in the Middle East, the rapid educational development of the Rulers' sons was mirrored by the rapid development of Dubai itself. Sheikh Rashid's massive construction boom, a thriving economy and enviable growth were all combining to inflate Dubai's population and stretch its services. During the first decade of the century the population was estimated as being close to 10,000, a figure that roughly doubled over the next two decades and trebled over 40 years. Despite the arrival of oil elsewhere, Dubai was years ahead in terms of infrastructure – and still booming. This was recognised in a rare reference to the Trucial Coast in a *New York Times* report, on February 23, 1961. While the writer, Richard Harris, painted a picture for readers unfamiliar with the area by noting a lack of roads and the recent arrival of cabbage farming in Ras Al Khaimah, he went on to say: "Big business in Trucial Oman is centred at Abu Dhabi, which has one rich oil field inland and another offshore, and at Dubai, where a clever Ruler is thriving on the fastest growing seaport in the Gulf."

For a region so isolated from the world for so long, it was a time of great publicity. Another newspaper clipping, from *Le Monde* in May 1961, reported on a part of the world that most westerners knew little about. *Le Monde* stated: "The people of the Trucial States live in the

In 1961 French national newspaper Le Monde reported that the international community was responsible for the poverty, disease and backwardness that afflicted the Trucial States.

Sheikh Rashid with Abdullah Saleh and Ali Al Owais, stalwarts of the Camelot Majlis (opposite page) The National Bank of Dubai played a key role in Dubai's development.

Dark Ages. The world has not only let them down, but also contributed significantly to their malaise. Yet times are changing. In Abu Dhabi the Ruler, Sheikh Shakhbut Al Nahyan, now has at his disposal the first significant monies from oil. Further along the coast, in Dubai, there is no oil, but the Ruler, Sheikh Rashid Al Maktoum, is a wily and clever man who has managed to overcome a lack of any natural assets and built a thriving port-town...

"Over 25,000 people live there, within a thriving economy that seems to thrive on nothing, yet it does indeed thrive..."

Le Monde's correspondent was not alone in his wonderment. Even some of those based in Dubai were baffled by the new found wealth. In his Annual Report for 1962, the British Political Agent commented:

> *Dubai's remarkable progress is unabated...in Dubai, which is the centre from which the others take their pattern, the progressiveness of the Ruler effectively removes the sting from any complaints...*
>
> *Dubai's economy continues to be as mystifyingly prosperous as ever. Imports are running at the rate of about £8 million a year and no-one knows where the money comes from – except the Ruler who, within his own circle, is virtually omniscient. Many new houses and blocks of flats and offices are being built...The Ruler is determined, against advice* [from the British] *to press on with the construction of a jet airport...More and more European and Arab firms are opening up and the future looks bright...*

Since a landmark 1946 agreement with the Imperial Bank of Iran (later the British Bank of the Middle East) which had brought banking services to Dubai for the first time, a great deal had changed within the community. Arab merchants had since learned that a bank was a safer place to store money than under the bed or buried in the garden. The arrival of a strong expatriate merchant community had seen a growing voice for competition to the sole banking institution allowed to operate in Dubai.

The commercial sector was crying out for a larger banking and financial sector, while the state itself, in common with most developing countries, was overdue an official banking institution. Throughout 1962 Sheikh Rashid's Majlis and government were humming with the prospect of a major new entry into the banking system, and one of Dubai's foremost home-grown finance men, Ali Al Owais, was for months seen as the prime contender for the chief executive's position.

"Ali Al Owais was a favourite of Sheikh Rashid. A man who had the drive to leave Dubai to seek a thorough education, in a sector which was to become increasingly important to the country," says Abdullah Saleh, present-day chairman of the National Bank of Dubai. "Sheikh Rashid was ardent in his encouragement of nationals who would play a future part in development, certainly those who could play a role in the major institutions he was planning."

Among the business community there were those who resented the virtual banking monopoly. The only alternative at the time was the Eastern Bank, which was based in Sharjah and had representatives who travelled into Dubai to do business. But things were set to change as Sheikh Rashid threw Dubai's banking sector open.

During 1962 Abdullah Saleh, then manager of the Sharjah branch of the British Bank of the Middle East, received a telephone call requesting that he meet Sheikh Rashid and Ali Al Owais. Within months he was behind the scenes preparing to launch the National Bank of Dubai (NBD).

"The British Bank of the Middle East had its headquarters in Bur Dubai, so it was decided that we would base ourselves in Deira, distinguishing ourselves from our opposition," he says. "Sheikh Rashid liked to be kept informed on everything, so we visited the Majlis nearly every day."

In 1963 Sheikh Rashid signed an order establishing the National Bank of Dubai. He instructed Ali Al Owais and David Mac, NBD assistant general manager, to fulfill the dual roles of setting the bank on course to be both pragmatic in its workings and aggressive in supporting business and commerce in Dubai.

"Sheikh Rashid followed everything and was so sharp that when you told him something on one occasion, he would perhaps ask the same question some weeks later, and would certainly pick up on any discrepancy in your answer. He was very sharp and I was surprised at his depth of knowledge in banking and finance," said Saleh. "He hated liars and loathed people who exaggerated simply to impress him.

"Of course, Sheikh Rashid championed all of the expensive projects on which Dubai embarked, and as a government-supported bank this could easily have placed undue influence on NBD to become involved as part of the financial package put together for most," recalls Saleh. "But he never put pressure on the bank. He would ask us to consider a project, explain the concept, but that would be the end of discussion."

The Dubai branch of a third banking institution, the First National City Bank of New York, was inaugurated on January 24, 1964 by Sheikh Rashid. He actively encouraged more banks, and by 1971 Dubai boasted eight, the same number as long-time oil producer Bahrain and more than Qatar, Abu Dhabi and Sharjah.

For its part, the National Bank of Dubai was at the centre of much of the country's development during the remainder of the 1960s and into the next decade. As a young, eminently qualified national, Saleh was soon spotted and drawn into the inner circle of the Majlis by Sheikh

Rashid. At the time, the Majlis was the think-tank where Dubai's Ruler introduced the ideas and concepts which would ultimately emerge as finished projects.

"There was a lot of energy in the Majlis. Sheikh Rashid was good at motivation and surrounded himself with people who were capable of achieving the tasks he set them," says Saleh. "He was tough and decisive, but at the same time he was kind-hearted and genuinely cared about everyone in his group."

Saleh recalls Sheikh Rashid's intense affection for his entourage. Although each was independent, the Dubai Ruler was sometimes offended when advisors failed to attend his Majlis for several days. "Once, I missed the Majlis for ten days," he says. "Sheikh Rashid was actually upset, so I had to exagerate a story about my wife being ill. Then he was placated. He knew the personal situation of all those in the Majlis and most of his staff, showing a genuine concern for their welfare."

Sheikh Rashid did have his favourites, usually those who were proven achievers. When it came to business, however, he was even-handed, taking great trouble to ensure a fair share of the plum contracts. Every project promoted by the government included earthworks, road building, construction and other sectors. Often, to the misery of his financial advisors, Sheikh Rashid would forego any form of competitive tendering, instead preferring to simply divide many jobs among those he knew and trusted to deliver.

"This system of deciding often major contracts was unusual, but worked well, and everyone knew that they simply had to perform to his expectations," says Saif Ahmed Al Ghurair. "If you fulfilled the contract, you could expect more. This was the only reason needed."

It was during the mid-1960s that names such as Al Naboodah, Lootah, Al Mulla and Khansaheb emerged as giants in domestic contracting.

Sheikh Rashid's method of awarding contracts might have been a relative boon, but could sometimes have an underside. He would set a price that usually was enough to cover the job and leave a profit, and offer the job to someone. On occasion, as Abdullah Saleh explains, the government's price was below cost. "No-one ever went back to Sheikh Rashid to ask for more money. The thought was that if you did the job well it would lead to more, so soaking up a small loss on one project was a modest sacrifice to make for more work."

This informality worked well in the climate of Dubai at the time. However, it was a different matter for foreign companies, many of which had never experienced anything, or anyone, like the Father of Dubai.

"Sheikh Rashid would deal with you personally. Then, when you were both satisfied with the arrangement, he would agree and expect you to get on with the job," explains Zakariah Doleh. "That was his way, the way of doing business in the Middle East for centuries, with a handshake."

Personal trust was proven to work among the peoples of the Gulf, but when valuable contracts were under way with corporations from abroad, Sheikh Rashid's time-honoured methods were often unsettling for those unacquainted with him.

"We were finalising a medium-sized contracting agreement through the bank with a German company, on the orders of Sheikh Rashid," remembers Saleh. "It was beyond their comprehension that anyone could deal on trust, but we were not going to go back to Sheikh Rashid and say they were unwilling. Therefore it was agreed that he would meet a delegation from the company in the Majlis. They were impressed, yet still unwilling to deal his way. Sheikh Rashid knew one man in the party spoke Arabic, so as they were leaving he told me, 'Give them until Monday to decide, then get someone else.' By Sunday they had agreed to proceed."

Today Sheikh Rashid is sometimes remembered for stretching his government's funds to the limit in pursuit of further development. But Saleh, in his senior position with the bank managing government funds, saw a fiscally prudent side of his leader.

"Sheikh Rashid was aware when the major bills were coming in. He would remind me a week before they were due, asking if we were sure there were funds to be able to pay. That we would pay on time he was always adamant," Saleh recalls. "Later, during the years of the Trucial States Council and United Arab Emirates, he would ensure that Dubai's payment into the federal budget was a week early. He felt responsibile and always insisted that there was no reason to pay bills at the latest possible time."

The Ruler's prudence was well known to those friendly governments that were inclined to aid development in the Trucial Coast through loans. Sheikh Rashid's first major loan, from Kuwait to pay for work on the Creek, was paid back early. This gave confidence to the major lenders and led to offers of further assistance.

Sheikh Rashid and his government had achieved a great deal during the five years since his accession. The sheikhdom had enjoyed an unparalleled period of steady economic growth, despite already being three decades behind Bahrain in joining the oil boom. The as yet untapped commercial reserves that were thought to be under Dubai were a source of continuing frustration to Sheikh Rashid. Nearby Abu Dhabi had been an oil producer since 1962.

In 1963 Dubai Petroleum Company (DPC) was formed, led by the the American Continental Company (Conoco) and including Total of France, Repsol of Spain, RWE-DEA and Wintersall of Germany. DPC's skills would propel Dubai into the oil boom.

Sheikh Rashid's customary inquisitiveness saw him briefed almost daily on developments at the various drill sites. Predictably he also wanted to see for himself. On January 10, 1962, Sheikh Rashid and his inner circle of advisors and friends gathered, soon after daybreak, up the coast at a site not far from Jebel Ali. A pipe had been connected to a drilling rig, anchored just off the beach, and there, at a little after eleven in the morning, around 40 people stood around Sheikh Rashid to see crude oil pumped ashore for the first time in the history of Dubai.

Those present included national and expatriate staff of the newly formed Oilfields Supply Centre, owned in partnership by Sheikh Rashid and itself a benefit to the local economy through large scale creation of employment. While they left the scene of the demonstration delighted at the apparent breakthrough, Sheikh Rashid himself returned to Dubai in silence, drawing on his guppti, a tiny Arabic pipe, a sure sign that he was deep in thought. The Ruler's frustration at the lack of progress in finding commercially viable fields had brought about the formation of the Dubai Petroleum Company, but much anticipated first commercial exports were to take several more years.

Throughout his life, Sheikh Rashid was seen referring to only three books: the Holy Koran; Al Mustatrif by Al Abshihi; and Al Mutanabi. The latter is the work of a poet from around 1,200 years ago, sometimes described as the Arabic Shakespeare, whose command of the language is still widely regarded as the most evolved of any figure in Arabic literature. Sheikh Rashid was far too occupied in his own world to spend

An offbeat photograph of Sheikh Rashid and American oilman Hal Nabors, president of Dubai Petroleum Company in 1969, exiting one of Dubai's unique Kazzans during their construction. These massive oil strage containers are unique to Dubai.

valuable time reading newspapers and scanning the various radio frequencies. Instead he employed the services of national Khalifa Kraif, who was paid to follow the media and report to Sheikh Rashid verbally.

"The only times Sheikh Rashid listened to the radio was when he knew the news was on," says Humaid bin Drai, a former Minister of Protocol. "His assistant Khalifa Kraif would immediately inform him of any major breaking news, or otherwise reprise the news stories of the day when it was convenient for Sheikh Rashid."

This said, Sheikh Rashid certainly recognised the value of a more accessible approach to literature, and was impressed by the major libraries he had seen in Tehran, Bombay and, especially, London.

The Prophet Mohammed said: "It is the duty of every Muslim man and woman to seek education." Arabs invented paper, which of course, gave rise to books and newspapers. Arab literature flourished under the Abbasids, who rose to power in Baghdad in the mid-8th century. The 'golden age' of Islamic culture and commerce reached its zenith during the reigns of Harun Al Rashid and his son, Al Mamun.

The Bayt Al Hikma for the Caliph Al Mamum (813-833 AD) and the Dar al-'Ilm of Cairo founded by Al Hakim (966-1021 AD) are the most notable libraries in the Islamic world. Books were collected from all over the world to create monumental libraries that housed volumes on medicine, philosophy, mathematics, science, alchemy, logic, astronomy and many other subjects.

"The people must be allowed to educate themselves," Sheikh Rashid commented to the Majlis on more than one occasion. He also talked at length on the subject with the British Political Agent to Dubai from 1955 to 1958, J P Tripp, a man whose education Sheikh Rashid admired. Undoubtedly from these talks, Dubai's Ruler learned more about the free public libraries found in Britain, a public service to the community of which his state could only dream at the time. In addition to buying books, he tackled this problem in a series of personal letters, sent in 1962 and early 1963, to the education ministers of the best developed Arab states of the time. In his communications, Sheikh Rashid appealed for support.

"He asked the ministries to send books, new or old, to help with the establishment of a public library, something unheard of in many of the countries he contacted, even though they were themselves comparatively wealthy," says Abdullah bin Jassim Al Muthairy. "But the response was tremendous. Over the next few months many large consignments were received, enough to establish Dubai's first library."

The British also responded to his requests with a container of English language publications, while the Indian and Pakistani merchant community donated books in Hindi, Malayalam and Pushtu. In just one year, the overwhelming response led to instructions from Sheikh Rashid to build library premises in Deira, overlooking the mouth of Dubai Creek. In 1963, he inaugurated Dubai's new multilingual public library, the first among the Trucial States. While it was not Bayt al-Hikma or Dar al-'Ilm, Dubai Library was nevertheless a major breakthrough.

As the Dubai government grappled with its own internal development during the 1960s, a wider and arguably more important picture was emerging on a regional level. The British had withdrawn from India in 1947 but maintained colonial domination in parts of the Middle East. They had received something of a diplomatic bloody nose, however, in 1949 when the sheikhs of the Trucial Coast issued an independently-produced proclamation of their rights. Though the proclamation changed little, it was significant in the history of the region, as this was the first time that the sheikhs had acted together on a peacetime matter, a precursor to moves toward a more formal union.

Throughout the late 1940s and 1950s, Britain had followed a course that would lead to diminished standing throughout the Middle East. The 1951 Iranian nationalism of the Anglo-Iranian Oil Company was an example of successful self-determination which nevertheless amounted to a major loss of prestige for the British. By this time – in the wake of the 1948 Red Line Agreement in which the USA signaled its willingness to defy British attempts to exclude other countries in the Gulf oil industry – the sheikhs were becoming increasingly vocal. Progress, though, was slow.

A wave of nationalism was spreading elsewhere in the Middle East, particularly under the patronage of Egyptian President Gamal Abdel Nasser. In 1956, the Suez Canal crisis weakened the regional standing of the colonial power and turned many against the British altogether. At that time, Sheikh Saeed and Sheikh Rashid had turned a blind eye when several hundred of their countrymen protested their support for Egypt. All along the coast, normally quiet townships took their lead from Dubai, as students, political activists and proud Arabs took to the streets to forcefully, but peacefully, register their opposition to British,

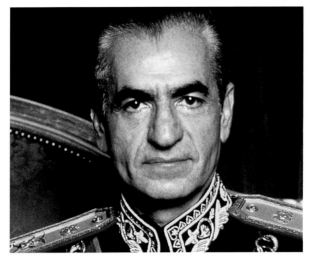

Sheikh Rashid consulted with the Shah of Iran in 1962, one of a number of visits to Iran.

American and French involvement. Along with many leaders along the Trucial Coast, Sheikh Rashid protested in the strongest possible terms to the British Political Agent when he next had the opportunity.

For once political opinion within the region was unified and this, along with the new nationalism, encouraged the Trucial States leaders to take more of a hand in their own affairs. Dubai's leader had long been on record as a believer in a certain level of self-determination. There was an intrinsic understanding in his arguments that the economic future of the Trucial States was far better run by the people concerned, than dictated by a general policy set in London.

Following his meetings with Edward Heath, then Lord Privy Seal, in Dubai and London in 1961, Sheikh Rashid was observed to be spending more time on the matter. He discussed a union framework at length within his own Majlis and mentioned this during conversations with British officials, who, he thought, would certainly have to play a major hand in the matter. He also travelled more and shuttled among the capitals of the region to develop consensus among his fellow leaders.

In the weeks following his return from the Heath meeting, Sheikh Rashid reportedly told the British Political Agent: "The British would be wise to enlist the support of the Ruler of Kuwait if you wish to pursue such a policy. Ajman, Umm Al Quwain, Ras Al Khaimah and Fujairah would immediately accept...Sheikh Saqr of Sharjah might struggle , but would eventually accept...as for Abu Dhabi, I cannot say what Sheikh Shakhbut's views will be since he is unpredictable."

Over subsequent years Sheikh Rashid was engaged in a frantic round of diplomacy in an attempt to build acquiescence between the major players in a proposed integrated entity. He was in constant contact with Sheikh Ahmed bin Ali Al Thani, Ruler of Qatar, Sheikh Isa bin Salman Al Khalifa, Ruler of Bahrain, and Sheikh Shakhbut of Abu Dhabi, while engaging all his fellow Rulers further along the coast.

Ploughing a relatively neutral furrow in terms of regional policy, Sheikh Rashid was one of the few whose relations with the Iranian government was anything more than stale. He hunted there annually and was often invited to visit as an official guest. His dialogue with the Iranians was of huge importance to the federal process, their tacit acceptance being necessary if the movement was to succeed.

Following an official visit to Iran in 1961, Sheikh Rashid returned in 1962 to consult the Iranian government and meet with the Shah, with whom he seemed to share a trusting relationship. Sheikh Rashid liked Iran as a country, and when an earthquake hit one of its outlying regions during his visit, he requested that an official banquet be cancelled and the cost of the event used to provide disaster relief.

This was not the first attempt at bolstering cooperation between the states. Over the preceding century there had been several meetings of the Rulers. The British had been the first to attempt a formal arrangement, convening a meeting in 1952 of all of the Trucial Rulers, from which grew the fledgling Trucial States Council.

This body made limited progress; several members blocked any attempts to set the council on a firmer footing. By the mid-1960s there was considerable frustration at this, prompting Sheikh Rashid to begin extolling the virtues of a new body (broadly similar in its composition). Although he was against a complete amalgamation, he was in favour of unifying areas such as inter-state development, foreign policy and defence. In a number of high-level meetings, Sheikh Rashid took trouble to promote his vision, winning support from several of those well-placed to push the process forward from outside the Trucial States.

In 1963, Sheikh Rashid decided it was time to see America. He had long been fascinated by the United States and had received many political and military emissaries from across the Atlantic. He had been invited on several occasions and was pressed to make the trip by the US-based Continental Oil Company, which had recently taken up a valuable land-based oil concession in Dubai.

After a cruise through the Mediterranean and a week in London, a group including his sons Sheikh Hamdan and Sheikh Mohammed, Ahmed bin Sulayem, Easa Saleh Al Gurg and Hamad bin Sukat, arrived unheralded in New York aboard the Cunard liner Queen Elizabeth on July 30, 1963.

They embarked on an exhaustive tour over the next two weeks, including visits to the Empire State Building, United Nations, White House and Hoover Dam, later also taking in the Rocky Mountains. Indeed, his American hosts took trouble to provide a varied and busy schedule which took in many of the major sights, while accommodating those of special interest to the visitors.

Sheikh Rashid asked to see the Islamic Centre in Washington, DC, site of one of America's largest mosques at the time, and was also shown a massive desert irrigation site in Phoenix, Arizona, in 1963 the most successful such project in the world.

Subsequent reports indicate that Sheikh Rashid was most impressed with the time he spent in the United Nations. On arrival he was met by the UN Head of Protocol and made an extensive tour of the Secretariat with an Arabic-speaking guide. He also sat through a debate in the Security Council, which was discussing the issue of Portuguese Territories.

"Sheikh Rashid appeared to find the whole experience an enjoyable one," reported a representative of the British Mission to the UN who accompanied him throughout.

In Washington, DC, he was contacted by the State Department and invited for talks, something which pleased him immensely, and was informed that a car would be sent to the hotel. To his acute embarrassment – understandable considering his confirmed hatred of pomp – Sheikh Rashid emerged into the street to find the sort of motorcade usually reserved for President Kennedy himself. Sheikh Rashid made his trip to the State Department riding in one of four black stretch limousines with a full complement of Secret Service agents bedecked in standard issue dark sunglasses, and an eight-strong entourage of motorcycle policemen, sirens blaring. One can only imagine the discomfort of the Ruler as the streets of Washington were brought to a halt by his cavalcade, traffic lights automatically switching to green to ensure smooth passage.

However, after two weeks on the road and in the air, the party cut short its visit and opted to return to Britain aboard the Queen Elizabeth

Sheikh Rashid and his party on the steps of the Capitol Building in Washington.
(inset) Visiting the United Nations in New York.

from New York. In a cable to inform London of Sheikh Rashid's early return, the British Consul-General in New York stated: "It appears that the Ruler had no idea of the distances to be covered in the United States, that he was not prepared to undertake long journeys by air, and has not, in the main, been very favourably impressed by what he has seen here, except for his visit to the United Nations."

Although this may have been the case, a different perspective on Sheikh Rashid's early departure was offered by a member of the British mission in New York, giving due consideration to the normal pace of life in his native Dubai. After dining with Sheikh Rashid he commented: "Sheikh Rashid was clearly appalled by the speed and noise of New York and arrived in Washington in an exhausted state after a whirlwind four-day tour of New York."

Back home, Dubai continued to boom, to the point where one observer, the British Political Agent, declared it "quite bewildering." The new improved Creek had become something of a magnet to shipping and, as early as 1962, it had been reported that all of Sharjah's seaborne trade was being funnelled through Dubai, where infrastructure was superior and access for larger vessels easier. All across the city, construction was going on; indeed, Deira was seen to double in size in little more than two years.

"The Creek project had been a massive burden on everyone concerned," says banker Abdullah Saleh. "But on completion of the work Dubai seemed to have jumped far ahead of its rivals in a commercial sense. The growth rate was unimaginable."

Other established Arabian Gulf trading centres were now taking Dubai seriously, such was the buoyancy of its economy and the pre-eminence of its infrastructure. By 1963 the British Trucial States Annual Review reported that companies from Kuwait (Al Gharabeli), Bahrain (Al Zayani) and Qatar (Al Darwish) were opening offices and shops. The same document went on: "Much capital undoubtedly comes from outside and it is certainly true that there exists at the moment a great deal of confidence in the future prosperity of Dubai. This confidence probably started with the wealth brought in by gold, was stimulated by the wealth brought in by the great success of the Creek dredging scheme and had been finally pushed to a remarkable – and possibly unwarranted – height by optimism about the prospects for the discovery of oil."

It likened Dubai's unprecedented growth to a "rolling snowball," and

Sheikh Rashid and Sheikh Maktoum receive iconic Egyptian President Gamal Abdul Nasser and future President Anwar Sadat.

though the metaphor may have been inappropriate for a desert sheikhdom, the sentiment was accurate. The report added that foreign corporations and trading companies were "racing one another to invest their money and start their branches, fearing in many cases, it seems, that if they do not get in now, they will be too late when the oil starts."

The promise of oil-fuelled progress certainly played a part in the boom and, oil or no oil, Sheikh Rashid was determined to capitalise on this and his state's massive advantage in terms of infrastructure. Year on year, Dubai extended its domination of the economies of the Northern Trucial States and much of the interior. The boom was dramatic and may even have surprised the ever optimistic Ruler himself. Nevertheless, Sheikh Rashid was determined that the people, business and wealth flowing into Dubai should be encouraged to stay.

While Dubai remained his preoccupation, wider notions of federation were also taking his time during this period. Sheikh Ahmed bin Ali, Sheikh Isa and Sheikh Shakhbut all visited Dubai during 1964 for private talks, while Sheikh Rashid's ideas found high-level support within the emerging Arab League. The League's Secretary-General, Dr Sayyid Nowfal, favoured a similar federal model. All the major players were involved in consolidation throughout 1964, and late in the year the Arab League sponsored a plan to unite the individual Trucial Sheikhdoms as part of the so-called Arab Fund. Dr Nowfal unveiled his plans in several face-to-face meetings with Sheikh Rashid, Sheikh Shakhbut and Sheikh Saqr bin Sultan Al Qassimi, Ruler of Sharjah, before going public.

"Even as early as the start of the 1960s, there had been several attempts at federalisation of states within the Arab world," says academic Abdullah bin Jassim Al Muthairy. "Sheikh Rashid was anxious to avoid any mistakes, which would actually weaken the strengthening position of the Trucial States. He was adamant that even a loose organisation must be made to work, and counselled the leaders that they should not enter into any arrangement without fully understanding that a joint organisation must entail following majority opinion in some issues and a resultant loss of sovereign powers over certain areas."

Late in 1964 the Arab League was envisaging a Trucial States Council, supported financially by Iran, Kuwait and Saudi Arabia as part of an Arab Fund, officiated from Sharjah and largely administered by the Arab League itself. This rough plan brought howls of protest from the British, who succeeded in ensuring the measure was watered down and responsibility for the Council was retained by the Trucial Sheikhs themselves.

Within the existing 12-year-old Trucial States Council structure, however, even at this juncture there seems to have been a problem with coherence. The records of the 19th meeting of the council, on June 23, 1964, indicate that its chairman, the Political Agent, was at a loss to explain the lack of cooperation between the seven member states, even to the point of speaking on the matter during his opening remarks. Staged in Dubai, the Council session was attended by Sheikh Rashid and his Prince Regent, Sheikh Maktoum. The Agent also records the presence of the other six Trucial Rulers, including Sheikh Shakhbut, a positive development as he had also attended the 18th session, five months earlier, the first that he had graced for three years.

The minutes of the meeting highlight the divergence of opinion among the seven states. Far from appearing as potential partners in a closer union, the Agent stated in his summary: "I am, more than ever, convinced that a federation or cooperation (it is better at this stage to avoid the former word which, I suspect, frightens some of the Rulers) will only come about through the introduction of specific and limited schemes in specific and limited spheres. Grandiose projects of unity, like grandiose words, will openly puzzle and dismay. Visa offices, unitary passports, central courts, cooperative roads: These are the key, not constitutions and federal buildings."

The June 1964 meeting was unremarkable in its actual content – an update on the Trucial States Development Fund and reports from Al Maktoum Hospital and Trucial Oman Scouts – going on to discuss the issue of passports and visas.

The latter was a particularly difficult point. By 1964 the growth of the economies of Abu Dhabi and Dubai was creating something of a gold rush mentality, particularly in Asia. A huge new demand for labour was resulting in mass immigration which the Trucial States themselves were finding hard to control, or monitor, with their basic Immigration Services. As early as 1962 it had been reported in Council that upwards of 900 Asians a week were landing by boat at Khor Fakkan on the East Coast and then making their way to Dubai, Sharjah or Abu Dhabi. Most found their way to Dubai, where there were more opportunities.

Although it was understood that a system of seven individual entities was unworkable, this was just what was being attempted. Sheikh Saqr bin Sultan of Sharjah suggested a joint visa section, based in Dubai, a plan that Sheikh Rashid took under consideration for the next Council meeting. He stated, however, that he was perfectly happy with the controls in place in Dubai. Indeed, administration and government apparatus in Dubai were, at this point, far ahead of the six others in their organisation and effectiveness.

At the end of the session, James Craig, the Political Agent, wrote: "Sheikh Rashid is in many things so amenable, so helpful and so apparently enlightened that it is easy to forget that often he is extremely obstinate…His personal talents and the state's resources are sufficient to make him, in every way, the leader of the Trucial Coast."

This 1964 meeting seems to have marked something of a change in the federal process. Whether it was that stinging rebuke from the influential Political Agent for their lack of cooperation, general circumstances, the Arab League's determined push, a perceived question mark over British intentions in the long term, or all of these factors, in the second part of this year things started to happen. A wind of change was noted, and, judging by his itinerary, Sheikh Rashid seems to have stepped up his own efforts. Before the end of the year he hosted more visits from Sheikh Ahmed bin Ali of Qatar (who was staying at his palace in Dubai throughout October), Sheikh Rashid bin Humaid Al Nuaimi of Ajman, Sheikh Ahmed bin Rashid Al Moalla of Umm Al Quwain and even his long-time adversary, Sheikh Saqr bin Sultan Al Qassimi of Sharjah.

The old rivalry between Dubai and Sharjah was, at last, giving way to more sustained relations. Even if this was triggered by the needs of the moment, Sheikh Rashid and Sheikh Saqr were set to be key players in a potential union and it was most certainly beneficial that their personal relationship was, seemingly, less frosty. On this basis, the British were working behind the scenes to bring Sheikh Rashid and Sheikh Saqr closer. Ultimately, though, this was to prove a false dawn.

Friction was counterproductive as both had been the most active in seeking further cooperation between the sheikhdoms, albeit taking different paths towards this. While Sheikh Rashid was inclined to proceed with work on the overall picture, Sheikh Saqr had made small inroads on a plan to install Sharjah at the head of a union of the Northern Emirates, ignoring both Dubai and Abu Dhabi. Earlier, in September 1958, Sharjah had concluded a 'common market'-style union with Fujairah and entered into discussions with Ajman, Ras Al Khaimah and Umm Al Quwain to join. Although the project was ultimately unsuccessful and went no further, the experiment showed that the political will for a union was evolving outside of Dubai, even if it was underscored by the Sharjah Ruler's desire for political paramountcy.

During the summer of 1964, Sheikh Rashid was also invited to Tehran for talks with the Iranian government, seen as a key element in the process. He briefed his Iranian counterpart and succeeded in breaching an apparent hostility on the part of the Iranian government.

Perhaps Sheikh Rashid's key aim during the second part of 1964, though, was to encourage Abu Dhabi further into the process. This was a tough assignment as, at the time, Sheikh Shakhbut was the most ardent supporter of the status quo. In previous reported discussions with the British, Sheikh Rashid was on record as identifying the Abu Dhabi Ruler's brother, Sheikh Zayed bin Sultan Al Nahyan, as the best hope of persuading Sheikh Shakhbut of the merits of even the most basic coalition. Sheikh Zayed was a man with whom he, and they, could do business.

On July 23 Dubai's head of state travelled with a small party to the oasis settlement of Buraimi, in the Abu Dhabi desert, where Sheikh Zayed was the Ruler's representative. Sheikh Zayed was more outgoing and politically astute than his brother, Sheikh Shakhbut, and enjoyed plenty of respect. This had been earned partly through infrequent diplomatic appearances on a regional level, but mainly for his achievements in Buraimi, both in handling outside intrusion into this key area and in developing the settlement. As early as 1963, during discussions with the Arabian Department of the Foreign Office, Sheikh Rashid had indicated that Sheikh Zayed was a man with whom he believed pro-unionists should work. The Political Agent commented in December 1963: "The Ruler said that Shakhbut was such a difficult character that he (Sheikh Rashid) would like to use Sheikh Zayed as an intermediary in breaching the subject with the Ruler of Abu Dhabi."

Sheikh Zayed laid on a great deal of entertainment for his guests, including a number of banquets and traditional horse and camel races. News of Sheikh Rashid's arrival travelled quickly, along with rumours that the purpose of the trip was to discuss union. The following afternoon Sheikh Shakhbut arrived unexpectedly from Abu Dhabi town. This tempered somewhat the main strand of conversation between Sheikh Rashid and Sheikh Zayed, although later the Dubai leader informed the Political Agent that the Ruler's brother was broadly more welcoming of the issue than the Ruler himself.

Further consultation came in November 1964 on the death of Saudi Arabia's King Saud ibn Abdul Aziz Al Saud. King Saud was a firm believer that the sheikhdoms of the Trucial Coast should eventually evolve into a single entity, and had on occasion consulted with Dubai's progressive Ruler by telephone or at occasional meetings. Although bigger and more powerful than its neighbours, the Saudi Arabian government had been generally benign. Politically, the peninsula had evolved considerably, and King Saud moved with the times and sought to resolve many of the land issues that remained. He had ended a dispute between his government and Bahrain over the Bu Safaa area in face-to-face negotiations with Sheikh Salman bin Hamad Al Khalifa. By and large, he conducted policy toward his neighbours in a similarly frank and open fashion.

His brother, King Faisal ibn Abdul Aziz, was equally warm in his greeting when Sheikh Rashid arrived in the Kingdom to offer condolences. Despite a full schedule in the days following the death of his brother, King Faisal was attentive in his talks with Sheikh Rashid, and the two covered a variety of topics, including the union. Later the new King met Sheikh Zayed bin Sultan Al Nahyan, who headed a mission of condolence on behalf of his brother, Sheikh Shakhbut. According to a Foreign Office report at the time, King Faisal reportedly used the opportunity to convey his hopes "that Abu Dhabi would play a full part in moves to bring the Trucial States closer."

Over ensuing months this emerging emphasis pushed the Rulers into a revamped model of the existing Trucial States Council. Most important, Sheikh Shakhbut had softened his position. The first meeting of a more formal Council was brought to order by the host, Sheikh Rashid, during March 1965 at his private residence, adjacent to the beach at Jumeirah, today called Union House. Against all odds the efforts of the British government and Arab League had ensured the attendance of all seven Trucial sheikhdoms, plus the Rulers of Qatar and Bahrain. Indeed, the assembling of nine leaders, at a time when transport infrastructure was limited, was a remarkable feat in itself. Several arrived in Dubai by boat.

The leaders in attendance included Sheikh Rashid, Sheikh Shakhbut, Sheikh Ahmed of Qatar, Sheikh Isa of Bahrain, Sheikh Saqr of Sharjah, Sheikh Ahmed bin Rashid Al Moalla of Umm Al Quwain, Sheikh Rashid bin Humaid Al Nuaimi of Ajman, Sheikh Mohammad bin Hamad Al Sharqi of Fujairah and Sheikh Saqr bin Mohammed Al Qassimi of Ras Al Khaimah. Also present was the British Political Resident, William Luce, a popular individual with the various leaders despite the prevailing attitude of anger toward his country and current government for its attitude on the Middle East in general.

This reformed body made a purposely slow start for, although it was armed with a broader range of powers, pro-unionists seemed to be well aware that those who viewed the concept more suspiciously were still somewhat nervous of the process they had entered. Sheikh Rashid seems to have checked his own enthusiasm and used this inaugural conference to encourage several of the more sceptical participants. By the time of the second Council meeting, later in the year, there was a new face at the table. Sheikh Saqr of Sharjah had been deposed as Ruler in a bloodless British-backed coup. The new Ruler of Sharjah was Sheikh Khalid bin Mohammed Al Qassimi, an ally of Sheikh Rashid and a man with whom the Dubai Ruler knew he could do business. Sheikh Khalid had owned a large paint shop in Deira souq and was well known throughout the town as an intelligent and down-to-earth man. Sheikh Khalid's tenure was to last until the creation of the United Arab Emirates six years later, and the personal warmth of the two ensured the neighbours enjoyed their closest relations for possibly 100 years.

"It was natural that Sheikh Rashid should get on well with Sheikh

Dubai was, at last, beginning to enjoy the fruits of some development, as can be seen from this picture of the Creek taken during the early 1960s. Sheikh Rashid now turned his efforts to regional development.

Khalid," says Abdullah bin Jassim Al Muthairy. "The new Sharjah Ruler was an energetic moderniser, very much in the same vein as his counterpart. He secured money from the Trucial States Development Fund and later the Abu Dhabi government, enabling Sharjah to embark on several badly needed infrastructure projects."

Within a year there was another new face at the Trucial States Council meetings, Sheikh Shakhbut having abdicated his rule – again under pressure from the British – in favour of his brother, Sheikh Zayed bin Sultan Al Nahyan. Once again this was a development of which Sheikh Rashid was fully in favour. "Sheikh Rashid had known Sheikh Zayed for a long time. He saw a man who was fully capable of leading Abu Dhabi, bringing out its potential," says Al Muthairy. "Sheikh Zayed was also a figure on whom you could rely. His judgment was sound and he was a stable Ruler who cared for development and the betterment of his people. While they may have disagreed on some issues, each fully respected the other."

With a pair of vibrant, new leaders at the table, the Trucial States Council began to make more of an impact. Sheikh Rashid urged all to understand the implications of a broad grouping and what it would mean to the area. He worked tirelessly to maintain consensus, and it was largely thanks to the efforts of both Sheikh Rashid and Sheikh Zayed that Council meetings began to work effectively. For a time the Trucial States Council basked in this unity. Ironically though, it was not from within that the first cracks began to appear, but from the benefactors who had originally offered to fund much of the new work. Iraq and

Kuwait withdrew support, while Saudi Arabia decided on funding several projects directly itself, including a first major tarmac road, which connected Ras Al Khaimah and Dubai.

In June 1965, in an effort to boost an undercapitalised and floundering grouping, the British government donated £2 million to its funds.

While this federal process dragged on during the mid-1960s, Dubai itself was on the verge of far more exciting times. The time consuming process of searching for financially viable oil fields continued.

In 1963, Sheikh Rashid had granted Dubai Petroleum Company a concession for the entire onshore area of the sheikhdom and DPC later acquired half of the offshore concession owned by Dubai Marine Areas. DPC's expertise had added momentum to a process which had begun in 1937 when Sheikh Saeed granted the first oil concession and by the mid-1960s reports filtering through from several DPC offshore drilling rigs were increasingly buoyant.

Yet patience was needed. In 1964 there were three unsuccessful exploration wells drilled. Optimism remained high, however, and the Ruler's Office was alive with excited geologists and weathered oilmen.

"On one occasion," says bin Sukat, "Sheikh Rashid had been engaging a group of businessmen from America in polite conversation in his broken English for several minutes. They must have certainly thought from his small office and relaxed manner that he was no more than a clerk. When one of the visitors interrupted him impatiently to ask how long they would be kept waiting to see the sheikh, they were shocked to discover that they were already sitting before him. They were amazed that they had been quizzed on their impressions of Dubai, the weather – and baseball – by the Ruler himself. He did, of course, know a great deal about America, having already visited that country."

But as the long hot summer of 1965 cooled to autumn, there were many more important issues being discussed in Customs House than baseball. As the weeks passed, Sheikh Rashid played host to a growing number of visitors from Dubai Petroleum Company. The news was increasingly bright. He would sit back in his old wooden chair and listen to progress reports, only breaking concentration to light up his small Arabic pipe.

"All year, we were hearing a lot of optimism from Sheikh Rashid. He

Dubai Petroleum Company test drilling was guided by strict environmental regulations, and utilised as little space as possible.

was constantly visiting the drilling operations," stated bin Sukat. "One evening he came to the Majlis and announced with a big smile that it was believed that a commercial oil field had been identified. The news spread like wildfire. That was probably the happiest I ever saw him. He knew then that he could go after the big projects he had always talked of."

DPC's perseverence finally paid off on June 6, 1966, when oil in commercial quantities was discovered 15 miles off the coast of Dubai. Sheikh Rashid decided to call the oil field Fateh, which in Arabic means 'good fortune'. Over the coming years more important discoveries were made. Two confirmation wells were completed in 1967 that proved the existence of a substantial field.

DPC developed Fateh rapidly and the commencement of production was announced officially on September 6, 1969. Discovery to export had taken just three years, a remarkably short period of time during the late 1960s. In November 1970 DPC would go on to announce the discovery of the 'Southwest Fateh' field.

Later the 'Falah' field was discovered in 1972 and production commenced in 1978, while the 'Rashid' field was discovered in 1973 and production commenced in 1979.

For Dubai, the oil boom had finally arrived.

Sheikh Rashid visiting a rig. Excitement grew in Dubai as news spread that the government was about to announce the discovery of commercial oil deposits.

Chapter Fourteen

Black Gold

Wealth unused might as well not exist.
– Aesop, Ancient Greek author

The oil industry began over 5,000 years ago. In the Middle East, oil seeping up through the ground was used for waterproofing boats and baskets, in paints, lighting and even for medication. The first oil wells were drilled in China in the fourth century or earlier. They had depths of up to 800 feet and were drilled using bits attached to bamboo poles, while in the eighth century the streets of the newly-constructed Baghdad were paved with tar, derived from easily-accessible petroleum from natural fields in the region.

The modern, industrial age had changed the demographics of demand and transformed oil from a folk industry in the Middle East into the region's primary source of income. Petroleum is used mostly, by volume, for producing fuel oil, which is the world's primary energy source and also the raw material for many chemical products, including solvents, fertilisers, pesticides, and plastics.

Oil lifted much of the region from penury. But at what cost and for how long? Other natural windfalls have, throughout history, harmed their beneficiaries. Gold and silver from the New World made Spain rich in the 16th century, but distorted its economy and ultimately weakened it. Peru enjoyed a boom in guano (used for fertiliser) in the mid-19th century, and later Brazil had a rubber boom. These made a few people rich but left no useful legacy – only some gaudy buildings, including an opera house in the Amazon jungle. Gold-rush sites in California and Alaska turned into ghost towns when the mining stopped. The trouble with booms is that they typically bring neither sustained

All over the world there are examples in history of natural windfalls being squandered and ultimately bringing disaster. Dubai's patrimony, however, was channelled into sustainable development of the city.

economic growth nor cultural improvements. The riches they create are spent with abandon, disrupting normal behaviour, fomenting unrealistic expectations, and inspiring envy. And booms always come to an end.

"It is striking how many countries have not used their natural resource wealth wisely," says Nobel Laureate Joseph E Stiglitz. "And as a result, the abundance of wealth has not enhanced growth."

Petroleum is a word derived from the Greek petra (rock) and oleum (oil). Crude oil, sometimes colloquially called 'black gold', exists in the upper strata of some areas of the Earth's crust. Another name is naphtha, from the Persian naft or nafátá (to flow).

The modern history of oil began in 1853, with the discovery of the process of oil distillation, and by 2002 the Middle East was responsible for over half of the world's proven oil reserves, and remains the centre of gravity in the global oil market. There is no doubt that the importance of the region is poised to grow.

After Abu Dhabi's entry into the elite club of oil exporters – following Kuwait, Saudi Arabia and Bahrain – it was now seemingly to be Dubai's turn. Yet the Dubai Ruler was still somewhat cautious. He needed oil revenues, but did not need the malaise that such wealth brought with it.

"Sheikh Rashid had seen what sudden wealth could do. He had also seen how wealth had corrupted those in power," says Sheikh Hamdan bin Rashid Al Maktoum. "He did not have that personality, but he was mindful that everything he had built in Dubai could come crashing down if the infusion of petrodollars was not handled in a way that brought long-term benefits to the people and did not spark corruption."

According to the anti-corruption campaign group Transparency International (TI), oil wealth is often a breeding ground for corruption, and in a report TI estimated that billions of dollars are lost to bribery in public purchasing, citing the oil sector in many nations as a particular problem. And corruption can often be seen to be either state-sponsored, or given tacit approval. A senior official of British Petroleum interviewed by journalist Andrew Duncan on such occurrences stated: "The authorities have taken the view that commission is a way of spending oil revenue...You have to have some mechanism, other than the dole, for pushing money round."

"The challenge of using oil wealth for poverty reduction in general and for agricultural and rural development in particular is not only an issue of political will, but also of the methods used for channelling of fiscal resources – with minimal leakage – to communities, local government areas, and civil society groups so that they can implement their own," says World Bank economist Hans Binswanger.

Of course, receipts for billions of petrodollars were still a long way away, yet the wealth that Fateh represented would unshackle Sheikh Rashid and allow him to embark upon a new round of ambitious projects and administrative developments. Since the turn of the century, when Sheikh Maktoum bin Hasher Al Maktoum Ruled Dubai, the sheikhdom had been positioned to become the Gulf's business hub. Throughout the lean years of the pearling industry – and the resulting depression that pervaded the Gulf economy – Dubai maintained a commercial awareness which in turn helped it emerge from the slump still an economic power.

Dubai Petroleum Company's 1966 announcement that commercial deposits of oil were indeed present in Dubai meant something else altogether. Over the next decade, the sheikhdom was to become one of the world's boom economies.

"Abu Dhabi's lead in 1957 was followed by Dubai in 1969 and, later, Sharjah. These years had witnessed the oil sector's surge to a pivotal position in the economy, providing vast revenues and dwarfing other sources of national income…The new direction of the economy naturally led to the progressive decline of some of the mainstays such as pearl fishing. The main pillars of subsequent growth, however, fuelled by oil revenue, were a mix of activities such as construction in line with a massive, sustained outlay for infrastructure development, the establishment of state-of-the-art health services, power plants, communication networks, ports and airports, industrial zones. Oil assumed dominance over the economy," says Mohammed Alabbar, director general of the Department of Economic Development, government of Dubai.

But despite estimates of commercial oil deposits sufficient to last up to half a century, Sheikh Rashid was by no means set to turn his back on Dubai's trade legacy.

In July 1965 he had enshrined the future of the sheikhdom as a commercial centre in a decree ordering the establishment of the Dubai Chamber of Commerce, the first such organisation on the Trucial Coast. Sheikh Rashid was adamant that the Chamber should both aggressively promote opportunities in Dubai and provide a wide range of services to

the local business community. The Chamber has not lost sight of Sheikh Rashid's instructions, and remains one of the highest-profile organisations in the Middle East, working hand-in-hand with the government.

Although it was to be almost three years before the first tanker loaded with Dubai crude would set sail, over the weeks and months following the confirmation of oil those used to life in the Majlis saw a distinct change in Sheikh Rashid.

"The arrival of the oil-producing era further ignited Sheikh Rashid," says Zakariah Doleh. "He was ambitious when times were hard. Now that there were ample funds set to come to the government he busied himself even more than before."

Friends in the Majlis warned him that he could not maintain such a work rate, to which Sheikh Rashid would often reply: "What you want to do, is too much; what you can do, is too little."

"He always believed he could find a middle ground between easing

By the early-1960s, the mere prospect of commercial oil deposits was fueling a construction and development boom in the sheikhdom. But Sheikh Rashid was careful to remain prudent.

off and working so hard that he burnt out," explains Doleh. "Even then Sheikh Rashid's pace was phenomenally high. He wore out many of his closest lieutenants."

"Sheikh Rashid worked at a frantic pace. There is no other way to describe it," said Sultan Ali Al Owais. "And he never let up. When the prospect of oil revenue arrived, this meant that he would work harder. His energy came from a reserve that most people do not have."

Sheikh Rashid also told the Majlis: "The living man, or more exactly a man who deserves to live, is the one who works for the present and the future of his country and adds new glories to those made by his fathers and grandfathers."

During the hardest of times, Sheikh Rashid had been able to fund part

247

of his most ambitious projects through revenue generated in customs duties. These had been boosted significantly by his project to dredge the Creek and build up the available wharfage, a project topped off during the early 1960s. The project soon paid for itself, and if a lesson in Sheikh Rashid's thinking was needed, this was it. He had ruled, or effectively ruled as Prince Regent, during the toughest economic downturn of the century. These were times when wasting funds was unthinkable. Even during the early 1960s when Dubai's financial position was improving rapidly, he personally kept – and demanded from his government – financial prudence.

After 1966, when it was finally confirmed that the oil boom was set to come to Dubai, he pressed on determinedly with a broadly identical policy.

"More funds were about to become available, but Sheikh Rashid hated waste and made it clear that there was not going to be unbridled spending," recalls Saif Ahmed Al Ghurair. "There was no extravagant spending. Every proposal or project still had to fulfill Sheikh Rashid's prerequisites for prudence."

Government apparatus had grown during the 1950s and 1960s. More services were provided and evolved into something resembling a civil service. Sheikh Rashid was adamant that the new breed of civil servants and technocrats should not stifle a mood of unbridled optimism that was attracting money and trade on a level comparable, in its effect, with that of the early years of the century and the demise of Lingah.

"As the population grew more civil government was required," recalls Abdullah Saleh. "He was acutely aware that some other Gulf States had enveloped the business community in red tape, new taxes and stifling regulation. He often reminded those of us concerned with the commercial sector to make it as easy as possible for legitimate businesses to trade here. It was Sheikh Rashid's open door policy and a lack of red tape which attracted many to do business in Dubai."

Thanks to earlier progress in basic amenities, such as water and electricity, living standards in Dubai had continued to improve, despite the fact that between 1956 and 1968 the population virtually doubled from 30,000 to 59,000. In other areas, the sheer speed of Dubai's

Sheikh Rashid consults with advisors on Port Rashid, a facility that would transform Dubai's economy. To the left is prominent businessman Abdullah Darwish.

Situated at the mouth of the Creek, Port Rashid would be an instant commercial success.

evolution put strains on facilities. The recently redeveloped Creek was floundering under weight of traffic, while it was patently clear that the economy was undergoing something of a metamorphosis. The old industries, like fishing, had been surpassed by events; commerce was now the key.

From late 1966 the Majlis began debating the concept of a new port, one that Sheikh Rashid envisaged as a world-class facility, attracting bigger ships and larger cargoes, boosting both imports and re-exports to the rest of the world. Improved facilities would inevitably also be needed by the oil industry if commercial deposits were to be fully exploited. At the time Dubai Creek was seeing a big growth in traffic, with estimates putting usage at upwards of 4,000 dhows each year. Larger vessels were forced to anchor one mile offshore and await their cargoes being unloaded onto smaller craft. Elsewhere in the Gulf larger ships waited at anchor, sometimes for weeks or months, for a berth at one of the better-developed ports. Dubai needed facilities of its own, while customers were queuing up elsewhere.

These two factors convinced Sheikh Rashid that a large modern port would be a natural progression to his city's expansion. As early as 1965 he had commissioned Sir William Halcrow and Partners to run a feasibility study into a deep water harbour. By 1967 designers were drawing up a plan for a port in the Shindagha area, selected because it was the deepest place within easy distance of the mouth of the Creek. Initial designs called for four berths able to take ocean-going vessels and oil tankers. It would be called Port Rashid and was to be the biggest earthworks project ever undertaken in Dubai.

Sheikh Rashid was also keen that Port Rashid develop as a free port. The most successful at the time on a similar model were those in Singapore and Holland, so government representatives were dispatched to each to complete a study. He reserved a massive area adjacent to the shipping berths for construction of giant cargo sheds.

Several months later, with plans well underway, Sheikh Rashid and his closest advisors were in a huddle when an attack of doubt surrounded them. The concept was undoubtedly valid, but questions surrounded the size. Knowing Dubai to be on a course of massive expansion, the following day Sheikh Rashid scrapped existing plans, confounding the designers when ordering them to draw up new plans for 16 berths instead of four.

(opposite page) Sheikh Rashid and his advisors Saif Ahmed Al Ghurair, Ahmed bin Sulayem and Hamad Al Futtaim, on a visit to the port. (this page) Sheikh Rashid tours a Pakistani frigate which called on Port Rashid in a fraternal visit.

"The port will be provided with the most modern equipment to handle 16 ships at a time," Dubai's Ruler now told newsmen. "We hope that this port will open Dubai to increased international trade."

Single-minded he certainly was, but never in his life was Sheikh Rashid seen to squander the government's money. Early in the Port Rashid project, he looked at the estimated bill of £13 million and, as was his way, sought to identify any unnecessary fat that could be stripped away.

"Let us first look at the possibilities," he cautioned, during a meeting at Customs House, aimed at finding savings. While Sheikh Rashid sat back to consider the overall picture, however, he certainly did not expect work to be held up.

"When he said 'get started', it meant just that," comments one consultant who worked on the showpiece port project. "He didn't mean he wanted you to sit down and draw up some plans, he wanted you to start digging. The plans could follow later."

The project required two large breakwaters, the stone for which engineers had thought would have to be shipped in from elsewhere in the Gulf. The areas identified as having suitable geology were principally in Ras Al Khaimah and the Sirri Islands. Sheikh Rashid, however, knew something of local topography. Over the years he heard Bedu complaining of the difficulty in drilling water wells in certain outlying areas of Dubai, due to hard ground. He set the experts the task of finding an alternative in Dubai, identifying several areas which he thought possible sources. Within weeks a site named Khraij Umm Biat, given a wide

berth by the Bedu, was found to have suitable limestone. The savings arising from this discovery were estimated, by Abdul Ghaffar Hashim Al Maimani, an advisor working on Port Rashid, at some £4.2 million.

Sheikh Rashid was often seen around Port Rashid, up to four times every day, taking a close interest as his vision gained shape. It was not uncommon for the workforce to begin arriving at 6.30 am to find him already there acquainting himself with progress. Three months into the job of transporting the limestone by truck from Khraij Umm Biat to the Port Rashid site, he was furious to discover the process falling behind schedule. Admonishing those responsible, he demanded round-the-clock efforts to catch up and also re-routed the constant stream of trucks past his own Za'abeel Palace.

"Sheikh Rashid was always a light sleeper. He could hear the sound of the trucks' movement and would wake up from his sleep if a truck did not pass for some time," recalls Abdullah Saleh.

Subsequent to the completion of the wharf at Port Rashid, the same limestone was used to construct harbours for fishermen at Hamriya, Jumeirah, Umm Suqeim and Mina Seyahi.

Even by Dubai standards the massive Port Rashid programme was remarkable. It had added one more major plank in the sheikhdom's plan for economic self-sufficiency and, in light of subsequent events, could not have come at a better time.

When Sheikh Rashid inaugurated the facility in October 1971, five years after initial earthworks began, his decision to expand the project looked like something approaching genius. Port facilities around the

Gulf were by now massively over-subscribed; waiting lists for berthing were common. At the same juncture, imports into Dubai had surpassed £100 million and merchants using the city were desperate for new and better facilities.

A second phase of development, which began in February 1976, was to add a further 20 berths to Port Rashid, including a five-berth container terminal for the biggest vessels of the day. At the same time the container storage area was raised to 30,000 square metres, including specialised areas for 400 reefers. During the same phase the Dubai government began work on major port development in the Hamriya area to cater to the busy traffic of medium-size vessels utilising Dubai Creek. Completed in 1975, Hamriya Port was largely created to service dhows and the wooden vessels that ply traditional trade routes between the Arabian Gulf states.

The year 1967, best remembered as the year in which work on the Port Rashid began, is also recalled by long time residents for a frightening medical emergency. Temperatures were searing and the city was relatively empty for the summer when a recently-arrived expatriate was admitted to Al Maktoum Hospital suffering from fever and suspected pneumonia. The patient was initially thought to have malaria, a disease which the World Health Organisation (WHO) reports at the time said existed in remoter parts of the Arabian Peninsula, but was not often seen in the coastal towns. However, there was no response to initial treatment, and when a severe rash and blistering covered his body, doctors began to think the unthinkable – smallpox.

The smallpox virus was soon confirmed, followed by a rush of admissions of people with whom the carrier had come into contact. The outbreak of smallpox – often fatal, hard to detect during its incubation stage and highly infectious – was immediately reported to Sheikh Rashid, who backed up Dubai medical authorities' call for urgent supplies of the vaccine with calls to the WHO and British Political Agent.

Smallpox is a serious, contagious, and sometimes fatal infectious disease, for which there is no specific treatment and the only prevention is vaccination. There are two clinical forms of smallpox. Variola major is the severe and most common form of smallpox, with a more extensive rash and higher fever and an overall fatality rate of about 30%.

Smallpox outbreaks have occurred from time to time for thousands of years, and only later was the disease eradicated after a successful

Sheikh Rashid in Scotland while on a private visit to Britain in 1966. Also pictured are Sheikh Hamdan (in suit), Habib Mohammed Habib, Ammer Al Majid and Buti Al Masoud.

worldwide vaccination programme. The last naturally-occurring case in the world was in Somalia in 1977.

Al Maktoum Hospital and a recently opened Kuwait-financed clinic were put on alert, while a government team organised the largest vaccination programme ever attempted in the region. The latter ultimately succeeded in preventing the outbreak from becoming an epidemic, but it was some days before authorities could say with confidence that they were winning the battle against the virus.

This close call with smallpox brought firmly into focus the need for developed medical facilities. At Sheikh Rashid's instigation, from April 1967 the Trucial States Development Fund, financed by the British, put extra funding into Al Maktoum Hospital and agreed to split the cost of running the facility. This freed additional funds, and in 1969 Sheikh Rashid announced a new manifesto for health care in the city:

"Besides the construction of Al Maktoum Hospital, the first phase of a Medical City in Dubai will start over the coming days. This will consist of a hospital with a capacity of 373 beds and a residential complex for doctors, nurses and other employees," he said.

Over subsequent years Medical City became Rashid Hospital. Sheikh Rashid was kept in close touch with the state of the city's medical services, and by August 1970, when Dubai and Ras Al Khaimah suffered the brunt of a serious malaria outbreak, capacity existed to manage the vaccination of upwards of 60,000 people.

Chapter Fifteen

Changing Times

*Whenever you take a step forward, you are bound to disturb
something. You disturb the air as you go forward, you disturb the dust,
the ground. You trample upon things. When a whole society moves
forward, this trampling is on a much bigger scale; and each thing
that you disturb, each vested interest which you want to
remove, stands as an obstacle.*
— Mahatma Gandhi, father of India

Britain had largely withdrawn from the Subcontinent in 1947
(it granted Independence to Ceylon – now Sri Lanka – in February 1948)
but had continued to exert a heavy influence in the Gulf, her interest
largely because of the region's emerging economic importance.
Britain's position had actually begun to weaken in the region since the
end of the Second World War, squeezed out by the stronger influence of
the two superpowers, America and Russia, along with the independent-
minded governments in Saudi Arabia and Iran. A renewed nationalism
among the population during the 1950s and 1960s had only served to
further inflate a sense of rift between the leaders of the area and the
predominant power.

Since 1949 and their joint declaration of partial self-determination,
the sheikhs of the Trucial States had not been afraid to defy British
authority. Sheikh Shakhbut of Abu Dhabi had taken this further in
granting an oil concession to the US-owned Super Oil Company in 1953.

By 1956 the British were facing a rising tide of niggling political
troubles in the Middle East when, as one of the protagonists, they had
blundered into Suez, an event which drew universal criticism around the
Arab world. Indeed, the growing unease over Britain's intentions

*Sheikh Rashid and Sheikh Zayed bin Sultan Al Nahyan, Ruler of Abu Dhabi, were to
be thrust into the spotlight as the political landscape was transformed following a
British government announcement that its forces were to withdraw from the Gulf.*

257

toward its responsibilities in the Gulf, coupled with the Suez crisis, was a large contributing factor to a growing disquiet over the direction in which Her Majesty's government was heading.

After the nationalisation of Suez, the situation settled and stabilised somewhat for several years in the Gulf and relations returned to normal. Unbeknown to many, however, the next steps in an unfolding process were already under way, not in the Middle East but in the corridors of power in London. Whitehall had begun to accept that Great Britain was part of a new world order. Policy documents from the time, particularly those produced in the Foreign Office, show a growing realisation that Britain's international standing was slipping. Within government there was a growing belief that Britain needed a rationalisation of its foreign policy, and spending. Britain, opinion decreed, needed to focus on European issues.

During the late 1960s the financial policies of Harold Wilson's Labour government had driven Britain toward its worst recession since the Second World War. 'Tax and Spend', a bedrock of Wilson's political manifesto, was failing. Combined with a world recession, this was enough to place the British economy in trouble and send most economic indicators into free-fall. Overseas commitments were an obvious target for review. As early as 1966 a motion signed by 54 Members of Parliament was submitted, claiming that the cost of maintaining Britain's 'east of Aden' military bases – at an estimated £317 million – made them an expensive anomaly at a time of domestic economic crisis. A government White Paper concluded much the same in February 1967. This was at odds with Wilson's official position as set out by George Brown, Foreign Secretary, in a statement made to Parliament on January 18, 1967, in which he sought to reassure allies in the Gulf by stating: "Britain most certainly will continue to honour its military commitments in the Gulf..."

Between these events and November of the same year, Britain's economy lurched into a worsening position. Unemployment was rising sharply, inflation was high and Wilson himself was the most unpopular Prime Minister for generations. These factors gave rise to rumours and even newspaper comment over the government's plans to continue with its treaty obligations in the Gulf. To silence this speculation, Goronwy Roberts, Minister of State for Foreign Affairs, was dispatched to the Trucial States where he visited all the Rulers in a bid to assure them that

Prime Minister Harold Wilson's economically disastrous tenure in Downing Street led directly to Britain's withdrawal from the Gulf.

Wilson remained committed to Britain's role in the Gulf.

It is easy to see why a majority of observers believed that Britain would wish to keep its influence in the Gulf, not least because the country was the guiding power to states that between them held a massive proportion of the world's known oil reserves. Britain was also obligated under the Central Treaty Organisation – previously titled the Baghdad Pact – while its strategic ally, the United States, was pressing for Britain to continue in the role to counter-balance Soviet interests in the region.

These factors might have been enough to deter Prime Minister Wilson from beating a retreat from the Gulf, yet his own domestic position grew steadily worse. Roberts had hardly returned to London from the Gulf when, on November 18, Sterling was devalued against the dollar, dropping to $2.40 from $2.80. This was a disastrous reflection of British economic policy, which forced the government into a desperate search for budget cuts. The Labour Party's own Overseas Policy Defence Committee had looked at the cost of Britain's 'east of Aden' commitments and thought these to be far in excess of the previous parliamentary estimate. The committee thought this figure nearer £800 million. From the moment of devaluation, Britain's commitment to its Trucial States allies was as dead as Wilson's subsequent General Election hopes.

On January 9, the *Daily Express* leaked the news that military forces stationed in the Gulf and throughout the Far East were to be brought home. One week later, so called 'Black Tuesday', Downing Street released a statement that confirmed the story, adding the footnote that the recall was to be completed by the end of 1971.

"While most people saw what trouble the British were in, I don't think we believed this would affect us directly," says prominent Dubai businessman Saif Ahmed Al Ghurair. "After the Daily Express story appeared, news of this filtered through quite quickly. No-one really knew what to believe. When we heard on the radio that Harold Wilson had issued a statement, everyone was in shock."

Shockwaves were also passing through the Majlis of every Ruler along the Trucial Coast. All knew they were unprepared to stand alone, while talks on federation had led to little tangible progress. Development in real terms, of any kind, had only begun around a decade before. A withdrawal would have profound effects on the balance of power in the region. Just across the Gulf from the Trucial Coast, a strongly nationalist Iranian government had emerged as a military and political force. The Shah of Iran was adamant that Bahrain was an Iranian island, and even in 1968 he was making plain his desire to annex the mid-Gulf Arab islands of Abu Musa and Greater and Lesser Tunbs.

The Shah also coveted Arab oil to prop up an economy that was geared towards building the biggest military force ever assembled in the Middle East. Indeed, according to his own book, *Mission of My Country*, the Shah had expressed the belief that God had set him a path to follow as divine saviour of Iran and the entire Gulf.

Arabs throughout the Middle East were nervous. The popular nationalist newspaper *Talia* wrote that there must be a "concerted effort to prevent the creation of another Palestine", hinting that danger would come from "a non-Arab country backed by Britain and America", a none-too-subtle comparison between Israel and Iran.

Two months after telling Sheikh Rashid that there was "no doubt about the government's continuing presence in the Gulf", Foreign Office representative Goronwy Roberts was back on a different mission. In Dubai, Sheikh Rashid learned of Britain's U-turn during a hastily arranged meeting on January 8. The Dubai Ruler spoke at length with his advisors, consulted with Crown Prince Sheikh Maktoum, and then telephoned Sheikh Hamdan and Sheikh Mohammed in Cambridge. There was much at stake and great shock at Wilson's decision.

Off the coast of Arabia lay the Arab islands of Abu Musa and Greater and Lesser Tunb. A British announcement that they were ending their security commitments in the region began the intrigue that would eventually lead to the annexing of these three islands by Iran.

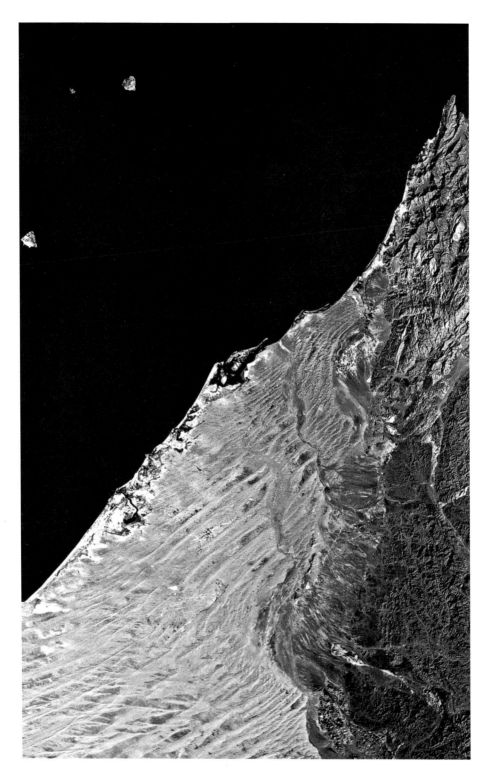

As a result of consultations between members of the Maktoum family, within a few hours Sheikh Rashid and the Ruler of Abu Dhabi, Sheikh Zayed bin Sultan Al Nahyan, had spoken on the telephone and agreed to start immediate talks. The seven sheikhdoms that would ultimately form the United Arab Emirates, plus Qatar, Bahrain and Oman, had been told that they had four years before Britain would cut them adrift, whatever their state of preparedness.

Indeed, the only good news for those in the region with a pro-British outlook was that Wilson decreed the pull-back would not be completed until the end of 1971. Many saw the task of those four years not simply as one of a gradual pull-out of forces, but for the British to help prevent a meltdown in the fragile peace of the Gulf. As much as the influence of the British Foreign Office was welcomed in some quarters, in others there was a resentment that a nation which had suddenly wrung its hands of its commitments had the audacity to continue meddling in internal Gulf affairs for more years.

Bahrain Ruler Sheikh Isa bin Salman Al Khalifa announced that a federation was "a national issue which we will decide and which will not be decided by anyone for us." A key player along the coast in the decision-making process, Sheikh Isa was in constant contact with Sheikh Rashid by telephone, sometimes daily, while he also visited Saudi Arabia and Kuwait for consultations.

Kuwaiti Foreign Affairs Minister Sheikh Sabah Al-Ahmed Al-Jaber Al-Sabah followed the Downing Street announcement by undertaking a whistle-stop tour of the potential federal states during the first half of February, offering the support of his country for the concept. He stopped off in Dubai for two days of talks with Sheikh Rashid.

Sheikh Rashid seems to have viewed news of the pull-out as an opportunity. The Trucial States Development Fund had in no small part been pieced together with the benefit of his diplomacy. This loose grouping had certainly worked for a time, but membership was effectively non-binding and several of its members had eventually begun to drift from a common path.

The British withdrawal was to bring the Council's nine members back to the table with renewed vigour, all recognising that their potential financial wealth, coupled with a military vulnerability, would make each a temptation to any sizeable country with less than peaceable intentions. This was largely understood, but still Sheikh Rashid and Sheikh Zayed, his most ardent ally in the strategy of mutual benefit through union, were frustrated in their attempts to shepherd the remaining seven sheikhdoms in even a relatively harmonious direction.

"My father was frustrated," says Sheikh Ahmed. "He wanted action on the issue."

Sheikh Rashid and Sheikh Zayed decided that they would only press the matter by taking the bull by the horns. Regional leaders were still trying to come to terms with Britain's decision, while Sheikh Rashid's position was that a union between Dubai and its neighbours was the only way to ensure their stability and future security. Two days after his meeting with Roberts, Sheikh Rashid received Sheikh Zayed at Za'abeel Palace in Dubai. This meeting was to define the union process, for although both leaders often had contradictory views, they became partners.

In the days after their meeting in Dubai, both Sheikh Rashid and Sheikh Zayed moved to broaden their contacts with fellow Rulers. These included the leaders of the five sheikhdoms to the north – Sharjah, Ajman, Umm Al Quwain, Ras Al Khaimah and Fujairah – and neighbours Bahrain and Qatar. All were responsive to a proposal for talks.

Nine sheikhdoms were part of the process at its outset. Bringing these economically and historically diverse entities together would prove a challenge and, to underscore the immediacy of the challenge, Sheikh Rashid and Sheikh Zayed decided upon a bold strategy. Their plan was for Dubai and Abu Dhabi to forge a fledgling state, unifying the two as one entity, and then to reach out to the remaining seven to persuade them to merge into this structure. Creating a federation would not be without significant compromise. The Maktoum and Al Nahyan families would be required to centralise authority into a joint structure. Foreign and fiscal policy had traditionally been exclusively those of individual Rulers.

Says Khalifa Al Naboodah: "Sheikh Rashid understood that for the good of the region and the people of the Trucial States, one could not cling to old concepts. Unity was the only way forward. From the very beginning, Sheikh Maktoum and his brothers supported Sheikh Rashid and threw their considerable weight behind efforts to unify the Trucial States."

With his sons supporting him, Sheikh Rashid agreed to this most decisive of steps forward. He met with Sheikh Zayed regularly during early February, and their most senior officials travelled between the two cities to negotiate.

Sheikh Maktoum and Sheikh Ahmed were based in Dubai during this period and were at hand for Sheikh Rashid. Both Sheikh Hamdan and Sheikh Mohammed shuttled between Dubai and Cambridge as their studies allowed, in order to participate in the process.

February 18 has a largely unspectacular place in history. In 1879 it was the day when Arab forces captured Egyptian premier Nabar Pasha and, five years later, the day when General Charles Gordon arrived in Khartoum. In 1921 British troops occupied Dublin, and in 1930 it was the day when astronomer Clyde Tombaugh discovered Pluto. February 18, 1968 was more newsworthy. Some 100,000 demonstrators assembled in West Berlin to rile against the Vietnam War, the Tenth Winter Olympic games closed in Grenoble, France, while in Britain the nation adopted year-round daylight saving time.

February 18, 1968 was also to mark the beginnings of a process that would lead to the creation of the United Arab Emirates (UAE). On that day Sheikh Rashid met Sheikh Zayed at a desert campsite specially erected in Al Samha, near the border between both states.

This was a historic meeting that set the tone for everything to follow. There could be no greater test of statesmanship, and both Rulers came to the negotiating table willing to settle the few issues that separated them: Sheikh Zayed agreed to give up land that had been disputed between their two states for generations.

With this and other matters settled, early that afternoon Sheikh Zayed and Sheikh Rashid sat down at a table to discuss forging an agreement to stipulate the beginning of a federation between Abu Dhabi and Dubai. As the only other individual sitting at this table, Sheikh Mohammed clearly remembers the few words that launched the beginnings of the United Arab Emirates: "So, Rashid, what do you think? Shall we create a union?" asked Sheikh Zayed. Without hesitation, the Dubai Ruler held out his hand and replied: "Give me your hand, Zayed. Let us shake upon an agreement. You will be President."

Their treaty included a unified flag, while the document called for federal unity in defence, internal security, foreign policy and common immigration, medical and education systems. This document has come to be known as the Union Accord and was the first real step towards a federation among the Lower Gulf sheikhdoms.

"A wall can be built only by laying one brick on top of the other," Sheikh Zayed had said. This was the first brick of many.

Aside from predictable condemnation by Iran, international reaction to the move was positive. Kuwait and Saudi Arabia welcomed the agreement, Britain wholeheartedly supported this achievement and King Hussein of Jordan recognised the Abu Dubai/Dubai union as a full-blown state.

After unveiling the Union Accord, Sheikh Rashid and Sheikh Zayed had been inundated by messages of support from the Rulers of the other seven sheikhdoms. All had wanted immediate entry into the union. Just one week later, on February 25, the nine Rulers attended a meeting at Sheikh Rashid's Jumeirah Beach Palace. This summit was to last three days, and such was the life which Dubai and Abu Dhabi had breathed into the federal concept that the Qatari delegation, previously seen as anti-union, opened discussions by circulating a draft constitution, a document which took talks on the first day of the meeting well into the night. The Qataris, led by Sheikh Rashid's son-in-law Sheikh Ahmed bin Ali Al Thani, proposed two unions in one. Under the banner of the United Arab Coastal Emirates (UACE), they grouped Ajman, Fujairah, Ras Al Khaimah, Sharjah and Umm Al Quwain in a larger state, with each ruled as a province by their present leaders, with a revolving Presidency. The UACE would then be represented as one unit, alongside Qatar, Bahrain, Dubai and Abu Dhabi, in a five-member federal body.

Sheikh Rashid was skeptical, but had encouraged his son-in-law to bring to the table his ideas in the knowledge that at the very least the document would open a flow of discussion and ideas. Predictably the Rulers envisaged as part of the UACE were unwilling to see either themselves sidetracked or their voices dissipated. But Sheikh Rashid was correct in his assumption that the emergence of a formula, however unacceptable it was to some, would bring about debate.

On the morning of February 26 the group resumed discussions, Dubai's Ruler opening the morning session with a call to continue the frank and earnest discussions of the previous day. The nine Rulers and their respective entourages emerged from the Jumeirah Palace only on limited occasions, for lunch and several short private consultations, and by the end of the second day most involved began to see progress on the central themes under discussion.

February 27 was scheduled to be the final day of the conference, and that afternoon the sheikhs emerged with a deal which astounded most neutral observers as to how far they had agreed to travel on the road to federalism. Although this was far from a working constitution, the document laid out many of the terms and provisions needed to gather the nine into a framework which had the potential to bring them together more formally. The Union of Arab Emirates was to be headed by a Supreme Council, made up of the nine Rulers, with a rotated one-year Presidency.

This was initially charged with solidifying the agreement by producing a more formal constitution, arranging greater integration and setting federal law. Under the Supreme Council there were to be three smaller councils, each with its nominated members charged with administering culture, defence and economic matters. This working administration was set to take on its role from April 30, 1968, only to be superseded at

On February 27, 1968, the Rulers of the seven Trucial States, plus Bahrain and Qatar, emerged from Union House in Dubai to announce that they were to create a new state - the Union of Arab Emirates.

a later date by an agreement taking the states into closer unity. This date was, by common consent, later brought forward to March 30.

Sheikh Rashid played an integral role in creating consensus at the meeting, and afterwards he declared in private his satisfaction at what had been achieved. He was aware that the richer states would be unlikely to rush into an arrangement which saw them take on financial responsibility for the smaller states. Equally he understood that individual sovereign powers, some of which had taken the sheikhs and their forebears centuries to win, were not going to be given away over the course of a three-day constitutional meeting.

Sheikh Rashid, Sheikh Ahmed of Qatar and Sheikh Saqr of Ras Al Khaimah used their final statements to urge their fellows onwards, all

*Sheikh Rashid greets
Sheikh Isa bin Salman Al
Khalifa of Bahrain.*

three appealing for work to begin immediately on cementing agreement
on key federal bodies.

"We have gone further than ever before," said Sheikh Rashid. "When
the British remove their forces from the Gulf we have to stand together
as part of a functioning body which guarantees our mutual security,
provides an umbrella for foreign policy and enables us to maintain
stability."

A communiqué was issued stating that:

> *Unanimity was reached on the creation of a federation embrac-
> ing all the Arab emirates in the Gulf, including the emirates of
> Abu Dhabi and Dubai. This is seen to be more fulfilling for the
> purpose adopted by these two emirates and cherished by the
> aspirations of the people of the whole region, in response to the
> desire of these people to strengthen the requirements for stability
> in their respective countries...in accordance with the objectives
> and principles embodied in the charters of the United Nations and
> the Arab League...*

The formation of the union was immediately welcomed by most
Arab states, Great Britain and the United States. Iran, which maintained
a territorial claim on Bahrain, was vitriolic in its denunciation, a Foreign
Ministry statement claiming: "There is no doubt that the colonialists'
and the imperialists' policies...cannot rest for a moment without trying
to exercise that hateful role through rear guard actions...[The

federation] is no more than an obedient instrument for the ambitions of the imperialists and colonialists..."

The *Voice of the Arabs*, broadcast from Cairo, was warmer in its reception: "Declaration of the federation last Sunday was a big step towards realising the aim of the Arab masses in the area...When the Dubai Agreement was concluded...the Arab peoples received it with great satisfaction and regarded it as another step on the path of unity."

Elsewhere in the Middle East, neighbours Saudi Arabia and Kuwait signaled their support, the former offering economic aid to hasten the process.

A little over a month was scheduled to pass before the federation came into being, but it increasingly seemed that little work was being done. Several of the Rulers returned to their respective states and found their enthusiasm cooling, so gradually the programme for establishing the major bodies enshrined in the so-called Dubai Agreement fell behind. The end of March came and went without any sort of fanfare, and when April passed without even a meeting of the proposed Supreme Council, the Dubai Agreement was in tatters.

Chapter Sixteen

Return to Camelot

*Fortitude is the marshal of thought, the armour of
the will, and the fort of reason.*
— Francis Bacon, author

The union process was to be another heavy burden on Sheikh Rashid, whose life was already filled with a myriad of pressures as he sought to transform Dubai. The Dubai Ruler had always trusted himself to get things right, only devolving responsibilities to a cadre of young nationals around him in the Majlis.

But the new reality of ruling Dubai was not one that could sit with one man and his 'Camelot'. The arrival of petrodollars in Dubai had caused an explosion of development work that was transforming the sheikhdom; on top of this, the demands of the union process were pressing. Sheikh Rashid simply had to devolve some decision making in order to concentrate on the bigger picture.

There were people around him on whom he could lean. Former Customs Head, Ahmed bin Sulayem, was now visible in the Majlis. Juma Al Majid and Majid Al Futtaim, two of Sheikh Rashid's favourites, who were also to become two of Dubai's foremost businessmen, were also there to take on responsibilities. All three would later represent Dubai's interests within the Provisional Federal Council of the Union of Arab Emirates that would later emerge.

"Sheikh Rashid had a great deal of trust for just a few men, including the likes of Abdullah Saleh," says Malcolm Corrigan, an expatriate Britain who served in the Ruler's Office in 1968. "Another emerging Majlis figure during this period was Ahmed Moosa. These were the sort of people he would spot, bring in, test and then, when they showed themselves talented, give authority to. He had an eye for talent."

Just in time, as the burden of nation-building became feverish, there

Sheikh Rashid and his entourage pictured during an official visit to India.

were other emerging figures set to play a role within Majlis, government and administration.

"Sheikh Rashid was always grooming his boys, giving them greater responsibilities," comments Hussain Khansaheb. "Sheikh Maktoum had always pleased him. He was a lot like his father in that he was not complicated. He listened to the people and was a good arbitrator. Sheikh Maktoum showed a lot of Sheikh Rashid's calmness and diplomacy."

Sheikh Maktoum, much trusted eldest son and Crown Prince, was now back in Dubai following a stint at the elite Gordonstoun school in Scotland and a term at the Bell School of Languages in Cambridge.

"Sheikh Maktoum had returned from England with a lot more experience," says Saif Ahmed Al Ghurair, "and Sheikh Rashid needed someone close to him who could speak fluent English given the increasing international aspect of the administration in its dealings with the outside world. Sheikh Rashid knew only a few words of English and trusted only a few people from his inner circle to sit with him when he was dealing with world leaders."

Sheikh Maktoum was only 25 years old in 1968, but was no stranger to the workings of Sheikh Rashid's famous 'Arabian Camelot'. As a child he had played at the feet of his grandfather as Sheikh Saeed bin Maktoum Al Maktoum had ruled Dubai. He had entered his father's Majlis as a young boy, and been present during the golden period when the vibrancy and energy of Majlis had earned itself the 'Camelot' moniker. Now, Dubai's future Ruler had returned from his further education to play a leading role within the administration.

"Sheikh Maktoum was an able young man on whom Sheikh Rashid relied a lot. I recall him interjecting with several points during my meetings with Sheikh Rashid. He was astute politically," says Edward Heath. "And then I had the pleasure of meeting Sheikh Hamdan on a number of occasions. I liked him. One could take an instant liking to Sheikh Hamdan."

Sheikh Hamdan had also returned full time to Dubai by 1968, following a stint at the Bell School of Languages. He was 23 years old in 1968, and already destined to head many of his father's economic projects in Dubai.

"Sheikh Hamdan is astute. He is sharp. He always was," says Issam Al Khayat, who was the Arabic-speaking staff member at the Bell School of

On his return from further studies in Britain, a heavy responsibility lay with Sheikh Maktoum assisting his father in government during one of the most crucial periods in the history of the city-state.

Languages. "I always got the impression that he was a heavy-duty thinker. If he was not born a Maktoum he would have been a chief executive."

"Sheikh Rashid always saw Sheikh Hamdan in the role he would eventually take on," says Hamad bin Sukat.

"Dubai's economy was shifting by the late 1960s from the traditional economy to something quite different," says Corrigan. "While Sheikh Rashid could see the opportunities that were coming, his status and indeed his experience could not see him take on day-to-day responsibilities for the commercial and the industrial projects that he had in mind. He had to have someone there he could trust implicitly. That was always going to be Sheikh Hamdan."

In Sheikh Mohammed, Sheikh Rashid had identified a leadership quality that he intended to use. His third son had also completed studies at the Bell School of Languages.

As the high hopes created by the Dubai Agreement dissipated, and several key signatories apparently cooled towards the concept, there was little forward movement. This forced Sheikh Rashid to give serious consideration to the possibility that Dubai might still be a separate entity when the British withdrew at the end of 1971. British records showed that during 1968 he clashed with British officials who sought to encourage a wait-and-see policy before establishing an independent defence capability. Despite the apparent failure of the union process, almost at its inception, the British believed implicitly that a union should be created. Foreign Office records show an emerging pattern of British attempts to undermine the ability of individual states to arm themselves properly.

The richer Union of Arab Emirates members – Abu Dhabi, Bahrain and Qatar – were already actively taking steps to ensure their own security should a union not materialise. In Dubai, which was expecting around £10 million as its first major return from oil in 1969, Sheikh Rashid was determined that the foundations of an army and navy be laid, in addition to a modern police force. The first step in this process had been taken on March 1, 1968, when Sheikh Rashid officially appointed his third son as Head of Police and Public Security, and made it clear to all that Sheikh Mohammed was intended to be the first head of his planned Dubai Defence Force.

Now it was up to Sheikh Mohammed to graduate from Mons Officer

Sheikh Hamdan meets with Pakistani President Zulfikar Ali Bhutto while on an official visit to Pakistan.

Cadet School. On May 1, 1968, Sheikh Mohammed drove himself from the Carlton Towers Hotel in London to Aldershot. In preparation he had studied all the material that he could locate on Mons and had worked himself into the best physical condition of his life. He would need it. The 26-week training course ahead had a failure rate of between 15 and 20%. Some would find the going too tough; at any time they could request a release. If visibly struggling, an officer cadet could be ordered to visit the Mons Commandant, Brigadier Phillip Heidenstram, CBE, from whom he would receive his marching orders.

Brigadier Heidenstram was an imposing character and military man, a veteran mentioned in dispatches while serving in Korea. It was Brigadier Heidenstram who would dispatch cadets who did not make the grade. Officer cadets had been trained at Mons since 1942, when a company was detached from the Royal Military College Sandhurst and renamed the 161 Royal Military College Officer Cadet Training Unit. Six years later, this was changed to Mons Officer Cadet School. The difference between Sandhurst and Mons was one of degree. Colonel R G H Chetwynd-Stapylton, who commanded Sheikh Mohammed's Company, explained: "Sandhurst took in raw fodder and after two years spat out men who could become generals, with few practical skills. Mons took in raw fodder and spat out officers who could command men, good and true. At Mons we offered practical training."

Mons was the principal training school for all potential officers for the British Cavalry and the Artillery until 1972, when it was re-absorbed by Sandhurst. Each intake of officer cadets was divided into two companies which were sub-divided into three platoons. Sheikh Mohammed entered Kohema Company, named after a Second World War battle in Burma.

He was greeted by Sergeant-Major Hillary Benney, a career soldier who had served in the Light Infantry for most of his life. A strict disciplinarian, Sergeant-Major Benney had a fearsome reputation. He had a booming voice and intimidating character – the stereotypical British army sergeant so beloved of film producers.

Sergeant-Major Benney, now retired in the Cornish town of Bodmin, recalls clearly his first encounter with Officer Cadet Rashid – as Sheikh Mohammed was known throughout his time at Mons – a sheikh from the remote Trucial Coast:

Sheikh Mohammed received his military training at Mons Officer Cadet School. His success there was viewed as vital for the future of his home state.

"There was something about him. You could not put your finger on it, but there was a presence that I clearly recall. Of course, I knew who he was. But I was there to do a job, to help develop his skills as an officer, so there was no question among any of the staff at Mons about favouritism or giving young Rashid an easy ride."

First stop at Mons was the Quartermaster, who issued Sheikh Mohammed with his kit. Along with full uniform, this included two pairs of army standard pyjamas, four pairs of 'all soldier' pattern woollen socks, one blue beret, one pair of braces and a grey raincoat. He was also given an ammunition allocation of 1,690 live rounds of various types, 7,400 blanks, 71 flares and 39 hand grenades. He then made his way to one of Kohema Company's barrack blocks, a home that he would share with 11 other men for the next six months.

In 1968, Kohema was a mini-United Nations with representatives from the Bahrain Defence Force, Guyana Defence Force and several other Arab and African states. Its British contingent represented some of the major branches of the British Army, nominated from the Royal Artillery, Royal Hussars, Royal Engineers, Light Infantry and Grenadier Guards.

At the start, there was some friction between British and African cadets. "We stamped on that pretty sharpish," says Sergeant-Major Benney. "That would not be tolerated."

Colonel Brooks recalls the same situation. He says:"One of my keenest recollections of Sheikh Mohammed is that he was not involved himself in this friction. He was accepted by all sides, and I recall that he, very maturely, used this to move between all the groupings. With his help, in a short space of time, we dampened down any friction."

Among Sheikh Mohammed's comrades was a young officer cadet from the Grenadier Guards, Charles Wiggin. Now retired, Wiggin joined Mons full of apprehension. "I arrived knowing no-one. We were all a little nervous at the tests that lay ahead. There was a mixed bunch of boys in Kohema, but we jelled pretty quickly," recalls Wiggin. "I remember Sheikh Mohammed. He just seemed to stand out. The first night we just milled around and got to know each other, especially in the mess where we ate together for the first time. Sheikh Mohammed was very interesting. His background was something different to us Brits and, although he tried to play it down, we pretty quickly got to know who he was."

Mons also had a strict policy that the background of an officer cadet should have no bearing on his time at the school. Indeed, while the British government kept a discreet eye on Sheikh Mohammed's progress throughout his time there, officially only Brigadier Heidenstram was briefed on the importance of his place in Mons. But others came to understand indirectly. Says Sergeant-Major Benney: "During Sheikh Mohammed's time, I came to believe that everything was being monitored, that we were being watched. There were some unusual faces on the base, officers not part of our regular staff."

For British and Western interests, it was strategically important that Sheikh Mohammed return to Dubai with the knowledge and experience that would allow him to lead Dubai's armed forces and police effectively. However, he entered Mons under no illusion that he was somehow immune to failure.

Brigadier Heidenstram showed no favours. This is apparent in his first briefing paper for the British government on Sheikh Mohammed's progress, dated May 24: "He will certainly not be treated differently to anyone else, and in fact the Regimental Sergeant-Major, who had no idea who he was, had him moving in very quick time within a short period from his arrival."

Colonel Brooks adds: "We had an ethic of strong discipline. Like all others, Sheikh Mohammed polished his own boots, cleaned his own living space. No-one escaped these basic duties."

Joining Mons on a Friday, Sheikh Mohammed and his comrades in Kohema were given two days of general base orientation. From Monday, training began in earnest with reveille at 6.30 am and Company muster parade at 8 am. Thereafter, a standard day would unfold through nine periods of training, covering every aspect of military life.

Sheikh Mohammed began the course at a considerable disadvantage to his fellow officer cadets, most of whom had prior military training. However, he was well prepared personally, which may have helped to make up for his lack of military experience. His peers recall his determination. Says Charles Wiggin: "He was very focused on the course. In other areas, such as physical training and anything that included shooting, he was one of the top officer cadets in Kohema."

Guns and ammunition were nothing new to Sheikh Mohammed; he had been handling them most of his life. Even in a technical environment, his experience and natural eye overcame the problems typically associated with being introduced to new weapons. He was also one of the best shots ever encountered by Colonel Brooks, and won many Company shooting

competitions. "I trained hundreds of officer cadets at Mons, yet Sheikh Mohammed stands out as being one of the top. He could pick up any type of rifle or handgun and, after a brief introduction, fire it with tremendous accuracy," says Colonel Brooks. "I remember speaking to him once about his shooting and he informed me that he had just been measured for a pair of Purdeys [the gun world's answer to a Rolls-Royce]. He was very keen on shooting and it showed."

Sergeant-Major Benney remembers his accuracy with a rifle. "I always recall one incident on the firing range. Sheikh Mohammed was explaining his preference for shooting at 800 metres. So I challenged him to prove his accuracy. The targets looked like a dot in the distance, but he proved himself. He hit the centre of the target again and again. We were all somewhat amazed"

During the initial weeks of their time at Mons, officer cadets were schooled in weapons handling, shooting and physical fitness. Other training

Sheikh Mohammed photographed with Kohema Company. Front row centre is Sergent-Major Benney.

covered such skills as map-reading and radio communications. And, of course, there was drill; square-bashing, or parading in formation, was a highly-cherished talent and most days included at least a little marching in formation.

It was a demanding time. Officer cadets were pushed to the limit of their endurance almost from the outset. Most days, the men of Kohema were challenged by a series of platoon exercise drills, night patrol exercises and unprogrammed drills, and endurance tests such as mammoth marches and assault courses while carrying 40 pounds of kit. Those who could not quickly reach and maintain a high level of fitness were soon culled from the course.

On a rare weekend off, Sheikh Mohammed made his way to London to meet friends. One of those in Britain at the time was Mohammed Al Naboodah. "When Sheikh Mohammed took off his boots we were horrified," recalls Al Naboodah. "His feet were a mass of blisters and blood. While he was coping well with the physical aspect of the course, the wear on his feet was quite awful to see."

The course was not all stiff military work. Periods set aside for physical pursuits were not used just for work in the gymnasium. Even in the late 1960s, British Army officers were expected to have basic skills in an array of sports, including boxing, fencing, tennis and cricket. Sheikh Mohammed was first introduced to cricket – 'the Empire's favourite export' – at Mons, but it was one of the few sports that failed to capture his imagination. Nevertheless he is remembered as an aggressive batsman who was not without merit in the slips or fielding at square leg thanks to quick reactions.

Other sports were more to his taste. He took well to Marquess of Queensberry Rules and was competitive in 'milling', three-minute single rounds of boxing. Milling bouts were short but could be bloody, as officer cadets did their best to rearrange their opponent's nose. At Mons, Sheikh Mohammed also became proficient at fencing and played team sports such as football, rugby and hockey.

Sheikh Mohammed had been at Mons for nine weeks before Brigadier Heidenstram offered a comprehensive assessment of progress. On July 19, he cabled the British Political Agent in Dubai with his report. It stated:

> *I am glad to say that he has improved a great deal...and showing signs of leadership qualities. He is quiet and a little shy, but he is popular with the staff and fellow officer cadets. He has done very well with his shooting, and today I was pleased to present to him several trophies that he had won in the Commandant's Shooting Competition.*
>
> *[Sheikh Mohammed] shows promise and I think he is going to do well in the course...In the field he should continue to improve if he continues to show the same determination that he is now displaying.*

After ten weeks, officer cadets had been given at least a brief taste of most disciplines that they would meet while based in Aldershot. At this point they faced their first big hurdle: Exercise Baskerville. In military jargon, this was a C-Type exercise, designed to give them experience of working in a hostile environment. The exercise was conducted over three days on the windswept expanses of Dartmoor National Park, where teams were exposed to the elements, were subjected to extreme sleep deprivation and pushed to the limits of their mental and physical capabilities. Just weeks earlier, two officer cadets attached to Salerno Company at Mons had become lost during Exercise Baskerville and died of hypothermia.

After taking charge of one of three Kohema platoons during Baskerville, Sheikh Mohammed showed his strength of leadership to Colonel Chetwynd-Stapylton in one incident that remains with the colonel to the present day.

"When Sheikh Mohammed gave the order to his men, someone questioned his plan. Obviously this is not done in the Army. Sheikh Mohammed picked this fellow up by the scruff of the neck and made it clear in no uncertain terms that he was in command and this was his order," says Colonel Chetwynd-Stapylton. "He stamped his authority and impressed me with his sense of leadership."

In the wake of Exercise Baskerville, Sheikh Mohammed was given a grading of 23 for his officer-like qualities, on a scale of 30 to minus 10. Only a couple of officer cadets in Kohema obtained a higher grade at this key part of the course. He was also within striking distance of the Stick of Honour, presented at Passing Out to the leading cadet in each Company, or the prestigious Sword of Honour, presented at Passing Out to the leading foreign and Commonwealth officer cadet in each course.

After Exercise Baskerville, Exercise Marathon, staged in the 14th week of the course, was comparatively easy for Sheikh Mohammed. Primarily a defensive exercise, it brought into play all aspects of war at Company level. After Exercise Marathon, in early September, Brigadier Heidenstram contacted the British authorities with a further update for Sheikh Rashid. He wrote that Sheikh Mohammed was:

> ...definitely benefiting from the course. He is much fitter than he was, and is a very good shot...in the field he shows leadership. He is popular with his fellow cadets and has tried his best. He is now approaching the end of the course and I have every reason to believe and hope that he will pass out...He has one further big test to complete and that is Battle Camp in South Wales...

By the time of this dispatch to Dubai, Brigadier Heidenstram had agreed to a decision made by those dealing directly with their young officer cadet from Dubai; Colonel Brooks, Colonel Chetwynd-Stapylton and Sergeant-Major Benney. During the latter stages of the six months, it was traditional to appoint one officer cadet as Senior Under Officer (SUO) and two as Junior Under Officer (JUO). SUOs and JUOs take on permanent responsibilities for organising the Company and assume partial leadership over it. Sheikh Mohammed was made SUO.

The Brecon Beacons cover some 519 square miles of Wales, more than half of it 1,000 feet above sea level. A national park, it is a beautiful area with dramatic scenery and varied wild life, a wild landscape of open moors and waterfalls, windswept mountains and sheltered valleys. The very remoteness and ruggedness that contributes to its beauty also made the Brecon Beacons ideal for the Mons Officer Cadet School's Battle Camp, the final and most difficult test of its officer cadets. Walkers, nature lovers and campers may relish the area, but officer cadets seldom recall anything but the brutality of the place from their days at Battle Camp.

Battle Camp finished just two weeks before the Commissioning Parade, meaning that it is virtually the last opportunity for officer cadets to show their commanding officers that they had mastered the skills expected in an officer. It was also the last chance for Mons to weed out those who had not achieved the necessary standard. Battle Camp, therefore, threw just about everything at officer cadets.

Returning to Mons after 12 days, officer cadets had to wait several days for confirmation that they had made the grade. Sheikh Mohammed had entered Battle Camp with a 22-plus rating and seemed to have produced an excellent performance.

Two days after returning from Wales, Kohema Company was notified of the final results. Each officer cadet was ushered into the office of Colonel Brooks, who would then pass judgement.

"Sheikh Mohammed was not given to public displays, but you could see in his eyes how delighted he was when I informed him that he had completed Mons successfully," says Colonel Brooks.

Not only had Sheikh Mohammed finished the six months at Mons with no drop in his rating, but he had also won the Sword of Honour for achieving the highest mark of any foreign or Commonwealth officer cadet in his intake.

During October 1968, Britain's Minister of Defence, Dennis Healey, had scheduled an inspection tour of Mons. The future of the school was at stake as the Wilson government struggled to make budget cuts at home as well as abroad. Determined to put on a sterling performance to show the minister the significance of Mons Officer Cadet School, on the day of Healey's visit the facility was at its finest. Buildings had been spruced up and restored, the grounds has been manicured, and the officer cadets had been drilled and redrilled to the peak of perfection.

Healey was due at 11 am. Shortly before this, row upon row of officer cadets were standing rigid in the parade square at Mons. As Senior Under Officer, Sheikh Mohammed stood slightly ahead of his fellow officer cadets. But when Brigadier Heidenstram appeared on the Mons Parade Ground a few minutes before Healey, this honour threatened to turn into a liability for Sheikh Mohammed. Heidenstram noticed Sheikh Mohammed was out of line with the rest of the Company. What followed has made its way into Dubai folklore as an illustration of leadership under fire. Brigadier Heidenstram informed Sergeant-Major Benney of his displeasure.

"Officer Cadet Rashid!" Benney bellowed: "Take two steps left!"

Sheikh Mohammed, thinking like a commander, immediately responded: "Kohema…two steps right!" And the 40 or so cadets quickly adjusted their positions.

Sergeant-Major Benney recalls his surprise. In Dubai the incident is today almost a legend, both an indicator of Sheikh Mohammed's abilities and as a principle of leadership.

The Commissioning Parade was held on October 18, 1968. As usual, a guest of honour was present. On this occasion, it was the Duke of Cumberland. Among the parents and relatives of these new officers was Sheikh Rashid, who had undertaken a time-consuming trip to be present at one of the defining moments of his son's life.

Those who were close to Sheikh Rashid testify that it was a defining moment in the Ruler's life, too. With the union process under way and Dubai undergoing a radical development programme, he rarely left Dubai, let alone on such a demanding journey to Britain. However, being at Mons for Sheikh Mohammed's Commissioning Parade was of personal importance.

"Sheikh Rashid would never have missed going to Mons for Sheikh Mohammed's Passing Out. He was so, so proud," says Hamad bin Sukat. This opinion is reflected by those who took the opportunity to meet Sheikh Rashid in England. Accompanied by a small entourage, the Dubai

Ruler held what was described as an informal Majlis in the Officers' Mess in order to meet those who had worked with his son.

"Sheikh Rashid had an intense presence. You could feel something of an aura," recalls Colonel Brooks. "I remember that Sheikh Mohammed was translating for his father. Sheikh Rashid told me that he was delighted that Sheikh Mohammed had passed through Mons successfully, very proud of him. Then he commented that Sheikh Mohammed was to return to Dubai where there was important work for him to do."

In a post-course report on Sheikh Mohammed's time at Mons Officer Cadet School, Colonel Chetwynd-Stapylton stated:

> *[Sheikh Mohammed] has benefited from the course at Mons. He has improved out of all recognition and has shown his instructors that he is capable of commanding and leading men. He has found his lack of expressiveness in English a small obstacle, but has made up for this by decisive action carried out with confidence and dash. He is well liked in the platoon and I'm sure will do well.*

Sheikh Rashid's confidence had been rewarded not only with a glowing report from Mons and his son's achievement in winning the Sword of Honour. By the winter of 1968, he had at his side a person who could effectively head the Dubai Defence Force and the Dubai Police Force. More importantly – with three years remaining before Britain withdrew its forces from the Gulf – Sheikh Rashid had the educated and able Sheikh Mohammed alongside him with Sheikh Maktoum, Sheikh Hamdan and Sheikh Ahmed, a quartet of men on whom he could rely when times got tough.

Sheikh Rashid with then Saudi Arabian Crown Prince Fahd ibn Abdul Aziz Al Saud. Despite pressing affairs of state Sheikh Rashid undertook an arduous round trip to Britain to attend Sheikh Mohammed's graduation from Mons.

Chapter Seventeen

A Long and Winding Road

Honest disagreement is often a good sign of progress.
— *Mahatma Gandhi, father of India*

After weeks of diplomacy and days of direct deliberations and negotiations, in February 1968, nine leaders had signed an agreement in Dubai to create the Union of Arab Emirates. It was a serious undertaking. Yet several returned to their palaces and disappeared off the political scene. The Union was to be headed by a Supreme Council and even this austere body did not meet ahead of the stated date on which the new state was to have been created.

The union was a false dawn. But there was too much at stake – perhaps the very existence of these nine small sheikhdoms – to let the union project, in whatever form, fail. Again Sheikh Rashid and Sheikh Zayed were left to pick up the pieces. The two were in regular and frequent contact by telephone, deciding the way forward to be a meeting between the most senior advisors of the nine Rulers. In inviting representation at the meeting, they insisted that the other Rulers send delegations able to genuinely act on their behalf.

This was set for May 18, and Dubai sent a three member delegation which included Sheikh Rashid's legal advisor, Uday Al Bitar, and two of his most trusted advisors, Ahmed bin Sulayem and Mahdi Al Tajir. This closed-door meeting, free of much of the distanced respect that the Rulers bestowed on each other, seems to have been a gloves-off affair. Many came to the table with differing views on what needed to be achieved before a formal constitution was adopted and this, as much as any fundamental difference of opinion, proved a major sticking point.

Despite agreeing on a method to pursue a constitution, the meeting

Sheikh Rashid fought to save the Union of Arab Emirates, which was almost still-born at birth and consistently faltered as many Rulers failed to follow through on key decisions.

was overshadowed by the concerns of the representatives from Ajman, Fujairah, Ras Al Khaimah, Sharjah and Umm Al Quwain, that the bigger four states sought to dominate them. Ras Al Khaimah's representatives were particularly adamant that a United Arab Coastal Emirates grouping, subservient to a larger federation, would not be allowed to happen. Indeed, Ras Al Khaimah's opinion of the whole federal process was coloured for some years by the proposed UACE formation.

The same state's proposal for the President of the federation to be democratically elected was supported by Bahrain, but defeated under vote, as were plans to recommend a federal capital and another setting out the parameters of the Federal Council. It was, however, decided that to move forward, a committee of five members would sit in Qatar to plot the future common currency, while another would be based in Dubai working on integrating the postal systems. In addition, Bahrain was to host a follow-up committee and Abu Dhabi a liaison committee. The follow-up committee was charged with proposing the formation of federal ministries, setting up a federal gazette and managing financial matters. Most significant, however, was the abandoning of what many saw as a wrong decision in Dubai that Federal Council motions could only be adopted by unanimous vote. This was understood to be impractical and was replaced with a simple majority voting system.

It seemed a progressive meeting, but too many decisions were put off and delegated to committees. The old adage, that a camel was simply a horse designed by a committee, was just as true for a union of nine sheikhdoms. The process needed decisive action, not procrastination in a time-consuming committee stage. Sheikh Rashid was reported to be furious at the outcome.

The Union of Arab Emirates had been due to come into being on March 30, 1968. That date came and went without so much as a meeting of the nine Rulers. Indeed, the next meeting of the nine did not take place until May 18, six weeks into the theoretical life of this federation. Staged in Abu Dhabi, it achieved little beyond confirming that the Northern Emirates – Sharjah, Ajman, Umm Al Quwain, Ras Al Khaimah and Fujairah – felt that the richer sheikhdoms were attempting to dominate the group.

Over two days and four sessions – one of which was so high-level only the nine Rulers themselves were present – they reached some measure of consensus. There was agreement that a draft constitution should be drawn up by several independent Arab experts, working with the retained legal advisors of the nine states. Even the standard buoyant final communiqué played down any progress, stating:

> *Between 25 and 26 May, the first meeting of the Supreme Council of the UAE was convened in Abu Dhabi. The Rulers of the emirates exchanged consultations on the best methods by which to implement the Dubai Agreement...From these consultations it transpired that there is some divergence of opinion regarding how this should be done. The Rulers were of the opinion that this meeting be adjourned, with another meeting of the Supreme Council to be convened on July 1, giving opportunity for more consultation in the hope of reaching agreement...*

Another meeting went ahead on July 7 and continued until the evening of July 9. Some progress was made this time. Qatar, now the most ardent federalist, unveiled its independently-advised draft constitution. This was loosely supported by Qatar's ally Kuwait, but most within the grouping saw the draft as biased in favour of the Qataris themselves.

Over and above the previous summit, this latest meeting invited the noted Egyptian constitutional expert, Dr Abdul Razaq Sanhuri, who drafted the Kuwaiti constitution, to take part in the process. In anticipation of this, the nine Rulers also finalised plans for the Provisional Federal Council (PFC) which had been set out in the original Dubai Agreement, charged with state affairs, drafting a federal budget and dealing with other key areas. Sheikh Khalifa bin Hamad Al Thani was appointed chairman of the PFC in an open vote, and the council at large set to comprise nine deputations, each headed by a member of the Ruling family. Sheikh Maktoum was to serve as head of Dubai's representation, with Ahmed bin Sulayem, Juma Al Majid and Majid Al Futtaim serving under him. The PFC met for the first time in September in Qatar.

But both Sheikh Rashid and Sheikh Zayed, the two leading players within the process, were now expressing doubts over the Union of Arab Emirates. Those in the Majlis at this time recalled that in private Sheikh Rashid was extremely worried. However, the two Rulers kept their reservations closely guarded. One of the few written references to their misgivings exists in British records of a visit that Sheikh Zayed made to London that summer. During a meeting with the Minister of State for

Sheikh Rashid pictured during a Union of Arab Emirates meeting. Next to him is seated Sheikh Maktoum, to their rear Ahmed bin Sulayem, part of the Dubai delegation. Also along the table are (l-r) Sheikh Saqr bin Mohammed Al Qassimi, Ruler of Ras Al Khaimah, Sheikh Hamad bin Khalifa Al Thani, Crown Prince of Qatar, and Sheikh Ahmed bin Ali Al Thani, Ruler of Qatar.

Foreign Affairs, he stated: "I had not realised that the process would take so long. Nearly a year has passed, but not a quarter of what was necessary has been achieved. A beginning on common defence should have been made well before this. I have tried everything possible..."

"Sheikh Rashid was one of the most ardent supporters of the concept of a federation or union," says Abdullah Saleh. "But he was frustrated at the lack of concerted action. When at last events brought about some movement, that had cheered him considerably.

"The impression I had from colleagues around the nine states was that Sheikh Rashid was really quite well respected. The other Rulers trusted him, understanding that he was not just looking at the federation from the point of view of boosting his own personal standing or power base," adds Saleh. "Certainly Sheikh Rashid wanted the best for Dubai. He told us as much. However he knew Dubai could not prosper in a climate of instability. The federation offered additional stability – both economically and politically."

With the future of their lands so uncertain, Sheikh Rashid and his fellow Rulers found themselves coming under sustained pressure from all sides. The people of the Trucial Coast, for so long without any voice in regional politics, were speaking out. They made it abundantly clear that they were deeply unhappy with events unfolding around the on-again, off-again Union of Arab Emirates. Fairly or unfairly, Bahrain and Qatar were blamed and many in the Trucial States wanted a union that excluded these two.

Significant pressure was also coming from across the Gulf in Iran. The self-aggrandising Shah, following his 'divine path' policy, claiming that God had told him to unite the region, pressed territorial claims against his neighbours, including Bahrain, Qatar, Sharjah and Ras Al Khaimah. To back up his claims, the Shah spent billions of dollars in building the Middle East's strongest military machine, while in Iran his people suffered through a worsening economic situation.

With his eye on 'uniting' the Gulf (presumably under an Iranian flag) the Shah welcomed Britain's decision to withdraw from the region. This would leave the smaller sheikhdoms divided, weak and largely undefended, easy pickings for Iran. Predictably, he was angered by talk of a union that would make them stronger and just a little more secure.

Denunciations of the Union of Arab Emirates became a regular theme of Iranian Ministry of Foreign Affairs' statements during this time. In October 1968, the ministry stated that Iran "has always been opposed to colonialism in all forms…[and] the so-called federation of the Persian Gulf emirates, by annexing the islands of Bahrain to it, is considered a matter which cannot be acceptable to the Iranian government…"

During the summer of 1968, Sheikh Rashid met with Iranian Prime Minister Amir Abbas-Hoveyda in Tehran. Abbas-Hoveyda's vaguely positive stance toward the federation contrasted with earlier angry and provocative statements. Without referring to Bahrain by name, Abbas-Hoveyda implied that Iran was dropping its territorial claim by saying that Iran wished well to "all the emirates". But the Iranians continued to cast a long and worrisome shadow over the Gulf.

Amid these pressures, Sheikh Maktoum, bin Sulayem, Al Majid and Al Futtaim would have their work cut out if they were to ensure that the Provisional Federal Council built upon the limited progress achieved.

Sheikh Maktoum was at the centre of Majlis discussions over the coming weeks as Dubai's leader discussed strategy. The Provisional Federal Council had been given limited powers to steer the general direction of the proposed federation, and mistakes at this stage would be paid for later.

"Sheikh Rashid had made it clear at all levels that he believed the future of the Trucial States depended on a positive outcome," says Hussain Khansaheb.

The Provisional Federal Council sat for the first time on September 8, 1968, in Qatar, following a quiet time during the summer utilised by most of the nine states to take stock of the overall situation. Rumours of a membership invitation for Kuwait proved unfounded, but most of the ruling families had dispatched senior members to London, Tehran and Jeddah for talks.

The Qatar meeting itself got the winter off to a flying start with what was unanimously agreed to be a constructive atmosphere. Much was agreed and Sheikh Maktoum returned with his team to Dubai full of optimism.

The next Supreme Council meeting was programmed for October in Qatar, only interceded by a previously arranged meeting of the seven-member Trucial States Council, at which they agreed on a £2 million British-sponsored budget.

Sheikh Rashid arrived in Qatar accompanied by Sheikh Maktoum and Sheikh Mohammed as part of Dubai's delegation. Delegates used the impetus created by the Abu Dhabi summit to further the aims of the union. The meeting in Doha was described by Sheikh Rashid as the most constructive gathering in which he had been involved since the Dubai Agreement eight months before. This spirit of optimism led to a third Supreme Council meeting on the peninsula in October. But the Maktoums were realists and left Qatar under no illusion that time continued to be wasted in futile debate over unimportant points.

One example was the issue of Union Commissions, a means of orchestrating common policy and unification in key areas. The commission structure was accepted and, after debate, it was decided that three should be based in Qatar (labour and social security, real estate, health), one in Dubai (commerce), one in Abu Dhabi (communications) and one in Bahrain (foreign policy). Bahrain objected, demanding that some of the commissions – specifically two of Qatar's three – be redistributed to the smaller sheikhdoms, despite the fact that they were ill-equipped. Others were clearly exasperated.

"Be it this or that," erupted a frustrated Sheikh Saqr bin Mohammed Al Qassimi, Ruler of Ras Al Khaimah, "the important thing is that the commissions should accomplish the tasks for which they have been set up."

Although this issue was subsequently settled, divisive and time-wasting debate over minor points drove home the fact that all was not well.

During this period, Sheikh Hamdan and Sheikh Mohammed became vital to the union process. Their father was one of the key players in the search for a successful formula. Their elder brother was integral in the Provisional Federal Council.

Sheikh Hamdan and Sheikh Mohammed were now in close contact with the eight Rulers in the Union of Arab Emirates, and with representatives from Saudi Arabia, Kuwait, Jordan, Egypt, Syria, Britain and the Arab League, to name a few. In a society and culture steeped in etiquette, politics involved direct contact at the highest level. With so many participants within the process, and many others who needed regular briefing, Sheikh Rashid now used his sons as roving ambassadors.

Sheikh Maktoum, Sheikh Hamdan and Sheikh Mohammed were regularly dispatched to meet with the Rulers of the sheikhdoms on their father's behalf, as well as to Kuwait and Saudi Arabia.

Sheikh Rashid came to rely upon his sons as roving emmisaries, representing Dubai in the union process.

"I was highly impressed with Sheikh Mohammed, even from a young age. In many ways, he is very much like his father," said Sheikh Saqr of Ras Al Khaimah. "Sheikh Rashid was our brother. His personality and ability were vital to the creation of a union. While we were attempting to build the federation, Sheikh Mohammed often travelled to Ras Al Khaimah to personally convey a message from Sheikh Rashid. Sheikh Hamdan was also acting on Sheikh Rashid's behalf."

The following month the nine met again, this time in Sharjah on November 26, where in addition to calling on the World Bank for help to produce an economic study, they tackled the thorny issue of defence and agreed ways of dealing with Iranian intransigence, even open hostility, towards the federation. The latter point, perhaps the trickiest, had improved slightly during the round of shuttle diplomacy that summer, when Qatar and Iran agreed to demarcate disputed territory.

Preceding months had given them a glimmer of hope because the nine sheikhdoms had appeared to be cooperating. However, those acquainted with the process understood that unity had been achieved by side-stepping the difficult issues that divided the nine.

Even before this meeting, Sheikh Maktoum and Sheikh Mohammed had found themselves working to restore calm within the body. The Provisional Federal Council had been due to sit on November 19. However, Sharjah was struggling to prepare for the meeting so the venue was switched to Qatar. Bahrain objected, stating that if the meeting went ahead in Doha it would boycott it. As a result, the meeting was postponed one week to give Sharjah time to arrange its facilities.

"Petty squabbling came to be the bane of the entire union process at this time," said Sheikh Saqr. "With Sheikh Rashid's full authority, his sons quietly worked behind the scenes to smooth the strains we were seeing."

When the meeting finally got under way in Sharjah, Sheikh Maktoum and Sheikh Mohammed had their father's clear and simple instructions as a guiding light: "Do not do anything against Dubai's strategic interests, but other than that, do anything that creates consensus. Time is running out."

That Sheikh Rashid, one of the fathers of the entire process, was expressing grave worries shows just how little actual progress had been made up to this point. Dubai's leadership hoped Sharjah would prove a watershed, but recognised that when greater issues were at stake, fighting over a venue was not a good omen. In the event, even the most pessimistic would have had difficulty in foreseeing just how badly the opportunities presented at the Sharjah meeting would be squandered.

Despite Sheikh Maktoum's insistence during this meeting that decisions should be reached, a majority vote deferred several crucial issues, such as how to approach defence and foreign policy. Even a scheduled debate on the union's education system was side-stepped. But after dumping all the contentious issues in favour of less difficult ones, consensus was still hard to come by. Both Sheikh Maktoum and Sheikh Mohammed were astonished as wrangling went on for several hours over the design of a union flag. Finally, when it became clear that agreement on a flag would prove impossible, the Provisional Federal Council ended its session in failure. It was abundantly clear that under present conditions, there was little hope of achieving anything of substance before the end of 1971.

What happened next, though, was a surprise to everyone. Once again several leaders got cold feet, and by March 1969 cracks were beginning to appear in the overall process. On March 17, Bahrain's Ruler, Sheikh Isa bin Salman Al Khalifa, told a group of visiting journalists that; "Conceivably there could be a situation in which Bahrain might not become a member of any federation. Bahrain is capable of going it alone. We are able to support our own statehood and could apply to become members of the United Nations..."

Bahrain's apparently growing disquiet sparked a flurry of diplomatic activity throughout the area, and by the fifth meeting of the Supreme

Council, in May, an earlier feeling of optimism had all but disappeared. Qatar continued to champion the federal cause, opening with an extensive agenda. The nine Rulers could not agree even on this, and much of the first day was spent clarifying a new formula for the meeting. Indeed, it has since been suggested that the Qataris' obvious determination to pursue a regional grouping could have been misinterpreted, with this leading to concern in other areas. Even when debate got under way, it soon became abundantly clear that little was being achieved. At the end of five days, the longest-ever summit, the result was a disappointment. The major issues, presidential election, ministerial appointment, defence integration, the naming of a capital and design of the federal flag, remained unresolved and were deferred.

"Both Sheikh Rashid and Sheikh Maktoum were constantly involved in meetings with fellow Rulers and Provisional Federal Council members in the run-up to the Doha meeting," says Humaid bin Drai. "They returned bitterly disappointed at the lack of progress."

As expected, Bahrain had been the most vocal in its unwillingness to bend on some issues, no more so than over a proposed Federal Parliament. Sheikh Rashid attended one more UAE Supreme Council meeting in Qatar in May 1969. Ras Al Khaimah's Sheikh Saqr commented: "Sheikh Rashid was a builder. He often dropped his own pre-conditions, in order to support a majority vote, in the hope that this helped. Sheikh Rashid was selfless and we appreciated his efforts. In the evenings, after the end of scheduled business, he worked into the night meeting with fellow Rulers privately."

Sheikh Mohammed was part of Dubai's representation and circulated around Qatar, visiting the Rulers and their closest aides and swapping ideas, in the search for common ground. He was a natural negotiator and haggled over issues with Sheikh Rashid's full blessing, often returning to his father's side with a different perspective on a problem.

Former UAE Minister of Education Dr Abdullah Omran Taryam says: "In many ways, Sheikh Mohammed could afford to be a little more blunt and hard-nosed than his father. Because of this, along with the understanding that he could speak for Sheikh Rashid, he was able to move among the various parties very effectively."

During the Doha meeting, the nine parties debated one of the most important and most divisive issues on the table, that of representation in a proposed parliamentary body, the Federal National Council (FNC).

The smaller sheikhdoms, wary of being sidelined, favoured a plan that would give four seats each to all nine. However the four biggest states – Abu Dhabi, Bahrain, Dubai and Qatar – were home to around 80% of the population of the proposed union. Dubai had a population of around 60,000 people, Bahrain three times that, with an estimated 180,000. At the other end of the scale Umm Al Quwain was home to 3,700 residents while Ajman had around 4,200. Under the equal representation plan, each Dubai delegate would theoretically represent 15,000 people, while each Bahraini had 45,000 constituents. By contrast, Umm Al Quwain would have a delegate for every 925 citizens and Ajman for every 1,050.

Clearly this could have been a major sticking point. Dubai quietly signalled it was prepared to set aside its own desire for equal representation in favour of limited proportional representation in order to satisfy the more populous states, especially Bahrain. While proportional representation was not necessarily in Dubai's interests, Sheikh Rashid altered his position to keep Bahrain on track.

The nine parties still left Qatar fundamentally divided by self-interest, but feeling that a breakthrough might be possible. With the arrival of summer and rocketing temperatures in the Middle East, the union process slipped into low gear as the main protagonists left for extended holidays in cooler climates. This included Sheikh Rashid, who had been invited to make a state visit to Britain several years before and saw an opportunity to fulfil his obligations as a Ruler, while also consulting his allies in London.

This politically sensitive visit began on July 20, with Goronwy Roberts, the Minister of State for Foreign Affairs, and Queen Elizabeth's representative, Lord Westmorland, greeting Sheikh Rashid as he stepped off a flight at Heathrow Airport. Having left Sheikh Hamdan in Dubai to run affairs of state, Sheikh Rashid's party included Crown Prince Sheikh Maktoum, Chief of Police and Public Security Sheikh Mohammed, senior advisors Bill Duff, Hamad bin Sukat and Easa Saleh Al Gurg. Al Gurg would subsequently serve a extended term as UAE Ambassador to Great Britain.

Ahead lay five days of official functions and political meetings. Predictably, however, Sheikh Rashid's enquiring mind was set on a different course. Among other sites, he had requested to be shown Felixstowe Port and the Royal Aircraft Establishment at Farnborough, both major installations serving industries that interested him. At this juncture he was rapidly developing Port Rashid and Dubai International Airport as lynchpins within Dubai's non-oil economy.

From Farnborough, the party flew by helicopter to RAF Fairford where they viewed the almost-completed 002 Concorde, the second prototype of this new supersonic passenger aircraft, just weeks before it flew for the first time. Brian Trubshaw, chief test pilot for commercial aircraft of BAC and Concorde's pilot, guided the Dubai party around the airplane.

The delegation also visited Scotland Yard and the Wexham Park Hospital in Windsor. Sheikh Rashid had been in London several times before, but always on fleeting visits. This time, after settling into the Dorchester Hotel, he used any gaps in his schedule to explore aspects of the city that intrigued him. One story from a previous visit has Sheikh Rashid abruptly stopping his official car outside the Knightsbridge Station of London Underground. Without warning, he and his party headed off across London by 'Tube', returning to Knightsbridge half an hour later, when an impressed Sheikh Rashid was satisfied and ready to continue with his official programme.

However, the undeniable emphasis of the trip remained political. Sheikh Rashid was less than pleased at Britain's handling of its Gulf policy. He sought to convey his unease directly to senior officials in the government, while also attempting to draw Britain's position closer to his own. On July 21, accompanied by his sons, Sheikh Rashid called on Foreign Secretary Michael Stewart in Whitehall. A day later they met for two hours with Goronwy Roberts at the Foreign Office, before taking the short journey to 10 Downing Street for face-to-face talks with Prime Minister Harold Wilson.

After some difficult times in office, Labour's fortunes had been on the rise as the General Election approached with some economic indicators showing positive signs. Wilson was optimistic of victory, but Labour's lead in the opinion polls was shaky. A year before, at the time of Britain's withdrawal announcement, Wilson had been a lame duck due to his government's handling of the economy. Now, Sheikh Rashid, Sheikh Maktoum and Sheikh Mohammed met a man confident of retaining his position. Wilson had little grasp of Gulf politics but had been well briefed. A scheduled 25-minute meeting was extended to 45 minutes as the two leaders – both straight-talking men – spoke frankly to each other.

The Arab world was none too keen on Wilson. With his outward demeanour and Yorkshire burr, hopes had been high that he would prove to be a good leader with the common touch. Instead, there had been disappointment. Worst of all, cited his critics later, he supported the US invasion of Vietnam with a passion that inspired US President Lyndon Johnson to describe him as "another Churchill". He made many mistakes in handling the Middle East too.

Yet, despite the failures of the Labour government, the Maktoums gained a favourable impression of Wilson. He was a man who got to the point and did not digress into platitudes. Wilson put on only the minimum of social graces, got to the point in any discussion and almost made a point of accentuating his Yorkshire accent to underline his working-class roots. His genuineness appealed to those who had direct contact with him.

In the few relaxed moments of their encounter, Wilson enquired about Sheikh Mohammed's time at Mons Officer Cadet School and questioned Sheikh Maktoum about Gordonstoun.

Later the same day, Sheikh Rashid, accompanied by his two sons, visited Buckingham Palace for a private lunch with Queen Elizabeth. The British Monarch and the Arab Ruler formed a friendship that day, unimpeded by language or cultural barriers, that lasted until Sheikh Rashid's death two decades later. At the end of the afternoon he insisted that she visit Dubai – an invitation she would finally accept in 1979 – and was himself invited back to Buckingham Palace.

"Of course the conversation was drawn out as it was running through an interpreter, but you could tell that Queen Elizabeth and Sheikh Rashid warmed to each other," says Humaid bin Drai. "Despite very different backgrounds they were very much alike, caring sincerely for the future of their people. Both had long espoused working against social deprivation and worked for the betterment of their respective countries."

Horses were a major topic. The adrenalin of thoroughbred ownership was still some years away for Sheikh Maktoum and Sheikh Mohammed, but both had a passion for horses. The Queen, on the other hand, was a highly competitive thoroughbred owner, having won her first Classic, the 2000 Guineas, a decade earlier with 'Pall Mall'. Sheikh Maktoum and Sheikh Mohammed, were adept in the saddle themselves, and

Sheikh Rashid and Queen Elizabeth II.

shared a love of all things equestrian with the Queen, who herself hunted and attended racing, polo and show jumping events. Equestrianism was probably the only common thread between the Queen of England and the Dubai Crown Prince and the Head of Dubai Police and Public Security, but it was a strong enough bond to spark a friendship that endured. A day after lunching at Buckingham Palace, the party attended racing at Sandown Park, a top class racecourse just outside London. Later in the trip, they enjoyed a visit to Earl's Court exhibition centre where they attended the Royal Tournament, accompanied by Goronwy Roberts.

After the end of this official portion of the State Visit, Sheikh Rashid stayed on in the United Kingdom and enjoyed a mini-holiday away from the pressures facing him at home. Sheikh Mohammed accompanied him by rail to Scotland aboard the Flying Scotsman. For a week, the Dubai party relaxed and took in some of Scotland's sites, including Edinburgh Castle.

Sheikh Rashid revelled in the beautiful Scottish countryside and warmed to the friendly people. Intrigued by the talk of a monster, Sheikh Rashid also made his way to Loch Ness to see what all the fuss was about. Whatever the claims of sightings through the years, in late July 1969, when Sheikh Rashid looked out over the Loch, 'Nessie' failed to put in an appearance.

At the beginning of August, the party flew back to Dubai. Sheikh Rashid and his advisors were delighted with the political progress made on the trip and – perhaps just as importantly as far as his sons were concerned – the trip had proven a useful opportunity to see that Sheikh Rashid had a break from his high-pressure schedule. Sheikh Rashid was in his late 50s at this juncture and worked 18 hours a day, overseeing all of Dubai's development with his own personal touch. On top of this, he was a central figure in the time-consuming process of attempting to form a union, leading those around him to express concern over the toll that stress could take on his health.

Sheikh Rashid enjoyed his first and only state visit to Great Britain, but the pressures of home never left him. Time was running out and, at the end of 1971, the sheikhdoms were to be cut adrift by the British. The future looked bright for Dubai, but a cloud of uncertainty was growing over the whole Arabian Peninsula. Concerted action was needed if disaster was to be avoided.

.

Chapter Eighteen

State of the Union

*If men would consider not so much wherein they differ, as
wherein they agree, there would be far less of
uncharitableness and angry feeling.*
- Joseph Addison, dramatist

During the winter of 1968 and into the early months of 1969, Sheikh
Rashid and his sons laboured to build consensus. Along with Sheikh
Zayed of Abu Dhabi, Sheikh Rashid believed that the nine sheikhdoms
should stand together in terms of both economics and security, yet
neither was blinded by the fact that the process was beset with problems.

Sheikh Zayed and Sheikh Rashid agreed that if a nine-member union
faltered, they would explore the possibility of a seven-member Trucial
States union, or a smaller grouping. Sheikh Zayed described it as
"riding three horses together until it could be seen clearly which one
was the best."

The individual sheikhdoms could simply not afford to sit and wait for
some degree of union to come their way. It was clear that a formula for
a successful union might not be found before the British withdrawal at
the end of 1971. If this happened and the colonial era ended with only
a fledgling union and no security apparatus, the potential for instability
would present irresistible opportunities to at least one expansionist
neighbour.

In Dubai, Sheikh Mohammed was building an effective police force
and laying the foundations for the Dubai Defence Force (DDF). He
began the process of acquiring fighter-training aircraft, tanks, personnel
carriers and small attack boats to defend the coast. He also began
recruiting men for both branches of the sheikhdom's security force. The
Dubai Police grew from 100 men to 450 within the two years between

*Sheikh Mohammed was charged with the sheikhdom's security, building
both the Dubai Defence Force and Dubai Police.*

1969 and the end of 1970. The DDF went from a concept to a body of 500 men over a similar duration.

"Sheikh Mohammed immersed himself in building Dubai's internal and external security forces," says Major General Dhahi Khalfan Tamim, chief of Dubai Police. "He had a strict deadline, Britain's withdrawal, and the very future of Dubai was at stake. As such, Sheikh Mohammed took his position very seriously indeed."

Sheikh Mohammed now had to take the skills, techniques and theory he had learned at Mons Officer Cadet School and apply them to Dubai's particular environment. Fortunately, the discipline of military life is much the same the world over, with just a few tweaks to take local conditions into account. In Dubai, the rigidity of Mons translated into a well-organised and highly-trained force. Aided initially by a number of expatriate officers, Sheikh Mohammed sought to use the limited resources at his disposal to ensure that his men were trained and armed to the highest standards. At the very least, he believed Dubai could quickly have an effective lightly-armed force, even if heavy weapons had to wait. Dubai's fledgling army soon set what were, at the time, the most rigorous entrance exams for potential recruits of any of the Trucial States. Men winning a place in either the DDF or Dubai Police could expect to face a testing regime that had its roots in the elite training at Mons.

Khalifa Al Naboodah, a close military aide to Sheikh Mohammed during the early years, says: "In a remarkably short time, early DDF platoons were marching on the parade ground like they had been doing it for years. Most were also being educated for the first time too. It was a fringe benefit, and a powerful attraction for new recruits."

The British Political Resident of this time reported: "Despite being founded later than the armed forces in several other sheikhdoms and not being the best armed, Dubai Defence Force was well respected and very much looked the part."

The DDF and Dubai Police had plenty of work at hand in a town that was bustling with activity. By the last years of the 1960s, oil receipts were filtering into the state's coffers. Since acceding to power in 1958, Sheikh Rashid had achieved a remarkable amount of progress without petro-dollars. With millions now at Sheikh Rashid's disposal, and a guaranteed income for the first time, the Camelot Majlis had the finances to make a greater impact on Dubai than Kennedy's White

House could ever have dreamed of making on the United States.

Between 1956 and 1968, the population had almost doubled from 30,000 to 59,000. This was directly attributable to Sheikh Rashid's pro-business outlook, coupled with the standard of living found in the sheikhdom through the provision of social services such as water and electricity.

"Dubai was growing at astonishing speed during the late 1960s," says Qassim Sultan, former head of Dubai Municipality. "It was incumbent upon Sheikh Hamdan to steer Dubai Municipality during a period in which we were both expanding at a dramatic rate and the demands placed upon Dubai Municipality were enormous."

Abdullah Saleh, one of Sheikh Rashid's young guns in the Majlis at this time, recalls the Ruler's mantra in the 1960s; "He was acutely aware that some other Gulf states had enveloped the business community in red tape, new taxes and stifling regulations. He often reminded those of us concerned with the commercial sector to make it as easy as possible for legitimate businesses to trade here. It was Sheikh Rashid's open door policy and a lack of red tape which attracted many to do business here."

This was a theme voiced consistently by Sheikh Rashid, particularly to his sons, whom he schooled in the principle of simplicity in government and administration.

"My father was convinced that the only way to attract businesses, and to keep them here, was to foster the correct environment. This was his first and last rule of business," says Sheikh Hamdan. "This attitude filtered down through the Majlis, through the government and ultimately became the mantra for Dubai."

Part of this environment, Sheikh Rashid understood, was to provide Dubai's trade base with the infrastructure necessary to support its efforts. The Dubai Creek Dredging Scheme was an early show of his determination in this regard. And as oil revenues began to change the economic outlook for Dubai, Sheikh Rashid's Majlis became ever more aggressive in its pursuit of development.

"Sheikh Rashid was a wily and clever leader. But he was never caught up in power and a belief that he knew everything," says Hamad bin Sukat. "He understood that times were changing. He had not been formally educated and had ruled with vision and an instinct as to what was best for Dubai. But times were moving quickly."

With his humble outlook, Sheikh Rashid did not think himself above taking advice from other people. He listened. Using the talents and knowledge of people who had been better trained and educated in a particular field, Sheikh Rashid was able to rule effectively at a time of great change. A simple man, he conversed as an equal with engineers, international politicians and business leaders with an ease that belied his basic education.

That he managed to guide an economy successfully through an oil boom was no miracle. He simply combined good briefing with a photographic memory and an exhaustive attention to detail. To function, Sheikh Rashid needed good people around him. His Camelot drew its strength from all levels of Dubai society. During the late 1960s, Sheikh Rashid's most dependable allies, his sons, gradually joined the 'family firm'.

"Sheikh Rashid trusted the judgment of his sons implicitly. Their devotion to him was unquestioned," says Sheikh Mohammed bin Khalifa Al Maktoum. "It was rare for Sheikh Rashid to go ahead with any major decision without discussing the subject at length with his sons. Most projects that came along in the late 1960s were a collective effort, shaped by those in the Majlis."

It was difficult to gain Sheikh Rashid's trust, but once earned he was not fickle. Loyalty was rewarded, yet he made it clear that sycophancy would not be tolerated in his Majlis. Dubai traded in certainties and could not afford to squander its limited resources.

Eric Tullock, an expatriate engineer whom Sheikh Rashid involved in most major Dubai projects, recalls: "Sheikh Mohammed and his brothers were not 'yes' men. All were brutal in condemnation of ideas that were viewed as foolhardy."

Sheikh Rashid's four sons, if they were very much against something decided in the Majlis, never – ever – argued with Sheikh Rashid in public, but quietly discussed ideas and concerns either in the Majlis or in private later. They were fiercely loyal to Sheikh Rashid.

That loyalty was reciprocated, and just as well – as Sheikh Rashid needed those around him to take on a widening load of responsibilities. All now took roles within the union process. While Sheikh Maktoum was most visible, his younger brothers worked alongside Sheikh Rashid in a family effort.

The union process was dominated by the four richer states: Abu Dhabi, Bahrain, Dubai and Qatar. The Ruler of Qatar, Sheikh Ahmed

Sheikh Mohammed discusses a point with his cousin, Sheikh Mohammed bin Khalifa Al Maktoum.

bin Ali Al Thani, was married to Sheikh Rashid's daughter, Sheikha Mariam. Sheikh Ahmed was seen as something of a loose cannon within the union process, so the remaining states looked to Dubai to ensure Qatar remained on track.

As such, when the Dubai Ruler needed an envoy to visit Qatar, his sons were natural candidates. Abdullah bin Mohammed Al Othman, Qatar's current Ambassador to the UAE, recalls these meetings. "Sheikh Ahmed had a healthy respect for his brothers-in-law. All behaved like seasoned diplomats."

As the union process lurched on, Sheikh Ahmed's ultimate intentions were questioned by some. Sheikh Rashid sought to guide his son-in-law toward a centralist position. This meant tough talking. When Sheikh Rashid thought it inappropriate to do this by telephone and could not visit Qatar himself, it was usually one of his sons to whom he turned.

The position of the nine sheikhdoms was hardly helped by events being played out in Britain at the same time. There, the poor handling of the economy that had forced the government of Harold Wilson to abandon its commitments to the Gulf was the overriding issue of an impending General Election. British voters were set to oust Wilson and the Labour Party from government, and the favourite to win the keys to 10 Downing Street was Edward Heath, leader of the Conservative Party.

Heath was no stranger to Gulf politics: He had visited Dubai on several occasions in the early 1960s when he was Lord Privy Seal. In the lead-up to the General Election, Heath decried Wilson's decision to abandon the Gulf and announced that, if elected, he would reverse the

Opposition leader Edward Heath opposed Britain's withdrawal from the Gulf. A General Election campaign further muddied the political waters in the Trucial States.

decision. Like other Gulf leaders, Sheikh Rashid respected Heath, who had served in both the MacMillan and Douglas-Home governments, and had led Britain's first application to join the European Community. He had also been awarded the Charlemagne Prize in recognition of his contribution to promoting international cooperation. Clearly, the man expected to be the next Prime Minister of Great Britain was a statesman capable of dealing with the sheikhdoms of the Gulf in a more pragmatic and stable manner. Many reasoned that if Heath announced that Britain would stay in the Gulf, the sheikhdoms would be best advised to stick with the status quo.

Yet, the likelihood of a Conservative victory seemed to have a further destabilising effect on the union process. Throughout 1969, and even into 1970, progress was limited, in no small part due to the belief that Britain would stay on in the region.

Behind the scenes, Qatar and Bahrain expressed reservations about the union. They seemed to believe that their respective futures could best be served by remaining independent under a British umbrella.

On October 21, 1969, Sheikh Rashid and his delegation flew to Abu Dhabi. He was tense and unusually silent during the half-hour flight, possibly mindful that 22 months had elapsed since the Union Accord and nothing tangible had been achieved in the interim. With each passing week the stakes were becoming higher and the potential for disaster bigger.

The agenda for Abu Dhabi included all unresolved issues: a draft constitution; the election of a President and Vice President; the appointment of a federal capital; and the make-up of the Federal National Council. Host Sheikh Zayed bin Sultan Al Nahyan opened proceedings by saying: "We have gathered in Abu Dhabi today, with a historic opportunity ahead of us. I believe we can face the uncertainties of the future with a strong common bond, a federation which serves our common needs and helps to provide a bright future for our people…Let us not forget the price that we may all pay for a failure to grasp the opportunities which lie before us…"

Over subsequent days, a spirit of cooperation was reborn. Sheikh Zayed was elected as President, Sheikh Rashid as Vice President (after first refusing the nomination) and Qatar Crown Prince Sheikh Khalifa bin Hamed Al Thani as Prime Minister. Abu Dhabi was named temporary capital city until a new city could be constructed on the Dubai-Abu Dhabi border. In a surprise move, Bahrain gave up its insistence on proportional representation in the Federal National Council, and full agreement was achieved on this key point.

One by one, the outstanding issues were settled and confidence seemed to emerge. Despite this, doubts remained about the intentions of some of the protagonists. Those present at the meeting give differing accounts, but to this day some continue to believe that circumstances almost led to a remarkable breakthrough and creation of the union.

Drama was never far from the surface during the negotiations on the Union of Arab Emirates, but no-one was prepared for the events on the final day of this ground-breaking conference.

On the afternoon of October 24, all the major hurdles to the creation of the nine-member federation had been cleared. The nine leaders used the final sessions to work on a communiqué. Sheikh Rashid, Sheikh Maktoum and their close aides were delighted with progress as they pored over an agreement that effectively gave a green light to the union's creation.

However, outside the meeting room, rumours were circulating around Abu Dhabi and other towns on the Trucial Coast that the nine-member union was on the verge of a final, decisive collapse. News of this reached the British Political Resident in Bahrain, Sir Stewart Crawford. Not known for his patience, Crawford decided to intervene with an ill-considered colonial-style slap on the wrist. He instructed his Political Agent in Abu Dhabi, James Treadwell, to read a statement to the Rulers on his behalf.

Efforts to revive the Union of Arab Emirates were at crisis point. Here the nine delegations meet to discuss a draft constitution. Ruler of Abu Dhabi Sheikh Zayed bin Sultan Al Nahyan can be seen right, Emir of Bahrain Sheikh Isa bin Salaman Al Khalifa, left. Dubai's delegation is seated in the centre of the table, headed by Sheikh Maktoum.

With the finishing touches to a communiqué still being debated, from outside Treadwell sent a message to the session chairman, Sheikh Zayed, requesting permission to address the floor. After a unanimous vote in favour, his request was granted. Treadwell read a statement that said, in part: "…My government will be extremely disappointed if these difficulties are not overcome…I strongly urge all the Rulers to do their utmost to find a way of resolving their difficulties…"

For reasons that are still disputed, this infuriated several of the parties present. Qatar's delegation left the chamber, followed by their counterparts from Ras Al Khaimah. The unsigned communiqué was consigned to the dustbin.

That night, with Qatar's Ruler having left for Doha, those still in Abu Dhabi struggled to achieve consensus. The following day a subdued and tragically weak end-of-session statement read:

The Supreme Council decided to adjourn its current meeting, and postpone discussion of what remains of the agenda to a further meeting, to be held in Abu Dhabi within two weeks from the date of this statement – 25th October 1969.

No further Supreme Council meetings were held and, after a couple of weak attempts at reviving the initiative, the Union of Arab Emirates effectively passed into history.

All Sheikh Rashid's efforts to create a nine-member union came to nothing. Instead he turned his attention to the seven Trucial States.

Chapter Nineteen

Success from the Jaws of Failure

Our problems are manmade. Therefore, they can be solved by man. And man can be as big as he wants. No problem of human destiny is beyond human beings. Man's reason and spirit have often solved the seemingly unsolvable...
— *John F Kennedy, statesman*

With Iran acting as something of a catalyst, after the collapse of the Union of Arab Emirates in October 1969, efforts to create a union continued. In the aftermath of the failure, Sheikh Rashid and Sheikh Zayed of Abu Dhabi agreed that they would not exclude the possibility of a nine-member federation, but that a more natural grouping, the seven Trucial States, should now be the emphasis of their efforts. As a result, the Dubai Ruler's sons were more active closer to home, often breaking from their domestic roles to shuttle to Abu Dhabi, or as far as Fujairah, over the Hajar Mountain range, to represent their father.

Sheikh Mohammed's helicopter became a regular sight in the major towns of the Trucial Coast and, on occasion, deep in the desert hinterland too. Dubai, and to a greater extent its much richer neighbour Abu Dhabi, also embarked upon a massive programme to give aid to the other five Trucial States during this period. Both sheikhdoms had only been enjoying the benefits of oil for a short time by 1969, but had been economic giants relative to the other Trucial sheikhdoms. These factors combined to see Abu Dhabi and Dubai boasting limited public services such as schools, electricity, water and hospitals. The five remaining sheikhdoms were significantly poorer in this regard and clearly needed help.

In 1968, Abu Dhabi had paid half of the funds available for the Trucial States Development Fund, and 90% the following year. Sheikh

Sheikh Mohammed greets King Hussein of Jordan. The Jordanian Monarch was particularly supportive of union efforts.

Rashid's Dubai preferred to channel its support directly. Both Rulers were hugely philanthropic.

When asked by financial advisors to show restraint, Sheikh Zayed reportedly responded by saying: "How can we be earning millions of dollars in Abu Dhabi while 200 miles from here people are drinking water from polluted wells, babies are dying because there are no medicines and children born into this poverty have no chance to get an education. In all conscience, I cannot allow this when it is in my power to provide clean water, medicine and schools."

While some social progress was being made in the Trucial States, it was clear that both Bahrain and Qatar were evolving and preparing to go their own way. On April 2, 1970, Qatar announced its formal constitution and cabinet while applying for membership of the Arab League. Bahrain seemed to be heading in the same direction.

However, once again, events in Britain were having a large impact on the evolution of the Trucial States. By the spring of 1970, the United Kingdom was immersed in a General Election campaign. The Labour and Conservative parties were neck-and-neck as the election approached; most pundits agreed that the outcome was too close to call.

From an Arab perspective, election uncertainties in Britain created doubts at home. While Britain's economy had improved, Wilson had fully committed his country to a withdrawal of troops. The Opposition Leader, Edward Heath, was an outspoken advocate of reversing this policy, believing that Britain should honour its commitments and, in doing so, protect much of the world's oil reserves.

In May, it seemed that Wilson might be elected for a second term, but a raft of poor economic figures, released just before the election, tipped the balance towards the Conservatives. Heath won a surprisingly thorough victory, landing himself a safe 30-seat majority in the House of Commons.

Throughout the period following Wilson's decision to pull British armed forces out of areas 'east of Aden', Heath had remained a staunch critic of this policy. He believed that Britain's strategic interests were best served by retaining a strong influence in the Gulf. Dubai's leadership was similarly inclined, taking into consideration the collapsed Union of Arab Emirates project. Sheikh Rashid worried that the Trucial States would simply not be ready to stand alone before the end of 1971.

In Britain, *The Sunday Telegraph* reported that the Trucial Rulers "were jubilant" and had sent telegrams to Heath congratulating him. The newspaper added that several visited the commanding officer at Britain's base in Sharjah to tell him of their relief, while others were hanging banners around their towns in Heath's honour. *The Sunday Telegraph*'s source for this story remains a mystery, because people living around the Trucial States recall no such jubilation. If anything, the ruling families felt relief that Britain's policy would quickly be settled after Heath moved into 10 Downing Street and that they could get on with preparing for whatever reality they were set to face.

On July 6, Foreign Secretary Sir Alec Douglas-Home told the House of Commons: "The urgent tasks now are, to create a climate favourable to the settlement of local disputes, some of them far reaching and important. The second is to consult the leaders of the Gulf as to how Britain can best contribute to the pattern of stability in the area. We shall go into fresh consultations with a completely open mind..."

During the election period, Sheikh Rashid had kept his opinions very much to himself. After June, however, while Heath was still finalising his cabinet and arranging his new government, he granted rare interviews to London-based media, in which he commented on the Trucial States' obvious state of unpreparedness and their lack of unity at this point in the protracted process. He was keen to encourage a more thoughtful approach from the British government.

On July 13, Sheikh Rashid spoke to Fleet Street writer David Housego. *The Times* published an interview stating that Sheikh Rashid was the first of the Trucial Rulers to "come out with open support for a continuing British military presence in the area".

In the interview, he said: "Abu Dhabi, Bahrain and in fact, the whole coast, people and Rulers, would all support the retaining of British forces in the Gulf even though…they may not give a direct answer out of a respect for the general Arab view."

If the British did indeed leave, the story went on, the Trucial Oman Scouts should "remain in existence, whether as part of a federal army or separately, even though we have to pay for the thing ourselves. He added that, in his view, a Union of Arab Emirates – encompassing the seven Trucial States, Qatar and Bahrain – was most likely to take the form of a 'confederation'."

Nearly one month later, Douglas-Home dispatched Sir William Luce to the Gulf on a mission to ascertain the exact situation. Luce flew into

*Sir William Luce,
Britain's envoy
throughout his
country's difficult
withdrawal.*

Dubai International Airport on the morning of August 9. He was met by
Sheikh Maktoum and Sheikh Mohammed. Later, during a meeting at
Za'abeel Palace, Luce discovered that the Dubai administration had
doubts about the sheikhdoms' readiness to stand alone.

Elsewhere on the coast, notably from Sheikh Zayed in Abu Dhabi, he
heard much the same, but also learned that attitudes had changed.
Having worked towards preparing for a British withdrawal, some leaders
had got used to the idea and wanted full independence. One influential
voice in the matter, Kuwaiti Crown Prince Sheikh Jaber Al-Ahmed
Al-Sabah, had stated on July 15: "We do not welcome any foreign
occupation in our region, British or otherwise."

After his trip to the Gulf, Luce became Britain's permanent envoy. He
was well respected in the region but, for whatever reason, continually
misinterpreted situations. He consistently steered Heath's policy
towards the formation of a nine-member federation, along the lines of
the failed Union of Arab Emirates. In a briefing with newspaper
reporters while in Tehran, Luce commented that "The nine-member
Union of Arab Emirates is a quite feasible possibility. My government,
along with those of Saudi Arabia and Kuwait, is exerting the utmost
effort in the belief that this can become a firm reality...I believe that
a smaller union of seven members, as proposed by some, will not be
plausible..."

In the wake of Luce's initial visit, Britain, Saudi Arabia and Kuwait
aggressively continued to pursue a Union of Arab Emirates encompassing
nine members. This led to a Union of Arab Emirates Deputy Rulers'

meeting in Abu Dhabi in late October. Sheikh Maktoum, representing Dubai, was mostly called upon to debate ground that had already been covered months before. Once again, controversial issues were deferred to committees, ignoring the fact that only 14 months remained before the British withdrawal and that firm decisions were needed urgently.

Despite the lateness of the hour, it was March 1971 before Heath's government declared that it would not change policy. Britain would definitely pull out completely from the Gulf. Heath was tackled on the issue on March 2 during Prime Minister's Question Time, when asked by an Opposition member: "If a union of Emirates is not formed, and the other things which are hoped for do not occur, will British withdrawal nonetheless occur at the end of 1971, or is British withdrawal conditional on the formation of a union?"

Heath stalled and replied: "This proposal to the Rulers and countries concerned in the union, and what we can do to help them for union, is being discussed with them. If necessary, the Foreign Secretary, or another minister, can visit the area to carry it further…we have changed the policy in the Gulf in the way our friends there believe can best help them to maintain stability."

Two weeks later, Sheikh Rashid told Housego of *The Times* of his "disappointment": "I am prepared to be frank with them [the British government], but they come along at times and say that 'this is our decision' and you are not given an opportunity to express your own view…the uncertainty of the past eight months, at the end of which the Conservatives had made virtually the same decision as the previous government, has been politically damaging in the area and has also reduced trade."

Housego went on to question the Dubai Ruler on the prospects of union. Sheikh Rashid's reply was a rare public statement for a leader who normally reserved his utterings for private discussions with fellow Rulers. He admitted: "I don't want to malign anybody, but if there was a union of eight there is a 99% chance that this may come into being at once. With Bahrain there are not any real differences but they simply do not want a union."

He also made his vision of a union clearer than ever. According to Housego he "suggested that he envisages a far looser federation with a weaker central executive, than either the British, the Saudi Arabians, or the Kuwaitis have been urging on the Rulers…The authority of the

Federal government should embrace defence, external affairs, health, education, the issue of passports and communications..."

In a subsequent article in *The Daily Telegraph*, under the heading 'Ruler says Gulf union is inevitable', Sheikh Rashid is reported to have told the newspaper: "There is no other choice but to form a federation when British forces pull out."

With less than one year remaining before British forces departed, all that had been achieved was a number of agreements that had quickly dissipated like the morning mist. Bahrain's leader, Sheikh Isa bin Salman Al Khalifa, was clearly embarking on preparations for statehood. Britain, Saudi Arabia and Kuwait, however, were still pushing for a union encompassing Bahrain and Qatar.

While Britain, Saudi Arabia and Kuwait could not be ignored, Sheikh Rashid had joined Sheikh Zayed of Abu Dhabi on a dual, or even three-track approach. On March 11 he brokered an informal meeting with Sheikh Zayed and Qatar's Sheikh Ahmed. While he undoubtedly would have liked to see Qatar in the union, it was clear that Sheikh Ahmed's enthusiasm for independence was growing.

Sheikh Rashid now concentrated on his fellow Trucial Rulers. During April 1971, he and Sheikh Zayed met six times to review the situation and assess their prospects. Other Trucial Rulers visited Dubai and Abu Dhabi. This was a sensitive time. The building process had begun all over again. A fear of failure hung over the Rulers like the Sword of Damocles. Throughout April and May, Sheikh Maktoum and his brothers were involved in talks with the Rulers of the five northern sheikhdoms. It was a time of stress for Dubai's ruling family as it struggled to rekindle the spirit of cooperation that had been apparent in the Dubai Agreement of February 1968, over two years earlier.

Most evenings, Sheikh Rashid's Majlis became the centre of attention in the sheikhdom. Sheikh Rashid, his sons and close aides would gather to discuss the developments of the day.

Despite the fact that they did not always see eye to eye on the nature of the union, Sheikh Rashid and Sheikh Zayed might have been able to renew their Union Accord of February 18, 1968. However they had learned from experience and they agreed to move on a pan-Trucial States level so that a wider and all-encompassing agreement could be reached. With this in mind, they chose a date for a summit of all seven Trucial Rulers. It was July 10, which was already the date of a Trucial

States Council meeting at the Trucial States Development Board (TSDB) offices in Dubai. The TSDB had done much for the people of the Trucial States. Now its humble offices in Dubai would be the venue for a make-or-break meeting that would decide the very future of the region.

While the union process continued, the leaders were also dealing with storm clouds emanating on the Iranian front. Throughout the non-life of the Union of Arab Emirates, the Shah had kept up his nationalistic sabre-rattling. He objected to a union of any kind. He objected to Bahrain being considered part of the union, as he claimed the island belonged to Iran. He objected to Britain protecting Abu Musa and the two Tunb islands, although historically they belonged to Sharjah and Ras Al Khaimah, respectively.

The Shah's list of grievances went on, albeit with an apparent softening of his position regarding Bahrain during 1970 and 1971. However, Iran's shifting stance on Bahrain was matched by new, even greater intransigence regarding Abu Musa and the two Tunb islands. Iran even threatened the British government on May 8, 1971 that its forces would fire on any Royal Air Force (RAF) aircraft infringing on Iran's airspace, including the three tiny Gulf islands. This drew an uncharacteristically subdued response from Her Majesty's government. Britain 'explained' that any aircraft near Abu Musa and the Tunbs were unarmed and on reconnaissance missions.

Very swiftly, the reasons for this weak rebuttal became clear. Before the end of May, Britain announced that the Shah was set to purchase a large number of British-made Chieftain tanks for around £100 million. It appeared to many observers that this huge order, which secured thousands of jobs in Britain during tough economic times, may have been placed with some political strings attached.

A month later, Luce returned to the Trucial States peddling a clearly outdated British proposal to revive negotiations toward a nine-member union. He also revealed that Britain was washing its hands of its commitment to handle the defence of the seven Trucial States. While visiting Sheikh Khalid bin Mohammed Al Qassimi, Ruler of Sharjah, and Sheikh Saqr bin Mohammed Al Qassimi, Ruler of Ras Al Khaimah, he 'recommended' that they each begin negotiating directly with Iran on the issue of the Gulf islands. What was more, Luce, a British official, was carrying with him an offer from the Iranian government under

which the Shah's administration would compensate the two sheikhdoms for agreeing to hand over the islands, and give them a share of any subsequent oil revenues.

Almost simultaneously, Iranian Foreign Minister Ardeshir Zahedi gave a speech in Tehran in which he demanded Britain hand over Abu Musa and the Tunbs, threatening that Iran would act to block creation of a federation. With military threats and economic influence, the Shah had delivered a coup de grâce that had all but achieved his ends.

On June 28, almost exactly six months before Britain's planned withdrawal, Sheikh Mohammed flew Sheikh Rashid to Abu Dhabi by helicopter for a meeting with Sheikh Zayed and the Rulers of Sharjah and Ras Al Khaimah. Two central issues for discussion were the proposed federation and the islands. They realised that there was little that the Trucial States, with their meagre armies, could do to defend themselves against the Iranian armed forces. International diplomacy

Accompanied by Sheikh Zayed, Sheikh Rashid inspects a guard of honour upon his arrival in Abu Dhabi.

was practically the only course of action open to them. They had to lobby the British to stand by their commitments and garner international support against an increasingly likely Iranian move.

On the subject of union, consensus was reached. Several sessions during the day were reserved for leaders-only talks, and the four found themselves in broad agreement on most issues. They returned to Dubai with much of the groundwork in place for a successful conclusion to be reached on July 10.

Sheikh Maktoum and his brothers now worked at a frenzied pace, shuttling among the seven sheikhdoms representing their father. Sheikh Rashid believed that to reach a successful outcome in this crucial meeting, consensus needed to be finalised in advance so that only a handful of strategic decisions would be left for the seven Rulers in Dubai.

From early morning on July 10, members of Dubai's ruling family hurried around the town to greet the delegations arriving by road and at Dubai International Airport. By 10 am, the seven Trucial Rulers and their entourages were seated in the central meeting room at the TSDB offices. Sheikh Rashid, flanked by his sons and close advisors, sat adjacent to Sheikh Zayed.

However, when proceedings began, those present were shocked. The agenda, prepared by TSDB officials, was dominated by procedural matters concerning development in the states themselves. Important, certainly, but less so when the very existence of the states was to be affected by the outcome of that day's deliberations. Many Rulers sat in stony silence through a morning of discussions on experimental farming, water desalination and traffic regulations. At the conclusion of the morning session, Sheikh Zayed sat forward in his chair and stated: "I can see that a lack of seriousness prevails..."

That afternoon, amid fears that Sheikh Zayed would leave for Abu Dhabi in frustration, a motion was carried unanimously that the prepared agenda be dispensed with in favour of discussions on union. Throughout the afternoon of July 10, the Rulers debated at length the issues that still separated them with what some recall as unparalleled frankness. Sheikh Zayed, seen by most as the natural leader of the federation, assumed this role in the meeting. Sheikh Rashid, with his deep understanding of each party present and what they required from a federation, pushed the debate along. With their own disagreements put to one side, Sheikh Zayed and Sheikh Rashid worked toward a broad, all-encompassing agreement. This they did with such success that the meeting was extended by a day, then another, and then another.

With expectations mounting in Dubai and around the Trucial States, pressure to reach an accord grew from outside of the meeting. Indeed, in the latter stages of this make-or-break meeting, public opinion was to play a role in ensuring that the leaders understood that it was imperative to conclude their summit with a tangible result. Public awareness of the political straits that the sheikhdoms found themselves in had grown inexorably since Wilson's announcement in 1967. As union efforts foundered, the unwritten taboo on open criticism of their leaders had become strained in the Trucial States. On more than one occasion, Sheikh Rashid was advised by his sons that the public were becoming disillusioned and even angry.

Increased access to radio and foreign newspapers had also instilled a new awareness into the population. An emerging local media corps offered information on the union process and locally-based newsmen were now creating local opinion. Sharjah based weekly, *Al-Shuruq*, commented at one juncture:

> *...more than two years have elapsed since the signing of the Union of Arab Emirates agreement...People were led to believe that those exchanged visits, consultations and bilateral meetings would inevitably lead to a federal union, but with every passing day their longing for union and a union state increases, while the union remains, until now, mere ink on paper. Responsible leaders should make up their minds frankly and clearly whether they want union or not...*

On July 17, eight days after the Rulers' meeting had begun, expectations of success were so great that it was agreed to conclude talks the following day. One major hurdle remained: the federation was projected to have a parliamentary body, the Federal National Council (FNC). This was to comprise eight representatives from both Abu Dhabi and Dubai, six from both Sharjah and Ras Al Khaimah and four each from Ajman, Umm Al Quwain and Fujairah.

However, Ras Al Khaimah Ruler Sheikh Saqr was unhappy, believing that representation on the FNC measured only modern economic realities while it should also reflect the historical status of each party. The Bani Yas towns of Abu Dhabi and Dubai would have a combined 16 seats, while the two Qawassim capitals of Sharjah and Ras Al Khaimah only had 12 seats under the proposal. He was also deeply unhappy about the Supreme Council, the proposed union's highest body made up of the seven Rulers. Abu Dhabi and Dubai insisted that a quorum of five apply in all decision-making, and that a quorum had to include the big two.

On Sunday, July 18, the seven Trucial Rulers met for a final day of union talks. Throughout much of the day, attempts were made to placate Sheikh Saqr, amid fears that Ras Al Khaimah might choose to remain on the sidelines. But when these efforts failed, the other six Rulers knew that they simply could not afford to adjourn in order to give time to develop a formula that was acceptable to Ras Al Khaimah. That afternoon, they issued a communiqué that stated:

In response to the desire of our Arab people, we, the Rulers of Abu Dhabi, Dubai, Sharjah, Ajman, Umm Al Quwain and Fujairah, have resolved to establish a federal state under the name of the United Arab Emirates. On this blessed day the provisional constitution of the United Arab Emirates was signed. Conveying this happy news to the Arab people, we pray the Almighty that this union shall be the nucleus for a full union to include the rest of the members of the family of sister emirates who, due to their current circumstances, were not able to sign this constitution.

Still ahead were months of hard work and diplomacy before the United Arab Emirates constitution could be signed and the UAE formed officially within international law. The Dubai meeting of July 1971 was just the beginning of a final push toward statehood.

"I had rarely seen Sheikh Rashid so happy. I suspect there was a degree of sadness in him that they had been unable to take Bahrain and Qatar with them, but he felt that the United Arab Emirates was a development which would benefit all six states," says Abdullah Saleh. "There seemed to be a feeling that, having taken this definite step, Ras Al Khaimah and Qatar could later choose to enter the UAE. The door was being left open for them."

Months remained in which Sheikh Zayed and Sheikh Rashid had to lay the foundations of an independent nation. Failure would mean that, whatever the intentions of the Rulers and the people, the UAE would be a failed state before it began. One example of the huge task that faced the union was in its diplomatic service. Britain had managed the Trucial States' international relations for nearly a century and a half. Between July and December 1971 the union had to be readied to handle its own affairs. The nation had no diplomatic service and no existing foreign representation – and most importantly of all no diplomats. An example of the ordered chaos that was evident in starting a nation from scratch is offered by Mirza Al Sayegh. Months earlier he had returned to Dubai from higher studies in Jordan with a BA. In late August he had secured a job with Dubai Petroleum Company, with a salary of Rs. 1,500.

Sheikh Zayed with Mirza Al Sayegh, one of the first wave of diplomats recruited to serve the UAE, even before its official inception.

On Al Sayegh's first morning he was accosted on his way to work and invited for an urgent meeting at the Abu Dhabi government office in Sharjah. Sheikh Zayed had sent out an urgent request for all BA graduates in the Northern Emirates to attend a meeting regarding the positions in the Diplomatic Service.

"I did not know what job, or what salary we were being offered," says Al Sayegh. "It was a risk. So I asked DPC if I could start the following day. It seemed an act of madness, but we were all feeling patriotic and saw it as a sense of duty."

Later the same day every BA graduate in Dubai and the Northern Emirates assembled in Sharjah. There was a paltry 25 (barring doctors). The UAE clearly had a long way to go.

At the meeting, the 25 were informed that Sheikh Zayed requested their presence in Abu Dhabi the following day.

"I had a choice to make and patriotism won," says Al Sayegh who, after obtaining a further deferment from DPC, travelled to the future federal capital where he and his fellow BA holders were briefed by Sheikh Zayed's chief advisor Ahmed Al Suweidi. Still it was unclear what position they were being offered – or what salary.

"We met with Sheikh Zayed the following day, and then Sheikh Rashid, as he was visiting Abu Dhabi," says Al Sayegh. "I think, although things were unclear, every one of our group agreed to join the Diplomatic Service. There was a palpable sense of national duty."

A third summer of intensive diplomacy ensued for Sheikh Rashid, who had hardly taken a break from the affairs of Dubai, or the all-consuming federation issue, for three years. By autumn he and Sheikh Zayed, by far the two most influential leaders of the six, had reached agreement in readiness to push the situation to its conclusion.

In the wake of the agreement on July 18, 1971, that led to the creation of the United Arab Emirates, two significant regional events occurred. On August 14, Sheikh Isa bin Salman Al Khalifa announced Bahrain's independence and applied for membership of the United Nations and the Arab League. The same day, the island state was recognised by the United Arab Republic, Jordan, Iraq and Iran. A fortnight later, on September 1, Qatar followed with a statement issued by Sheikh Ahmed bin Ali Al Thani. Qatar was recognised by most major Middle East nations immediately and later joined the United Nations and Arab League.

Most intriguing in the tangled web of Gulf politics was Iran's speedy recognition of Bahrain. Although the Shah had laid claim to the island and its mineral wealth for years, a gradual shift had been under way and, as Tehran changed its position toward Bahrain, it had stepped up its campaign for Sharjah's Abu Musa island and Ras Al Khaimah's two Tunb islands. Now it became clear to the Arab governments concerned that the British had absolved themselves of their defence commitments. A £100 million deal to supply British made Chieftain tanks to the Iranian army, coupled with British insistence that Sharjah and Ras Al Khaimah should 'negotiate', made such a conclusion possible.

After the triumphant agreement to create the UAE, the islands issue hung like a black cloud over the political landscape. Six Rulers had signed the document that created the UAE. Several months passed while the details were thrashed out ahead of a full constitution-signing ceremony that would officially form the United Arab Emirates in the eyes of international law.

Of the seven Trucial States, the Dubai administration was closest to the Iranians. With its large trade base, Dubai enjoyed long-standing and close commercial links with Iran. Both Sheikh Rashid and Sheikh Maktoum had made official visits to Tehran. Now, these ties were renewed in an effort to stop what Sheikh Rashid thought was inevitable – the Iranian seizure of Abu Musa and the Tunbs.

The governments of Sharjah and Ras Al Khaimah, with minimal international ties, had nowhere to turn for help. Sharjah opened direct negotiations with Iran on the future of Abu Musa; a mistake, as it turned

The Shah of Iran delivered his coup de grace with a timely military deal and the siezure of three Arab islands.

out. Meanwhile, Sheikh Zayed used his well-established contacts with international leaders to campaign strenuously and seek help from Middle Eastern and Gulf powers such as Egypt and Kuwait. Little feedback was received. With the predator circling in for his kill, none of the Arab world's influential voices, it seemed, was willing to strain relations with the Shah over three small islands.

By the beginning of November 1971, the six founding states of the UAE were sufficiently advanced in their negotiations to schedule a constitution-signing meeting for Thursday, December 2. In view of its doubts over union issues, and concerns over the future of the Tunb islands, Ras Al Khaimah continued to remain on the sidelines although involved in an ongoing dialogue.

On November 29, Sharjah announced that it had concluded an 'agreement' with Iran over Abu Musa. After landing on Abu Musa, the Iranians occupied the island and made it clear they had no intention of keeping to this arrangement. That same afternoon, Iranian troops landed on Ras Al Khaimah's Greater Tunb island and annexed Lesser Tunb. Around the Trucial States, there was fury among the general public. Demonstrations broke out in most towns. In Dubai, Sheikh Mohammed deployed the Dubai Police and units of the DDF to guard Iranians and their property against any revenge attacks.

On December 1, the British Political Resident began a final official tour of the seven sheikhdoms, during which each of the Rulers signed a document that nullified all the treaty agreements concluded with Britain since the 1820 General Treaty of Peace. These included Britain's

December 2, 1971 and Sheikh Zayed bin Sultan Al Nahyan, Sheikh Rashid and Sharjah Ruler Sheikh Khalid bin Mohammed Al Qassimi prepare to sign the United Arab Emirates' Provisional Constitution, formally creating the new state. Sheikh Maktoum and Sheikh Hamdan can be seen adjacent to the Dubai Ruler.

commitments to defend the Trucial States. London's *Financial Times* commented: "From the point of view of international law, the responsibility for protecting these islands certainly rested with Britain..."

The world could see that Britain had reneged on its responsibility, but no-one was prepared to challenge Iran.

On December 2, 1971, the Rulers of Abu Dhabi, Dubai, Sharjah, Ajman and Fujairah and the Crown Prince of Umm Al Quwain, representing his father, met at Union House in Dubai. They were presented with a draft constitution that would bring the United Arab Emirates into existence.

Sheikh Rashid opened proceedings. In a closed session, the Rulers unanimously elected Sheikh Zayed as UAE President and Sheikh Rashid as Vice President. Dubai Crown Prince Sheikh Maktoum was named as Prime Minister. A little after 11 am, with business completed, the meeting room was opened to VIPs and the media. Reporters and photographers from as far afield as North America and the Far East had assembled to watch as the six signed a draft constitution that "bound them together in a common destiny".

A joint declaration said:

> *On this day, Thursday the Second of December, 1971, in the emirate of Dubai, the Rulers of Abu Dhabi, Dubai, Sharjah, Ajman, Umm Al Quwain and Fujairah, as co-signatories of the provisional constitution of the United Arab Emirates, met in an atmosphere in which brotherly sentiments, mutual confidence and profound determination to realise the aspirations of the people of these emirates prevailed, and issued a declaration in accordance with the provisions of the aforesaid constitution will take effect as of this date.*
>
> *The Rulers then continued their meeting as the Supreme Council of the Federation. With the help of the Almighty, in this meeting H.H. Sheikh Zayed bin Sultan Al Nahyan, the Ruler of Abu Dhabi, was elected as President of the State of the United Arab Emirates, for a period of five Gregorian years, and H.H. Sheikh Rashid bin Saeed Al Maktoum, the Ruler of Dubai, was elected as Vice President, for the same period. Both took the constitutional oath of office according to the provisions of the constitution. Sheikh Maktoum bin Rashid Al Maktoum, the Crown*

Prince of Dubai, was appointed Prime Minister. The Council will convene its second meeting in Abu Dhabi on Tuesday 7 December 1971.

The Supreme Council brings glad tidings to the people of the United Arab Emirates, to all fraternal Arab nations, to friendly nations and to the world in general. The United Arab Emirates has been established as an independent, sovereign state, part of the greater Arab Nation. Its aim is to maintain its independence, its sovereignty, its security and its stability, in defence against any attack on any member of its member emirates. It also seeks to protect the freedoms and rights of its people, and to achieve co-operation between the emirates for the common good. Among its aims, in addition to the purposes above, is to work for the sake of the progress of the country in all fields, for the sake of providing a better life for its citizens, to give assistance and support to Arab causes and interests, and to support the charter of the United Nations and international norms.

The Federation condemns the use of force and regrets that Iran has recently occupied part of the Arab nation. Therefore it deems it necessary to honour legal rights and resolve disputes between nations by means that are internationally recognised.

The Supreme Council of the Federation on this blessed historic occasion turns to Allah, the Almighty, with praise and thanks for His granting of a happy outcome and for His help. It also turns to the people of the Federation with congratulations and blessings on the achievement of security, having faith with the Council that any unity or unification in this part of the world is a step on the way to the true call for complete Arab unity. The Council emphasises that it is keen to welcome other countries to join the United Arab Emirates, and especially brother emirates who have signed the Agreement of the Union of Arab Emirates in Dubai on 28 February 1968.

Chapter Twenty

We Pledge

Progress lies not in enhancing what is,
but in advancing toward what will be.
— *Gibran Khalil Gibran, philosophical essayist*

"The establishment of the federation was necessary to push forward the wheel of development in economic and social sectors, through pooling the country's resources. We do not claim perfection," said Sheikh Rashid. "Our primary aim in shouldering this responsibility is to work more and to produce more. Those who do not work will not make mistakes. God has given us great resources. These should be exploited for the well being of our people in all emirates, without exception. I, and the cabinet, do not claim that we can achieve miracles, but we pledge to do our best to serve the federation."

Around the UAE there was understandable jubilation that the uncertaintities of the past were over and that the nation could now move forward with a sense of optimism. Days after the formation of the UAE a teenage Anita Mehra Homayoun arrived in Dubai for the first time. "Everywhere there was a sense of euphoria" she recalls. "The major families were hosting huge celebratory lunches and dinners. The people were just so happy and elated. Dubai was a very joyous place to be."

On December 6, four days after its formation, the United Arab Emirates was formally accepted as the 18th member of the Arab League. On December 8, the United Nations Security Council approved the UAE as a member of the UN. The 128th UN member took its seat the following day.

As far as the UAE's leadership was concerned, the union project was finally completed not in the chambers of these world bodies, but when Ras Al Khaimah, having applied to join the UAE on December 8, was

Newly elected UAE President Sheikh Zayed stands in front of the Emirates flag following its symbolic first raising at Union House in Dubai.

President Sheikh Zayed, Vice President Sheikh Rashid and Prime Minister Sheikh Maktoum face the press with members of the Cabinet and the Federal National Council.

formally accepted as the seventh emirate on December 24, 1971.

The *Guinness Book of Records* states that 31-year-old Roosevelt Skerritt, when appointed Prime Minister of Dominica on January 8, 2004, was the world's youngest Prime Minister. On December 2, 1971, Sheikh Maktoum was 28 years old when handed the same office.

Despite his relative youth, Sheikh Maktoum had been handed an awesome responsibility. Not only was he to appoint the first cabinet, with a mandate that this reflect the UAE's constituents, but that cabinet was to assume power without any formal government apparatus, established ministries or government buildings, and no civil servants and no history of such national structures. It was a blank slate.

On top of that, Sheikh Maktoum's government would preside over a 1972 budget of a mere 115.5 million Bahraini dinars. The 82,880 square kilometres that made up the seven emirates were almost untouched in terms of modern development outside of the main towns of Abu Dhabi, Dubai and Sharjah. Beyond them there were no public services such as water supplies, hospitals and education. Electricity supplies were confined to the towns. Tarmac roads were rare. Housing was poor. The employment market was, outside of Dubai and to a lesser extent Abu Dhabi, stagnant.

"There was an extraordinary amount of work to be done, hurriedly as well as to be done well, in order to raise the living standards of the people of the UAE," says UAE Minister of Agriculture Saeed bin Mohammed Al Ragabani. "This was 1971 and the standard of living in the UAE as a whole was shocking. The government had a big, big responsibility."

The federal agreement between the emirates called upon Sheikh Maktoum to divide portfolios among the seven, with many key posts demarcated to a certain emirate. The Ruler of each would have a preference for a nominee, but the final decision on each cabinet member stayed with the Prime Minister.

In the days after December 2, Sheikh Maktoum began putting together a cabinet. These were extraordinary times that called for individuals with special talents. Only Abu Dhabi and Dubai possessed any formal government apparatus. Members of the UAE cabinet would each be required to build a pan-Emirates body from scratch, among seven entities, most of which had no direct telephone links between them and were not connected by tarmac roads.

"Sheikh Maktoum tapped into a vein of what was largely young talent," says Dr Abdullah Omran Taryam, who was the UAE's second Education Minister. "Sheikh Maktoum was the world's youngest Prime Minister, and he was ultimately to have serving under him the youngest cabinet in the world.

"This was neither an advantage nor a disadvantage, as the UAE was in a quite different situation to nearly every government formation in the last half century. There was no ministerial experience on a pan-UAE level, as there had never been a government before."

"Sheikh Maktoum drew around him a young team. Yes," said the late Sheikh Abdulaziz bin Mohammed Al Qassimi. "But every one was dynamic, committed and consumed by a zeal born of their youth and enthusiasm."

On December 8, Sheikh Maktoum visited Sheikh Zayed in Abu Dhabi, where he presented the list of proposed cabinet members. Among those included were his brothers, Sheikh Hamdan, as Minister of Finance and Industry, and Sheikh Mohammed, as Minister of Defence.

A day later, the UAE President ratified this inaugural cabinet, and on December 10 the new Prime Minister flew by helicopter to Abu Dhabi to preside over the UAE's first cabinet meeting.

"They were a dynamic group," says Sheikh Ahmed bin Saeed Al Maktoum, "but there was an awesome responsibility on the shoulders of everyone in that first cabinet."

At 22, Sheikh Mohammed was also a record-breaker, the world's youngest Minister of Defence. He took on a portfolio that presented its own set of unique challenges. The state of affairs over which the new minister presided was probably unique.

The scope and size of the armed forces of each emirate varied wildly from the multi-million-dollar Abu Dhabi Defence Force to the untrained armed retainers that provided security in Ajman and Umm Al Quwain. The contrast could hardly have been greater, yet the armed forces of each emirate had to be assimilated into a single body.

One of his first acts as minister was to appoint Khalifa Al Naboodah as his assistant in the ministry, later as under-secretary. Al Naboodah recalls the situation that lay before them: "The ministry started with nothing. Not an office. No central staff. Just a definitive plan of what must eventually be achieved. We took over an office in the complex that was the Dubai Rulers' Office, in Bur Dubai, ahead of building our own office block. Sheikh Mohammed had a blank piece of paper and was told to build an army. It was quite a daunting task."

Before the end of 1971, Sheikh Mohammed was airborne again, hopping by helicopter across the UAE to visit each of the emirates where he met with commanding officers and inspected their men, facilities and armaments. "It was a bewildering and eye-opening tour during which we went from viewing a handful of Bedouin retainers armed with pre-Second World War Mauser rifles to displays of the latest thing in ground-to-ground missiles," says Al Naboodah. Unity demanded not only a common command structure, but also a gradual consolidation of procedures and, eventually, strength.

Ahead of Sheikh Hamdan, at the age of 26, loomed a terrific responsibility. The Ministry of Finance and Industry was charged with implementing all fiscal, monetary and industrial policies for the UAE's overall economic development.

"The Ministry of Finance and Industry is a major component in government," says Minister of State for Financial and Industrial Affairs, Dr Mohamed Khalfan bin Kharbash. "Sheikh Hamdan was in a position that held a great deal of importance to the success of the federal project."

Among other things the ministry was charged with formulating fiscal and government accounting policies, preparing the national federal budget and keeping all federal accounts. The Ministry of Finance and Industry also administers revenue collection, supervises purchases, expenditure control and asset administration. Its industry function includes the preparation and implementation of polices for the development of industries; this was important as the UAE sought to diversify its economy away from such massive reliance upon oil revenues.

As Sheikh Maktoum could not afford to fail, Sheikh Hamdan's position left no room for error. To a great degree the United Arab Emirates depended upon their efforts. A stalled government could easily have led to a collapse of the fledgling state.

Under Sheikh Hamdan's ministry, the UAE was among the first countries in the region to adopt liberal economic policies.

The country further sought to enact legislation that encouraged foreign investments by creating a conducive climate and less bureaucracy. The World Bank would go on to hail the UAE's economic diversification

As Minister of Finance and Industry, Sheikh Hamdan's portfolio required him to spend a great deal of time outside of the country, including many trips accompanying Sheikh Zayed to meetings of the major global institutions.

and welcome its "marked success" in reducing its dependence on oil. The UAE's non-oil exports were 52.3% of the total in the five years from 2000 to 2004 compared with 31.9% in the 1970s and 29.5% in the 1980s. They were as low as 5.7% of GDP in 1975.

One of the early achievements of the Ministry of Finance and Industry, and in the UAE as a whole, was the monetary integration of the Emirates, which culminated in May 1973 with the establishment of the UAE Monetary Agency and the issue of the UAE national currency, the Dirham, which replaced both the Qatari/Dubai Riyal circulating in the Northern Emirates and the Bahraini Dinar circulating in Abu Dhabi.

"The UAE government exceeded all expectations in its success," says Denis Healey, who served as Chancellor of the Exchequer (British Finance Minister) from March 5, 1974 to May 4, 1979. "Sheikh Hamdan emerged as an adept administrator, while the Ministry of Finance and Industry played a key role in the speedy advancement of the UAE."

The first major test of the federation came not within Sheikh Maktoum's cabinet, or in the Ministry of Finance, but for Sheikh Mohammed's Ministry of Defence less than two months after he took office.

As night fell over Sharjah on January 25, 1972, a group of armed mercenaries slipped into the outskirts of the town. They were headed by Sheikh Saqr bin Sultan Al Qassimi, a former Ruler of the emirate who had been unseated in 1965.

Sheikh Saqr's successor, supported by Sharjah's ruling family, was

345

Almost Sheikh Mohammed's first task as Minister of Defence was to deal with the murder of the Ruler of Sharjah. He is pictured here consulting with his number two, Khalifa Al Naboodah. (opposite page) Sharjah Fort.

Sheikh Khalid bin Mohammed Al Qassimi who, until his accession, had been a successful merchant. After 1965, Sheikh Khalid showed a great deal of panache in adapting to leadership. With little finance at his disposal, he nevertheless reinvigorated Sharjah's souq and redeveloped its port. Because of these successes, he was a popular leader, both in his own emirate and throughout the UAE.

Despite this, Sheikh Saqr, who was living in exile in Egypt, believed that he could force his way back into power. The seaside Ruler's Palace and adjoining Sharjah Fort, seat of power in Sharjah, were protected only by a handful of armed retainers despite the perceived threat to Sheikh Khalid. They were surprised and overcome by the well-armed force and the compound was taken with hardly a shot being fired.

However, sporadic gunfire and the commotion from within alerted people living near Sheikh Khalid's home that something was wrong. News quickly reached UDF personnel at Al Qassimi Base, former headquarters of the British battalion, who notified both Vice President Sheikh Rashid and Minister of Defence Sheikh Mohammed by radio in Dubai.

Sheikh Mohammed was at the MoD office in Bur Dubai when the door to his office burst open. A communications officer, assigned to handle radio communications to the Minister of Defence, blurted out that an emergency situation was being reported in Sharjah, and that the life of the emirate's Ruler might conceivably be in danger. Sheikh Mohammed paused only to order that units from Al Qassimi Base be scrambled before leaping into his jeep and tearing along the roads of

Dubai in the direction of Sharjah, siren blaring.

On the way to the scene, he spoke by radio telephone with President Sheikh Zayed in Abu Dhabi and with his father, Sheikh Rashid. Sheikh Zayed reacted by sending three units of the Abu Dhabi Defence Force to Sharjah to support the UDF, placing these units under Sheikh Mohammed's command. Abu Dhabi also put the remainder of its army, navy and air forces on high alert. Dubai did the same with the DDF.

Within 20 minutes of receiving news of the emerging crisis, Sheikh Mohammed was on the scene. The force had barricaded themselves into the fort, while outside the walls people milled around in confusion, in open view of the armed gunmen stationed on the high walls above them. Groups of Bedu, visiting Sharjah and hearing news of the threat to Sheikh Khalid, had also made their way to the scene and were preparing to enter the melee by shooting at the men they could see on the ramparts. Clearly, this was a situation that could quickly get out of hand. The UDF's first task was to clear the area, then to attempt to contact the man leading the insurrection.

Inside, Sheikh Saqr, showing the lack of judgment that had led to his being ousted, believed that most Sharjah citizens still saw him as the legitimate Ruler. He reasoned that as news of his return spread, the people would rally in his support. In reality, however, no such thing would happen.

After communication had been established between the UDF and those inside the fort, Sheikh Mohammed spoke with Sheikh Saqr and was troubled to learn of his plan. Among the 30 hostages was the Ruler,

Sheikh Khalid. Considering his popular support, Sheikh Khalid's life would be in grave danger when Sheikh Saqr realised that he was no longer wanted.

In order not to endanger Sheikh Khalid's life, Sheikh Mohammed proceeded with caution. He could not launch the UDF against Sharjah Fort; not because the men inside were a match for the UDF, but because in the few minutes that it would take to capture the fort, it was likely that Sheikh Khalid and any number of other hostages would be killed. Sheikh Saqr and his men had trapped themselves. They were surrounded and, without the popular uprising that Sheikh Saqr had predicted, friendless.

Around the fort, Sheikh Mohammed deployed heavy armour as a show of strength. UDF helicopters circled constantly. Overhead, jet fighters periodically made their presence known with high-speed, low-level passes. In the sea off Sharjah, and within plain sight of the fort, fast attack craft were on standby. For the men inside, there was no way out.

Throughout the evening there were occasional exchanges of gunfire. Several rebels and a UDF man named Captain Cameron were injured. But as Sheikh Mohammed embarked on talks with Sheikh Saqr inside, the situation calmed considerably. The two knew each other from happier times, when Sheikh Saqr was Ruler of Sharjah and Sheikh Mohammed was nothing more than a teenage sheikh from a neighbouring sheikhdom.

"Once we were returning from a hunting trip, through the desert outside Sharjah, when we encountered Sheikh Saqr," says Mohammed Mirhashim. "It was customary to offer a gift to the Ruler. We had nothing except some cans of fruit. So we sat on the desert sands to share slices of pineapple with Sheikh Saqr and talk."

A decade later, Sheikh Mohammed used his acquaintance with Sheikh Saqr to build a dialogue. He worked on guaranteeing Sheikh Saqr's personal safety if he abandoned the coup attempt. Only after 16 hours of negotiations, throughout the night, did Sheikh Saqr agree to end his insurrection. Around mid-morning, the doors of the fortress opened and the gunmen surrendered into UDF custody.

All the hostages were freed unharmed except one who had been killed. Sadly, this was the Ruler of Sharjah, Sheikh Khalid. Conflicting reports from those involved make it unclear whether Sheikh Khalid was murdered in cold blood during the siege, or felled by accident when the palace was being occupied. What is clear is that the tragedy robbed Sharjah of a man who was probably its finest Ruler in generations. A popular man on a pan-Emirates level, his loss was felt keenly.

Sheikh Maktoum was dismayed that a man whom he respected could be cut down in his prime in such a manner. He reflected, as did many in the government, on the irony. The last Trucial States Rulers to be murdered had been Sheikh Saqr bin Zayed Al Nahyan of Abu Dhabi in 1928 and Sheikh Hamad bin Ibrahim Al Moalla of Umm Al Quwain in 1929, over four decades earlier. Now, less than two months after the creation of a national entity, which was supposed to propel the country into the modern era, one of the founding leaders had been struck down in an episode borrowed from the unruly past.

As the crisis ended on January 26, the UAE's Supreme Council met in emergency session in Dubai. There they ratified a decision made by the Al Qassimi family that Sheikh Sultan bin Mohammed Al Qassimi, brother of the deceased Ruler and UAE Minister of Education should accede.

Just a few months later, the UDF was called into action for a second time on domestic duty. On the morning of June 11, 1972, the office of the Ruler of Fujairah sent an urgent radio message to the Ministry of Defence. A night-time clash between rival Bedouin tribesmen affiliated to Fujairah and Sharjah had escalated. The dispute had started over grazing rights for sheep and goats in an area on the UAE's eastern coast where Sharjah's three enclaves – Dibba, Khor Fakkan and Kalba – had loosely defined borders with Fujairah. A couple of deaths had angered both tribes, who had called more armed men to the scene. By dawn, hundreds of Bedouin fighters were roaming the area and threatening to turn the incident into a major conflict that could encompass thousands of men.

Once again, units of the Union Defence Force were rushed to the scene. However, with roads poor to non-existent and only tracks on which to negotiate the Hajar mountain range, the bulk of the UDF took over half a day to get to the scene from Sharjah. An advance party was sent by helicopter and Sheikh Mohammed dispatched other units to establish contact with the leaders of the tribes that had begun the conflict so that he could deal with them directly.

It took around 24 hours for UDF forces to position themselves between the combatants, after which tensions eased. In the intervening

period, 22 men had been killed and a further 12 seriously injured. On July 17, the UDF escorted the leaders of both tribes to Abu Dhabi where President Sheikh Zayed brokered a settlement.

This issue was settled reasonably quickly, yet it provided useful lessons for the UAE's leadership. While those on the relatively affluent and forward thinking coast easily accepted the idea of statehood, the Bedu remained suspicious and unwilling to accept imported ideas. National boundaries were an alien concept to them, as was nationhood. But the Bedu made up a large segment of the population. If they were ignored, they would become a disenfranchised underclass.

President Sheikh Zayed and Vice President Sheikh Rashid, who were respected by all Bedouin leaders, had made it one of their projects to fully encompass the Bedu in the union experiment. Throughout the process that created the union, they had spent time in the desert hinterland with Bedouin leaders, talking over the reasons for union, seeking their support. The events of June 1972 showed that there was still much work to do in this regard. Sheikh Zayed continued his efforts, and pushed his colleagues on the Supreme Council to do the same. Prime Minister Sheikh Maktoum's government also had a role in this process, as showing the Bedu the tangible benefits of nationhood, such as reliable water sources, electricity and health care, would create a sense of acceptance and eventually belonging to the new union.

The Fujairah crisis also represented an early watershed for the UDF and Sheikh Mohammed's pan-union members' emirates. For the first time, they had faced an armed conflict between two sides. In the pre-union past, loyalties would have been divided strictly down ethnic and tribal lines. As a unified military force, the UDF could not split along such lines and remain loyal to its command. Six months into the life of the UAE, the Sharjah/Fujairah Bedu dispute had presented such a challenge: Of the several hundred men sent in as peacekeepers, dozens came from Sharjah and Fujairah. The results were encouraging.

"We were delighted," says Khalifa Al Naboodah. "There was no question of factionalism. The troops there worked as UDF men first and foremost, setting aside their traditional loyalties. Of course, this is how it should be, but this was very early in the life of the UAE."

The UAE's leaders overcame the first crisis in the young life of the country and Sheikh Sultan bin Mohammed Al Qassimi (behind Sheikh Zayed), brother of the deceased leader of Sharjah, joined the Supreme Council.

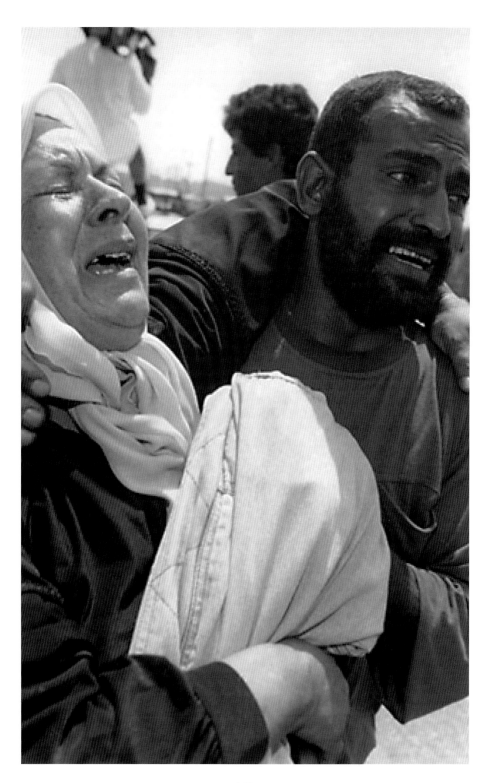

Chapter Twenty-One

"We fight to move ahead the peace…."

> He who controls the past commands the future.
> He who commands the future conquers the past.
> — *George Orwell, author*

Sheikh Rashid was 59 years old when the UAE was established through the federal agreement. Since his teens he had played a role in affairs of state, and from the late 1930s had effectively ruled over Dubai. Taking on a back breaking workload, he had laboured to develop the sheikhdom through the pre-oil years, a pace which only increased when the petro-dollar opened the way for even bigger and better development. And through the late 1960s he had also vigorously pursued the federation, in an energy sapping three years of ongoing diplomacy.

One could have expected the newly installed UAE Vice President to be tired of his responsibilities, but instead those around him at the time saw a new Sheikh Rashid, charged by the need to adapt his city to the realities of its position within a larger state, and manage development of this larger entity.

"His workload during this period was enormous, but he loved his work," says Khalifa Al Naboodah. "On top of Dubai there was also the federation to consider. There were roads to be built, houses to construct and more. He would often visit project sites before the contractors had arrived in the morning and be waiting for them with comments. He would go on working all day and in the evening we would all meet at the Jumeirah Majlis until late in the night. We called the Jumeirah Majlis Dubai's version of Hyde Park Corner, as it was open for anyone to come and express an opinion. Ideas were discussed and refined between politicians, engineers and military leaders, all nationalities and walks of life. This was true democracy.

Palestine and the fate of the Palestinians remained a key issue for the leaders of Dubai and the UAE.

Sheikh Rashid had a packed diary of public commitments, yet dismissed concerns for his personal safety although many Arab statesmen had paid the ultimate price for their life in politics.

"How Sheikh Rashid kept up his schedule we did not know, and men a lot younger than him used to escape for a couple of hours' sleep. As I said, it was his love for his work which gave him this energy."

There was a lot of work to be done, for as UAE Vice President he had taken on far wider responsibility than when it was his burden simply to care for the people of Dubai. This new position had also added a new element to Sheikh Rashid's life. Those around him considered his life was now in danger. Yet he insisted on maintaining his simple style and that the people had open access to him.

Keen expatriate horserider Anita Mehra Homayoun encountered the nation's Vice President many times during early morning hacks around the town with her father, Dr Abu Torab Mehra, who was responsible for bringing the Iranian Hospital to Dubai.

"Sheikh Rashid would arrive in his car, sitting next to his driver in the front seat, the pair alone," she recalls. "He was very informal and relaxed, asking my father questions. I remember his piercing, yet soft eyes. He was always asking questions and interested in what was going on in the finest detail. His zest and enthusiasm for Dubai and its development were amazing."

While Dubai's Ruler shunned additional security, Sheikh Khalid's death had only served to highlight the uncertainties surrounding those in power throughout the Middle East. Regional politics were a minefield, which regularly claimed the lives of Rulers and senior politicians. In 1971 alone – the year before Sheikh Khalid's death – senior officials including Iraqi Prime Minister, Air Marshal Hardan Takriti, and

Jordanian Prime Minister, Wasfi al-Tall, were assassinated despite being very well guarded.

Dubai and the UAE clearly played a more reserved role and were, by comparison to Iraq and Jordan, relatively neutral and therefore less likely to make enemies. The UAE, though, was asserting its national identity and opinions on a wide range of issues affecting the Middle East. Many senior UAE officials had only light protection, and clearly the Emirates were not considered immune from the malaise of terrorism. This was borne out by the extremist killing of Khalifa Ahmed Al Mubarak, UAE Ambassador to France, on February 9, 1984. Closer to home, the March 1975 slaying of King Faisal ibn Abdul Aziz Al Saud of Saudi Arabia, by a disenfranchised relative during an open Majlis, was ample proof of the burden of power.

As UAE Vice President, later with the dual portfolio of Prime Minister, Sheikh Rashid was now a far higher-profile player on the regional stage. His reputation as a serious politician only enhanced the security threat perceived by Dubai and federal officials. As a relative neutral, at one time or another Sheikh Rashid met major leaders and political figures from virtually all sides of the splintered divide. Americans, Iranians, Palestinians and Jordanians, all seem to have considered him someone who would see past the rhetoric. As Khalifa Al Naboodah put it, "He was accepted by all the Rulers of the Arabian coast, of the Gulf and the major players from Europe, Russia and North America. From what I saw, when he talked people would take his opinion seriously and know he meant exactly what he said. There were not enough politicians like him."

As such, Sheikh Rashid must always have been in a measure of danger, particularly when exposed in public. However, to the disquiet of those charged with his security, he dismissed such trappings of power, claiming that they restricted his free movement and access to people.

"Sheikh Rashid absolutely refused security, or a bodyguard," recalls Al Naboodah, who in 1971 was assistant Minister of Defence to Sheikh Mohammed. "Eventually a compromise was reached with soldiers in his bodyguard dressed in plain clothes, and keeping their arms well hidden. We argued that you could never properly assess the dangers to his security, certainly those which came from outside the UAE, but Sheikh Rashid would never be persuaded."

Even then, Sheikh Rashid would often stop his car by the side of the road, flag down his bodyguard following in a car behind his, and then send them back to the palace or instruct them to wait at his office. Relatives and officials were often sent into a spin as the Ruler and his close friends disappeared into Dubai to review projects, without any security cover or, indeed, anyone knowing exactly where he was.

The seeds of the discontent that swirled across the Middle East like a violent summer shamal had been sown three-quarters of a century before at the first Zionist Congress, held in the Swiss city of Basle in 1897. Its organiser, Theodor Herzl, had stated: "At Basle I founded the Jewish state. In 50 years everyone will perceive it."

Fifty years and 85 days later, on November 29, 1947, the United Nations approved the partition of Palestine. In doing so, the world community laid the foundations for a divisive and bloody conflict that has dragged on until the present day.

The UAE was never going to be a front-line state in this struggle. But from its creation, the UAE's leadership has supported the Palestinian cause. Through the national treasury, the UAE remains one of the Palestinians' biggest supporters. The UAE offers financial, political, moral and relief aid to the Palestinians.

Both Dubai and Abu Dhabi also gave to the Palestinian cause from their own funds. Sheikh Rashid was a noted supporter within the Arab world, and his sons have continued to channel major funding to the Palestinian National Authority and directly to the Palestinian people.

Sheikh Maktoum and his brothers, without fanfare, began their own work for Palestinians in the Occupied Territories around this time, supporting many families whose breadwinners had been murdered by the Israelis. They continue this aspect of private help to the present day, in some cases having paid the living expenses of a refugee family for decades. The Al Maktoum Foundation and Mohammad Bin Rashid Al Maktoum Charitable and Humanitarian Establishment are two organisations under the brothers, which have made significant impact upon the lives of tens of thousands in the Occupied West Bank and Gaza. Through these organisations, and often through undisclosed back channels so as to retain anonymity, Sheikh Rashid and his sons have sponsored orphanages, a number of village schools and clinics in the Occupied Territories and in refugee camps in Lebanon and Jordan.

During the remainder of 1972 and into 1973, tensions grew with increasingly bitter actions by both Palestinian groups and Israeli forces.

Sheikh Mohammed in the Control Tower at Dubai International Airport speaking to the hijackers. (inset) The JAL Boeing 747 on the tarmac.

In July 1973, this emerging international crisis found its way to Dubai. On the morning of July 20, a Japan Air Lines (JAL—now Japan Airlines) Boeing 747 took off from Amsterdam en route to Tokyo. Aboard were 137 passengers and the usual complement of crew. Shortly after the aircraft reached its cruising altitude, five passengers – four Palestinians and one Japanese – seized control. The five, who had smuggled small arms and a number of bombs on board, instructed the pilot to set a course for Dubai International Airport.

The Japanese hijacker was Osamu Maruoka, an experienced field operative of the Japanese Red Army (JRA). The leftist JRA had formed an alliance with militant elements of the PLO around 1970, and members were believed to be in a Syrian garrisoned area of Lebanon's Bekaa Valley. The JRA's stated goals were to overthrow the Japanese government and monarchy and help ferment a world revolution. Palestinian militants perceived Japan and Holland to be supporters of Israel. Therefore a Japanese airliner, flying from Holland, was an ideal target for both organisations.

Shortly after noon, the UAE government was informed that a hijacked Boeing 747 was apparently heading in the direction of Dubai. Within an hour, both Sheikh Zayed and Sheikh Rashid had decided that the UAE's Minister of Defence should take direct responsibility for the crisis. He was summoned from the UDF base on the outskirts of Dubai and briefed by officials, including the Japanese ambassador.

By the time the captain of the JAL aircraft had radioed the control tower at Dubai International Airport requesting clearance to land, the airport had been cleared. Other aircraft heading for Dubai had been diverted. UDF troops were discreetly deployed around the perimeter of the airport. In the control tower, a skeleton staff of volunteers remained with a small number of officials and worried observers. Sitting at the main control desk was Sheikh Mohammed. He gave the pilot clearance and watched the aircraft land. Over 140 lives were now directly in his hands.

Former civil aviation official Mohidin bin Hendi recalls the scene: "There was a great deal of tension in the control tower. We were still unsure as to who the hijackers were and what they were demanding. Sheikh Mohammed looked calm, but we were all nervous. Nothing like this had ever happened in the UAE or the Trucial States."

After the aircraft had taxied to a halt a distance from both the terminal building and control tower, the long process of developing a dialogue with the hijackers began. First to speak with Sheikh Mohammed was Maruoka, the most experienced of the five hijackers and described as a cold and calculating character, a ruthless killer. Appealing to the UAE's pro-Palestinian stance, he insisted, among other demands, that the hijackers be allowed to disembark with guaranteed free passage so that they could escape. Although the UAE was indeed ardently pro-Palestinian, there was no way a young state that prided itself on its position in the international community could allow this. Negotiations began.

In the face of dark hints that passengers might be sacrificed to prove the hijackers' seriousness, Sheikh Mohammed talked into the night with Maruoka and the senior Palestinian hijacker on board. President Sheikh Zayed arrived to show solidarity, while Sheikh Rashid consulted with his son by telephone several times each hour. The Japanese ambassador was on hand throughout the crisis as most of the passengers on board the aircraft were his countrymen. Anti-JRA officials flew into the UAE from Tokyo to join the effort.

This stalemate continued for a second day and into a third. Throughout, Sheikh Mohammed remained in the control tower. During periods of quiet, he catnapped in a chair. For nearly 72 hours, the time that the 747 was on the tarmac in Dubai, he struggled to build trust with Maruoka. The Japanese hijacker was angry that his demands had not been met, yet did not go through with threats to murder passengers. Experts said that this was probably because he never felt threatened and received a quick response to his demands for food and new movies on board. The UDF stayed well away at the fringes of the airport. Deliveries of food and supplies were managed carefully to avoid giving the nervous hijackers cause for suspicion.

But while Maruoka was relatively comfortable, Sheikh Mohammed was not. One wrong move might have led to wholesale slaughter. In the annals of aircraft hijacking, there are dozens of bloody incidents that started with a misunderstanding or with the negotiator taking too hard a line. These situations were unpredictable. "Sheikh Mohammed was unwilling to see any lives lost. This was his overriding concern – his bottom line," says bin Hendi. "All his actions over nearly three days of contacts with the hijackers were primarily motivated by the need to preserve life."

Against this backdrop, he also needed to protect the reputation of the UAE so that terrorists did not see it as a safe haven. This would invite more hijackers to head for the Emirates in future. Nearing the end of three days on the ground, Maruoka and his fellow hijackers found themselves getting nowhere. Sheikh Mohammed's security forces had not threatened them, but neither was he proving a soft touch. He had set his negotiating position and had stuck with it: the hijackers, he said, should surrender and face justice.

This they would not do, and subsequently resolved to look elsewhere for a safe haven. There now came a crucial decision. The hijackers, who were known to have explosives, threatened to blow up the airplane. Reluctantly, Sheikh Mohammed decided to avoid bloodshed and allowed the 747 to be refueled. On the morning of July 23, the JAL aircraft took off and headed towards Benghazi Airport in Libya. There, around 87 hours after the hijack began, passengers and crew were released and the aircraft was set on fire and ultimately destroyed.

The fate of the Palestinian hijackers is not recorded. However, some 15 years later Maruoka, by then the leader of the JRA, was arrested and, on December 7, 1993, sentenced to life imprisonment for his role in hijacking two JAL flights, in 1973 and 1977.

The hijacking drama added to Sheikh Mohammed's growing reputation. He had slept for less than three hours during the three days that the Japanese airliner was in Dubai, yet he had maintained a cool head throughout. Later the Japanese government showed its appreciation for his efforts by extending an official invitation to visit Japan.

Weeks later, Sheikh Mohammed was again involved in a drama, only this time one that would have even more profound repercussions for the UAE and the Arab World at large. At the beginning of October 1973, official business took Sheikh Mohammed to Cairo. The Egyptian capital – dubbed 'Umm al-Dunya', the mother of the world – remains one of the region's favourite cities, a riotous cacophony of contrasts where donkey carts vie with Mercedes-Benz cars for right of way on narrow roads and suited businessmen share coffee shops with peasants dressed in traditional gelabiya. From his favourite hotel, the Nile Hilton, Sheikh Mohammed used every opportunity to explore this most vibrant of cities and to pray in the city's historic mosques: Ibn Tulun, Al-Azhar and Muhammad Ali.

Sheikh Mohammed's schedule was dominated by consultations with his counterparts in the Egyptian government and military. Egypt had been one of the UAE's leading supporters after its formation and nowhere was this more apparent than in terms of military cooperation. Egypt had trained by far the largest proportion of UDF's men in addition to seconding officers to the UAE to aid the Ministry of Defence. Sheikh Mohammed enjoyed close ties with many senior officials. During this visit, Sheikh Mohammed also held talks with Egyptian Foreign Minister Ismail Fahmy.

On Thursday, October 4, after a meeting with General Saaduddin Al Shazliy, the influential Chief of Staff of the Egyptian armed forces. After this, Sheikh Mohammed hurried hurried back to Dubai where he formed new medical units and organised drills and equipment checks for them. Although it was the Islamic Holy Month of Ramadan, leave was cancelled for all UDF personnel and UDF bases were put on standby. At this stage of its development, the UDF was not yet trained and equipped to take part in open warfare but, if necessary, senior officers were confident that the UAE's armed forces could play a significant support role in the war effort.

On October 6, 1973, Egypt and Syria launched a coordinated surprise attack against Israel. That morning, UAE President Sheikh Zayed telephoned both Egyptian President Sadat and Syrian President Hafez Al Assad to say that all the UAE's resources were theirs on request.

For two days, with the Israelis in turmoil, the Arab armies pushed deep into territories lost five years earlier. At one time the Syrian armour was only a few hours away from Tel Aviv. The Egyptians achieved something miraculous in successfully managing an unopposed penetration through the Barlev Line. This was the biggest Arab success in decades of conflict with Israel.

One week into the conflict, Israel had mobilised its reserves and stopped further penetration on either front. In the battle zones, there were heavy casualties on both sides and the fighting was fierce. In the UAE, tension mounted as it seemed increasingly likely that the Emirates would be asked to participate in the Arab effort. On October 11, Vice President Sheikh Rashid reiterated that the UAE was ready to do whatever was asked of it by Sadat and Assad.

Sheikh Rashid stated: "The UAE follows, with great concern, news of the fighting that our brothers have launched on the Egyptian and Syrian fronts in order to liberate our land and our nation's dignity. The

Sheikh Zayed, Sheikh Rashid and Egyptian President Anwar Sadat greeting Egyptian Air Force pilots.

UAE believes this war concerns the whole Arab nation, which should place all its means at the disposal of this effort. The international community has to shoulder responsibility for the Palestinians."

The same day, Sheikh Mohammed was asked to send medical teams to both Cairo and Damascus and, within hours, two teams were in the air and heading for the battle zones.

On October 15, the US began a major airlift of arms to Israel. With the full might of the US military machine backing them, the Israelis quickly gained a battlefield advantage and turned the tide. Unable to match the assisted Israelis, Sadat realised the effort was doomed. On the Egyptian front, peace came on October 23 under the terms of a United Nations-brokered ceasefire. Two days later peace descended on the Syrian front, but not before Israeli bombers got in the last word by dropping tonnes of ordnance on civilian areas of Damascus, killing hundreds of women and children.

Sheikh Rashid had commented: "The UAE believes this battle concerns the whole Arab nation." He, Sheikh Zayed and the government would place an ever greater emphasis on helping the Palestinians through the provision of social support in areas cut off from the world and ravaged by poverty inflicted upon them.

Yet the October War of 1973 had changed the Arab world. The perceived success of Arab forces redressed the imbalance caused by the events of 1967. Now it was time to build upon the peace that followed. For Sheikh Rashid and his sons, that meant more work on the most vibrant economy and nation in the modern Middle East.

"WE FIGHT TO MOVE AHEAD THE PEACE..."

Chapter Twenty-Two

What is the point?

*The rung of a ladder was never meant to rest upon, but
only to hold a man's foot long enough to enable him to
put the other somewhat higher.*
— Thomas Henry Huxley, biologist

"...what is the point of keeping it in the bank?..." Sheikh Rashid
wondered aloud in the Majlis. The Dubai Ruler was careful with his
emirate's money. Government reserves were invested wisely.

It was similar to a generation later when amidst one of the most
extraordinary construction booms ever seen in the world, his son,
Sheikh Mohammed, would comment: "I would like to tell capitalists
that Dubai does not need investors; investors need Dubai. And I tell you
that the risk lies not in using your money, but in letting it pile up."

But for the time being, Sheikh Rashid's emphasis was in laying the
foundations for Dubai's growth in the 21st century. His investment
portfolio was carefully chosen and administered only by those he trusted
most. And, indeed, Dubai had one of the most advanced banking
systems in the Arabian Peninsula.

The longest established was the British Bank of the Middle East, now
called HSBC Bank Middle East, which had opened in Bahrain in 1944
and, in 1946, its first branch in Dubai. Among other prominent names,
or later to be leading names, was the National Bank of Dubai, which had
been established in 1963 with one branch in Deira. The bank had been
an immediate success and in 1970 a new headquarters, inaugurated by
Sheikh Rashid, opened beside the Creek. Attracted by the growth of
Dubai, a number of foreign banks had also sought and won permission
to open branches in the sheikhdom.

*By the early 1970s the youngest of the four Maktoum brothers, Sheikh Ahmed,
had returned to Dubai, having completed his schooling abroad and was taking
on a role in the emirate, both as Deputy Head of Dubai Public Security and
within public life in general.*

Dubai Petroleum Company's Fateh oil field was the primary source of the emirate's 300,000 barrels per day of production. (right) Production in Dubai was notable for three 'Khazzans', the first floating oil storage vessels in the world.

In 1969 the Commercial Bank of Dubai was established as a public shareholding company by an Emiri Decree issued by Sheikh Rashid. In the beginning, this bank was owned by Commerzbank, Chase Manhattan Bank and Commercial Bank of Kuwait, with UAE businessmen holding a minority stake.

"Sheikh Rashid was keen to build a healthy banking sector to underpin the commercial sector," says Abdullah Saleh, chairman of National Bank of Dubai.

But, to Sheikh Rashid, banks were alien in the sense that he wished to make Dubai's revenue work. In 1973 the Gulf Arab oil exporters were Saudi Arabia (7.3 million barrels per day), Kuwait (2.8 million bpd), Iraq (2 million bpd), Abu Dhabi (1.3 million bpd), Qatar (600,000 bpd), Dubai (300,000 bpd), Oman (60,000 bpd) and Bahrain (60,000 bpd).

On January 19, 1974 the Gulf states reacted to a major Iranian deal that inflated the oil price, by announcing that they were doubling the price of crude to between $11.65 and $13 a barrel. Even going on the lower figure, this gave Dubai oil revenues of close to $3.5 million per day, or $1.28 billion a year. It was money that he believed needed to be used.

The emirate's oil revenue was being boosted by a booming commercial sector. Its non-oil trade was growing at a healthy pace, and an influx of immigrants boosted the economy. From 1968 to 1975, a wave of immigration boosted the population across the seven emirates from 180,000 to nearly 560,000, a majority of this influx heading to the booming city under Sheikh Rashid. Most immigrants – then, as

now – were Indian, Persian, Baluchi, and Arabs from other Gulf and Middle Eastern states, although there was also a surge in Europeans and North Americans

The increase in oil prices meant that Sheikh Rashid and his administration could move more quickly and decisively than ever on local and national levels, with much more control over their destiny. Although he was the Vice President of a nation, and Ruler of a quickly evolving emirate, Sheikh Rashid still ran his state in a simple manner.

"When he was once addressed to support the construction of a hospital in another emirate, he sent me the same day to examine the situation and report back to him," states Khalaf Al Habtoor, then a young national drawn by Sheikh Rashid into the Majlis, who would go on to be a prominent businessman. "That emirate desperately needed a hospital. I told Sheikh Rashid the same afternoon. He ordered the construction of two hospitals there, and detailed plans were presented two weeks later."

Dubai was expanding at an unprecedented rate. Sheikh Rashid, after devoting most of his attention and efforts toward creating the federation, was free to consider the development of Dubai and of the Emirates as a whole.

Economic and social development were his speciality. Surrounded by his capable sons, Sheikh Rashid was full of confidence, a fact mirrored in his projects, which grew in size and scope during the same period. The biggest and most audacious was the port. His Port Rashid project had attracted business and generated revenues far beyond projections. But Sheikh Rashid recognised that the Gulf still had a massive shortfall in capacity. He believed that with oil continuing to infuse the regional economy, Dubai could only benefit if it were positioned to meet that demand.

During 1970 and 1971, amid the tribulations of the union process, he grappled with a quandary. Although there was a need for additional port capacity, the shipping lanes around Dubai were already overcrowded. Sheikh Rashid brought up the issue of a new port in his Majlis many times. In private, his sons were also consulted.

"I'm not looking forward to next year, or even the next five years," explained Sheikh Rashid. "I'm looking ahead perhaps 50 years. We've got money, so what is the point of keeping it in the bank? Eventually we will definitely need more port capacity and in 20 years this could cost us double or triple the price to build than it will cost us now."

Although the cost of an undertaking on the scale that Sheikh Rashid was considering was huge enough to make most of his closest advisors baulk, he persevered.

"Sheikh Rashid confounded everyone around him," says Abdullah Darwish, private secretary to Sheikh Zayed, a position which often took him to the Dubai Ruler's Majlis. "His ideas were so far ahead. He was looking at what Dubai would need a few decades on. Some believed that he was building white elephants, projects with ridiculous over-capacity. But he knew what he was doing. While most people were all thinking for now, he was thinking a generation ahead."

One morning in 1972, just before dawn, Sheikh Rashid woke one of his closest European advisors, Neville Allen, with a telephone call. Allen was summoned to a hillock around 35 kilometres outside Dubai's city limits. He was met by Sheikh Rashid who drew his attention toward the shoreline.

"Down there," he said, "I want to build a port."

"I gave him a rough estimate," Allen recalled. "Then and there he told me to go ahead with the project. He was an exceptionally brilliant man who worked with lightning speed."

Within days, planning for Jebel Ali Port – Mina Jebel Ali in Arabic – was underway. There were many sceptics in the Majlis. It was not that Sheikh Rashid had to appeal to a constituency that could block his decisions, but that he believed in 'Arabic democracy'. Those he drew into his Majlis, from all walks of life, represented something of a

Sheikh Rashid launched the ambitious Jebel Ali Port project in 1972.
His decision was to be proven visionary.

parliament for Dubai. There was an inherent advantage in that they were not career politicians but society's high achievers and brilliant thinkers. They were there to give good advice to the Ruler. Their collective opinion mattered to him and he rarely pulled rank.

However, few in his Majlis could see any need for Jebel Ali Port. "I think reaction in the Majlis was, frankly, incredulous," says Abdullah Saleh. "Most thought the idea of a port way out of Dubai in Jebel Ali was foolhardy."

Such was the scale of the project that it took four years, until August 1976, just to complete planning for Jebel Ali. The initial phase, comprising some 66 berths, was not fully completed until 1983.

With the benefit of hindsight, Saleh says: "Not for the last time, Sheikh Rashid was proven quite right. In fact, if you consider that ultimately Dubai would have had to have additional port facilities, the eventual bill of $1.7 billion was minuscule compared with one of perhaps six times that if you attempted to build Jebel Ali today."

The same can be said of the Dubai Dry Docks project. A similar plan had been proposed in Sheikh Rashid's Majlis in the late 1960s and had found few supporters. Sheikh Rashid had dropped the idea, but had not forgotten it. In 1973, such was his confidence in the idea that he revived the concept. On December 30, he signed a contract worth £95 million to construct a massive dry dock, which opened in 1979 and was the biggest in the Middle East. It boasted three basins, one of which accommodated vessels of one million DWT (dead weight tonnage).

Dubai Dry Docks was expensive to build and a long time in repaying the investment. It was just one of many ambitious projects that Dubai launched during the first half of the 1970s. During those years, the Majlis was thronged with financiers, architects, land developers and officials from Dubai government and municipal departments that had not previously existed.

Sheikh Hamdan was appointed chairman of Dubai Municipality on July 10, 1974 and presided over a growing local government.

"Dubai Municipality had been formed by Sheikh Rashid in 1956," says Qassim Sultan. "Of course, times had changed and by the mid-1970s the Municipality had a far greater role to play in Dubai's development. The town was becoming a city. Development needed to be guided and the inhabitants of the city needed services. Sheikh Hamdan brought a lot of impetus to this process and guides Dubai Municipality

This ariel view shows the mouth of the Creek, dominated by Port Rashid and (above) Dubai Dry Docks.

371

until the present day. That the city is what it is in 2006 has a great deal to do with Sheikh Hamdan's demands that we play a pro-active role."

Sheikh Hamdan and Sheikh Mohammed now effectively took on roles of lead advisors to Sheikh Rashid, while their brother, UAE Prime Minister Sheikh Maktoum, spent much of his time on federal matters.

The fusion of Sheikh Rashid's ability to seize an opportunity with a new modern administration brought an increasing number of projects to the fore. Jebel Ali Port and Dubai Dry Docks were quickly followed by the inauguration of the Dubai International Trade Centre (later renamed the Dubai World Trade Centre). Sheikh Rashid gave the green light to this £56 million project on October 15, 1974. The Middle East's tallest building at the time, the Trade Centre was constructed at a site on the town's outskirts, thought quite inappropriate by most observers at the time.

"Preposterous," says George Chapman, an expatriate who was part of the 1970s boom. "That is what most people called the World Trade Centre when Sheikh Rashid started building. Some questioned Sheikh Rashid's continued sense of vision, ironic when in fact the lack of vision was on the side of those who remained doubters."

"Many people, particularly expatriates, laughed at what was going on," says Anita Mehra Homayoun. "It was exciting to see so much development underway, but few people who lived here saw the need for so many big new projects. Yet later they did have the effect of creating confidence in the future."

From its opening, the Dubai World Trade Centre was fully occupied by commercial tenants. More than a quarter of a century later, although overshadowed by new, taller buildings like Emirates Towers, the Dubai World Trade Centre remains a towering monument to Dubai's status as the region's commercial capital.

The 1970s were also years during which Dubai embarked on a number of industrial undertakings. The first was the development of a £150 million aluminum smelter (later named DUBAL), for which Sheikh Rashid signed a contract on May 6, 1975. He laid a foundation stone on October 15 the same year. Construction of the smelter itself started in 1977, the first metal was tapped and poured in 1979, followed by initial metal sales in 1980. It was a project that was a huge investment

The Dubai World Trade Centre was the tallest building in the Middle East when opened and became a symbol of the emirate's progressive outlook.

for Dubai and had to go right. Sheikh Rashid placed Sheikh Hamdan in charge.

Today Dubai Aluminum Company Limited (DUBAL) is one of the world's largest single-site aluminum smelters.

"If visionary is a word often used to describe Sheikh Rashid, then the successes of DUBAL perhaps sums up what that vision was all about," says Ahmed Al Tayer, vice chairman, DUBAL.

Recognised as the industrial flagship of the region, by 2006 DUBAL contributes a huge slice of Dubai's non-oil revenue and is a multi-billion dollar, state-of-the-art smelter complex consisting of seven potlines, a 1,645 megawatt power station, a large carbon plant, two cast houses, a 30 million gallon-per-day desalination plant, laboratories, research facilities, and port and storage facilities.

A quarter of a century after its inauguration, the company produces 686,000 tonnes of primary aluminum per annum.

"Although much has changed since the decree of Sheikh Rashid announcing the beginning of DUBAL's operations, the company's driving vision remains much the same. Under these guiding principles, DUBAL has blazed its fast-track industrial triumph and has become one of the UAE's great business success stories," says Sheikh Hamdan.

In 1975, Sheikh Hamdan took charge of another major industrial development in the form of Dubai Natural Gas Company (DUGAS), set up to process gas from offshore oil fields. The majority of natural gas produced as a by-product of oil drilling around the world is flared; in many cases the remainder is re-injected to aid in oil recovery. Sheikh Rashid's government was opposed to wasting this valuable natural asset and developed a Gas Master Plan to harness the flame, processing this into liquefied petroleum gas (LPG). DUGAS's liquid natural gas (LNG) plant was the only one in the world to use associated gas as its primary feedstock.

DUGAS's Jebel Ali plant came on-line in 1980 with a capacity of 20,000 bpd of natural gas liquids (propane, butane, and heavier liquids) and 2.1 million cubic metres of dry gas (methane) a day.

Dry gas is piped to DUGAS, where it fuels a large electric power and desalination plant. A small portion of the LNG output is locally bottled and consumed, but most is exported to Japan. A gas terminal was opened at Jebel Ali in 1980, which can handle tankers of up to 48,000 tons.

This was followed by the Dubai Cable Company (DUCAB), a project inaugurated in 1977 by Sheikh Rashid. Sheikh Hamdan was also handed responsibility for this, another of Dubai's vital non-oil industrial projects. Established in 1979, DUCAB is owned by the governments of Dubai and Abu Dhabi, and is the leading manufacturer of electric cables in the Middle East.

Today, the DUCAB factory in Jebel Ali extends over 54 hectares. Plant enhancements and extensions in 1985, 1988, 1991, 1998, and the most recent expansion in 2001 – to manufacture medium and high voltage cables – have helped DUCAB keep pace with the steady growth of the economy. Factory floor space and production capacity has more than tripled since 1979.

During the same period, the emirate placed great emphasis on infrastructure and embarked on large scale road, bridge and tunnel building programmes. A second Dubai Creek dredging project was undertaken, at a cost of $71 million. Some $55 million were allocated for homes for UAE nationals in 1975. These and other projects boosted the local economy, created jobs and developed Dubai further. In this way, the Maktoum family believed that Dubai could continue to evolve and sustain itself as a regional commercial centre even after the end of the oil-producing era.

'What is good for the merchants is good for Dubai' is a statement often attributed to Sheikh Rashid. Today, his sons recall that their father continued to remind them of this basic principle throughout their time at his side in government. One influential book from 1975, *A Hundred Million Dollars A Day*, penned by a senior writer from London's *Financial Times*, states: "...the emirate's development has been stimulated [through]...liberal commercial and financial regulations, and almost total absence of civil servants, paperwork and restrictions of foreign ownership of local industrial and commercial enterprises."

A hearty distaste for bureaucracy was another of Sheikh Rashid's traits that he took pains to pass on to his sons. As Dubai grew, so did its administration, out of necessity. His sons retain some of their father's attitude, resulting in both a carrot-and-stick approach toward bureaucrats, with awards for top Dubai government performers and dismissal for those found ineffective.

There are two forms of charity in Islam – obligatory and voluntary – called zakat and sadaqa, respectively. Zakat, from the verb zaka, which signifies 'to thrive', 'to be wholesome', 'to be pure', and means purification. One of the most important principles of Islam is that all things belong to God, and that wealth is therefore held by human beings in trust. Zakat is the amount of money that every adult, mentally stable, free, and financially able Muslim – male and female – has to pay to support specific categories of people.

The only difference between sadaqa and zakat is that while both kinds of almsgiving are necessarily voluntary (that being the reason for the word 'sadaqa', covering both forms of contribution), the former is the result of an inspiration on the part of the donor.

Both forms of charity are underscored by a strict set of principles: that the giving must be done in the way of God; that the giver must not expect reward in this world; and that such acts of charity must not be followed by references or reminders to the acts of charity, the latter meaning that there should be no public relations value sought from such gestures.

Sheikh Rashid and the Dubai government took seriously their commitments in this regard. And Palestine was a continual project.

Since 1948, well-intentioned United Nations and European organisations and charities have succeeded in perpetuating the refugee state through three generations, a unique feat in the history of the UN.

There are almost 7.2 million Palestinians scattered in every corner of the globe. The West Bank is inhabited by approximately 2.4 million, while 1.4 million live in the Gaza Strip, a narrow strip of land that is one of the most densely-populated territories on earth, often called the 'biggest jail on the planet'.

The majority of the Palestinians are direct descendants of refugees who fled or were expelled from Israel during the 1948 Arab-Israeli War. Poverty, unemployment, and poor living conditions are widespread, exacerbated by the imposition of generalised border closures which disrupted previously established labour and commodity market relationships between Israel and the Strip. The most serious negative social effect of this downturn was the emergence of high unemployment.

Independent health studies have revealed very high levels of dietary deficiency among the Palestinian population, as much as 17.5% of children aged 6 to 59 months suffering from chronic malnutrition. Some 53% of women under 40, and 44% of children, were found to be anaemic. The healthcare system continues to face severe challenges.

Sheikh Rashid and Sheikh Ahmed oversee a military presentation ceremony. Both were key supporters of efforts to prop up the education system in Gaza and the West Bank.

A highly evolved and modern Palestinian identity has defiantly emerged despite an often high degree of prejudice, adversity and negation. National institutions are under constant threat. In addition to health services, education is constantly undermined by Israeli actions.

Sheikh Rashid and his sons have, over the years, supported the construction of thousands of homes, a number of orphanages and hospitals. This was always done quietly and without fanfare.

"Sheikh Rashid believed that it was a duty," says Khalaf Al Habtoor. "He insisted that such things were done quietly."

The Dubai Ruler believed passionately that when statehood eventually came the Palestinians needed to be ready, but, as Al Habtoor says: "Even this visionary never foresaw that by the beginning of the 21st century this would still not have happened".

The Dubai Ruler fervently believed that the only way that the Palestinians would be in a position to govern themselves properly when statehood arrived was to ensure that there was an educated base of talent into which Palestinian government could tap. Education, therefore, was a pet project of his. In 1985 he discovered that Birzeit University was facing a crisis due to a lack of funding and ongoing harassment from the Israelis.

A decade earlier, in 1975, Birzeit College, in the village of Birzeit north of Ramallah, became Birzeit University after adding third- and fourth-year college-level programmes. Birzeit was widely considered the foremost educational institute in the Palestinian territories, and has played a significant role in political affairs.

Former Birzeit University students include prominent Palestinian intellectuals and political figures such as Hanan Ashrawi, Sari Nusseibeh, Ibrahim Abu Lughod and Azmi Bishara.

On November 13, 1985, Sheikh Maktoum donated $2.4 million to build a new student complex on campus.

"The Maktoum family have been generous to Birzeit University," says Dr Sami Al-Sayrafi, Vice President for Administration and Finance. "In addition to the student complex, many smaller donations have been made and within the student body I know of many who were sponsored by Sheikh Rashid, his sons, the Dubai government or charities emanating out of Dubai."

The Israeli authorities closed the university by military order on numerous occasions between 1973 and 1992. During the years from 1979 to 1992, the university was closed 60% of the time, including a closure of 51 months, although it continued to operate underground during that period.

"Education has flourished in Palestine in spite of efforts to deconstruct it," says Dr Al-Sayrafi. "This has been achieved in no short measure thanks to our friends abroad, and among these we certainly count Dubai."

Around this time, Sheikh Rashid said: "The UAE fully supports all Arab causes, with the Palestinian cause at the top of the list, putting its financial resources at the service of such issues and participating in all Arab summits and contacts, aiming at harmonising the Arab stand in such issues."

In the late 1970s, the Dubai government donated tens of millions of dollars to the PLO (Palestine Liberation Organisation) privately and without fanfare. The Maktoum family believed that such support was simply their duty; any news of donations made by Dubai came from the Palestinian side. In October 1979, for instance, it was reported that Dubai had donated $5.5 million to the Palestine National Fund. Months later, donations of $275,000 and $2.2 million were sent to organisations supporting Palestinian families bereaved as a result of Israeli aggression in the Occupied Territories.

During this period, the Maktoums made a personal commitment to the Palestinian cause that has grown with time. Stories of the brutality and acts of depravity meted out to the Palestinians by the Israeli army of occupation could not be ignored. They had seen the terrible conditions in which half a million dispossessed Palestinians lived in refugee camps around the region. It was a situation that could not fail to touch a person and, at least to some degree, a little of the suffering could be alleviated.

"As Prime Minister of the UAE Sheikh Maktoum had led the nation's efforts, politically and economically, to support the Palestinian people," says Saeed Khalfan Al Ghaith, Minister of State for Cabinet Affairs. "It was a cause that was close to his heart."

"Sheikh Hamdan has supported literally dozens of causes in the Occupied Territories, like clinics, schools and orphanages," says Mirza Al Sayegh. "He considers this a duty of someone in his position, but does not treat the issue like that. It is close to his heart."

Former Cabinet member Dr Abdullah Omran Taryam recalls: "Sheikh Mohammed concerned himself with the Palestinian issue. In Dubai, many local support initiatives were a direct result of his influence. In the Federal Cabinet, he spoke out fervently in favour of moves to support the Palestinians."

"Sheikh Ahmed has reached out very privately to the victims in Palestine. He sponsored hundreds of children through their education," says Dr Al-Sayrafi. "He has also sponsored text books and other school equipment for dozens of schools, especially at kindergarten level."

Over the years Sheikh Rashid and his sons have done their best to extend help directly to the victims of the occupation and their families. This has been one of their least-publicised efforts since the mid-1970s. Without publicity of any kind, various charities funded and managed in Dubai began supporting a variety of causes in the Occupied Territories and in the refugee camps dotted around Jordan, Lebanon and other Middle Eastern states. Children's charities have been foremost among those receiving support, because much Israeli emphasis has been on stifling education and forcing Palestinian youngsters to live under a punitive set of rules.

PLO leader Yasser Arafat once famously described the youth of the Occupied Territories as "yet another generation of Palestinian children on the verge of being lost..." Successive generations have gone the same way for over half a century.

In response, a network spreading out throughout the Occupied Territories has sponsored impoverished families. By meeting the living expenses of a family, this enabled the children in the home to pursue an education instead of seeking ways to eke out a living on the barren and often dangerous streets of the Occupied Territories. This required a long-term commitment while the child was going through school; otherwise such support would have been pointless.

Since the late 1970s, children as young as eight have been offered this support. In some cases, this has extended to support for their families while they went to university. Over the years, thousands of children have passed through primary, secondary, college and university thanks to Sheikh Rashid's patronage.

One unique aspect of this philanthropy has been its delivery. None of the families or children involved has any idea of the identity of their benefactor. Sheikh Rashid was now spending vast amounts of money, albeit quietly and without fanfare.

Despite the overwhelming number of statistics and indicators, global poverty is hard to measure. Although it is simple to characterise abstractly the living conditions of the world's impoverished population, there is no widely accepted, standard method of identifying the poor and, therefore, of measuring the exact extent of global poverty. Nonetheless, whatever the bias of the analyst or the method used to estimate the number of global poor, the statistics are appallingly high, almost beyond comprehension. Consider, for example, *UN Chronicle* of September 1990, which stated that one billion people live in absolute poverty, 100 million persons are completely homeless, 800 million persons go hungry every day, 1.75 billion people are without access to safe drinking water and 1.5 billion persons are without access to primary health care.

"Sheikh Rashid never forgot the days when life was not so good on this peninsula," observes academic Abdullah bin Jassim Al Muthairy. "Particularly during the years of depression following the decline of the pearling industry, he had seen for himself the effects of crushing poverty, while he also knew life before proper education and medical facilities. As the leader of an increasingly wealthy Muslim state, he also knew of his responsibilities."

Of the projects Sheikh Rashid championed, he was particularly proud to have funded the construction of a vitally needed emergency ward and operating theatre complex for the Bahawalpur city hospital, in the Punjab region of Pakistan. The area had long suffered from a crippling lack of medical facilities, in parallel to Dubai and the Trucial Coast several decades before. Sheikh Rashid was a regular visitor to

Pakistan for hunting, was friendly with many of the nation's most influential leaders, and certainly aware of the plight of many in the state.

His friend and regular travelling partner, Hamad bin Sukat, says that as he crossed Pakistan, Sheikh Rashid would often overwhelm national and local officials whom he encountered, asking without warning for a suggestion on what he could do to help build or supply. Around Pakistan the Dubai Ruler arranged the construction of dozens of mosques, several schools, an orphanage and the Bahawalpur medical complex, for which he laid the foundation stone in January 1979. When the building was completed in February 1982, the Rashid Wing of BV Hospital in Bahawalpur boasted the most modern operating theatres in Pakistan.

That same year Sheikh Rashid also reacted to international appeals from aid agencies as the war in Afghanistan forced hundreds of thousands of Afghani civilians to flee. An unexpected wave of refugees had begun pouring into Peshawar in Pakistan over the freezing winter months. Media reports indicated that thousands might perish in freezing conditions. Sheikh Rashid scrambled his government to react, and within 56 hours of hearing of the emergency, an aircraft had left Dubai International Airport, filled with tonnes of supplies including food, blankets, tents and winter clothing. Other consignments followed.

While the Dubai government had an established plan and budget for foreign aid, this incident sums up Sheikh Rashid's personal approach. It was much the same in July 1985 when, in response to the global Live Aid appeal for the starving millions of Africa, the Dubai government donated £1 million to the fund, administered by Irish rock star Bob Geldof. This was the largest single donation to Live Aid, which prompted the United Nations Children's Fund (UNICEF) to say, in a media release, that the leadership of Sheikh Rashid and his sons "provided the world with an admirable example. Their action proves their belief in the common destiny of all people on earth and their effective support for the concept of humanitarian assistance from people to people, irrespective of race, colour or creed."

Chapter Twenty-Three

Growing Pains

By union the smallest states thrive.
By discord the greatest are destroyed.
— *Sallust, Roman historian*

Nearly five years into the life of the United Arab Emirates, all was going relatively well in Dubai. But on a federal level, fundamental problems were emerging that were to test the resolve of the Maktoum family and, indeed, threaten the existence of the state that they had worked so hard to create. During the early 1970s, it was generally accepted that each individual emirate would gradually melt, over time, into a strong, centralised authority, the Federal government.

However, while a national identity had indeed formed, each emirate had also scrupulously maintained a separate political and economic integrity. Was the UAE going to evolve into a union or a loose federation? This was the question many asked.

This issue would come to a head during the constitutional crises of 1976 and 1979.

In 1976 this materialised through calls for a more unified state and the abolition of Article 23 of the Provisional Constitution, which stipulated that local ruling authorities should control local resources. When it was formed in 1971, the UAE was set on a five-year cycle. The terms of the President and Vice President, the highest offices, were half a decade. Similarly, the provisional constitution had a five-year mandate before it could be renewed or replaced by a permanent version. The federal budget for 1976 allotted funds for the construction of 5,000 new homes nationwide, 43 water and electricity projects, 100 new hospitals and health centres and 134 new schools. The education budget for 1976 was $142 million, almost nine times that of the $16 million allowed for

From a virtual standing start, in just half a decade the UAE had developed an extensive education infrastructure.

education in 1972. Incredible progress had been made.

"As we found so often in Britain, having money to spend is one thing, spending it correctly and efficiently is another matter," said Sir Edward Heath. "The UAE had spent its federal funds wisely and achieved startling progress."

But the UAE was on the brink of a crisis that would rock its very foundations. During the creation of the federation, and its subsequent growth, certainly no one had a greater impact than the President, Sheikh Zayed. The Abu Dhabi Ruler's presence hung over the Emirates like that of a benign father figure, to expatriates as well as nationals. His impact on the regional and international stages had grown in equal measure, his influence far outstripping the UAE's military or economic importance. As a symbol of nationhood to Emiratis, Sheikh Zayed was the glue that held the seven emirates together during their early days as a single entity. By 1976, few could imagine a UAE without him at the helm. But as his five-year mandate as UAE President drew to a close in the second half of 1976, in private at least, Sheikh Zayed could see just that eventuality.

In 1975 and 1976, the UAE suffered its first economic slow-down. The people of the country, many of whom had gone into business in a post-1971 boom, had no experience of recession and failed to cope. Local markets lost much of their liquidity, and people blamed the government. This had stung Sheikh Zayed and Sheikh Rashid whose government had given the people the public services and civic infrastructure denied them for so long. During the summer of 1976, Sheikh Zayed listened to these complaints against his government in silence. Perhaps the only public display of his disquiet came in an interview in early 1976 during which he said: "May God be my witness, I am uninterested in the Presidency. From the depths of my heart I wish that my brothers, the Rulers, relieve me of its burden. I shall be the first one to co-operate in all understanding and endearment with a new President."

Few people believed that the UAE President was serious.

In addition to his unhappiness, Sheikh Zayed thought that the Presidency had been given little tangible authority. He believed that a President should hold strong executive powers and be able to make a real difference. He also held strong views on Article 23 of the Provisional Constitution.

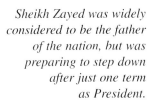

Sheikh Zayed was widely considered to be the father of the nation, but was preparing to step down after just one term as President.

On August 1, one of Bahrain's leading daily newspapers, *Akhbar Al Khaleej*, published an interview with Sheikh Zayed in which he revealed that he had decided not to accept a second five-year term as UAE President. This triggered a five-month crisis that cast the very future of the union into doubt.

August 2, 1976, was scheduled to be a red letter day in the modern history of the emirate of Dubai, the inauguration of a first phase of the showpiece $750 million, 74-berth Jebel Ali Port. Sheikh Rashid's greatest project had taken just four years from inception to inauguration of a first section, and provided the most modern port facilities in the region at a time when demand was far outstripping capacity.

Although it was a Dubai initiative, the opening of Jebel Ali Port was a national event, such was its importance to the nation's infrastructure and economy. The Dubai Ruler had invited Sheikh Zayed to officiate, and the rest of the UAE Supreme Council to attend.

Coming one day after the news that Sheikh Zayed intended to refuse a second term as President, the opening of Jebel Ali Port presented the first opportunity for consultations. Sheikh Humaid bin Rashid Al Nuaimi, Crown Prince of Ajman, summed up reaction best when he told reporters: "We cannot let our father decline to remain as President. We shall mobilise the people who love him so that they can ask him to stay on."

Sheikh Zayed, however, was adamant. At one point early in the crisis, he is reported to have said: "My fellow Rulers are aware of the need to give the Presidency some teeth, powers which can be used to take decisions, which would free the President's hands to effect change. I personally have come to this difficult decision for the simple reason that being President is worthless when it means little more than being a feather in my cap."

Days later, Sheikh Zayed travelled to Somalia on an official visit, continuing on to Sri Lanka for a summit of the Non-Aligned Movement and private trips to India and Great Britain. He was away from the country for a month.

Behind the scenes, senior members of the Supreme Council and Cabinet struggled to pursuade Sheikh Zayed to reverse his decision. Among those were Sheikh Zayed's Prime Minister, Minister of Finance and Industry and Minister of Defence. On August 5, the day Sheikh Zayed left for Somalia, Sheikh Mohammed told newspaper reporters: "Sheikh Zayed was instrumental in the creation of the union and instrumental in the continued process of building the UAE and its national institutions. This is why it is imperative that he reconsiders his resignation. Can anyone really contemplate a United Arab Emirates without Sheikh Zayed as its head of state? I have to say that I cannot."

During these tense weeks, Sheikh Zayed and Sheikh Rashid, the Vice President representing the Supreme Council, worked hard to find a solution to the President's complaints. They met several times each week and had lengthy telephone conversations ahead of an emergency session of the Supreme Council on October 16 and a scheduled meeting on November 6.

As contacts between President and Vice President continued, once again Sheikh Rashid called upon his sons. It was, of course, necessary for Sheikh Rashid to consult with, and report to, his fellow Rulers, and now his sons took on the role of roving ambassadors. As Sheikh Zayed's position became clear, in order to retain him as President it would be incumbent upon the Supreme Council to agree to changes. With such a sensitive and complex issue, this was a gradual process.

On the morning of November 6, Sheikh Mohammed flew his father to Abu Dhabi for a key event. This was to be a meeting that not only decided the fate of the Sheikh Zayed Presidency, but the shape of the UAE over the next stage of its development. Sheikh Rashid brought a set of proposals crafted by himself and the five other Rulers over weeks of contacts.

The seven Rulers voted unanimously to amend the Provisional

Constitution to state that the federal government was the only entity able to establish and maintain a military force. The President was also handed sweeping powers in the areas of immigration, border security and others. A new internal security apparatus was to be created under his command. New powers were also given to a unified Federal Ministry of Information.

These changes placated Sheikh Zayed. On November 28, the UAE President accepted the resignation of the Cabinet. Four days later, on the fifth anniversary of the UAE's creation, Sheikh Zayed's office issued a statement that read: "I have renewed the vow I took to shoulder the responsibilities of President of the United Arab Emirates. With a strong commitment, I approach these duties with the concern demanded of a parent for his children, with the sincerity of a leader towards his people..."

The threat of Sheikh Zayed's departure may have produced a national crisis, but it also offered insight into the union process. Perhaps the most positive was the show of unity that the near loss of Sheikh Zayed had inspired. While the trappings of nationhood – the bricks and mortar of ministry buildings, government meetings and armed forces comprising men from different emirates – were all well and good, they amounted to nothing if the people continued to think of their emirates as separate entities.

As the UAE's Minister of Defence observed: "If the people themselves don't identify as being part of a union, there is no union."

Three years later, a second and final constitutional crisis arose with the Supreme Council's rejection of a memorandum that recommended the abolition of internal borders and an end to arms purchases by individual emirates.

Many in the pro-union government believed that this process should be accelerated. Other influential figures, among them Vice President Sheikh Rashid, were happy to see a gradual progress.

After simmering for some time, the issue was debated in the open for the first time during a Federal National Council meeting on June 27. The result was a joint committee under Deputy Prime Minister Sheikh Hamdan bin Mohammed Al Nahyan. The committee met for the first time on July 5, after which members made a series of visits to the UAE's seven Rulers. They followed up, on February 13, 1979, with a report that encompassed recommendations on the unification and

Sheikh Zayed and Sheikh Rashid overcame their differences through statesmanship and the crisis of 1976 led to a strengthening of the federation.

389

command of the UAE armed forces, internal security, contributions to the federal budget, immigration, planning and other key issues.

This document brought into the open a divergence of opinion within the ruling elite and ultimately exposed differences between the union's two leading protagonists. Within a fortnight, Sheikh Zayed and Sheikh Rashid had met four times to discuss their respective positions. Despite their personal relationship, which was consistently hailed as warm and full of mutual respect, the two men struggled to find common ground.

This was a crisis that tested both leaders and those around them.

On March 12 the two Rulers met at a campsite in the Ghantoot area of Abu Dhabi, close to the Dubai border. This could easily have resulted in a meltdown of the federation, but they both understood that this would be catastrophic for the region. Both men gave ground and agreed on some points, but they remained divided in key areas, notably the integration of many government departments and public institutions.

Historians have made much of the fact that on March 19, the UAE's Supreme Council met in Abu Dhabi and both Dubai and Ras Al Khaimah were under-represented. On the surface, this appears to indicate a serious slide into disunity, but Dubai and Abu Dhabi were communicating throughout this period: the two leaders exchanging daily telephone calls.

On April 22, the two leaders and Sheikh Sultan bin Mohammed Al Qassimi, Ruler of Sharjah, met with Sheikh Sabah Al-Ahmed Al-Sabah, the Kuwaiti Minister of Foreign Affairs, who was in the UAE as part of a joint Kuwaiti/Saudi Arabian mission. A day later, Sheikh Sabah met with the Rulers of Ras Al Khaimah, Fujairah and Ajman, along with the Crown Prince of Umm Al Quwain.

During Sheikh Sabah's visit, a compromise formula began to take shape. As per Sheikh Rashid's wishes, a variety of government institutions including the UAE armed forces remained on a 'slow-track' toward unification. As Sheikh Zayed wished, Dubai began to pay some of its oil revenues directly into the federal treasury.

On April 30, the Supreme Council unanimously voted in favour of appointing Sheikh Rashid as Prime Minister, in addition to Vice President.

Sheikh Rashid said: "To be entrusted by my brother, Sheikh Zayed, and his brothers, the members of the Supreme Council, to form the Cabinet, is a responsibility which I will not shirk, especially at a key point in the history of the union from a domestic, regional and international point of view..."

As observers had hoped, in his new role as Prime Minister Sheikh Rashid brought to bear all of his simple and practical style. He got things done. Two months later he unveiled a new 23 member Cabinet, in which Sheikh Hamdan retained his portfolio as Minister of Finance and Industry and Sheikh Mohammed remained Minister of Defence.

Stepping down as Prime Minister, Dubai Crown Prince Sheikh Maktoum would take on a greater role at home to compensate for Sheikh Rashid's involvement in national affairs. Sheikh Rashid now steered the federal government in much the same way as he had run Dubai. When bureaucracy slowed things down, he would immediately circumvent normal procedures to get things done quickly.

Roads, electricity, water and housing programmes were all accelerated through his intervention. He would personally track the work of contractors who fell behind on their schedules and would appear unexpectedly on project sites to review progress.

The UAE had a federal budget of $266 million in 1979. A year later, with Dubai paying $463 million into national funds, Sheikh Rashid embarked upon one of the most dramatic development booms seen in the region.

Historians differ in their views of the federal crisis of 1979 and its ultimate resolution. Many consider the compromise as procrastination by the UAE's leaders, putting off key issues for later. Hindsight allows a different interpretation. In the years following 1979, the UAE grew stronger. Unification might have taken longer in some areas, but nevertheless it did happen.

In 1979, the UAE's oil production stood at 668 million barrels. Per capita income in 1978 was $5,260 – the world's highest. Sheikh Rashid would drive a national programme to diversify the economy away from a reliance on oil, as he had done in Dubai. The federation was about to enter the same Sheikh Rashid-driven period of hyper growth that had so transformed Dubai a generation earlier.

Sheikh Zayed and Sheikh Hamdan on an official visit to Pakistan,
hosted by President Zulfikar Ali Bhutto.

On an official visit to India, where Sheikh Zayed and Sheikh Hamdan were principally hosted by Prime Minister Indira Ghandi.

Chapter Twenty-Four

The Colonel

My father contended that, in the animal world, there is no creature so noble or intelligent as the horse. It is a belief that I have never had cause to question.
— *Sheikh Hamdan bin Rashid Al Maktoum, Statesman*

Sports are full of surprises, and none more so than horse racing. One of the biggest surprises of the modern era was a small bay colt with three white stockings and a crooked blaze. Unsaleable as a foal in 1961, he became virtually priceless as a stallion. A surprise champion and winner of two legs of racing's legendary Triple Crown, he was retired to stud in 1964 and sent back to his native Canada to stand for $10,000 per live foal – a bargain. Just as he was a surprise champion during his racing career, the stallion was to prove a dramatic and spectacular success at stud, shaping the modern sport to a greater degree than any horse in the last half century.

Within three years of his arrival at stud, his progeny began to appear on racecourses and it was immediately apparent that this stallion was passing on his ability – and more – to his offspring. He produced champions from his first season at stud, and went on to become leading sire in North America in 1971 and 1977 and leading sire in Britain in 1970, 1977, 1983 and 1984. Significantly, he attracted the attention of racing's most influential players, including a small group of horsemen from the other side of the world.

In October 1976 Sheikh Mohammed set out on a private mission to Britain. This was a trip that would have huge significance for him and his brothers and would ultimately change the face of one of the world's oldest sports – horse racing. He was in England to attend Tattersalls' October Yearling Sales in Newmarket.

Newmarket racecourse was the first European track that Sheikh

Colonel Dick Warden.

Hamdan and Sheikh Mohammed had visited, nearly a decade earlier, for thoroughbred racing. The family had a long history with horses in the Gulf, where riding and breeding Arabians are viewed as the pastimes of nobility. Dubai's Ruling family had maintained stables at Al Fahidi Fort, its seat of power, since arriving in the sheikhdom in 1833. Sheikh Rashid had been a noted horseman in his youth and had taught his sons about horses. Sheikh Hamdan recalls his father showed him what to look for in a good horse, and the way to examine its head, neck and legs.

In 1969, Sheikh Maktoum had constructed a small Western-style racecourse in Dubai at a site in Al Ghusais, now part of Dubai International Airport. Al Ghusais had a simple grandstand and tight oval racecourse, complete with wooden running rail. Crown Prince Sheikh Maktoum maintained a stable there, while Sheikh Mohammed opened his own yard, a complex that also boasted a sandy track with wooden running rail, in the Za'abeel area of Dubai. The brothers raced their horses, ridden by expatriate jockeys, but it was also not uncommon for Sheikh Mohammed to ride full-blown races against friends.

During this period, horses also played a part in Sheikh Mohammed's working life. Dubai was still far from becoming the paved metropolis of today. Even in the city, there were sandy areas unsuitable for the decidedly suburban Mercedes-Benz patrol cars of Dubai Police, so it maintained a mounted division – as it does to this day.

With his interest in horses, Sheikh Mohammed had a particular affinity for this area of his command. When a batch of new animals from Britain arrived in Dubai in early 1976, a contract handled by the

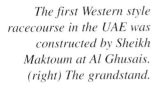

The first Western style racecourse in the UAE was constructed by Sheikh Maktoum at Al Ghusais. (right) The grandstand.

Curragh Bloodstock Agency (CBA), he was on hand for its arrival.

It was here that Sheikh Mohammed encountered one of the men who would most influence the course of his life. Accompanying the horses was Colonel Dick Warden. Silver-haired and neatly balding, Warden was a World War II hero renowned for his exploits working with the Resistance behind enemy lines in Occupied France. In peace time, the Old Harrovian was something of an enigma. Sometime thoroughbred trainer, amateur race jockey (he rode his own horse, 'Harewood', in the 1932 Grand National), gambler and general raconteur, Warden was above all a gentleman from the old school. He is remembered by those who encountered him as being superb company. Sheikh Mohammed was charmed by the 68-year-old veteran horseman and, almost immediately, the two struck up a friendship that would last until Warden's death in 1990.

Sheikh Mohammed was intrigued by Warden's stories and his successes as a trainer. Warden particularly delighted in relating his exploits with 'Ballisland', joint top-rated filly in the 1948 Free Handicap and winner of the Seaton Delaval Stakes and Cherry Hinton Stakes, and of other superb animals that he had trained. Almost inevitably, the subject of ownership came up. The young sheikh was attracted to the sport and the two talked at length about the possibilities. Warden told colleagues at the CBA on his return to Europe: "I've met this charming Arab who would like to buy a few horses. I think that one day he could be a very big owner."

Over subsequent months, the two men stayed in touch while Sheikh

Mohammed considered becoming an owner. Some months later, with Sheikh Maktoum also having expressed an interest, he contacted Warden and agreed to visit Newmarket for the October Yearling Sales at Tattersalls, the world's first and leading thoroughbred sales firm. Having decided to become an owner, Sheikh Mohammed was keen not to miss the sale. Despite a political crisis at home, he headed for Newmarket for a couple of days.

The atmosphere of a thoroughbred sale can be intoxicating, and Tattersalls' coliseum-like indoor sales ring is the most thrilling in the world. The whinny of young horses and the rolling brogue and falling hammer of the auctioneer fill the air. Around the sales ring, a buzz of anticipation from buyers lifts and energises the atmosphere.

Warden promised his new clients that for a relatively small outlay they could try their hands at the sport, have a great deal of fun and, hopefully, win a few races. With a great appreciation for the history and tradition that underpins British racing and breeding, Sheikh Mohammed accompanied Warden to Tattersalls.

The result was three purchases. Two came in the space of ten minutes from a consignment of seven yearlings from Mount Coote Stud, an Irish breeder based in County Limerick. All three horses went into training with John Dunlop, another man who was to play a major role in the Maktoums' first quarter-century in the sport. 'Hatta' and 'Haddfan' were registered as being owned by Sheikh Mohammed, and 'Shaab' was registered to Sheikh Maktoum.

Soon after, Dunlop had his first opportunity to meet his new owner when Sheikh Mohammed visited the historic Arundel Stables in Sussex, a few miles inland from England's south coast. He recalls: "My recollection of meeting Sheikh Mohammed for the first time was that he was a charming and polite man. But my overriding initial impression was that here was a man who knew horses. He asked many questions about the training and preparation of thoroughbreds. Horses, as a species, he understood implicitly and he was attempting to reconcile his own understanding of the subject to the principles of caring for and training thoroughbreds, finely-tuned equine athletes."

In the months that followed Dunlop were happy with the progress made by 'Hatta', 'Haddfan' and 'Shaab' and looked forward to the following spring in the belief that the trio could provide their owners with a few winners and encourage them to buy a few more horses.

Hatta (blue colours) claims the Molecomb Stakes.

Sheikh Mohammed had his first wins in 1977 when Dunlop saddled 'Hatta' to four successes, topped off by victory in the Group Three Molecomb Stakes at Goodwood. A year later, he celebrated four victories with three thoroughbreds: 'Haddfan', 'La Silentiaire' and 'Swanlinbar', part of his growing string of racehorses.

In 1979, Sheikh Maktoum celebrated his first winner, with four-year-old 'Shaab', his first Tattersalls purchase three years earlier. 'Shaab' won four races that summer, including the prestigious Gordon Carter Handicap.

A year later, in 1980, Sheikh Hamdan added his name to the family roll of honour. His first winner, 'Mushref', also went on to finish third in the listed Champion Two Year Old Trophy.

"A lot has changed in the quarter century since Mushref first carried my silks into the winners' enclosure," says Sheikh Hamdan. "The sight of a newborn foal struggling to its feet, or a powerful thoroughbred showing his paces on the gallops, continues to be as enchanting to me as it was when this journey began."

The late Major Dick Hern, one of Europe's most respected thoroughbred trainers, recalled the era. "Rarely in my career did I ever see any owners who involved themselves in British racing so purely for the pleasure," he said.

Major Hern was one of the Maktoums' first choices to handle a number of the thoroughbreds on their behalf. "All the Maktoum brothers were knowledgeable. Their understanding of the intricacies of training horses allowed them to be patient with the horses and myself.

Of course, this allowed us time to bring out the best in the horses," added Major Hern.

In 1981, 16 horses won races in Britain for the Maktoum family. Six of those were Sheikh Mohammed's, and he ended the season with nine wins. This was the first season during which his horses emerged with the quality to be genuine competitors in the season's pattern races. 'Jalmood', a star in subsequent years, won three races as a juvenile and took third in the Group One William Hill Futurity. In the spring, Sheikh Mohammed's 'Taufan' claimed second in the European Free Handicap.

But it was in 1982 that the family made its big breakthrough. That year, 36 horses won races in England for the three sheikhs from Dubai, 20 of those taking 30 races in Sheikh Mohammed's increasingly familiar maroon-and-white silks. His stars were 'Jalmood', which took the Group Three Derby Trial Stakes and the Scottish Derby, listed winner 'Henry's Secret' and 'Noalto', which placed in three group events. One of 'Noalto's' most significant races that season was a third at Newmarket in the Dubai Champion Stakes. This end-of-season race was sponsored by the Dubai government for the first time that year, the start of a sponsorship that has lasted until the present day, making it one of the longest ongoing deals in modern British racing.

The biggest of Sheikh Mohammed's stars in 1982 was undoubtedly 'Awaasif', a three-year-old filly rated as one of the most talented of her generation. After finishing fourth in the Oaks at Epsom – Sheikh Mohammed's first showing in a Classic – she took the Group One Yorkshire Oaks. Later in the season she finished third in the Prix de l'Arc de Triomphe at Longchamp. 'Awaasif's' owner was in Paris to see her run possibly the best race of her career and was impressed by her performance as well as the charm and prestige of Europe's end-of-season middle distance Classic. The Prix de l'Arc de Triomphe became, and has remained, one of his favourite events on the calendar.

Weeks before 'Awaasif's' powerful showing in Paris, however, the family reached a milestone in its first six years in British thoroughbred ownership. This came courtesy of 'Touching Wood', a three-year-old son of 'Roberto', one of the leading thoroughbreds in Europe in modern times. 'Touching Wood' had run several outstanding races in 1982 in the blue-and-white colours of Sheikh Maktoum; in June, he had finished third in the Derby at Epsom, at that time the world's greatest and best known race.

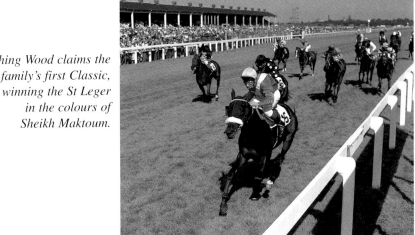

Touching Wood claims the family's first Classic, winning the St Leger in the colours of Sheikh Maktoum.

The atmosphere at Epsom on Derby Day was nothing new to any of the Maktoum brothers. They had attended the race and had runners on several occasions. But to see 'Touching Wood' in contention was an adrenalin pumping thrill to match no other. With a crowd of 40,000 people cheering and Sheikh Maktoum's colours among the leaders in the closing stages of the race, this was something special.

By September, the colt had another target. 'Touching Wood' had stayed on strongly in the latter stages at Epsom, suggesting that a race over a longer distance would suit him better. The biggest long-distance race for three-year-olds was the final Classic of the season, the St Leger, over one-and-three-quarter miles. One sunny September afternoon, the Maktoum brothers were in Doncaster, an industrial town in Northern England. They were not disappointed. As the field rounded the final bend into the long home straight, 'Touching Wood' was settled in behind a pacemaker and moving smoothly. With three furlongs remaining, the colt swept into a commanding lead and was never challenged. His winning time in the Classic was the fastest since that of a colt named, coincidentally, 'Bahrain' in 1935. Sheikh Maktoum later told a British writer of the thrill of his first Classic success. "I could not feel my legs, I did not know if I was sitting or standing," he said.

The scene that day embodied the spirit later carried over into the modern day Godolphin organisation. The brothers celebrated as one. Each saw 'Touching Wood's' win as a family affair. Sheikh Mohammed, in an interview with *Pacemaker*, the journal of the British thoroughbred breeding industry, said: "Of course I want my horse to win. But if he can't then I want my brothers' to come first."

The thrill of 'Touching Wood's' Classic successes (he later added the Irish St Leger, becoming the first to collect an English-Irish double since 'Trigo' in 1929) and 'Awaasif's' exploits encouraged the Maktoum brothers toward greater involvement in the sport. A year later, their combined string numbered around 250 horses; Sheikh Maktoum collected two more Classics with 'Ma Biche' (1000 Guineas) and 'Shareef Dancer' (Irish Derby) and youngest brother Sheikh Ahmed enjoyed his first racecourse success in Europe with 'Wassl', a gift from Sheikh Mohammed, in no less prestigious a race than the Irish 2000 Guineas. The Maktoum brothers had fallen in love with the 'sport of kings' and were about to enter their first golden era in the sport.

The aforementioned stallion, with his three white stockings and a crooked blaze, was 'Northern Dancer'. By the early 1980s, Sheikh Mohammed's initial interest in thoroughbred racing had grown into a passion. After he and his brothers had shared in the thrill of 'Touching Wood's' St Leger success in 1982, Sheikh Mohammed's involvement in the sport grew quickly and he became champion owner in Britain for the first time in 1984. That year, 54 horses piloted by jockeys wearing his familiar maroon and white silks won races in Britain. His brothers Sheikh Maktoum, Sheikh Hamdan and Sheikh Ahmed, and his cousin Sheikh Marwan Al Maktoum were also gaining prominence as leading owners.

This was the year the British press began referring to 'The Maktoum Phenomenon', and the phenomenon began to gain pace. Their love of the sport knew no bounds. While at first they wished simply to own winners, it was a natural progression to move on to breeding their own winners. To achieve this, Sheikh Mohammed purchased two British properties, Dalham Hall Stud near Newmarket and Aston Upthorpe Stud near Didcot. He and his team then retired some of his highest-class mares from racing and purchased others to create a broodmare band of around 30 horses.

In 1984, one British publication estimated that the brothers from Dubai would have over 250 horses in training by the following summer. The brothers had great respect for the traditions on which the sport was built but were unencumbered by any notion that they had to follow blindly the same route as generations of owners before them.

For decades, the training, campaigning and care of thoroughbreds had remained largely unaltered. But as times changed, so did theories on equine nutrition, on the capabilities of a thoroughbred and on a horse's ability to travel and perform. Someone seeking a competitive advantage in horse racing – as in business – could be expected to look at the industry from different perspectives. It was this lateral thinking that allowed Sheikh Mohammed to follow his individual path to success.

The late Dr Michael Osborne, former chief executive of the Emirates Racing Association and Dubai World Cup Organising Committee, put it in a nutshell when he commented, many years later: "Nothing is impossible for the Maktoum family. They have the vision. They are not tied to tradition. They have a totally open mind."

The early 1980s were years of tremendous change in world racing. A new professionalism that would quickly shape the sport into a global industry was taking root. Sheikh Mohammed, having fallen in love with thoroughbred racing as a sport, was also attracted by the industry: he was intrigued by new ideas and interested in people who took a different approach. At a time when he was preparing to participate in the sport on a larger scale, his competitive nature was quickly to become apparent.

Racing was also waking up from decades of stagnation and beginning to modernise. The first major manifestation of this fresh direction came in the form of the Breeders' Cup in America in 1984, a single day of championship racing, offering millions of dollars in purses.

A year later, Sheikh Mohammed underlined his emerging status as a major international owner when superstar filly 'Pebbles', trained in Britain by Clive Brittain, travelled to the United States to claim the Group One Breeders' Cup Turf. It was a year when Sheikh Mohammed 'arrived' in terms of racecourse success. In addition to this ground breaking triumph for the Europeans in America, Sheikh Mohammed's silks were carried by other notable winners such as 'Bairn', 'I Want To Be', 'Sure Blade' and 'Oh So Sharp'.

Away from the racecourse, the first stirrings of globalisation were changing the sport. Major British owner Robert Sangster and his partners were among the first to recognise the importance of the new North American market. With the expertise of Dr Vincent O'Brien, one of the finest trainers of modern times, they changed the face of the major international auctions such as Keeneland in Kentucky and Tattersalls in Britain.

This group played by its own set of rules. They believed that by buying the best young horses available each year they stood to produce at least

The sale ring at Keeneland.

one outstanding champion colt from among them. This horse could be retired to stud and would earn tens of millions of dollars through the sale of breeding rights or syndication. O'Brien advised them to seek out strong-looking individuals, with an outstanding pedigree. What was more, O'Brien, Sangster and their partners believed that there was only one stallion which could consistently produce at least one star performer with each crop, and that was 'Northern Dancer'. Finally, and crucially, the consortium believed that only by holding all the cards – every one of the gems from 'Northern Dancer's' crop each year – could their plan be guaranteed success.

At its inception, the Sangster/O'Brien consortium was unique, well-organised and probably the strongest financially in world racing. At first, without any consistent competition, they succeeded in securing the best 'Northern Dancer' yearlings that came on the open market.

However, another force was emerging. In 1980, the brothers from Dubai had their own plan. They wished to win the best races with the best thoroughbreds of each generation. Then they would retire these stars to Maktoum-owned stud operations, where they would repay the investment through stud fees and by siring future Maktoum winners.

It was not dissimilar to the Sangster plan; the only real difference was that Sangster and his partners would syndicate their retired champions, some standing at Coolmore Stud in Ireland, which was owned by the consortium, while Maktoum champions would remain in-house.

The first that Keeneland knew about the arrival of the Maktoum phenomenon was a telephone call from New York. Ted Bassett, then president, now chairman of Keeneland, recalls: "We had a call from Hyatt Hotels in New York, saying, 'A very important client of ours is coming, and somehow you need to find accommodation.'"

It was September 1980 and the time of Keeneland's Yearling Sale, when the most blue-blooded of blue-blooded yearlings come under the hammer. All the premium hotels in Kentucky were full. It took all the diplomatic persuasion and arm-twisting that Keeneland officials could muster to obtain a suite for Sheikh Mohammed and rooms for those in his entourage. Still largely unknown in the USA, this gentleman from Dubai created an immediate impression and repaid Keeneland's efforts by purchasing many horses.

But this created yet another headache for the company. Bassett says: "One of the disconcerting factors was our inability to obtain financial credit information prior to the sale." Keeneland Association had to take it on faith that Sheikh Mohammed could pay. However, testimonials from many of the British contingent at the sale that day, along with the knowledge that they were dealing with Arab nobility and a cabinet minister of an oil-rich Middle Eastern state, certainly could not have done any harm.

What the people at Keeneland didn't know then, however, was that the shrewd Sheikh Mohammed had been there before. In September 1979, he had used scheduled flights to arrive in Kentucky incognito. As all the major hotels were full, he checked into a motel near the Keeneland complex, and sat through several sessions of bidding, keeping to the back of the arena to avoid the few bloodstock people there who knew him. At the time, his sole 'black type' success as an owner was 'Hatta's' win in 1977. By the end of 1979, he had enjoyed a total of just 11 winners as an owner.

His mission in 1979 had been to get a feel for Keeneland and observe the workings of the sale. By character, he is competitive and instinctively he knew that he wanted to build a great bloodstock and racing empire. His military training told him to get to know 'the enemy', or at least the competition and that was what Sheikh Mohammed had been doing that previous September: observing the scene, soaking up the atmosphere. Sangster and his partners were there. So were the major American owners and a sprinkling of wealthy Japanese.

He was also there to learn, to assimilate the theories within the industry on what to look for in a thoroughbred to those he had learned as a child from his father, and to what he himself believed as a horseman and thoroughbred owner.

Looking back on 1979, Sheikh Mohammed recalls that Keeneland impressed him. His motel did not. "If you asked for coffee, they said: 'You can get it yourself'," he recalled.

In 1981, Sheikh Mohammed returned to Keeneland with a carefully thought out plan, and with the help to achieve it. Both Sheikh Maktoum and Sheikh Hamdan were to participate. Together, the brothers determined that sufficient investment could materialise into a sustainable bloodstock empire. It was, and is, a sound approach if the right horses materialise. For example, one of the great stallions of modern times, 'Nureyev', won only $42,522 on the track, but earned an estimated $100 million at stud.

The Maktoums and their advisors were not simply in Keeneland seeking winning racehorses, but animals who could go on to become giants as stallions too.

It was clear that offspring of 'Northern Dancer' were emerging as the leading racecourse performers of the day. Therefore the Maktoum family was certainly in the market for his elite yearlings. The cream of the crop. With Sangster and his consortium, and other buyers, all angling in the same direction, the stage was set for a collision of demand that would push the bloodstock industry into an unprecedented boom.

Auction prices in America had gone through the roof in the early 1980s, and million-dollar milestones were passed with regularity. Mostly this was in pursuit of 'Northern Dancer' blood, but the boom had a knock-on effect and the entire market grew apace. As 'Northern Dancer' yearlings were in short supply on the open market, demand grew for the yearlings produced by his sons and daughters already at stud; all the more so when it became apparent that 'Northern Dancer' genes were being passed on to his grandchildren.

In 1984, 40 of the yearlings on offer at public auction passed the million-dollar mark, and the lucky owners who sold one of 'Northern Dancer's' 14 yearlings on the open market received an average of $3,320,357. 'Northern Dancer' blood was so intensely sought that his stud fee had rocketed to more than $1 million with no guarantee.

'Northern Dancer' remained productive at stud until 1986; he was retired the following year at the age of 26 with only one of two mares in foal. But the brothers' decision to invest in the best resulted in a wealth of racecourse successes in the 1980s and laid the foundations for a thriving bloodstock empire.

Today, Sheikh Mohammed's Darley enterprise, a global operation with interests as far afield as Australia, Japan and South Africa, remains heavily influenced by 'Northern Dancer' blood.

For Sheikh Mohammed, what started as a hobby – creating a racing and bloodstock empire – proved a valuable escape from the tensions of an increasingly demanding public career. When circumstances allowed, he shuttled to Europe for one or two days to attend big meetings at which his equine stars were racing. He made the time to sit quietly and read *The Sporting Life*, or speak by telephone with his trainers. As the breeding season approached, he liked nothing more than to sit with his advisors and discuss the possibilities.

"Horse racing and breeding offered Sheikh Mohammed one of his few outlets for relaxation at times of stress," says Mohammed Al Naboodah.

Long-time bloodstock advisor John Ferguson says: "The final decision of matings belongs to Sheikh Mohammed. His knowledge is vast and he understands the complexities of pairing stallions and mares. Although he listens to his own experts, a quarter of a century in the sport has given Sheikh Mohammed his own insight."

Sheikh Hamdan's Shadwell operation spans the world, with three main units – Shadwell Farm in Kentucky, Shadwell Estates in Britain and Derrinstown Stud in Ireland – breeding thoroughbreds that will compete at the highest level all over the world. Sheikh Hamdan holds the distinction of breeding two Epsom Derby winners in 'Nashwan' and 'Erhaab', along with a roll call that includes the winners of Black Type races all over the world, among them 'Salsabil', 'Dayjur', 'Shadayid', 'Unfuwain' and 'Harayir'.

"Shadwell's global success is the result of hands-on management," says Rick Nichols, vice president and general manager of Shadwell Farm. "Under Sheikh Hamdan's direct supervision, Shadwell built an outstanding facility on the best land available and is home to many of the world's top broodmares.

"Sheikh Hamdan is the best all-round horseman I have met. He possesses a tremendous eye for a good individual animal as well as superior knowledge of pedigrees and breeding concerns."

(top) Nashwan claims the Epsom Derby.
(bottom) The colt is led in by his owner.

*(top) The picturesque Shadwell Farm in Kentucky.
(bottom) Derrinstown Stud in Ireland.*

409

Sheikh Maktoum began his owner-breeder interest in racing with the purchase of the historic Harwood Stud in Britain in 1981. At the time there were five broodmares and 15 horses in training. Since then the renamed Gainsborough Stud was been completely re-furbished and re-built and was the worldwide operation centre for Sheikh Maktoum's bloodstock enterprise, comprising of Woodpark Stud, County Meath and Ballysheehan Stud, in County Tipperary, Eire, and Gainsborough Farm, and Dubai Millennium Farm, both in Kentucky. Among the racecourse stars he campaigned around the world were 'Ma Biche', 'Shareef Dancer', 'Shadeed', 'Balanchine', 'Green Desert', 'Ezzoud', 'Hatoof 'and 'Cadeaux Genereux'.

The link between the Arabian horse and modern thoroughbred racing was established some 1,000 years after the death of the Prophet Mohammed. Although 103 Oriental stallions were registered in the General Stud Book as the founders of the thoroughbred breed, only three bloodlines have been maintained to the present day. By 1850, all traces of the others had been obliterated. Only these three – 'Byerley Turk', 'Darley Arabian' and 'Godolphin Barb' – can be considered genuine founding sires.

Like most of the Oriental stallions at the time, they bore the names of their owners. 'Byerley Turk' was used as a cavalry horse by a Captain Byerley in 1683 at the siege of Vienna. 'Darley Arabian' was bought by a Thomas Darley, the British Consul in Aleppo, Syria, as a present for his brother Richard, and reached Britain in 1704. 'Godolphin Barb', the third of the founding sires, found his way into the Cambridgeshire stud of Lord Godolphin, where he lived a productive life until 1753.

With a nice touch of symbolism, Sheikh Mohammed decided on Darley as the umbrella name for his first British breeding operation which he bought in the late 1970s. Fifteen years later, he returned to the sport's origins for a name for the operation that would revolutionise racehorse training – Godolphin.

The origins of the Godolphin concept and operation can be traced back to Derby Day, 1968. Held on the first Wednesday in June every year, Derby Day was a red-letter day in British sport when the country traditionally stopped for ten minutes to watch on television, or listen on the radio, to the race unfolding at Epsom Downs.

In 1968, Sheikh Mohammed was still around a decade away from becoming a racehorse owner, but he had developed an interest in the sport by attending meetings at Newmarket while he studied in nearby Cambridge. That year, events at Epsom pricked his interest for the first time: The newspapers in Britain were full of speculation about 'Sir Ivor', a colt handled by Irish trainer Dr Vincent O'Brien and to be ridden by the world's greatest jockey, Lester Piggott. What was unusual was the colt's preparation. The preceding winter, 'Sir Ivor' had been sent from Ireland to Pisa in Italy, his trainer believing he would be better for some winter sunshine, rather than remaining in the cold and damp Irish climate. 'Sir Ivor' proved O'Brien right: on his return, he took the 2000 Guineas at Newmarket and was routed toward the Derby, where Sheikh Mohammed was in the stands to witness 'Sir Ivor' collect a Classic double, winning by a length and a half.

By the early 1990s, however, Sheikh Mohammed had developed a plan that would bring together his hobby – horse racing – and his passion – Dubai. He believed that advances in equine transportation, and the control and eradication of equine diseases had opened a way for the sport to return to its roots. The Arabian horse had left the Middle East and founded the thoroughbred; now the thoroughbred could leave the West for the Middle East: The wheel could turn full circle.

Horse racing has existed in one form or another in Dubai and the Emirates for centuries.

In Dubai, the first proper race meeting is believed to have been staged at Dubai Camel Track on October 1, 1981, organised by Sheikh Mohammed's Office. Three thoroughbred races were run: a sprint, a mile race and a mile-and-a-half race. Sheikh Mohammed was watching as Za'abeel Stables won two events.

Later, enthusiastic amateurs built and managed a track adjacent to the Metropolitan Hotel in Dubai. Coincidentally this 'Al Met' track was a stone's throw from the site where Sheikh Mohammed later established Al Quoz Stables, home of Godolphin.

The 1980s also saw the emergence of racing elsewhere in the Gulf. Bahrain, which boasted two grass tracks and a modern, well-equipped stadium, hosted several invitational meetings that attracted entrants from the GCC (Gulf Cooperation Council) states. Oman also hosted pan-Gulf meetings. Sheikh Mohammed's Za'abeel Stables and Sheikh Maktoum's Nad Al Sheba Stables, run by British trainers Paddy Crotty and Bill Mather respectively, usually brought home the majority of cups on offer.

The great Mtoto racing in Sheikh Ahmed's yellow and black silks. (inset) Both as an owner and through his popular Jebel Ali Racecourse, Sheikh Ahmed is a key patron of racing in the UAE and in Britain. He is photographed here in the winners' enclosure with his private trainer Dhruba Selvaratnam.

By 1990, horse racing in the UAE still consisted of a loose programme of up to a dozen meetings each winter. At the time, Abu Dhabi Equestrian and Racing Club, the most advanced facility in the Emirates, ran only private meetings. This was managed by 1963 Grand National winning jockey Pat Buckley

Modern racing in Dubai began to take off in earnest in the early 1990s. Sheikh Mohammed's brother Sheikh Ahmed opened a track in the Jebel Ali area of Dubai, while Nad Al Sheba, where an 800-seat stadium had been built in 1988, was upgraded and its track relaid. During the winter of 1991-92, progress was being made at last. Dubai's premium yards, Za'abeel Stables and Nad Al Sheba Stables, had been joined by Sheikh Ahmed's Jebel Ali Stables under Sri Lanka-born Dhruba Selvaratnam, a former pupil trainer of Dr Vincent O'Brien. Sheikh Mohammed had installed a new trainer, Satish Seemar, at Za'abeel. He had met Seemar while in the United States to see equine behaviour guru Monty Roberts. Za'abeel Stables had been refitted and more boxes added to accommodate a larger number of thoroughbreds, Arabians and crossbreds.

That winter, the sport began to benefit from proper organisation, although technically still not being run under international rules. Sheikh Mohammed installed new officials in a variety of positions, importing expatriate expertise but also involving a number of nationals he had encountered through his racing. Among the most notable was Ali Khamis Al Jafleh, a UAE air force officer who had owned horses in Britain during the 1980s. Al Jafleh attended several programmes on racing and racecourse administration in Britain as Sheikh Mohammed groomed him for the future.

Al Jafleh recalls: "Sheikh Mohammed kept his actual plans very much to himself, but we all understood that he was planning to go much further. The opening of Nad Al Sheba early in 1992 underscored that Dubai had the scope to become a notable home for the sport."

On February 29, 1992, Sheikh Mohammed staged a soft opening at Dubai's showpiece venue. One month later at the official opening, appearances by riding stars Willie Carson and Lester Piggott made the headlines.

During the summer of 1992, there were more changes. The Emirates Racing Association (ERA), the sport's governing body in the UAE, was formed and gained the recognition of the International Racing

Conference. Nad Al Sheba evolved into the Dubai Racing Club; Al Jafleh took senior roles in both association and club. A weekly racing programme throughout the winter of 1992 and 1993 attracted leading European jockeys such as Richard Hills and Johnny Murtagh.

This season was the breakthrough for racing in the UAE. Sheikh Mohammed, attempting to restore the popularity of the sport in a region that had all but turned its back on equestrianism, was at his most visible attending nearly all meetings at Nad Al Sheba and some at Jebel Ali and Abu Dhabi. His presence stimulated additional media interest, but crowds remained small, with numbers mainly in the hundreds during the early months of the 1992/93 season.

Equally significant, however, were the developments behind the scenes in Dubai and the UAE. The Middle East had a bad equine health record, particularly with African Horse Sickness (AHS). During the 1960s, a series of wet winters had helped the virus spread through the Middle East from North Africa, carried by the culicoides fly. Tens of thousands of horses and donkeys died. Over subsequent decades the virus continued to be reported throughout the Gulf, although it never reached the epidemic proportions of the past. The mere suspicion of the disease's existence anywhere in the UAE meant that the areas of the racing world accepted as disease-free – notably North America, Europe, Australia and established racing states in the Far East such as Japan and Hong Kong – would never allow the free movement of horses between their territories and the Gulf.

Moving horses in and out of the UAE remained a key aim of Sheikh Mohammed. During this period, the Ministry of Agriculture and Fisheries embarked on the first of regular serological surveys of the Emirates that ultimately would prove that the UAE was free of AHS and a variety of prohibited equine ailments. By 1994, the ministry's evidence was accepted internationally.

In March 1993, with the free movement of horses still some time away, Sheikh Mohammed wished to make a statement of intent; a bold move that would say that Dubai had arrived as a racing centre. As horses could not be shipped to the Emirates, the Dubai Racing Club went for the next best thing – jockeys. On March 26, Nad Al Sheba hosted the inaugural Dubai International Jockeys' Challenge. Five groups of two jockeys were invited to compete, senior riders representing the UAE, the United States, Europe, Australia and Japan.

It was not the top-class horse race to which Sheikh Mohammed aspired, but it was a strong step in that direction. For three seasons, the Dubai International Jockeys' Challenge brought major names such as Gary Stevens, Yutake Take, Thierry Jarnet, Chris McCarron and Pat Eddery, some of the world's most successful and renowned jockeys, to compete for honours in a country that had only just begun its life as a racing nation.

As the building process continued, after the summer of 1993 another racing development in Dubai occupied Sheikh Mohammed. Always competitive, he had not forgotten the lessons of the double Classic-winning campaign 'Sir Ivor' mounted in 1968 after a warm winter in Italy. Sheikh Mohammed wondered whether an entire winter in the pleasant climate of Dubai, rather than that of Europe, could speed the development of a young thoroughbred. He was certain that a thoroughbred could go into its spring and summer campaigns in Europe significantly better prepared than its Europe-based opponents by virtue of having been able to undertake a complete training regime.

It was a theory that would take time to explore, but Sheikh Mohammed resolved to test the water. During the winter of 1993, he quietly had a pair of two-year-olds shipped to Dubai. Both had been reasonable performers during their juvenile seasons, but nothing outstanding. One colt, 'Blush Rambler', was placed in the care of American trainer Richard Conway. A filly named 'Dayflower', which had behavioural problems in addition to abundant talent, was put into the care of Seemar at Za'abeel Stables. Over the course of the winter, the two horses were put through their respective training programmes, the only sign of their significance being almost daily visits from their owner.

Recalls Seemar: "Sheikh Mohammed helped develop, and personally followed 'Dayflower's' training programme throughout her time in Dubai. Most mornings when she worked he was there to see for himself, and many evenings he would visit Za'abeel Stables to see her in her box. The experiment with her was a very personal thing and he was not content to hear the conclusions of others. It was his project and he made up his own mind."

In the spring of 1993, with much of her temperamental problems corrected, 'Dayflower' finished a disappointing second in a specially arranged 'prep' race at Nad Al Sheba. As a result, she was shipped to Newmarket

Dayflower proved Sheikh Mohammed's theories correct and paved the way for the creation of the revolution that is Godolphin.

to take part in the first Classic race of the season, the 1000 Guineas, where she was sent off a 33:1 outsider under jockey Frankie Dettori. She struggled during the early stages, running downhill, but soon after hitting rising ground near the finish of the mile race she ran on strongly to finish a close-up fifth.

Later in the summer, 'Dayflower' won a small conditions event at York under jockey Walter Swinburn, to cement her place in history as the first UAE-trained horse to win a race in Britain. Sheikh Mohammed was watching on the television at home in Dubai when his filly won. By this time he had won a hatful of Classics, dozens of Group and Listed races and literally hundreds of others. The prestige of a minor York conditions race was minuscule in comparison with many of his successes. But in terms of significance, 'Dayflower's' win was to prove a potent lesson that Gulf-wintered horses could be campaigned internationally. Seemar says: "Sheikh Mohammed called immediately after the race and was delighted with her performance. He had selected her personally to go to Dubai, overseen her training programme, made her travel arrangements and directed her campaign in Britain. It was very much a personal success."

From Sheikh Mohammed's point of view, the 'Dayflower' experiment raised as many questions as it answered. One of the biggest challenges was the resistance he met. Some sections of the media were, if not scornful, less than positive towards the idea of doing things differently. Tradition dictated that horses bred in thoroughbred heartlands were trained in the accepted and time-honoured fashion by socially acceptable trainers. The cream of the three-year-olds, the majority trained in Newmarket, were brought out of their winter off-season in spring and prepared for the Guineas at Newmarket. Others would join them from Ireland and possibly even France.

The very idea of a thoroughbred wintering in the Middle East and travelling back to compete in Britain was ridiculous. Few around Sheikh Mohammed, including many of his trainers, racing managers and bloodstock advisors, were enthusiastic.

Fundamentally Sheikh Mohammed was a horseman. Over time, he had gained knowledge and experience of the thoroughbred. He had invested substantial sums in pursuing his dream of a sustainable racing and breeding empire. He believed that this gave him a right to opinions, after listening to his retained experts, on all aspects of the operation. This extended from which stallions were utilised by his mares and which animals were bought at the sales to which races were targeted. To racing traditionalists, this was sacrilege. An owner was expected to pay his training bills each month and leave the rest to his trainer and racing manager. How could someone like Sheikh Mohammed – an Arab who was new to the sport – understand the psyche of a thoroughbred?

This was not an unusual situation for Sheikh Mohammed, who had encountered moss-covered thinking since the beginning of his involvement with thoroughbreds. *The Washington Post* captured the sentiment when, in a profile of Sheikh Mohammed, the interviewer wrote that: "…to many racing insiders, the idea of developing a world-class stable in a desert country where betting was forbidden seemed strange and silly…When he bought three horses at Newmarket, one of his hosts wondered, 'Why don't you sit in your tent and buy camels?'

"When I wanted to start Godolphin...they said, 'What are you going to feed them, sand?'"

Always unorthodox, but never rash, Sheikh Mohammed had his own views and acted on them in the name of competitive advantage. Sheikh Mohammed started Godolphin because he wanted a more personal role in overseeing the training of his horses – and because he thought his horses would have an edge in fitness if they trained in the warm climate of Dubai during the winter.

At a family meeting on December 25, 1993, Sheikh Maktoum,

Sheikh Maktoum greets Queen Elizabeth II after a success in the King George VI and Queen Elizabeth Diamond Stakes.

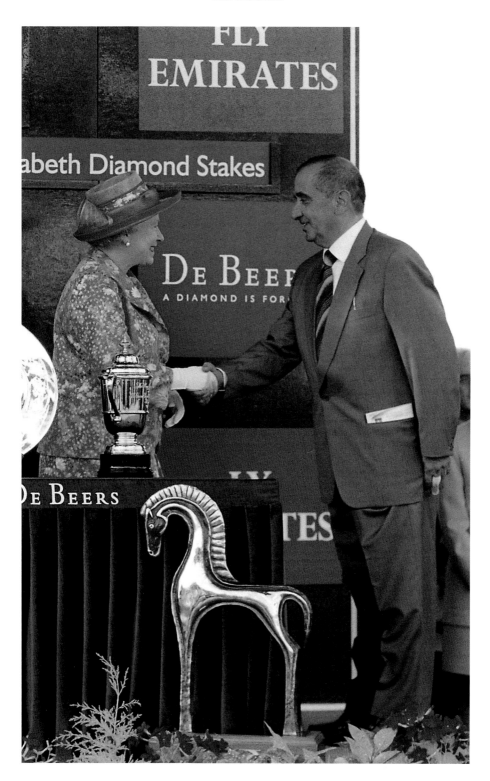

Sheikh Hamdan, Sheikh Mohammed and Sheikh Ahmed discussed the idea and decided to pool their best resources in search of even greater success. The brothers decided upon the name Godolphin, after 'Godolphin Barb'.

Coincidentally, it was 241 years to the day since 'Godolphin Barb' had passed away. The stallion's identity may have been lost to more than a few thousand racing and breeding aficionados nearly a quarter of a millennium after his death – but his famous name was set to make a spectacular return.

Sheikh Hamdan's famed blue and white silks.

Chapter Twenty-Five

Flying High...and Low

Never give in! Never give in! ... in anything great or small,
large or petty... never give in except to
convictions of honour and good sense.
— Sir Winston Churchill, statesman

The last months of 1976 brought a milestone in the history of the Emirates, albeit in tragic circumstances. In 1973 Sheikh Mohammed had been in charge of the UDF when medical teams had been sent to Egypt and Syria to support Arab efforts in the October War. Exactly three years later, he sent men into active service abroad for the first time. What led to this was the tragic unfolding of events in Lebanon.

Long a gateway between East and West, Lebanon has always been strategically important. Moreover its capital, Beirut, lived up to a reputation as the 'Paris of the Middle East'. The population of the country was evenly balanced between Muslims and Christians living together peacefully, creating a melting pot of cultures and lifestyles that gave Lebanon much of its vitality. By the early 1970s, the bright lights of Beirut shone throughout the East.

Arabs were attracted by the opportunity to holiday or do business in a Western-influenced environment where Arabic was the first language. The Maktoums were regular summer visitors to Lebanon in the early 1970s. It was a place where they could escape the rising temperatures of a Gulf summer, while remaining close enough to Dubai to hurry home should duties require.

But from the beginning of 1975, the social equilibrium in Lebanon began to waiver; before long it descended into civil war. The first shots of the war were fired on April 13, 1975. During an ambush in Beirut aimed at Pierre Gemayel, a popular Phalangist leader, four members of his guard were gunned down. The Phalangists were enraged and aimed

Now in his mid-60s, Sheikh Rashid continued to maintain a busy schedule.

their retaliation against Palestinian targets. The same day a bus carrying Palestinian passengers was stopped by militiamen and 26 people were murdered in cold blood.

Divided along ethnic and religious lines, the government was itself paralysed. As various groups took sides, the fighting spread to other areas of the country, forcing residents in towns with mixed populations to seek safety in regions where their group was dominant. By the end of 1975, neither side held a military advantage. The rest of the Arab world watched in horror as Lebanon destroyed itself.

From Abu Dhabi, President Sheikh Zayed led many efforts to bring all the parties to the negotiating table and he kept in contact with his Minister of Defence as proposals for pan-Arab military intervention were mooted.

The Arab League attempted to put together an Arab Deterrent Force (ADF) charged with manning positions between the warring sides to restore calm. This was a difficult, demanding and dangerous task, such were the anger and divisions between the communities. Few governments wished to commit troops to a tense situation that could quickly boil over.

The UAE was one nation that dared. Sheikh Maktoum's government offered to pay 15% of the costs incurred by any nation which participated in the ADF and itself committed troops to serve in the effort. For the Emirates, this was yet another major milestone: A diplomatic presence on the international stage was one thing, but a willingness to participate in international, military policing actions underlined the country's growing maturity.

It was also a source of worry for Sheikh Mohammed, not through any lack of confidence in the ability of the UAE's armed forces but for the simple fact that this was a first – effectively the UAE armed forces' debut on active duty.

"Sheikh Mohammed was almost paternal toward our troops. He was aware that they were going into a danger zone," says Khalifa Al Naboodah. "He took it personally and throughout the time that men from the UAE were stationed in Lebanon, stayed in daily touch with their commanders on the ground, and liaised with those in overall command of the ADF."

By the end of January 1977, the ADF consisted of 30,000 men. A majority were from Syria, with divisions from the UAE, other Gulf states and Sudan. Libya had withdrawn its small force in late 1976. During ensuing months, Sheikh Mohammed twice travelled to Lebanon to view the situation and review UAE troops, reporting back to President Sheikh Zayed with a first-hand account.

Mohammed Mirhashim recalls: "Sheikh Mohammed was devastated to see a country so needlessly ruined. He believed that nothing had been achieved other than to kill and maim and to throw away years of progress that had created a vibrant and attractive nation. Since his younger days, he had enjoyed an affection for Lebanon and its people."

The ADF's policing helped to restore relative calm to Lebanon after more than one-and-a-half years of madness. Although the exact human cost of the war will never be known, the toll is believed to have reached 44,000 dead, 180,000 wounded and many thousands displaced, left homeless, or forced to migrate. Much of the once magnificent Beirut was reduced to rubble and the city divided into Muslim and Christian sectors, separated by the so-called Green Line. However, Lebanon's civil strife was not over. This would not be the last time that Sheikh Mohammed and his men would concern themselves with the fate of this once great nation.

At home in Dubai, the second half of the 1970s brought huge strides in development. A strong oil price worldwide meant that the emirate was able to spend more on its infrastructure and services, in addition to developing its industrial base. One good indicator of the spurt of growth was the 1976 budget allotted to Dubai Municipality: $115 million, some 20 times more than during the previous 12 months.

This was a period when Dubai's great industrial projects were coming on line. DUBAL, DUGAS and DUCAB were set to transform the economy. Unusually for the Middle East, private investment flowed to the emirate, attracted by a regime that worked to accommodate business.

In 1977, Sheikh Mohammed also began what would become a long association with civil aviation, an industry that has held its fascination for him. On August 25, Sheikh Rashid announced the formation of a committee, under Sheikh Mohammed, that would take over the administration and future development of Dubai International Airport. This was a task that Sheikh Mohammed relished. He was well travelled and understood well the impact that aviation could have on the economic prospects of a country, especially one that boasted a tourism infrastructure.

Mohidin bin Hendi, then head of the Airport Customs Department and later director-general of the Department of Civil Aviation, said: "Even in the mid-1970s, Sheikh Mohammed had a plan that ultimately would lead to the situation we are in today. He never sat down and spelled it out in full, but we were aware of his designs for Dubai as a tourist destination that could compete with the best in the world."

At this juncture, Dubai International Airport was growing, but it was hardly a high-flying facility. In 1977, some 15 airlines flew into the airport and there were direct connections with 42 destinations, mainly around the Middle East and Europe. Central among those companies serving Dubai was Gulf Air. The UAE's flag-carrier, Gulf Air had been formed on January 1, 1974 after the governments of Abu Dhabi, Bahrain, Oman and Qatar purchased Gulf Aviation in 1973 from British Overseas Airways Corporation. Gulf Air's fleet of Lockheed TriStars and Boeing 737s made it the region's most advanced civil airline.

By the mid-1970s, Dubai International Airport was already becoming a regional hub.

From the outset, Sheikh Mohammed saw that his role at Dubai International Airport should encompass more than just the aviation business. Broadly, it was a tourism brief. The Dubai Tourism and Commerce Promotion Board, another of his pet projects, was still many years away. But he and Sheikh Rashid were persuaded that tourism was another sector in which Dubai could advance its quest to lessen dependence on oil revenues. After 1977 Sheikh Mohammed was given almost free rein to work on this brief – as an unofficial Minister of Tourism – with the full weight of the Dubai government behind him to develop Dubai as an established destination serving what he described as "the top end of the market".

Dubai already had a number of five-star hotels, the privately-owned Sheraton and Inter Continental among them. Both remain landmarks on

A Lufthansa Boeing 737 on the tarmac at Dubai International Airport. (right) Sheikh Mohammed strategises with German government officials. (below) As lead negotiator, Sheikh Mohammed was in contact with the cockpit.

the Creek today, but their location makes them suitable mainly as business hotels. To attract holidaymakers, the emirate needed resort hotels and other infrastructure. Sheikh Mohammed encouraged the private sector and invested government money to this end in the knowledge that by the late 1970s many 'top end' travellers in Europe were looking beyond destinations such as Spain and the South of France. In addition, he made it abundantly clear to those with investment capital in the emirate that the Dubai government would look favourably on projects that created tourist facilities. A long road lay ahead to develop Dubai's name as an established destination and to set in motion the developments required to cater for millions of people each year.

But first Sheikh Mohammed planned to create an airport of world standing, a hub between East and West that could handle tens of millions of passengers a year. From 1977, he renewed Dubai's 'open skies' policy, encouraging carriers to put Dubai on their route networks. Millions of dollars of improvements were undertaken in the late 1970s, boosting both the quality of the airport and its capacity to efficiently handle passengers.

Such investment is invariably a long haul, but within a short time better-established regional hubs, such the traditional Gulf stop of Bahrain, began to feel the competition. As one senior official involved in the airport put it: "Before Sheikh Mohammed got involved, all you used to hear abroad about the Gulf was Bahrain... Bahrain... Bahrain... Pretty quickly after he got involved, it was Dubai... Dubai... Dubai..."

However, aviation-related news was not all positive. In 1977, Sheikh Mohammed was forced to handle another hijack crisis. On October 13, a Lufthansa Boeing 737, bound for Frankfurt, was hijacked shortly after takeoff by supporters of Germany's notorious Baader-Meinhof gang. Most of the passengers were German vacationers. Including the crew, there were 91 hostages.

The jetliner was diverted to Rome's Fiumicino Airport. A day later, it landed in Bahrain, refueled, and headed for Dubai. This presented a problem for UAE authorities: Sheikh Zayed and Sheikh Rashid had adopted a policy that hijacked aircraft were not to be allowed to land at airports in the Emirates. Prevented from landing, the airplane circled UAE airspace, but with its fuel rapidly running out and a crash-landing a growing possibility, permission to land was reluctantly granted.

"This is 'Captain Martyr Mohammed' speaking," announced one of the hijackers as the aircraft came to a halt on Dubai's tarmac. "The group I represent demands the release of our comrades in German prisons. We are fighting against the imperialist organisations of the world."

On October 14, Sheikh Mohammed also had every reason for wishing the Baader-Meinhof leaders were free. After the failure of a $15 million ransom drop to the InterContinental Hotel in Frankfurt, the hijackers were on edge as they flew into Dubai.

"It was clear that the hijackers were in an unstable condition. They were backed into a corner and desperate," said Mohidin bin Hendi. "Sheikh Mohammed needed to keep his cool because he would not offer them a clear way out of the mess into which they had placed themselves but, by the same token, those briefing him were of the clear opinion that they would certainly murder passengers to make a point."

For nearly 48 hours, Sheikh Mohammed remained in the control tower at Dubai airport. 'Captain Martyr Mohammed' spoke Arabic as a first language and was more inclined to deal with an Arab than anyone else. High on adrenalin and missionary zeal, the lead hijacker did not sleep. He wanted to talk, and this meant that his contact point on the ground had to be present.

"The tension in Sheikh Mohammed was visible. The lives of 91 people depended on him. One false move during all this time and disaster might have struck," said bin Hendi.

Sheikh Mohammed remained firm in the face of threats that people would be killed should demands not be met. After two days, realising that there was little to gain from staying in Dubai, 'Captain Martyr Mohammed' began negotiating for fuel. Unless Sheikh Mohammed agreed to supply fuel, the hijackers threatened they would kill a hostage every ten minutes. With their key demands denied and no escape route in Dubai, they had nothing to lose. As subsequent events showed, the authorities in Dubai were correct in agreeing to provide fuel, a decision that probably prevented a bloodbath.

On October 16, the Lufthansa aircraft flew from Dubai to Aden. After it landed, 'Captain Martyr Mohammed' shot and killed the pilot, Jürgen Schumann, in cold blood. His body was dumped onto the tarmac. A day later, with the terrorists still desperate to find a friendly country, the refueled 737 took off, landing a few hours later in Mogadishu, Somalia. Under cover of darkness, a Boeing 707 carrying the German military's crack GSG-9 commando team landed unnoticed. After an hour of preparation, a GSG-9 unit stormed the airplane, killing three of the four hijackers and seriously wounding the final one. None of the passengers was injured.

Just ten days after Sheikh Mohammed had managed a hijacking crisis at Dubai International Airport in October 1977, foreign politics again cast a dark shadow over the UAE. However, on this occasion a terrorist act would bring bloodshed to the UAE and the tragic death of one member of the cabinet.

During the early 1970s, one of the rising stars of the cabinet was Saif Said bin Ghobash, who assumed a portfolio as Minister of State for Foreign Affairs in 1973. During this period, bin Ghobash emerged as one of the UAE's foremost politicians on an international stage. He travelled around the region representing the President, and addressed the United Nations General Assembly in New York on a number of occasions.

As part of his ministerial duties, bin Ghobash played host to his Syrian counterpart, Foreign Minister Abdul Halim Khaddam, who visited Abu Dhabi on October 25, 1977. After a full day of meetings in the UAE capital, Khaddam made his way to Abu Dhabi International Airport accompanied by bin Ghobash. As the two men got out of their official car, which was parked beside a Syrian government aircraft, an assassin shot and hit bin Ghobash, injuring him fatally. Despite frantic efforts to revive him as he lay on the tarmac, he was pronounced dead on arrival at hospital minutes later.

"Saif Said bin Ghobash was a gentleman and a very, very capable politician who had served the government well," says Mirza Al Sayegh. "He was set to play a key diplomatic role for the UAE well into the future. And aside from this he was a friend to anyone who knew him. His loss was felt acutely."

The incident brought the nature of political unrest in the Middle East into sharp focus. Although the UAE remained scrupulously neutral in regional politics, and despite the peaceful role the UAE government chose to play, political extremists remained a threat to the state. The UAE's security apparatus – particularly its military – would have to remain in a constant state of vigilance.

Towards the end of the 1970s some of Sheikh Rashid's more controversial projects were beginning to come on line. In July 1979, he symbolically opened the already functioning Jebel Ali Port, a facility the

Jebel Ali Port and Jebel Ali Free Zone were a boon to Dubai's economy. (left) Sultan bin Sulayem, who is responsible for Jebel Ali.

sheer size and cost of which was still troubling many in the Dubai government. The largest manmade port in the world, Jebel Ali initially encompassed some 70,000 square metres of warehousing and 850,000 square metres of uncovered areas. It had taken nearly three years to create, transforming 25 acres of desert and requiring the excavation of 160 million cubic yards of sand, gravel and stone. It was certainly a working port, but the $3 billion project still suffered from an impression among outsiders that it was a lame duck.

Over subsequent months shipping into Jebel Ali Port did indeed increase, a fact undoubtedly boosted by the Dubai government's visionary, if almost completely unexpected, next move.

It is necessary to go back nearly 80 years to the turn of the century and the rule of Sheikh Maktoum bin Hasher to pinpoint the moment when Dubai was first set on course to becoming the Gulf's trading capital. At the turn of the century 1901 Sheikh Hasher had sought to capitalise on the imminent fall of Lingah, on the Iranian coast, by effectively declaring Dubai a free trade zone. His masterful tactic stole the initiative from under the noses of his neighbours and the bulk of the Lower Gulf's merchant community set up shop in Dubai.

In May 1980, Sheikh Rashid took a leaf from his grandfather's book in what was at the time a truly bold move. He signed a decree establishing a Free Trade Zone at Jebel Ali, adding to the port a major trade and industry zone, eventually extending to some 7,500 acres. In the decades leading up the new millennium, the site had become one of the biggest in the region, administered by the Jebel Ali Free Zone

Authority, a corporate body formed by the Ruler on January 9, 1985.

But even then Sheikh Rashid could not have envisaged the reasons that would help propel Jebel Ali into the number one shipping destination in the Gulf. Throughout 1979 and 1980 tensions between the new Iranian government in Tehran and the Iraqi regime of Saddam Hussein were on the rise.

On September 9 and 10, 1980, Iraq claimed to have "liberated" two small areas of previously Iranian territory between Naft-e Shah and Qasr-e Sherin. Later in the month, Iraqi troops made incursions into Iran. Several Iranian airfields were targeted by the Iraqi air force. The following day Iran, having earlier called up all military reservists, responded by bombing a number of military and key economic targets, its first response in a war of attrition which was to rage for eight divisive years.

The bloody conflict between these two regional powers had inevitable consequences for the whole Gulf. Trade was badly hit, the conflict taking little time to reach Gulf waters when the two states fought a desperate battle for the Iranian port of Khoramshahr, just two months after the beginning of hostilities. International vessels were clearly at risk in the 'Higher Gulf' area, if not directly targeted by the combatants, and seamen were being asked to work in increasingly dangerous waters. Insurance rates went sky-high. When shipping companies were forced to look for an alternative, only one port in the Lower Gulf enjoyed the spare capacity and facilities to cope – Jebel Ali. The port's business took off during the early years of the Iran-Iraq War and by the time hostilities ended, in 1988, the Dubai facility was fully established and growing.

The year 1979 was also a special one personally for Sheikh Rashid. The UAE government formed under his Prime Ministership was performing well, the federation was functioning at its best and its constituents were visibly better aligned than ever before.

At home, Dubai was booming. The 1970s had been kind to his emirate. The infrastructure that Sheikh Rashid had put in place during the 1960s was ready to serve the city-state when oil receipts began to rise. With that head start, Dubai had spent the 1970s in a furious pace of development. By 1979, many of the grandest projects ever to be undertaken in the Middle East were coming on line. Jebel Ali Port was awaiting inauguration, as were Dubai Dry Docks. Both were completed during the mid-part of the year, ahead of a special event in the annual calendar, and one much anticipated by Sheikh Rashid himself.

Since their June 1961 meeting at a Buckingham Palace garden party, Sheikh Rashid and Britain's Queen Elizabeth II had struck up a friendship. On that occasion a scheduled 'introduction' had extended to a 25-minute discussion. Sheikh Rashid subsequently met the Queen for an official banquet during his State Visit to Great Britain in July 1969. During the intervening period, they had stayed in contact and Sheikh Rashid had visited Buckingham Palace privately several times, the Queen promising to reciprocate when her programme allowed.

Queen Elizabeth was to make her long-anticipated visit to the UAE in 1979, during which she inaugurated the new Dubai Municipality building, adjacent to the Creek, Jebel Ali Port and Dubai Dry Dock. Her Majesty's visit lasted several days, including a Sunday when, as head of the Church of England, the Queen traditionally attends services wherever she is. In Dubai, she planned to attend Holy Trinity Church.

"Out of courtesy, Sheikh Rashid insisted on taking Queen Elizabeth to church personally," recalls Humaid bin Drai, then Head of Protocol. "It was an extraordinary display of friendship. The Ruler's car stopped near the entrance of the church and Sheikh Rashid got out to escort Queen Elizabeth up some stairs and to the church door."

On another occasion during the visit, Sheikh Rashid was escorting the Queen around work in progress on the second phase of development at Port Rashid when the workforce began a quite unexpected show of support for the Dubai Ruler.

Sheikh Rashid and Queen Elizabeth II on a dhow tour along Dubai Creek. Prince Phillip, the Duke of Edinburgh, is seen waving.

"Naturally work on the site was interrupted, although all the staff were on site," recalls property developer Zakariah Doleh, who joined the party. "Suddenly they started singing 'For He's A Jolly Good Fellow' in the direction of Sheikh Rashid. He was embarrassed personally, but nevertheless it was a testimony to his popularity."

Later that year Sheikh Rashid travelled to the Sultanate of Oman for an official visit. He flew from Dubai to Muscat on September 16, and immediately drove to Sultan Qaboos' majestic palace for a round of talks. It was a time of heightened political tension around the Middle East. Across the Gulf, in Iran, the Shah's regime had been swept away by the Iranian Revolution while, in Iraq, Saddam Hussein had gained power. Tensions between the two were escalating, prompting Sultan Qaboos to send emissaries seeking to ensure protection for international shipping using the Straits of Hormuz, the southern coast of which is Omani territory.

Dubai's Ruler stayed in the Sultanate for three days touring Salalah and several development projects, including Oman's award-winning Arzat experimental vegetable farm. Most important, over several sessions with Sultan Qaboos the Rulers strengthened their own ties and built a broad policy consensus on the issues of the day.

"The meeting between Sultan Qaboos and myself has shown that relations between the UAE and Oman are very good and will continue to improve," said Sheikh Rashid. "It has given us the opportunity to acquaint ourselves with the outstanding achievements in Oman under the wise leadership of Sultan Qaboos bin Said."

What no-one could control, however, was the worsening situation between Iran and Iraq. By September 1980 vocal attacks had given away to military skirmishing, and later the same year all out war had started. In a rapidly worsening situation, the conflict constantly threatened to escalate to include other Gulf states.

The UAE worked tirelessly to seek peace between the protagonists, while itself studiously maintaining neutrality. This was a war of which there was no accurate picture, both governments releasing contradictory information on the state of the war. This left pertinent questions to be answered on the subject of public reportage on the war.

"Sheikh Rashid knew it was important to be impartial and not offend either side," recalls bin Drai. "He personally called Dubai Radio to instruct them to broadcast both versions of the news, those released by the Iranians and the Iraqis."

Aside from this worrying regional development, by the beginning of 1981, Sheikh Rashid was probably happier than at any time in his 69 years. The UAE, a union which he is widely credited as having played an important part in creating, was almost a decade old and thriving. Dubai was riding high on a wave of petro-dollar-induced prosperity and beginning to emerge as a modern entity. Its success was founded and, at this point, driven by the infrastructure projects that Sheikh Rashid had set about putting in place from the 1960s.

His sons had followed him into office and held key portfolios within the government carrying forward Sheikh Rashid's vision of the larger state. Dubai Crown Prince Sheikh Maktoum was Deputy Prime Minister of the UAE, Sheikh Hamdan was Minister of Finance and Industry and Sheikh Mohammed was Minister of Defence. Sheikh Ahmed was Commander of Dubai's Central Military Command. Each was continuing the legacy of their father in some way, while also managing the affairs of Dubai in the shape set out a generation before.

"Sheikh Rashid was proud of his boys. He had worked at a blistering pace for decades. By the time he was in his seventies he was watching his sons take on an increasing role in Dubai and the UAE, in the knowledge that, although they were four independently minded men, they were going to continue the work which he began," recalls Hamad bin Sukat.

At 69-years-of-age, Sheikh Rashid continued to maintain a tight

Sheikh Rashid with British Prime Minister Margaret Thatcher upon her arrival at Dubai International Airport.

Sheikh Rashid and Indian Prime Minister Indira Gandhi. Their meeting was to mark the tragic end of an era for Dubai.

schedule of meetings and commitments. On February 7, 1981 he visited Pakistan, along with Sheikh Hamdan and Sheikh Mohammed, for talks with Pakistani President General Mohammed Zia ul-Haq and, the following month, visited Britain for a short holiday, interrupting this to involve himself in a chemical waste-dumping scare in Umm Al Quwain and Ras Al Khaimah. Returning home he continued on a taxing round of engagements, among them meeting a delegation from the Palestinian Liberation Organisation (PLO) and senior ministers from the Philippines and Bangladesh, among others, all during April. At the end of the month, he toured parts of the Creek and ordered the Municipality to draw up plans to shift all industrial installations to specially designated 'industrial zones' outside the city.

There was also hectic behind-the-scenes negotiations going on toward the formulation of a pan-Gulf body, a concept on which Sheikh Rashid had constantly touched with his regional associates. As early as June 13, 1973 he told reporters: "The economy is of such importance that we have to look not just on a local level, but a regional level, to secure stability. I would like to see the UAE as part of a wider Gulf Arab organisation, perhaps on the lines of the Common Market in Europe."

The Iran-Iraq War had underlined the need for just such a grouping and in May 1981 it became a reality when the UAE, Bahrain, Kuwait, Oman, Qatar and Saudi Arabia established the Gulf Cooperation Council (GCC). As Sheikh Rashid had envisaged nearly a decade earlier, the GCC sought to boost cooperation in economics, industry, agriculture, transport and communications, energy, defence and external relations.

One of the most important diplomatic events of the year in the UAE was the visit of Indian Prime Minister Indira Gandhi between May 11 and 13. Mrs Gandhi had often conferred with Sheikh Rashid by telephone and her visit was in response to a personal invitation. He insisted on hosting a banquet for the Indian Prime Minister during her visit, and honoured his ally at a banquet attended by 200 community leaders at the Ambassador Hotel in Bur Dubai. In many ways, this poignant occasion showed Sheikh Rashid at his best.

"Although they were speaking through an interpreter, he and Mrs Gandhi were noticeably engrossed in conversation during the entire time they sat together," recalls L R Lulla, owner of the Ambassador. "Since the Ambassador opened in 1969, Sheikh Rashid had often staged banquets at our hotel. He was always charming. I remember thinking that he must have liked Mrs Gandhi. His eyes that evening were glowing and he was smiling in that way of his which lit up his face.

"As usual, he himself only ate little and drank orange juice sparingly."

Photographs of this event show a relaxed and happy Sheikh Rashid. He occasionally smoked his Midwakh – a small-bowled Arabic pipe – and chatted at the head table with Mrs Gandhi throughout the evening. Those within earshot recall that although they had to speak through an interpreter, their conversation was full of anecdotes and laughter.

The dinner over, Mrs Gandhi left for her hotel at 11 pm. Sheikh Rashid, though looking tired and a little drawn at the end of the evening, thanked management at the hotel profusely for a job well done, as was his custom. Sheikh Rashid entered his car and waved warmly to L R Lulla as he pulled away from the front entrance of Ambassador.

"He was smiling broadly," says Lulla. "I remember those moments clearly, like they were a dream, as I never had the opportunity to see Sheikh Rashid again."

Chapter Twenty-Six

Double Blow

*True heroism is remarkably sober, very undramatic. It is not
the urge to surpass all others at whatever cost, but the
urge to serve others, at whatever cost.*
— Arthur Ashe, sportsman

On a warm and sultry evening in May 1981, Sheikh Rashid had
entertained Indian Prime Minister Indira Gandhi at a banquet at Dubai's
Ambassador Hotel. The dinner had been a great success, a personal
empathy between the two Prime Ministers building upon a relationship
forged during several of the Dubai Ruler's visits to India.

Sheikh Rashid, however, was tired. He had punished his body with a
frightening workload and schedule since his teens. At 69-years-of-age,
he still fought through a demanding 18-hour working day.

"His energy was amazing," says Sheikh Ahmed bin Saeed Al
Maktoum. "Far younger men, those who worked in Sheikh Rashid's
office or around him in the Majlis, could simply not keep up with him."

Those close to Sheikh Rashid saw something different on the morning
of May 10. The Dubai Ruler was strict in his adhesion to Fajr Salaat
(congregational dawn prayers), but on this particular morning he
remained quietly in his private quarters. He usually took a light, simple
breakfast of fruit juice and some Arabic bread, perhaps some yoghurt.
This Sheikh Rashid left untouched.

For a few days the Dubai Ruler struggled on with something of a
schedule. But he was not himself and his full diary of commitments was
impossible to fulfill.

Tired and unable to force himself back into his routine, Sheikh
Rashid decided a short break was in order and travelled with several
friends by car to Hatta, an enclave of Dubai in the Hajar Mountains that
was always a favourite with Sheikh Rashid. He retreated to his palace at

Sheikh Rashid with Majlis stalwart Saif Ahmed Al Ghurair.

The Ruler of Dubai is presented with a model submarine by a foreign delegation visiting the emirate.

Hatta several times a year and was normally refreshed. Hatta's history dates back more than two millennia and remained a traditional mountain village set amid an oasis.

It was common that when Sheikh Rashid was in the town he would receive visitors and make a visit to the souq, sitting with people there and at Al Hadeera, passing the time relaxing drinking coffee and nibbling dates.

But on this occasion Sheikh Rashid stayed remote in his small palace complex. He was called upon by his personal physician, who could find nothing specifically wrong and suspected a virus. The Ruler felt generally unwell.

Hatta's mountainous location means that the weather there is normally more temperate than on the Gulf coast. A day or two in Hatta, away from the pressures of office, was all it normally took Sheikh Rashid to recharge his batteries.

His sons stayed in touch by telephone and were informed by their father that the mountain air was having its usual rejuvenating effect. But those accompanying Sheikh Rashid were not so sure.

After a few days respite and despite not feeling at all rejuvenated, Sheikh Rashid knew that work was mounting up back in the city. There were duties to attend to and the UAE was preparing to host a meeting of the GCC (Gulf Cooperation Council). Duty, as ever, was his primary concern. But it was during this journey, of less than two hours, that Sheik Rashid's health suddenly worsened. He was physically sick several times and arrived in Dubai pale and evidently suffering from much more than a virus. His health worsened. The following morning, a stroke had been diagnosed.

Over 2,400 years ago, Hippocrates was first to describe the phenomenon of sudden paralysis, which we now know, is caused by stroke. A stroke occurs when the blood supply to a part of the brain is suddenly interrupted. In brain tissue, ischemia – a reduction of blood flow – leads to an ischemic cascade that can damage or kill brain cells. Death of brain tissue can lead to loss of the function controlled by that tissue. Thus, stroke is the third leading cause of death and leading cause of adult disability in the United States and industrialised European nations.

It is an unwritten rule observed by all ruling families throughout the world that a public face is maintained as a matter of course, while personal matters remain private. In the Middle East, privacy is everything, especially when it comes to illness. Among the Arabs, any form of sickness of those in power is treated with utmost secrecy. This, of course, was a necessity in less-settled times when a leader's illness could provide an opening for those who sought to gain power by force.

Well loved and widely respected, Sheikh Rashid was a public person. He made himself accessible to his people and was seen in their midst nearly every day. News of his illness was quickly carried far from the centre of the Ruler's court. Within a day the whole of Dubai had heard rumours that all was not well, and in days the truth was widely known, even if it was unconfirmed through official channels. Sheikh Rashid was public property and his health was a national concern shared by everyone from UAE President Sheikh Zayed to the most humble of expatriate workers.

"It was quite a shock as Sheikh Rashid became ill suddenly and without warning. Until then he was as strong as ever," recalls Hamad bin Sukat.

Over the next 24 hours, Sheikh Rashid's four sons maintained a vigil at their father's bedside, while efforts were made to ensure that best possible care and treatment were available. Dubai had sufficient expertise within its medical community to provide top-class care. Had this not been the case, help was at hand: President Sheikh Zayed and other GCC and regional leaders had been quick to call Za'abeel Palace, offering to send the best doctors at their disposal. Present-day UAE President Sheikh Khalifa bin Zayed Al Nahyan arrived in Dubai in order to speak with Sheikh Maktoum personally and reiterate that he and his father

Happier times: Sheikh Rashid meets French President Valéry Giscard d'Estaing. When the Dubai Ruler fell sick d'Estaing called personally to enquire about his status.

would stop at nothing in their support of the family at this dark time. Emir of Bahrain Sheikh Isa bin Salman Al Khalifa telephoned every day. Calls flooded in from around the world, including from Pakistani President Mohammed Zia ul-Haq, President Anwar Sadat and Vice President Hosni Mubarak from Egypt, King Hussein of Jordan, and outgoing French President Valéry Giscard d'Estaing. There were also messages from the Reagan White House and British Prime Minister Margaret Thatcher in Downing Street, while on behalf of his government, British Foreign Secretary Lord Carrington offered any assistance necessary. Queen Elizabeth, who had shared such a warm relationship with Sheikh Rashid over the years, requested that she be kept informed of his progress.

When not at his father's bedside, Sheikh Maktoum was fielding calls from Jaafar Muhammad al-Nemieri of Sudan, Mohammad Ali Raja of Iran and Hafez Al Assad of Syria, among many others. This and other gestures of support did not go unnoticed by the Maktoum family. Sheikh Rashid had never been slow to step forward in offering Dubai's help to its neighbours and Arab and Islamic friends. In his time of trial, it was a source of comfort that Sheikh Rashid's friends did the same.

However, it was not so much the immediate aftermath, but the profound, long-term debilitation that a stroke can cause that was a concern. Despite being fit and comparatively healthy for a man of his age, Sheikh Rashid faced a long road to recovery.

The best specialist treatment was sought. This was something that his sons undertook personally and, for months after Sheikh Rashid's stroke, it was not unusual to find foreign experts visiting the Majlis. Later, he and his sons travelled abroad extensively seeking care and advice.

In time, Sheikh Rashid's medical team grew to include physical and speech therapists, nurses and doctors. He made significant progress in the first three to six months, and continued to grow stronger. His rehabilitation, however, was not easy; few people regain 100% of their original health and physical capacity after a stroke. That said, Sheikh Rashid proved adaptable and learned new ways of functioning.

Within ten days there was firm progress. Sheikh Rashid was able to take telephone calls from UAE President Sheikh Zayed bin Sultan Al Nahyan and several members of the UAE Supreme Council, all seeking news of his recovery.

Sheikh Rashid was conscious and – crucial for his long-term prospects for recovery – soon after the stroke could communicate clearly with doctors and family members. Despite his advancing age, which inevitably would mean that he would take time to recover, it was indications like this that he retained all his mental faculties that gave rise to hope.

"Within only a few weeks we were happy to see Sheikh Rashid showing good progress. His appetite, although never great, was returning and as he grew stronger we were able to sit and talk for long periods, just like before," said bin Sukat.

Khalifa Al Naboodah recalled: "He looked so healthy at times, it was hard to think that he was technically still ill. Being Sheikh Rashid, he was unable to rest his mind, constantly inquiring from everyone about the progress of projects and news of what was happening in his city."

On June 20, Sheikh Rashid was well enough to fly to Britain for treatment at Wellington Hospital in London. The following day Thatcher visited him at his London residence, during which the two discussed relations between their countries and the political situation in the Gulf. After returning to Dubai, during August, Sheikh Rashid took a short private tour of Britain, Spain and the United States, returning to London in September for a further visit to the Wellington. Following that visit, the hospital's director issued a statement saying that "Sheikh Rashid is improving remarkably. He showed great progress even within two weeks of treatment."

Sheikh Rashid was always keen to get back to his home, and as summer cooled into autumn he became increasingly active again, albeit staying in the relative privacy of his palace. On November 7, Sheikh Zayed travelled to Za'abeel Palace to call on his friend, Vice President and Prime Minister. Sheikh Zayed's visit proved a watershed in Sheikh Rashid's recovery; although he was still a little frail, he began to insist on a thorough briefing of affairs of state.

The following day, in Abu Dhabi, the Rulers of Abu Dhabi and Dubai were both re-elected by the Supreme Council as President and Vice President, respectively, for a third five-year term. Deputy Prime Minister Sheikh Maktoum represented his father. Sheikh Hamdan, who held the key UAE Finance and Industry portfolio, was also present.

During 1982 and early 1983 there was considerable hope within the Maktoum family and the Ruler's closely-knit inner circle. Sheikh Rashid's strength appeared to be returning.

"He was almost back to being the normal Sheikh Rashid, although a little greyer in the beard. The doctors were delighted with his progress," said bin Sukat, perhaps the only man to have visited his friend every day during the dark times following the Ruler's stroke. "He was anxious to go out more and see what developments were going on in the city. Mentally he was often still sharp as a knife."

By mid-1982 Sheikh Rashid was following developments closely once again. On May 9 he braved high temperatures to visit Margham 1, a promising new onshore oil and gas field, just off the Dubai-Hatta road.

On June 19 he made his first full public appearance during the inauguration of five new road underpasses in the centre of Dubai, built at a cost of Dhs. 300 million. Travelling by car, he toured the tunnels as a symbolic gesture. Sheikh Rashid had, indeed, gone a touch grey, as the crowds that lined the streets could see. But as his car crossed the city, the mood of the population was captured by the spontaneous displays of affection. Sheikh Rashid's appearance had been widely publicised in the press and by 4.30 pm, a full 30 minutes before he was due to appear, shops and offices all over the city closed. His route was easily visible, as the roads had been cleared and closed by police. For most of the way the streets were lined with people of all nationalities, all social groups. Promptly, as was his way, Sheikh Rashid's car appeared at the appointed time from Za'abeel Palace and slowly made its way to the centre of the city.

"It was sort of an impromptu public holiday," says long-term expatriate resident Anthea Grainger. "I saw some nationals actually weeping after his car had swept past. It was that sort of emotion that swirled around. We expats, all nationalities, cheered and hollered."

It was a remarkable scene, a genuine outpouring of affection in which he was greeted with cheers and applause virtually the entire route. In an emotional afternoon, the city turned out to applaud its creator, perhaps even to mark the occasion it got him back.

"Sheikh Rashid was, I suppose, a little bemused," recalls bin Sukat. "He never liked a fuss and here were a great many people from his city lining his route. He was moved."

A few weeks later, during August, Sheikh Rashid made a further public outing, visiting the Jebel Ali Free Zone, including DUBAL, the port and a new water desalination plant. He also went on a short private visit to West Germany in September 1982, accompanied by Sheikh Mohammed. During that year, Sheikh Rashid had continued his recovery and gradually appeared more often in public. At the beginning of December he gave a rare press interview to *Dar Al Watan* magazine, to mark the occasion of the UAE's eleventh National Day.

"I feel great joy to see the UAE people united in one state achieving its hopes and aspirations in its march towards general progress and advancement in all aspects of its economic, social and political life," he said.

His health made further progress, and he travelled to London and later the United States for treatment. The United States government organised appointments with the best doctors in both Chicago and Houston.

But a second blow was about to hit the family. In May 1983, Sheikha Latifa, Sheikh Rashid's wife and partner of 44 years, was in London. Fit and healthy for a woman her age, she was visiting the UK for routine medical treatment. She spoke by telephone several times a day with Sheikh Rashid, who was always uncomfortable when she was absent.

After their wedding in 1939, Sheikh Rashid and Sheikha Latifa had grown close. Sheikha Latifa was reserved; a homemaker, she doted on her children. She also held her own Majlis and took many of the concerns and problems that she heard there directly to the seat of power in Dubai, becoming a bridge between Sheikh Rashid and the women of the community. She was still active in the early 1980s although, like Sheikh Rashid, she was taking life at a more sedate pace.

On May 17 tragedy struck when she passed away suddenly. Sheikh Rashid was still struggling to overcome his own illness, and doctors had warned that he should not be subjected to any trauma in order to avoid a setback in his recovery process. It was left to Sheikh Mohammed to break the awful news gently to his father. Hamad bin Sukat later recalled: "In around 40 years of knowing Sheikh Rashid, this was the only time that I ever saw him cry. He loved Sheikha Latifa so much."A day later, the government in Dubai issued a statement that read:

With our hearts full of grief for what Almighty God had ordained, the Court of HH Sheikh Rashid bin Saeed Al Maktoum announces the death of Sheikha Latifa bint Hamdan bin Zayed Al Nahyan yesterday. May her soul rest in peace and God console our hearts for the grave loss."

Following Islamic custom, Sheikha Latifa's body was immediately flown back to her homeland for burial. A report in the *Khaleej Times* said 10,000 people were present as she was buried in a Maktoum family plot in the heart of the city.

Unusually for a woman who played her role from the background, full state mourning was accorded to Sheikha Latifa. National flags were lowered to half-mast, seven days of mourning were ordered, UAE Embassies the world over were closed for three days and all public engagements cancelled.

Hundreds of citizens and expatriates offered their personal condolences to Sheikh Rashid and his sons. UAE President Sheikh Zayed and the Rulers of Sharjah, Ras Al Khaimah, Ajman and Fujairah called on them at Za'abeel Palace. The Iranian Deputy Prime Minister, Mirza Taheri, flew in to pay his respects, as did the Qatari Foreign Minister and representatives of the Rulers of Kuwait and Oman.

The death of Sheikha Latifa was a blow to her husband. Hamad bin Sukat recalls that it took several months before Sheikh Rashid seemed to return to normal, adding: "I'm sure it was not my imagination, but he never seemed quite the same."

Although his health was improving, Sheikh Rashid never did return to his public visibility of old. He insisted on following developments in his city and in his country, but by the mid-1980s was content to devolve power to his sons.

Freed somewhat from his heavy schedule, he also holidayed more. He visited Pakistan three times in 1984. A man with little time for himself previously, he also took a close interest in camel racing for the first time and visited Dubai's Nad Al Sheba Camel racetrack on numerous occasions.

Most of the UAE's Rulers also took trouble to visit Dubai in order to offer their respects, while in May 1985 Pakistan President General Mohammed Zia ul-Haq and his family flew into Dubai especially to pay a private call on Sheikh Rashid.

"I had not seen him for a while and he has not been keeping well," General Zia told the media. "Sheikh Rashid has pioneered an excellent relationship with Pakistan and I pray to God to give him good health."

In the wake of May 1981 an adjustment in leadership had occurred in Dubai. It was clear after consultations with President Sheikh Zayed that there was no question of asking Sheikh Rashid to step down as Vice President or Prime Minister. Yet paradoxically no-one would risk Sheikh Rashid's long-term health by entertaining the thought that he go back to work full time.

So, on a federal level, as in Dubai, others simply assumed his duties. Much of his federal work went to Sheikh Maktoum, Crown Prince of Dubai and former UAE Prime Minister. With his experience Sheikh Maktoum was able to slip naturally into both roles, supported by his brothers.

In Dubai, Sheikh Rashid's sons formed something of a collective when it came to decision-making. Where the Dubai Ruler usually took advice before making up his mind, his sons consulted each other and, more often than not, went the way of the majority. As eldest son and Crown Prince, Sheikh Maktoum became de facto Ruler of Dubai. This was not merely in deference to his seniority, but also because of his reputation as a thinker. Much of the business conducted by Sheikh Hamdan, Sheikh Mohammed and Sheikh Ahmed was first discussed with Sheikh Maktoum.

This collective decision-making process would prove a successful model on which the Maktoum brothers and Dubai would come to depend during Sheikh Rashid's illness, and after his death nearly a decade later.

Chapter Twenty-Seven

Double-Dip

It is not for him to pride himself who loveth his own country,
but rather for him who loveth the whole world. The earth is
but one country and mankind its citizens.
— *Mírzá Husayn-'Alí, religious leader and writer*

Many analysts make the link between high oil prices and global
recession. Recessions in the 1970s, the early 1980s and the early 1990s
were all preceded by a rise in the oil price. A second oil shock in 1979,
combined with the 1979 Iranian revolution and the beginning of the
Iran-Iraq war sent prices higher.

'Double-Dip' is a term used by economists to summarise back-to-back
recessions. In 1980, the first slump of a Double-Dip hit the world economy.
Even in the petro-dollar infused Gulf there was no shelter.

Dynamic forces of oil supply and demand led to excess supply in
world markets, which in turn led to a de facto decline in the price of oil
even before OPEC's London agreement of March 1983 in which the
official price was reduced by approximately 14%. Paradoxically, high
oil prices, an increase in production, and reduction in demand were the
three enemies of OPEC (Organisation of Petroleum Exporting Countries)
oil-producers as they led to a reduction in demand.

Worldwide recession in the early 1980s led to a decline in growth
rates and gross national products of the developed countries by an average
of 0.5%. The decrease in the United States was 1.8%, that of Canada
was 5%, and all of West Germany 1.3%.

World oil supply peaked in 1979, at a level of approximately 66 million
barrels a day, but the 1980 economic recession, which plagued the world
economy and which had markedly reduced the productive capacity of
industrial nations by its greatest percentage decline since World War II,

*Sheikh Hamdan (foreground) and Sheikh Mohammed. The Minister of Finance
and Industry watched over the UAE's economy during a quick-fire double
world recession.*

451

Sheikh Rashid with a class at the newly opened American School in Dubai. Improving education remained a national priority.

reduced demand for oil even further. In this way, even the oil-infused economies of the Gulf were not inflation-proof.

Add in another factor, the increasing burden of international debt, and one can see why the world economy was heading for an uncertain period, even if no-one could have predicted a dreaded Double-Dip. The world confronted recession with a massive debt hanging over it, a debt that would rise to $1.362 trillion in 1991.

The government of the UAE faced something of a crisis. Standing in for his father, Deputy Prime Minister Sheikh Maktoum chaired a cabinet that, two decades into the life of the UAE, still had a lot of work to do. Astonishing progress had been made in developing the economy, building infrastructure, and developing services such as education, electricity, health and water. Yet, as the nation grew, so did the demands of the nation. The population had rocketed, as had its needs.

Could the UAE government possibly cut back its investment? Could spending on new schools, homes, roads, and electricity and water projects be slashed in order to ride out the global slump and a dip in federal revenues?

The prospect of implementing austerity programmes amid severe policy constraints caused fiscal imbalances and balance-of-payments problems was an issue that went to cabinet, but the issue reached much farther. From the office of the President, through the Federal National Council and down to the man in the street, a debate ranged on what course the UAE should take.

"Sheikh Maktoum, among many in the government, only had one

mind," says Saeed bin Mohammed Al Ragabani. "Spending could not be slashed across the board, not when there were hospitals and schools that needed building, others that needed improving, nationals who needed better homes, a hospital system that was still expanding, just some many of the issues that the government was tackling."

In terms of economy, the 1980s introduced a grim period of declining incomes in most countries. During the 1980s, the buzzwords of 'stabilisation' and 'structural adjustment' became commonplace around the world. They were a politician's way of telling constituents there were to be cuts, but without mentioning that 'C' word. Cuts to welfare. Cuts to social services. A freeze on investments.

For many developing countries, the 1980s was certainly a period of frustration. But the UAE was in a special situation. Two decades had seen remarkable progress from the chronic situation in which the new federal government found itself upon formation in 1971, but much more was needed.

"The Deputy Prime Minister, as acting Prime Minister, was an advocate that social spending had to remain untouched in these key areas, in so far as possible," says Dr Abdullah Omran Taryam. "The government had to look for savings elsewhere, to prevent waste and postpone spending in areas that are unnecessary. But where many governments around the world saw education, for example, as something that could be starved of new money in lean times, this was never the attitude of Sheikh Maktoum's administration. In so far as possible, basics like health and education were never prevented from being allocated new money."

Section 17 of the UAE constitution states that education is fundamental to the progress of society and is to be compulsory at the primary level and free at all levels. Uniforms, books, equipment, and school transportation are also free. In the first seven years of the UAE's existence, education was second only to defence in the federal budget. The Deputy Prime Minister was not only protecting the children of his country, but also defending the constitution.

In 1983, the federal budget allowed for a $1.5 billion deficit, the biggest in the history of the UAE. But the UAE was not alone in running a deficit. The influential *International Finance* magazine forecast that the UAE, Kuwait, Qatar and Saudi Arabia would have a combined deficit approaching $10 billion in 1984, with the latter accounting for the biggest share.

The burden for ensuring that these fiscal aims were possible fell to a great degree on Sheikh Maktoum's cabinet colleague and brother. Sheikh Hamdan's Ministry of Finance and Industry had under its responsibilities the implementation of all fiscal, monetary and industrial policies.

The formulation and management of sensible and sustainable fiscal policy, within a national federal budget, was paramount. The Ministry administers revenue collection, supervises purchases and expenditure control. In order for Sheikh Maktoum's government to remain able to invest in its services and prevent either unbridled national borrowing or a severe budget crisis, the Ministry of Finance and Industry had a major responsibility.

Still only 35-years-old in 1980, Sheikh Hamdan would need to tap into all the fiscal sense for which he is so renowned. Indeed, the techniques of fiscal management and, within the limits that the Ministry had set, his programme of economic stability succeeded. Financial solvency was achieved by balancing the national budget without recourse to undue borrowing. This required a strong government capable of holding public expenditures and reducing domestic consumption by controlling credit and trade. In a few years the Ministry had single-mindedly achieved a favourable balance of trade, and surpluses both in foreign reserves and in the national budget.

The UAE would ride out this Double-Dip in the global economy relatively intact. Stable government and a solvent economy would eventually attract foreign investment.

And investment during the 1980s, amid a global recession, would pay off spectacularly over future years. For example in education, where the system was able to expand dramatically thanks to a greater number of teachers being trained and new classrooms being opened. In 1972 there were only 140 schools around the UAE. By the 1990-91 scholastic year there were about 760.

The early 1980s were also a period in which Sheikh Mohammed, in his role as Minister of Defence, was called upon. In July 1979, Saddam Hussein was made President of Iraq and chairman of the Revolutionary Command Council following the resignation of Ahmad Hassan al-Bakr. Changes of leadership in both Iran and Iraq, by far the most populous and militaristic countries of the region, affected many spheres of life in the Arabian Gulf. Initial hopes that the new administrations would herald an era of stability and prosperity were quickly dashed as the politics of division continued. On September 4, Iraq issued a statement saying that Iranian forces were shelling the towns of Khanaqin and Mandali. Days later Iran announced that its forces had 'liberated' two areas between Naft-e Shah and Qasr-e Shirin. In response, on September 22, Iraq launched a full-scale invasion of Iran, crossing the border at eight places. A day later, Iran bombed military and economic targets throughout Iraq.

Sheikh Mohammed and his team had already drawn up plans to protect the UAE's borders and offshore assets should fighting spill over.

Khalifa Al Naboodah notes: "The Iran-Iraq War brought terrible tensions to the region that threatened everyone. As Minister of Defence, Sheikh Mohammed's job was to respond to this threat. There was a great deal of emphasis on him at this time. People were obviously worried and the Ministry of Defence had a key role to play in developing measures that helped retain confidence."

It was a responsibility that would drag on for eight long years, while the Iran-Iraq War would claim a horrific one million lives from the populations of both protagonists.

The war would also bring devastating economic and social consequences for the region as a whole, stifling the Gulf economy that was already reeling from world recession.

If there was one lasting and positive development that came from the Iran-Iraq War, it was to reinforce the need for closer cooperation among the comparatively small Gulf states which were the combatants' neighbours. For decades, President Sheikh Zayed had gone on record pressing for a pan-Gulf body. Sheikh Rashid was similarly supportive of the concept.

"Sheikh Rashid brought up the issue of a pan-Gulf body regularly. On fraternal visits abroad, or hosting Gulf leaders in the UAE, he was on record pressing for more effort to create the conditions necessary for such a grouping," says Dr Abdullah Omran Taryam. "Sheikh Rashid was one of the first influential leaders to pursue the matter."

Little progress had been made since then, but during the tribulations of the second half of the decade, closer cooperation became a live issue and the governments of Kuwait, Saudi Arabia, Oman, Qatar and Bahrain began serious dialogue as a matter of policy.

What eventually emerged was a proposal to form the Gulf Cooperation Council (GCC), a bloc comprising the UAE, Kuwait, Saudi Arabia, Oman, Qatar and Bahrain. This was initially formed to strengthen economic, industrial, agricultural, transportation, communications, energy, defence and external relations.

On February 4, 1981, Sheikh Mohammed's cabinet colleague, Foreign Minister Rashid Abdulla Al Nuaimi, represented the UAE at a meeting in Riyadh of foreign ministers from the proposed GCC states. They were in Saudi Arabia to put the final touches to this new grouping. Later that day, the impending formation of the Gulf Cooperation Council was announced officially.

On May 25, President Sheikh Zayed welcomed his five counterparts to Abu Dhabi for the inaugural GCC summit: King Khalid ibn Abdul Aziz Al Saud of Saudi Arabia; Sheikh Isa bin Salman Al Khalifa of Bahrain; Sheikh Khalifa bin Hamad Al Thani of Qatar; Sheikh Jaber Al-Ahmed Al-Sabah of Kuwait; and Sultan Qaboos bin Said of Oman. The six leaders – the Supreme Council of the GCC – sat at an ornate circular table. Behind each was a small retinue of ministers, close advisors and senior government officials. Sheikh Hamdan and Sheikh Mohammed were seated just behind Sheikh Zayed.

Behind the smiles on that spring day in 1981, however, the brothers were reeling. Indeed, on the sidelines of the GCC Conference, all six leaders and many in their entourages had taken Sheikh Hamdan and Sheikh Mohammed aside to offer their personal words of support. The subject of their concern was Vice President Sheikh Rashid who, just days earlier, had suffered a massive stroke.

On June 2, under Defence Minister Ariel Sharon, Israel launched the sinister 'Operation Peace for Galilee' offensive. At dawn the full might of the well-armed Israeli forces crashed through a Lebanon that was defenceless aside from a relatively weak and unprepared Arab Deterrent Force. Sharon aimed to oust Yasser Arafat and his PLO from the country and had convinced his government that this could be achieved in one swift action, followed by a speedy withdrawal of Zionist forces back within Israel's borders.

While Sharon's overall plan was reviewed by his cabinet colleagues, what seems not to have been approved or even looked at by the Israeli government were his tactics. Israeli guns were soon overlooking Beirut where the PLO was headquartered, mainly in Muslim districts. In an

The UAE armed forces rushed supplies to Lebanon in order to bring aid to those displaced by the Israeli invasion.

effort to break PLO and Arab military resistance, Sharon ordered a bombardment of civilian districts that had few precedents in its ferocity. Thousands of women and children were killed. Homes were reduced to rubble by the shelling and burned by cluster bombs and other indiscriminately fired incendiary devices.

Within hours of the Israeli invasion, Sheikh Mohammed had flown himself, a number of generals and Ministry of Defence officials to Abu Dhabi for urgent consultations with Sheikh Zayed.

Tens of thousands of Lebanese civilians made a dash for safety to the north of the country, often risking their lives under Israeli fire. Most left their homes with nothing more than the possessions they carried. Refugees in their own homeland, they urgently required tents, blankets, food, medicines and other essential supplies. Their plight rapidly turned into a massive humanitarian crisis, to which the UAE was the first to respond.

In typical style, Sheikh Zayed led the relief effort personally to ensure a sense of urgency. He was supported by Sheikh Mohammed, who marshalled the UAE armed forces. Giant military transport aircraft were leased and flown to the UAE, while thousands of tons of supplies were shipped to selected airports by convoys of military vehicles. It was a massive operation, coordinated personally by Sheikh Mohammed. He had only days to put into effect one of the UAE's largest logistical operations. Such was the scale of the Lebanese people's needs that even UAE armed forces' supplies – including tents, blankets and food packs – were commandeered. On June 7, five days after the beginning of the

Sheikh Mohammed at the controls of a transport aircraft bound for Lebanon with aid supplies.

Israeli aggression and within two days of Sheikh Zayed issuing an order, the first UAE aid flight took off for North Lebanon.

Over the next few weeks, the UAE's military organised dozens of aid flights to the people of the embattled country. The UAE government also sought to support the forces defending Lebanon. The Ministry of Defence helped to organise an urgent blood donation effort throughout the Emirates.

On June 10, Sheikh Maktoum announced that the Dubai government was donating $5.5 million to charitable organisations managing refugee support in Lebanon. A day later, Sheikh Mohammed accompanied Sheikh Zayed as part of the UAE delegation to an emergency Arab Summit in the Moroccan city of Fez.

Meanwhile, after shelling Beirut for two months, the Israelis entered West Beirut. The Israeli invasion now entered its blackest phase. Sharon gave personal approval for his forces to assist their allies, the Phalangist militia, to enter Palestinian refugee camps at Sabra and Chatilla, ostensibly to search for guerrilla fighters. It was the day after Phalangist leader and Lebanese President Bashir Gemayel had been assassinated, and the militiamen were in an ugly mood. Prominent Palestinian author Said K Aburish later wrote:

> What happened there did not involve any fighting and was simply the slaughter of civilians. Nor was the entry of the Christians [militias] in to the camps a secret; they were ushered in by the Israeli troops...At some points [over the 36 hours of the massacre, the Israelis were within 600 yards of the camps and therefore able to hear the gunfire, if not the shrieks of the victims who included babies, pregnant women and old men...the bayoneting of pregnant women was commonplace...the butchering did not stop until some of the Israeli army officers tired of hearing the screams and ordered an end to it all."

Unrepentant, Sharon later became the focus of an international storm of protest and was forced to give up the defence portfolio. An independent inquiry mildly criticised his role in the atrocity, passing over the fact that his troops had been ordered to illuminate the night skies over Sabra and Chatilla so that the militiamen inside could continue their deadly task after dark. In all, around 1,000 Palestinians and hundreds

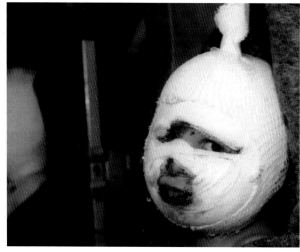

A Lebanese child hurt in fighting: The Dubai and UAE governments worked frantically to bring relief to the people of the beleagured state.

of Lebanese were massacred in the camps with the logistical support and tacit approval of the Israeli army.

The UAE wrote to the five permanent members of the United Nations Security Council demanding action. The Foreign Ministry publicly denounced the United States for not ensuring that its Israeli allies were made to follow the acceptable norms of war.

The 70-day siege of 'Operation Peace for Galilee' left as many as 14,000 Lebanese and Palestinian civilians dead in Beirut alone. According to one estimate, from the *Reuters* news agency, many thousands of Palestinians and Lebanese were killed and many times that number injured.

Worse still, the Israeli invasion worsened the situation in Lebanon. Internal divisions were sharpened and civil strife intensified, bringing the death toll even higher. As the country faced meltdown, the UAE and Dubai continued to support Lebanon, participating in a number of reconstruction plans and funding refugee re-housing programmes.

The Dubai government has consistently helped the Lebanese cause. Over the years, while Israel maintained its military presence in the south of the country, dozens of badly injured civilians have been flown to Dubai for treatment. The emirate also supported many social causes in South Lebanon in the face of Israeli attempts to disrupt education, health and economic systems.

There was also help for the large Lebanese community at home. In 1984, as the Civil War took its toll, what remained of the central Lebanese government had no reliable income. To pay for desperately needed hospitals and schools, cuts had to be made. Among the first to go were Lebanon's diplomatic missions abroad. In 1984, the Dubai government was informed that the Lebanese Consulate in Dubai was about to close. In response, the Dubai government 'sponsored' the Consulate, and has continued to do so until today.

Chapter Twenty-Eight

Camelot Continued

No matter how good you get you can always get better.
That is the exciting part.
— *Tiger Woods, sportsman*

It seemed to many that the Camelot Era was now over in Dubai. The extraordinary bubbling cauldron of ideas and energy that existed around Sheikh Rashid for the last half century had inevitably dissipated with the illness of the remarkable Ruler. Or had it?

By early 1982, much to the relief of the Maktoum family, Sheikh Rashid had recovered sufficiently from his stroke to appear in public once again. Greyer than before, and noticeably frailer, he paid a visit to an onshore drilling rig at Margham 1 on May 8, only one day short of a full year since his last appearance before his people. He was visiting the site of a new gas discovery just off the road between Dubai and Hatta that would be extremely important to the economy of the emirate over subsequent decades. Equally important, the visit showed his people that their beloved leader was emerging from a long period of convalescence.

In better health, Sheikh Rashid had started to play a more active part in government. Although, for the most part, he was content for his sons to continue to carry the responsibilities they had assumed when he became ill.

For Dubai, it was an era of consolidating the infrastructure and industrial base that Sheikh Rashid had put in place. Just that year, Dubai Municipality had a budget of $410 million; 5,000 new housing units had been ordered for Dubai's residents and a ten-year, $950 million sewerage and storm water development plan was initiated.

But the new feeling of optimism in Dubai was about more than money and bricks and mortar. Just as Sheikh Rashid had instilled

Although in faltering health, Sheikh Rashid was not content to sit back and he set ambitious plans for development for the UAE and Dubai governments.

the office of the Ruler with a renewed sense of purpose and energetic leadership when he succeeded his father in 1958, so his sons were now bringing new vigour to an old sense of direction. The Ruler's old friend Hamad bin Sukat says: "His [Sheikh Rashid's] period of illness had served to underline the fact that his sons were highly capable leaders in their own right. He was enthusiastic about the progress that they represented."

Camelot, as Sheikh Rashid's Majlis had been so memorably dubbed, was not dead. Sheikh Rashid, the John F. Kennedy or King Arthur figure who had been the catalyst to this remarkable entity, was not always there in person, but the spirit of his Majlis was alive and well.

Sheikh Rashid had planned well into the future: Jebel Ali; The World Trade Centre; Port Rashid; Dubai International Airport; all were infrastructure that were put in place with an eye on the future.

But Sheikh Rashid had not thought only in terms of bricks and mortar. He had also astutely planned for the future leadership of his land. His sons were ready to step into the breach when their father could no longer keep up his extraordinary 18-hour working day and was unable to sit at the centre of his Camelot.

"Sheikh Maktoum had begun preparing for the role that he would now assume when he was a boy. Sheikh Rashid had often brought him to the Majlis. He had worked with his father in the Ruler's Office. Even in his early teens, Sheikh Maktoum was experienced and a mature figure within his father's administration," says Hussain Khansaheb. "Sheikh Rashid had guaranteed continuity as the torch of leadership, in a way, symbolically moved to the new generation."

The centre of power had shifted to the Dubai Crown Prince, but such was his long-standing immersion in the Ruler's Office, that shift was as seamless as when Sheikh Rashid had succeeded his father in 1958.

"Nothing changed," said Mohidin bin Hendi. "The same calm sense of progressive leadership emanated from the Ruler's Office. Sheikh Maktoum had served what one could say was his apprenticeship under his father. He was ready for the new responsibilities that now rested on his shoulders."

Sheikh Maktoum had his own identity, his own people around him, but kept in his circle and in senior positions within the Dubai government all of those in whom his father had identified talent, nurtured their ability and then given responsibility.

Sheikh Maktoum and Sheikh Mohammed greet then Bahrain Crown Prince Sheikh Hamad bin Isa Al Khalifa on his arrival at Dubai International Airport.

"Sheikh Maktoum had a very thoughtful style, like Sheikh Rashid," says Qassim Sultan former director general of Dubai Municipality. "He was never rash and when he gave an order, his decisions were based upon an opinion formed having heard the views of people he trusted and then carefully considering the options."

"The respect in which Sheikh Maktoum was held was not because of his position, but the sort of man he was," said the late Sheikh Dalmouk bin Juma Al Maktoum.

Around Sheikh Maktoum were his brothers who, likewise, had been astutely prepared by Sheikh Rashid for the responsibilities that would be theirs.

The early 1980s were tough times for the world economy as not one, but two recessions bit into growth. Dubai was far from immune from the resulting dip in oil prices, but the effects of this slump were now offset by a diversification away from a reliance of oil that had always been government policy. In particular, Sheikh Hamdan now had a role to play. Under his charge were DUBAL, DUGAS, DUCAB – three of the industrial projects that he had turned into major sources of wealth for the government. These were the foundation on which the Maktoums were set to build an economy free from reliance.

"Sheikh Hamdan built the same efficient management structures at all the projects that fell under his responsibility," says Mirza Al Sayegh. "He personally involved himself in these projects in order to ensure that these were run to his liking. In every way, the success of these companies can be attributed to leadership from the top."

465

Sheikh Hamdan was also heading Dubai Municipality during this important phase of the emirate's development. Sheikh Rashid was famed for his dislike of red-tape and bureaucracy, but in the new reality of a growing city-state a balance was needed. A bureaucracy was necessary, yet could not be allowed to stifle the enterprise, and can-do culture on which Dubai had been founded and then thrived.

"Arab government is notoriously bureaucratic, beset by reams of regulations and underscored by a terrible attitude among government officials," says Malcolm Corrigan. "Sheikh Hamdan had a major job on his hands. For Dubai to progress in the way it did during the 1980s and until the present day, it needed a strong bureaucratic wing. But Dubai was never a place of bureaucracy. And the pitfalls that foul most government institutions in the Arab world needed to be avoided.

"It was a very tough assignment that needed adept management. Sheikh Hamdan provided that leadership and, during the period I was there certainly he was bringing in some talented and well-educated young nationals, grooming them through work experience at various levels, and then promoting them into senior positions."

The municipal structure had been designed in the 1950s for a population of approximately 50,000, but was creaking at the responsibilities it was now undertaking.

"Dubai holds the top position worldwide for both population and employment growth at 5.8% per annum, and 8.3% per annum," stated the report *Winning Cities of the Decade* between 1991 to 2001. "Much of its success derives from a drive to create a favourable environment for business, and in providing the physical infrastructure to match."

During the early 1980s the UAE was at the beginning of a population explosion that would see it nearly quadrupled in 25 years. Dubai's population was amid a spurt of growth that would see 50,000 in the 1950s become around a million in 50 years time.

In combining rapid urbanisation with economic diversification, Dubai Municipality developed a highly responsive and efficient urban management reform process. In a bottom up approach, the Municipality has integrated structural change with administrative improvement, including a system of delegation of authority, decentralisation of services, human resource development and the introduction of a proper legal framework.

"Local government is the engine room on which all private sector

Dubai Municipality was taking on an increasing burden as Dubai and its population grew apace.

and government development function. Without a good local government, you can forget any sustainable development," says Corrigan. "That is why Sheikh Hamdan's success was invaluable. Without it, you can forget the Dubai of 2006 being like it is."

Sheikh Mohammed's field of responsibility was also widening considerably. His federal defence portfolio continued to make heavy demands, while in Dubai he was charged with, among other things, Dubai International Airport and several of Dubai's heavy industrial projects. He had also begun to take over responsibility for Dubai's oil; this was one of the key tasks within the Dubai government, given the importance of oil to the economy.

"Taking control of Dubai's petroleum sector was a huge responsibility handed to Sheikh Mohammed by his father," says Saeed Al Ghandi. "It was a brief that involved a tremendous amount of technical understanding, so that he could fully embrace the subject. For months, Sheikh Mohammed used nearly every spare moment to read books and papers concerning the industry, everything from exploration and storage and shipping, to knowing how international markets functioned."

Within a relatively short time, Sheikh Mohammed began to assert his authority over the industry in Dubai. It was a period of optimism, with the emirate's major Fateh offshore oilfield now joined onstream by Margham. Breakthroughs in technology increased the chances of success in the search for oil, particularly offshore, and were changing the face of the industry.

With every passing year, exploration companies around the world

467

were able, with new techniques, to reach more remote locations, test more definitively and bring hydrocarbon deposits on line faster and cheaper. A broadly strong oil price, aided by periods of relative unity within OPEC, also made exploration a more attractive risk.

Keeping abreast of technical developments is time-consuming. Nevertheless Sheikh Mohammed managed to keep up with details such as evolving design of drill bits so that he was well informed.

Commenting on a long standing relationship, which spans more than 40 years, ConocoPhillips CEO Jim Mulva says: "It has been a great honour to serve Dubai. From inception, the late Sheikh Rashid and the late Sheikh Maktoum have shown great interest in the progress of Dubai Petroleum Company and have always helped it to achieve its success and potential.

"I must say the opportunities that have been given to interact with Sheikh Mohammed have been a great inspiration and value for both our company and the country. Sheikh Mohammed is an incredibly forward thinking man and a true believer in international business and cooperation. I am proud of the history of Dubai Petroleum Company and look forward to its exciting future and our involvement in the Dubai offshore concession. There are a lot of opportunities that we can see and when the time arises we can forge ahead with confidence and the full support of Sheikh Mohammed."

Amid their burgeoning responsibilities, each brother attempted to divide his day to allow more personal time. When in Dubai or the UAE it was rare they did not spend at least an hour with their father. Hamad bin Sukat says: "Even at his lowest ebb, Sheikh Rashid was probably happiest when his sons were around him. His overriding wish was not to lose touch with what was going on."

Without the burdens that had been his for all of his adult life, Sheikh Rashid was somewhat different now. Instead of day-to-day duties, he was able to sit back and see the bigger picture. He was full of new ideas. Another major change in the Dubai Ruler was that he now enjoyed reflecting on the past. For his children this was a rare opportunity as their father followed the tradition of passing on anecdotal history to the next generation through storytelling. They were now companions on a nostalgic walk through Dubai and Maktoum history.

And Sheikh Rashid also used this period of recuperation to spend more time with a new generation of the family. Sheikh Maktoum's eldest

Sheikh Rashid and Sheikh Hamdan return to Dubai following a hunting trip abroad. Sheikh Mohammed bin Hasher Al Maktoum is pictured holding a falcon

son, Sheikh Saeed, spent a great deal of time with his grandfather now, as did Sheikh Rashid bin Mohammed Al Maktoum and Sheikh Hamdan bin Mohammed Al Maktoum.

There was a definite sign of recovery in Sheikh Rashid when he returned to the desert as part of a hunt. For six decades virtually Sheikh Rashid's only outlet for relaxation from the pressures of rule was during his twice-yearly hunting trip abroad. He had a passing interest in game, such as Persian Pasang (Bezoard Goat) in the challenging Alborz Mountains, or the fabulous Cop-e-Dagh (Urial Sheep) along the northeast mountains of Iran. But his affection for this traditional Arab pursuit rested with falconry and the houbara bustard, a migratory bird that flies between Pakistan, Iran and Central Asia. The bird is widely popular among Arab hunters thanks to traditional beliefs, starting with the old customs and traditions and ending with the houbara's meat qualities.

Within 18 months of his stroke, Sheikh Rashid was sufficiently well to hunt again. It was a good sign. And falconry is a passion that Sheikh Rashid and his sons shared in equal measure.

"The Arabs now fly falcons because they enjoy it, because it's fun; but they are also upholding a part of their heritage that could go back as far as two and half thousand years," says Dr David Remple, a falcon specialist, who helped establish the Dubai Falcon Hospital.

To the uninitiated, the traditional Arab sport of falconry looks like a few days of driving in the desert. Aficionados describe the sport as a cerebral game of chess between houbara bustard and its pursuers. The search for a single bird can take days and the outcome can be decided

in minutes, often in favour of the houbara.

"The layman often regards it as a blood sport which it is not," says Dr Remple, "because the wild falcon is a specialised predator which kills to eat every day. The sport of falconry simply borrows this bird as a hunting partner. Our major concern in falconry is not in the prey but in witnessing what the falcon is doing every day. We concentrate on its spectacular flight and beauty. As it is a hunting bird, the falcon is at its best when hunting. It is a very intelligent bird and among the birds of prey, the falcon could be the one that could be tamed."

One feature in the *Lexington Herald-Leader* perhaps conjures up the rustic pleasures that come from hunting, a far cry from the pressures that surrounded the brothers and their father:

...Perhaps there's nothing like it in the Western world: as many as 100 falcons are loaded with as many people into about 30 open-air, four-wheel-drive vehicles and the convoy sets out over desert dunes...The quarry Sheikh Hamdan was seeking this day was a rare bird prized by Arab falconers: the houbara bustard. It comes from the crane family, looks like a streamlined turkey and tastes a bit like goose...At each day's end, perhaps as many as 20 bustards were piled at Sheikh Hamdan's feet, awaiting his nod of approval. Then they were off to the cooking pots.

The evening meal of bustard and rice is served around the campfire where the deeds of the falcons are extolled over coffee and tea long into the night. "I think this is one of the few times he enjoys himself," said Dr David Remple.

Opened in 1983, the Dubai Falcon Hospital is at the forefront of not just falconry. According to one BBC report, "Falcons in Dubai in the United Arab Emirates have been the key to a number of recent developments in avian medicine..."

A typical examination of a bird includes endoscope test of the lungs, parasite tests – from both faecal and swab samples, blood tests for anemia and underlying infection – and X-rays.

"(With) this routine, the clients expect the medicines to be a pretty

Like his brother, Sheikh Ahmed bin Saeed Al Maktoum has a passion for hunting.

high standard, and because the training starts immediately, they don't want to wait," Tom Bailey, a vet at the Dubai Falcon Hospital, told the BBC.

A connection between the hospital and Dubai's Department of Health has meant that a number of developments in human medicine have crossed directly into avian treatment. The latest example is aspergillosis. It affects many birds, but some types of falcon are particularly vulnerable to the illness, which causes the growth of fungus in the lungs. Falcons that contact aspergillosis have their ability to fly fast and hunt degraded – so a way to tackle it is of particular interest in Dubai.

Since aspergillosis also affects humans with immuno-suppression diseases such as HIV/AIDS, researchers at the falcon hospital have been testing the efficacy on the birds of voriconazol, a new drug used on humans. So far the results are very promising. And work done at Dubai Falcon Hospital is being watched throughout the world for its potential application not just in birds used for sport, but in flock birds, which has massive implications for food production around the world.

Sheikh Mohammed is renowned for his hunting skills, but even time spent away from the UAE does not afford the opportunity to relax completely. In the evening, the hunt comes to a halt and the group makes camp. As he and his companions sit around a campfire, it is not unusual for him to have a diplomatic bag full of official papers to attend to. At other times, his companions, invariably including many close advisors, have projects and plans to discuss. In these surroundings, discussions may evolve at a slower tempo but they take place over a longer duration. Dubai and the UAE remain foremost in Sheikh Mohammed's thoughts, even when relaxing, and the 'down time' spent hunting is an opportunity to strategise. Mohammed Mirhashim says: "Late at night, I have often woken to find that Sheikh Mohammed has propped himself up in his camp bed and is reading some papers, or sometimes even writing poetry. He never fully switches off. He is always thinking of something new."

Another friend recalls: "Even in the remote desert, he is constantly receiving telephone calls. Sometimes you can see in his face that he is not with us, his thoughts are elsewhere as he turns over an issue in his head."

At home in Dubai, Sheikh Rashid's sons had carried on from where their father had left off. Hamad bin Sukat recalls: "After he won his battle with illness Sheikh Rashid was told by his doctors that if he continued to press ahead with same the degree of energy as before, he would be reducing his life expectancy. Of course, Sheikh Rashid was not a young man at this point and could really not have gone back to how things were before anyway."

Sheikh Rashid held his formal Majlis less frequently now. However, the lessons learned from that heady mix of thinkers and achievers that the Ruler had brought into his circle were not lost on the new generations. All of Sheikh Rashid's sons drew similar circles around them – a new Camelot generation. The Majlis of each became a potpourri of individuals from all walks of life: bankers sat next to Bedouin poets, while property developers shared a sofa with camel breeders and falconry experts. The leaders of all strands of society have an open invitation.

"Sheikh Hamdan conducts his Majlis along the line of his father, it is an open forum, a consultation point between the people and senior government," says Mirza Al Sayegh. "People are free to speak their minds."

Saeed Al Ghandi comments: "From the early 1980s, one could see striking similarities between the Majlis of Sheikh Mohammed and that of his father, some time before. There was the same vibrancy and passion."

Sultan bin Sulayem, son of one of Sheikh Rashid's foremost lieutenants says: "Sheikh Mohammed set about surrounding himself with the best and brightest. Unlike Sheikh Rashid's days, when emphasis was on Dubai surviving, and then competing on a regional scale, Sheikh Mohammed believed that his father had placed Dubai in a position of becoming an internationally renowned, world-class city. This is the direction in which he dares those around him to set their minds."

Following his illness, Sheikh Rashid would never return to the political centre of life in Dubai from where he had operated for, effectively, more than half a century. But the spirit of Camelot endured.

474

Chapter Twenty-Nine

In Flight

These days no one can make money on the goddam airline
business. The economics represent sheer hell.
— C.R. Smith, President, American Airlines

Throughout the second half of the 1980s, the Gulf was a crowded theatre of military operations. At least ten Western navies and eight regional navies were patrolling the area, including that of the UAE. The Iran-Iraq War was into the dark phase of the Tanker Wars and the protagonists were well on their way to fueling a body count that would eventually rise past one million.

Dubai also had a key role in repairing many of the victims of Iraqi and Iranian attacks. Only two facilities in the region catered for major repairs to shipping, the Arab Ship Repair Yard (ASRY) in Bahrain and Dubai Dry Docks, and such was demand that they could not carry out full repairs on all casualties. The Dubai Dry Docks took on extra workers and arranged round-the-clock shifts. Many vessels, towed into Dubai by tugs and taking on water, waited months at Jebel Ali Port or Port Rashid for a berth at Dubai Dry Docks. Others that could be patched up temporarily were sent to repair yards outside the Gulf.

The Iran-Iraq War had lasted nearly eight years, from September 1980 until August 1988. Of the issues generally cited as causes of this conflict, virtually none had been resolved.

The war years had not been kind to the Gulf. Oil exports had been interrupted, and the GCC states had been forced to invest billions in their armed forces to defend themselves and guarantee security. The war had caused a general contraction in business and commerce. Non-government investment had fallen dramatically. As the markets slowed and liquidity dried up, companies inevitably folded. With no jobs, large sections of the expatriate community were forced to leave.

Sheikh Mohammed at the controls of a trainer aircraft belonging to the
UAE Air Force.

Consumer markets contracted as a direct result. It was a vicious downward spiral played out throughout the GCC. Dubai, with its heavy dependence on commerce, suffered its first sustained recession since the death of the pearling industry in the 1930s.

This was a challenge that Dubai attempted to meet through greater government investment, which would not only boost the economy but also lay the foundations for Dubai after the current period of uncertainty.

"Under Sheikh Hamdan's personal guidance, the municipality had put together a plan of development over a decade that would transform Dubai," says Kamal Hamza. "This was a blueprint document. A map to the future. It was also very ambitious."

Sheikh Hamdan discussed the document with Sheikh Maktoum, Sheikh Mohammed and Sheikh Ahmed during one of the four brothers' many meetings during this period. With Sheikh Maktoum at the helm, decision-making on such a grand scale was a collective.

Later, Dubai Municipality used this period to unveil a development plan that would take it to the year 2005, encompassing some $3 billion in infrastructure projects alone. Financial analyst Clinton Jones of leading British institution Faber Callibus said: "There was a self-belief within the Dubai and federal governments. The Maktoum family in particular was not content to tread water and wait until regional stability returned. Indeed, there was a trend regionally to increase holdings in Europe and North America. Dubai bucked this trend. To boost the local economy there was greater spending on infrastructure projects. In doing so, Dubai showed its overwhelming confidence in itself and the future. This helped to calm the Dubai economy."

During this period, Sheikh Mohammed also showed his commitment to the future with a series of audacious new initiatives in aviation. Since the late 1970s, the Dubai government had coupled an interest in aviation and the development of Dubai International Airport with a strong belief that the emirate should position itself as a global player within the tourism industry. These interests, of course, went hand in hand.

But progress was slow and, although traffic through Dubai airport was burgeoning, the facility was still really only a regional airport. Bahrain was more economically advanced and was therefore preferred by airlines operating from, or through, the region. Bahrain was still very much the Gulf's aviation hub. There was little tourism development in Dubai during the 1980s when it was only the most adventurous of holidaymakers who were willing to spend their vacation time on the fringes of an unpredictable theatre of conflict.

However, with the foresight that would increasingly become its trademark, the Dubai government lost none of its enthusiasm for tourism. Its response to the economic slowdown caused by war was to increase investment in the country. In addition to the municipality's grand plan, civil institutions such as hospitals and schools were developed and work began on a long-term road-building plan. The brothers guided Dubai's spending programme in order to lay the foundations for tourism infrastructure, including new hotels and beach resorts. But it was clear that establishing Dubai as a competitive up-market tourist destination would be a long-term effort, especially with war raging.

If this vision were to come about, from the outset the priority of the Dubai government would have to be to develop the principal entry point to the emirate, Dubai International Airport.

Like so many of his greatest projects, Sheikh Rashid had developed the airport against the prevailing political and economic tide. Inaugurated on September 30, 1960, nearly a quarter of a century later the Dubai Ruler had been proven entirely correct.

Dubai International Airport had opened with Heron and Dakota aircraft of Gulf Air as regular visitors. Kuwait Airways and BOAC also began using Dubai. From this minor league start, Sheikh Rashid's open skies policy had quickly begun to make a major league impact on the industry. By 1984 some 42 airlines were scheduling regular flights to Dubai.

"There was a steadly flow of new carriers wishing to take slots into Dubai. Sheikh Rashid's vision was already starting to pay off," says Mohidin bin Hendi.

Sheikh Rashid's foresight had created the airport to support the merchants of Dubai and create a gateway into the emirate. Now his sons needed to propel Dubai into an entirely different sphere.

In the decade since he had assumed responsibility for the airport, Sheikh Mohammed had set in motion a far-reaching modernisation programme. As a seasoned traveller, he understood the frustrations of bureaucratic immigration and customs procedures, and worked relentlessly to cut red tape. The airport building was expanded to accommodate an expected increase in passenger traffic once a more settled political climate returned.

But while Dubai International Airport was a work in progress, the Dubai government remained less than happy with the network of airlines serving it. No airport in the Gulf had grown as quickly in terms of infrastructure development and passenger flow during the 1970s and 1980s, despite the economic challenges the region faced. With Dubai's open skies policy and improved facilities, the airport had attracted new carriers from around the world.

Everything was possible, but one problem remained. The UAE's flag carrier was Gulf Air. In 1973 the governments of Abu Dhabi, Bahrain, Oman, and Qatar purchased BOAC's shares in Gulf Aviation and, on January 1, 1974, a Foundation Treaty was signed. The Gulf Aviation Company became Gulf Air.

Dubai's relationship with Gulf Air had always been somewhat ambiguous. By the 1980s Dubai was Gulf Air's most profitable centre. The airline operated more flights into Dubai than any other destination.

Yet, despite this, some friction existed. Gulf Air was unhappy with Sheikh Rashid's open skies policy, a sharp contrast to the protectionist policies operated by its partner governments. Gulf Air persistently lobbied Dubai for protection for itself and for restrictions to be placed on other airlines.

The Dubai government had other ideas. Its open skies policy was working. It pressed Gulf Air to increase services into the emirate. Demand for seats consistently outstripped supply, a bottleneck.

The dynamics of the state-airline relationship changed abruptly in 1984. Late that year Gulf Air published its spring/summer schedules for the following spring. This included a huge shock for Dubai. Instead of increasing services into Dubai, Gulf Air had drastically slashed capacity. Dozens of services had been withdrawn. There was some media comment noting that Gulf Air was ready to hit Dubai — and its own balance sheet — in order to make the point that it ruled the skies over Dubai. As it would find out to its cost, this was far from the case.

"The Gulf Air situation could not be ignored," recalls Maurice Flanagan, then head of DNATA, which was general sales agent (GSA) for Gulf Air. "This would have an extremely negative impact on Dubai's economy, on the tourism sector and on business travel. We had either to throw our successful open skies policy out of the window, find an accommodation with Gulf Air and protect that airline, or find another solution… urgently."

Dubai International Airport faced a crisis as Gulf Air slashed services.

Flanagan set about preparing an urgent briefing paper detailing the options available to Dubai. Among the several solutions suggested, this document made reference to Dubai developing its own airline. But Flanagan freely admits he did not believe the Dubai government would choose this high-risk route.

"In DNATA, we initially believed a solution would be found to satisfy Dubai's needs, balanced with Gulf Air's demands. But the curtailing of services into Dubai was a radical stance by Gulf Air that could not be ignored," he says. "Dubai's attitude is shaped by that of Sheikh Mohammed."

After a short period of reflection Sheikh Mohammed surprised even close advisors with his final decision. While urgent efforts would be made to solve the Gulf Air crisis, he asked for more details on the possibility of starting an airline. He later took delivery of a brief, which outlined possible approaches to entering the airline industry.

"There was a little talk of Dubai starting her own airline, but the consensus was that Gulf Air would climb down. Its position was financially unsound, to remove services to its most profitable destination," said Mohidin bin Hendi, then DCA director general.

As time went on, however, both sides were just as far apart. By the turn of the year Sheikh Mohammed was ready to launch one of the boldest initiatives Dubai had ever seen.

"I was in the InterContinental Hotel one afternoon in late 1984," recalls Flanagan of the moment he began to get a clear picture of which way Sheikh Mohammed was leaning. "To this day I have no idea how

(opposite page) Sheikh Mohammed appointed Sheikh Ahmed bin Saeed Al Maktoum to head Emirates. (left) Maurice Flanagan had a pivitol role in the carrier from its inception until the present day.

Sheikh Mohammed knew I was there, but I was having coffee and was paged to answer the telephone."

On the line was the UAE Minister of Defence.

"When did you say was the date on which we should launch an airline?" he asked.

After a little hesitation to collect his thoughts, Flanagan replied: "October 25, sir."

"Thank you," replied Sheikh Mohammed.

Abruptly, the line went dead.

On 25 March 1985, Dubai International Airport went into a significant phase in its history. At the beginning of the spring/summer schedules, services were curtailed and passenger traffic was down markedly. Gulf Air flights dropped by 84 per week to just 39. Instead of Dubai, a majority of these lost flights began landing in Sharjah and Abu Dhabi. Some international airlines had spotted an opportunity and, as they were freely able to do under Dubai's much touted 'open skies' policy, requested additional slots. Yet despite this Dubai International Airport lost valuable capacity.

By now Sheikh Mohammed had in his possession a favourable report on the proposed airline from Deloitte and Touche and he himself nurtured a growing belief that developing a Dubai-based airline was the right thing to do for the future of the emirate.

Two weeks after the spring/summer schedules began, Flanagan was called urgently to Za'abeel Palace for a meeting. After a very brief exchange, Sheikh Mohammed wasted no time in getting to the point.

"I have looked closely at your proposal for an airline," he stated, leaning forward to present the startled Flanagan with a piece of paper that was to transform his life forever. "Here is a cheque for $10 million. Tomorrow an account will be opened with the National Bank of Dubai where this can be deposited. What is the next appropriate date on which you can launch?"

Flanagan replied that the autumn/winter schedules started on October 25.

"That is when we should begin then," stated Sheikh Mohammed. "Keep me informed."

With that the meeting was over. Flanagan retreated to his office to contemplate launching an airline, from scratch, in just five months. Perhaps no one in aviation had ever embarked upon such an ambitious timetable, yet established norms were never to be a factor for Emirates.

"There was a sense of euphoria, but mixed with trepidation," recalls Peter Hill, who was charged with commercial operations for the audacious new carrier. "Dreaming up how to start an airline is one thing. Implementation of those plans, in such a short space of time, was positively frightening. The clock was most certainly ticking."

Sheikh Ahmed bin Saeed Al Maktoum joined Emirates airline as chairman during 1985 and took on the role of president of the Dubai Department of Civil Aviation later that year. In an interview in 2000, Sheikh Ahmed said: "I have been involved with both the commercial aspects of running an airline and the demanding logistics of running an airport for 15 years. In the beginning, we had to overcome many

481

objections to setting up Emirates, both regional and international.

"I have been honoured to hold a position that has allowed me to play a part in finding solutions to those objections. I have also always loved airplanes. I think most people do, as it is not hard to appreciate the speed and beauty of them, and the glamour of the industry.

"The objective behind establishing Emirates was not only to have our own airline but to use it as part of an overall marketing plan to promote Dubai and tourism, and to create jobs. It was also decided that, unlike other airlines in the region which have a history of either losing money or being subsidised by the state, Emirates would have to stand on its own, to serve the region and be commercially viable."

This extended to the question of favourable trading status. Today, Flanagan admits that Sheikh Mohammed's team proposed that Dubai 'protect' its airline commercially. In an expensive high-risk industry, no national airline in the world is thrown into a free market situation. All

INTER

The formation of Emirates would be the key to an era of remarkable development of Dubai.

were given commercial priority at home through preferential allotment of landing rights and other means.

But Dubai had always operated with an open skies policy and Sheikh Mohammed believed that to make Dubai a hub for trade and tourism, as many airlines as possible had to be encouraged to operate through Dubai International Airport. He turned down favourable status for Emirates and, what was more, demanded that the airline post a profit, making it clear that subsidies were also not an option.

"It was a far-sighted decision," says Flanagan as he looks back on a journey which has seen Emirates claim some 200 international awards and remain profitable every year since its formation.

Emirates was launched on October 25, 1985, with its first flight, to

Karachi, taking off on schedule from Dubai International Airport. At first it used two aircraft on wet lease from Pakistan International Airlines. To preserve pre-launch secrecy, both aircraft were painted with the Sheikh Mohammed approved livery inside a locked hangar on the edge of Karachi airport. In addition to its own evolving programme of aircraft leasings and purchases, Emirates was also given two lightly used Boeing 727s from the Dubai Ruling family's private fleet.

The late 1980s also witnessed a rich harvest of initiatives from Dubai. Typically, the emirate was able to build on one of its strengths – aviation – to support what was to become one of its largest and highest profile international events, the Dubai air show. This was launched in 1989, aimed at both a burgeoning civil aviation sector in the Gulf and military aviation. At the time, the Middle East was the world's fastest growing market for military technology, while the industry recognised that Dubai was a staging point, convenient for the African and Asian markets.

Inaugurated on January 29, 1989, the first Dubai air show attracted close to 200 exhibitors, including industry leaders such as Boeing, Airbus, Lockheed Martin and Westland. Twenty-five military and civilian aircraft were on show. It was a small beginning by comparison with the established international airshows at Farnborough and Paris. But the event marked a breakthrough for the aviation industry in the Middle East and buyers came from as far afield as Japan, China, Russia and some Eastern European states.

Today, the Dubai air show stands alongside Farnborough International in Britain, the Paris air show at Le Bourget and Asian Aerospace as one of world's top four events.

There were also big strides made in tourism. Even in the late 1980s, Dubai and tourism were largely strangers. Few people had heard of this small Gulf-destination. While the emirate continued to attract a limited number of tourists each year during the 1980s, few shared Sheikh Mohammed's vision that it could become a major destination.

The Middle East was hardly a big player in an industry estimated to be generating up to $100 billion annually at the turn of the decade. Within the region, only Egypt and, to a lesser extent, Jordan, were considered 'big league'. A sizeable portion of Egypt's GDP came from tourism and it was abundantly clear why Egypt continued to attract so many millions of visitors each year: With its colourful history, monuments and oriental flavour, it had a great deal to offer tourists.

Dubai, on the other hand, had no such ancient treasures and was comparatively unknown. Even as recently as 1989, few could envisage Dubai playing host to hundreds of thousands of tourists a year. Khalid bin Sulayem, recalls: "People scoffed when you spoke about Dubai as being a major centre of tourism, even ten or 15 years ago. They believed that the climate was not conducive during the summer, at the peak of the tourism season, and that Dubai had nothing to offer. Many people even commented that Dubai's best attribute, its beaches, could easily be matched by those in Spain or the Mediterranean."

Even during the petro-dollar boom years of the 1970s and 1980s, Dubai was looking over its shoulder. With oil resources far smaller than those of some of its neighbours, the Dubai government's position, as early as the 1960s, was that petro-dollars should be put to use developing non-oil related commerce. While encouraging private enterprise within this sector, the government also invested – in the airport, Emirates airline, new hotels and tourist facilities. It was a long process. With most five-star hotels catering for businessmen, it needed a sea change in perception. Through government spending and gentle encouragement for the private sector, the 1980s saw a move toward resort hotels bordering Dubai's clean, golden beaches. In the late 1980s, the strategy showed signs of paying off as tourist numbers began to grow.

Recognising the industry's potential was just the first step. Equipping the emirate with the necessary infrastructure, using public and private money, was a massive undertaking that encompassed many government departments. As the industry grew, so did the many entities which were involved. Recognising this, centralising the industry under one umbrella before it grew too unwieldy became of paramount concern, and this led to the creation of the Dubai Tourism and Commerce Promotion Board (DTCPB) in 1991.

DTCPB concentrated on the international promotion of Dubai, later adding a second main stream of responsibility as the principal authority for the planning, supervision and development of the tourism sector in the emirate. In its marketing role, the DTCPB managed an integrated programme of international promotions and publicity activities, including participation in exhibitions, marketing visits, presentations and roadshows, familiarisation and assisted visits, brochure production and distribution, media relations and enquiry services. So successful were

*Khalid bin Sulayem led
the Dubai Tourism
and Commerce
Promotion Board.*

its efforts that the DTCPB became the template against which other states have subsequently planned their own efforts to break into the industry.

Under its director-general, Khalid bin Sulayem, the organisation became – and has remained – one of the most proactive in the world. Within a short time, it boasted international offices in Philadelphia, Los Angeles, London, Paris, Frankfurt, Stockholm, Milan, Moscow, Nairobi, Johannesburg, Mumbai, Hong Kong and Tokyo.

Today, as the Department of Tourism and Commerce Marketing, the organisation handles the licensing of tourist accommodation, tour operators, tourist transport companies and travel agents and in a supervisory role also covers all tourist, archaeological and heritage sites, tourism conferences and exhibitions, the operation of tourist information services and the organisation and licensing of tour guides.

At the end of the 1980s, tourism was well on its way. During 1990, more than 600,000 guests stayed at hotels in Dubai, of which there were 11 in the so-called deluxe category and 12 in the first class category. At the time Dubai had 70 hotels with 5,378 rooms. Just five years later, in 1995, this figure would be up by nearly 170% to 1.6 million guests. The number of deluxe class hotels would double to 22, and the number of first class hotels to 22. In just this five year period, the total number of hotels would rise from 70 to 233 with 12,727 rooms.

The government's belief in tourism would be vindicated where it counts the most. The bottom line. Hotel revenues alone in 1990 were $71 million, while in 1999 they would stand at around $271 million.

Since 1990, the total number of guests checking into Dubai's hotels annually has increased year-on-year to reach 2.5 million by the end of the millennium – all this achieved from a virtual standing start in 1989.

A more settled political scene settled over the Gulf following the cessation of hostilities between Iran and Iraq. This certainly helped when reaching out to tourists. The 1980s as a whole had been dubbed "the lost decade" by UAE President Sheikh Zayed. Although evidence suggests that there was a significant loss in the momentum of development as the region was pulled apart by war, there was, nevertheless, a great deal of progress.

Just in terms of population, the UAE was progressing swiftly. Between 1980 and 1985, the population of the Emirates grew by more than a quarter. The bulk of the additional 600,000 people were made up of expatriate labour and this figure gives an illuminating insight into the speed of the growth. Sheikh Rashid's federal administration had forged ahead with its building programme regardless of war. Government contracts had kept much of the private sector afloat.

In no small part due to the confidence of its government, Dubai remained the most robust of the seven emirates in economic terms. The decision of the Maktoum family to speed up programmes and to increase spending sent powerful signals to local and regional investors. In the months after the end of the Iran-Iraq War, Dubai was the first regional market to see the green shoots of recovery. What was more, due to the government's spending programme, the emirate possessed by far the best infrastructure to support the boom that was predicted by analysts.

One of the best examples of this was Jebel Ali Free Zone. Established in 1985, at the height of the Iran-Iraq War when commerce in the Gulf was at its lowest ebb, it is an industrial area centred around the Jebel Ali port terminal. Its development was typical of Dubai's response to the war: It was fully functional by the end of the conflict and ready to welcome new businesses looking for an entry point into the Gulf market.

The port had been championed by Sheikh Rashid in the 1970s, against all advice and flying in the face of prevailing thinking. Opened in 1976, it quickly became one of the UAE's leading commercial and industrial locations, contributing hundreds of millions of dollars in profits to the national economy and creating jobs and opportunities for UAE-owned companies.

Sultan bin Sulayem, chairman of Jebel Ali Free Zone Authority

(JAFZA) as well as head of Dubai Ports Authority (DPA), says: "One of the main points that Sheikh Mohammed stressed was the need to keep things simple. He worked to ensure that JAFZA was served by the best in infrastructure, that would empower us to offer the best services possible."

Echoing one of Sheikh Rashid's central themes of government, it was decreed that JAFZA should also adopt a streamlined 'business friendly' administration. As such, the Free Zone was linked first to the Jebel Ali Port Authority and then to its successor, DPA, which manages both Jebel Ali and Port Rashid terminals. The Free Zone and the port were planned as complementary organisations. The Free Zone helped to build traffic through the port and the port provided ideal facilities to attract investors to the Free Zone. The entire project has been an overwhelming success.

For example, Dubai Municipality statistics showed that the manufacturing industry sector had grown tremendously, with the number of companies based there rising from 1,386 in 1980 to 3,687 in 2000 - an increase of over 160% at an average annual growth rate of 5%. The number of employees within Jebel Ali Free Zone grew from 21,971 in 1980 to 81,272 in 2000.

And the port – labelled a Sheikh Rashid-inspired White Elephant by skeptics when he first decided upon the project – was at the centre of a massive amount of economic activity. In 1995, total input into the manufacturing sector was over Dhs. 4 billion while total output was more than Dhs. 8 billion. Annual capital formation ran at around Dhs. 221.6 million while total invested capital was about Dhs. 2.9 billion.

Jebel Ali Free Zone has contributed to the development of the manufacturing sector, as it attracted foreign direct investment that was seeking a hub in the regional market.

An example of the cohesion at the heart of the Dubai government during the expansion of 1980s was the development of Dubai International Airport's capability to handle cargo. One of the few worrisome points as far as foreign investors were concerned was the fact that Jebel Ali is some 35 kilometres from Dubai International Airport. In markets where red tape and administrative hold-ups are endemic, this would be a problem. Dubai saw it more as an opportunity to show the business-orientated nature of the emirate. Everything from customs systems to transport links were synchronised by various departments in order to ensure an attractive business environment

Bin Sulayem says: "By ensuring that departments were working together, and smooth systems were implemented, administrative delays were kept to a minimum. Dubai Ports Authority and Dubai International Airport were given the opportunity to invest in the most efficient cargo-handling equipment available, so that the task of turning around cargoes was as efficient as possible."

With this investment, Dubai quickly boasted the world's fastest sea-air transfer times. By the late 1980s, Jebel Ali was also fully integrated into Dubai's highly-developed transport infrastructure, helping it gain international recognition as a distribution hub for the whole region.

Considering these factors, as international confidence in the stability of the Gulf grew, so did the attractiveness of Jebel Ali Free Zone.

After his stroke in 1981, Sheikh Rashid had been forced to lighten his workload and become more of an elder statesman in the UAE and Dubai. He took well to the change in pace. Saeed Al Ghandi recalls: "Sheikh Rashid kept his finger on the pulse of Dubai. Although he was less visible himself, his friends and family were quizzed on the goings-on within the emirate on a daily basis, whenever anyone visited him."

Throughout the 1980s, Sheikh Rashid's health went up and down. For long periods he would be in good spirits, only for his physical well-being to decline. Each time he fought back but each time, his sons were aware, that a little less of their father's old vitality returned. For his part, even at times of frustration when his body could not match the continuing vigour of his mind, one of Sheikh Rashid's only desires was not to lose touch with the city that had been his life's work.

Hamad bin Sukat continued to visit Sheikh Rashid daily. He says: "There was a small rise near Za'abeel Palace, from where one could see far into the distance, all the way to Dubai's high-rise buildings. Even on bad days, when he was in a wheelchair, Sheikh Rashid would sit on this rise for hours, looking out over the city, over his creation."

"He was very happy," says Sheikh Mohammed bin Khalifa Al Maktoum, "that Dubai continued to progress smoothly and seamlessly under his sons."

Sheikh Rashid had seen first-hand the result of allowing divisions within a ruling family to develop. By the time he was forced into taking a back seat, his biggest project was complete: Seamlessly, his sons took over most of the reins of power.

Nor is their unity of purpose a false front. Mirza Al Sayegh says: "Sheikh Maktoum, Sheikh Hamdan, Sheikh Mohammed and Sheikh Ahmed were in regular touch, every day, often dozens of time each day. There is nothing of importance that went on without all knowing about it. Information was shared and collective decisions were taken."

In this way, the brothers have managed a rare feat in pooling their talents in the pursuit of a common goal. One of the best placed to see this is Sheikh Mohammed bin Khalifa, their cousin, who observes: "There is an intimacy, a bond, between them. This was nurtured by Sheikh Rashid and has grown over time. Nothing major happened without Sheikh Maktoum approving it. But similarly there is a collective decision-making process. All participated fully in administering Dubai. The energy we see in development, and that which drives many of the new, innovative projects around Dubai, is a result of that collective effort."

Sheikh Rashid is greeted by Dubai Police chief Dhahi Khalfan Tamim. The Dubai Ruler increasingly withdrew during the late 1980s as his health faltered.

Chapter Thirty

End of an Era

Why, man, he doth bestride the narrow world
Like a Colossus, and we petty men
Walk under his huge legs and peep about
To find ourselves dishonorable graves.
Men at some time are masters of their fates:
The fault, dear Brutus, is not in our stars,
But in ourselves, that we are underlings.
— *William Shakespeare, 'Julius Caesar', Act I, Scene II*

Sheikh Rashid never did return to his public visibility of old following his stroke in 1981. He insisted on following developments, but was content to devolve a great deal of power to his well proven sons. This said, he remained active in some areas of personal interest.

"My father never lost his keen interest in education. Both on a federal level, and within the Dubai government, he followed developments in education closely," says Sheikh Ahmed bin Rashid Al Maktoum.

Sheikh Rashid, of course, had found his genius imbibed in him. It had to be, as nothing in his formal education equipped him for the responsibilities that were his. As a child he received the finest education available in the region. Attending the Al Ahmadiya School in Dubai Sheikh Rashid's subjects included Islamic studies, Arabic and arithmetic. Yet half a century later he could count among those he could call friends Royalty and political leaders from around the world. Queen Elizabeth of England remained in touch. Global figures such as Gamal Abdul Nasser of Egypt and King Hussein of Jordan spent time in Dubai being hosted by the Dubai Ruler, while his hospitality was reciprocated in visits to Cairo and Amman.

In his Majlis, the Ruler moved easily between Bedu leaders and congressmen. His simple, humble style remained the same for all-comers.

Sheikh Rashid with his great nephew Sheikh Saeed bin Mohammed bin Khalifa Al Maktoum.

Sheikh Rashid still maintained a public schedule when his health allowed: (opposite page, top) Reviewing plans for a cement plant with Ahmed Baker and Sheikh Ahmed Mubarak (opposite page, bottom) Visiting an industrial project. (this page, top) with Saeed Ahmed Lootah. (this page, bottom) Accompanied by Mohammed bin Dhahi Sheikh Rashid is confronted by a full size suit of armour when opening a trade exhibition.

Now, in his dotage, instead of concentrating on multi-million dollar infrastructure projects and billion dollar ports, his emphasis seemed to have turned full circle. The 1940s and 1950s had been largely about survival for Dubai, while its then Crown Prince did what he could to change the economic face of the sheikhdom while alleviating the woeful living conditions that his people suffered. When Sheikh Rashid had begun his career his emphasis was on fundamentals – health and education being primary considerations.

"Schools," says Minister of Higher Education and Scientific Studies Sheikh Nahyan bin Mubarak Al Nahyan, "were of great importance to Sheikh Rashid. As Prime Minister, Sheikh Rashid had a great many responsibilities, yet the Ministry of Education always had his ear."

Sheikh Rashid always held the belief that education centres of the highest level were vital to the development of the country and would provide the necessary foundation for the modernisation of Dubai. With less day-to-day responsibility for the UAE and Dubai governments, during the late 1980s he was freed to take a more active interest in this area. As well as following the Ministry, Sheikh Rashid was placing his private funds into a number of projects, especially in education for children with special needs.

A man of his stature, however, could not be allowed to fade away politically and when the need arose Sheikh Rashid was not slow to set aside his own condition. There were territorial problems to contend with when relations between Ras Al Khaimah and the neighbouring Sultanate of Oman suddenly worsened in late 1988. Ras Al Khaimah and Oman shared a long, rugged and woefully ill-defined border that was the cause of mounting tensions between Sheikh Saqr bin Mohammed Al Qassimi and Sultan Qaboos bin Said of Oman, both of whom knew the Dubai Ruler well. For a time in early 1989 it seemed that either could move to escalate the crisis. Several efforts at mediation failed and when the situation suddenly worsened, Sheikh Rashid, as UAE Vice President and Prime Minister, stepped into the fray.

"Sheikh Rashid called on Sheikh Saqr and told him that he would work to resolve the situation peaceably," recalls Khalifa Al Naboodah, a close advisor of Sheikh Rashid who was present during the crisis.

His intervention could not have come at a more crucial juncture. The UAE was positioned as one of the most politically moderate states in the Gulf, one which enjoyed dialogue with all the many sides of the Middle

Eastern landscape. Its position, though an asset, would have been under threat had relations with Oman worsened. Within the UAE government there probably could have been no better mediator, judging from the close relations which Sheikh Rashid kept with Sultan Qaboos.

"Sheikh Rashid did not simply get involved to wash his hands of the affair when negotiating got difficult. He spent a great deal of time mediating, bringing the two sides together, helped by the fact that Sultan Qaboos and he had extremely good personal relations," recalls Humaid bin Drai.

In time, the positions of both Ras Al Khaimah and Oman softened, allowing the start of broad-based discussions which all but settled the matter. On April 8, 1989 a spokesman for the Prime Minister's office issued a statement saying that the UAE and Oman had agreed to negotiate a formula for re-demarcation of the border.

The turn of the decade saw Sheikh Rashid turn 78. His once upright figure was slightly bent, the lines were etched deeper in his craggy, charismatic face and his hair was grey. Although his mind was often still as sharp as ever, his body was giving out on him. He seldom ventured into public and had come to rely on friends and family for news.

From Za'abeel Palace he loved to sit and watch the city go by. The nearby Dubai World Trade Centre, Hilton Hotel and busy Dubai-Abu Dhabi Road offered something of a comfort. In the distance he could also see much of the Bur Dubai quarter and the city centre bristling with construction cranes, evidence of the continuing boom. To someone who had been something of a workaholic throughout his life, Sheikh Rashid often found his forced inactivity frustrating. To a man who could always see unfinished business, it was maddening.

By 1990, Sheikh Rashid's medical team remained close by, but it was clear that age rather than illness was attacking his vitality. Most evenings in winter, when temperatures were mildest, Sheikh Rashid would sit on a terrace at Za'abeel Palace and look out over Dubai. There, he would receive close friends and family members. Bin Sukat recalls: "I visited Sheikh Rashid nearly every day and the first thing he would always ask was for news of what was happening in Dubai and of the people that he knew. His appetite for information was still insatiable. We would sit and talk about the old times, or he would tell me of his hopes for Dubai in the future."

During late summer Sheikh Rashid was comfortable, although at times he was notably distant. On October 7, Hamad bin Sukat made his

By 1989 Sheikh Rashid was rarely seen and on his fleeting appearances was noticeably weaker. (opposite page) Sheikh Zayed was a regular visitor to his old friend.

daily visit to Za'abeel Palace. Sheikh Rashid was weak, but he spoke quietly, if falteringly, with his longtime friend. Close by were Sheikh Hamdan and other Maktoum family members. Sheikh Ahmed, a close companion of his father during his quieter years was, as ever, by his side. After half an hour, Sheikh Rashid was tired. Bin Sukat made to leave, promising Sheikh Rashid he would return the following day. Sheikh Rashid smiled thinly and raised his hand slightly off the bed, indicating that he should go. "Inshallah," Sheikh Rashid said, almost whispering.

That evening, Sheikh Rashid slipped into a deep sleep and passed away at 10pm, his sons at his bedside.

Bin Sukat recalls the immediate aftermath. "Sheikh Mohammed called to inform me that Sheikh Rashid had died. It was a shock and I was in something of a panic. I had to sit down. Few people in Dubai had ever known a time when Sheikh Rashid was not around. I could not believe that he had finally gone."

Moments later, a police car, dispatched on Sheikh Mohammed's orders, arrived at bin Sukat's home to take him to Za'abeel Palace. Sheikh Rashid had always considered him like a brother. Sheikh Mohammed thought that 'family' should be together at a time of grief. It was a personal kindness that bin Sukat has never forgotten.

Despite a deepening regional crisis following the Iraqi invasion of Kuwait the death of Sheikh Rashid bin Saeed Al Maktoum, architect of modern Dubai, prompted a pause. Indeed, his death marked a rallying point for a nation which had been brought to the brink of war, had been

inundated with refugees and had seen an influx of foreign troops on the Arabian Peninsula as an international coalition grew.

Islamic tradition decrees that the deceased be buried before the first sunset after death. The new Ruler, Sheikh Maktoum, who had been in London on official business, rushed home.

Despite their grief, Maktoum family members steeled themselves for a public occasion and a very open show of national mourning. As word of Sheikh Rashid's death spread, a steady stream of people, uncertain of what to do, assembled outside Za'abeel Palace. Within hours hundreds were there, a mixture of nationals and expatriates, most standing in silent contemplation of a beloved figure. It was an extraordinary scene.

British expatriate Anthea Grainger, who joined the throng in Za'abeel with friends, described it as unforgettable and moving. "I've never seen so many people in one place, so quiet. No-one really knew what to do, but we all felt a sadness and wanted to show our respect for Sheikh Rashid, and show our solidarity with the ruling family."

At daybreak, the people who had maintained an informal vigil overnight were joined by thousands more, drawn from all sections of the community. This crowd grew as news spread of Sheikh Rashid's death, and as staff arrived at offices and shops throughout Dubai to find them closed as a mark of respect.

"I was in India when I heard the news that he had passed and it is no exaggeration to say that it felt as though I had lost my own father," says Abdul Qadir Mohammed, chairman of the Express Group and a stalwart of the Indian business community in Dubai. "My first thought was to

call my office and instruct them to close, as a mark of respect. My second was to return so that I may offer my condolences to his sons."

Around 10.30 in the morning, the funeral cortege emerged from the Za'abeel Palace grounds and a procession of vehicles made slow progress toward Umm Hurair Cemetery in Dubai. Sheikh Hamdan drove the hearse, while UAE President Sheikh Zayed bin Sultan Al Nahyan led mourners in a car behind. Police estimated that there were between 7,000 and 8,000 people near Za'abeel Palace at the beginning of the funeral and thousands thronged the streets along the route.

Within 20 minutes the cortege arrived in Umm Hurair. Thousands of people watched from every possible vantage point as Sheikh Rashid's bier, his body wrapped tightly in a plain white shroud, was carried to its final resting place. Sheikh Hamdan and Sheikh Mohammed helped place their father's body into a freshly dug grave. A silence fell over the cemetery as Koranic verses were read aloud by a cleric.

Led by Sheikh Maktoum, the brothers emerge from Za'abeel Mosque at the beginning of an emotional journey to bury their father.

Throughout, his sons faces remained masks of anguish and grief. But the death of their father was also a political occasion and had to be handled as such. Even at a time of sadness, the brothers were bound by duty.

Among the mourners were most of the Rulers of the other emirates and representatives of dozens of foreign governments. Sheikh Zayed paid tribute to his old ally.

"Sheikh Rashid contributed and accomplished much throughout his life, exerting a great deal of effort. And this is not my opinion alone, but we have all witnessed these facts. His loss demands that we all follow suit along the same road as he travelled, with renewed vigour, towards strengthening the federation and the foundations of the country," stated Sheikh Zayed.

"Sheikh Rashid was one of the most remarkable leaders I have ever met. Modern Dubai is a testimony to his vision. It is also true that the UAE would not have become what it is today without his efforts. He was my friend... Now that we have lost such a great man, the country has been compensated in Sheikh Maktoum and his brothers."

After the funeral, Sheikh Zayed publicly told Sheikh Rashid's four grieving sons: "As Sheikh Rashid was my brother, may God be my witness I consider you my sons."

Traditionally, senior members of a ruling family in mourning receive condolences from ordinary people. Accordingly, the doors of Za'abeel Palace were opened. Amid many emotional scenes, Sheikh Maktoum and his brothers stood for hours over subsequent days receiving and shaking hands with around 12,000 people.

Among those offering condolences were Sheikh Khalifa bin Hamad Al Thani, Ruler of Qatar, and Sheikh Isa bin Salman Al Khalifa, Emir of Bahrain, along with representatives from governments around the world. Elsewhere, Qatar and Pakistan ordered three days of official mourning, and the Omani and Bahraini governments announced that flags would be flown at half mast. Across the world in New York, both the United Nations General Assembly and United Nations Security Council observed a minute of silence, while the representatives of Kuwait, Poland and the United States were granted time by the chair to make statements of tribute before the world body on Sheikh Rashid's life and achievements.

The government announced a 40 day mourning period, ordering UAE missions abroad to shut and closing federal ministries for six days.

In Britain, the news media reported his death. *The Daily Telegraph* published a lengthy obituary which stated that Sheikh Rashid "led his pocket-sized Gulf emirate to an unprecedented prosperity based not only on oil but also on trade..." Another influential broadsheet, *The Independent*, called him "the merchant prince" and added that he "leaves behind a Dubai that far outclasses any other Middle Eastern city as a place to live and do business and that bears comparison with Hong Kong and Singapore, its economy re-stimulated by the current surge in oil prices."

The international news agency *Agence France-Presse* observed that he moulded Dubai into "a strong candidate to take over Hong Kong's position in world trade in the 21st Century."

Chapter Thirty-One

A Heavy Burden

Other nations of different habits are not enemies: they are godsends.
Men require of their neighbours something sufficiently akin to be
understood, something sufficiently different to provoke attention,
and something great enough to command admiration.
We must not expect, however, all the virtues.
— Alfred North Whitehead, mathematician and philosopher.

Sheikh Maktoum bin Rashid Al Maktoum had acceded as Ruler of Dubai, the ninth member of the family to hold the position in a lineage that stretched back nearly 160 years. On October 22, 1990, during a meeting of the UAE Supreme Council in Abu Dhabi, he was unanimously elected Vice President of the UAE and appointed Prime Minister, with a five-year mandate.

He and his brothers hardly had time to draw breath following the sadness that enveloped the family, and Dubai as a whole, before they were consumed by pressing business, the most urgent of which was shaping a response to the Iraqi invasion and occupation of Kuwait. The UAE threw its weight behind an emerging United Nations sanctioned political and military coalition to oust the Iraqis and restore Kuwait's rightful Rulers to power.

As Prime Minister, this was to be one of the most trying periods in Sheikh Maktoum's life, while, as Minister of Defence, Sheikh Mohammed was called upon to serve the nation in one of its darkest hours.

On September 2, following a meeting with British Foreign Secretary Douglas Hurd, Sheikh Mohammed reiterated the UAE's position, and answered criticism from a small number of Arab world states about the involvement of foreign forces in the crisis: "Once the reason for these foreign armed forces being stationed in the Gulf is removed, they will

Sheikh Maktoum bin Rashid Al Maktoum was the ninth member of the
family to rule Dubai.

withdraw. But the international community had made a commitment to defend the sovereignty of Kuwait. Freeing Kuwait will be the only end to this troubling scenario.

"Let me be perfectly clear. The UAE is participating fully and strenuously in the search for a political solution to this crisis. We wish to guarantee an immediate withdrawal of Iraqi armed forces from Kuwait, after which the UAE will work to see the beginnings of a new phase of stability and co-operation within this region."

On January 11, United States Secretary of State James Baker flew into Abu Dhabi to meet with President Sheikh Zayed, Sheikh Maktoum, Sheikh Mohammed and other senior Emirati officials. His message was not promising, and the coalition struck on January 16. On February 22 an intense ground offensive began and, four days later, Iraqi troops were ordered out of Kuwait.

Within days of the war ending, the UAE government had directed efforts to send 250 tonnes of aid from the UAE, while, under Sheikh Mohammed, the army rushed medical teams to Kuwait City to revive the devastated health service. With the city's desalination plants destroyed, the UAE air force also carried emergency supplies of bottled water for residents.

The UAE was still home to thousands of Kuwaitis and other refugees from the crisis, and it was months before the situation would calm, some semblance of normality would descend upon Kuwait and people would return home.

But Kuwait was the beginning of a series of international crises that would test UAE President Sheikh Zayed, Sheikh Maktoum's federal government and heavily involve the country's Minister of Defence Sheikh Mohammed throughout the 1990s.

When the UAE was established as an independent state, circumstances dictated that its policy-makers focused on the Gulf and then the broader Arab region. Gradually, however, as the country's domestic and regional situation strengthened and stabilised, its political horizons expanded. This process accelerated markedly during the 1990s. As a result the country was projecting the pursuit of its political interests far further afield than many might have anticipated only a few years earlier.

During its fledgling years the UAE has emerged as a state with distinct characteristics and a very real role to play within international affairs. That, in turn, had brought benefits in winning support for its own position on key issues. Conciliation, consensus and diplomacy form the bedrock of this characteristic style of foreign policy; established by President Sheikh Zayed, it has now become a fundamental component of the state's persona. But it is also notable because this is likely to be the long-term nature of Emirati foreign policy. Influential figures such as Sheikh Maktoum, Sheikh Khalifa bin Zayed Al Nahyan, Sheikh Mohammed and Lt-General Sheikh Mohammed bin Zayed Al Nahyan were instinctively humanitarians by nature.

All have supported the active involvement of the UAE's armed forces in international crises and policing actions. One US-based military think-tank appraised the UAE's foreign policy approach in a report, which commented:

> *The UAE carefully reviews issues and options before any action is taken, generally adopting a policy of promoting conciliation and of defusing confrontation and conflict. This derives from the nature of tribal society in Arabia that is essentially communal, requiring general consensus in order to survive.*
>
> *At the same time, the UAE is prepared to act swiftly when the situation requires, and to stand alone on controversial issues. In August 1990, following the Iraqi invasion of Kuwait, the UAE was among the first of the Arab states to support an international military response.... The UAE is tolerant of different lifestyles as long as these do not threaten the basic values of the country and its people.*

The UAE has devoted considerable attention to efforts aimed at encouraging international aid efforts, motivated in each case by humanitarian concerns. The UAE's foreign policy is based on the principles outlined in the Charter of the United Nations and the Charter of the Organisation of the Islamic Conference (OIC). This foreign policy aspect can be traced back to the 1970s, when the UAE provided a contingent for the Arab Deterrent Force in Lebanon during that country's civil war. Such intervention represented an evolution in UAE government policy. The UAE government recognised that its civil and military apparatus was ready and able to play a leading role on the international stage.

Sheikh Mohammed has been at the forefront of change. As Minister of Defence, he consistently pushed for the UAE to define for itself an

Two off-duty UAE army personnel with some displaced Bosnian children in an emergency camp. (opposite page) A UAE Air Force transporter loading emergency relief supplies destined for the Balkans.

active political and military role.

The fruits of this 'coming of age' process were later seen in 1999, when peacekeeping operations in Kosovo were undertaken by a special international force, KFOR. The UAE was the only Muslim state to participate; in addition, the UAE and Russia were the only non-NATO participants. It was the first operational deployment of UAE forces outside the Middle East and a landmark in the history of the Emirates.

The years following the Gulf War were a time for introspection for both the UAE military and its political leadership. Globally, it was an era of change as the Cold War 'thawed' and half a century of military and political stalemate came crashing down with the Berlin Wall in November 1989. Former protagonists, as well as those who had nervously attempted to stay on the sidelines, could contemplate other uses for the billions of dollars they had been forced to spend on arms.

Earlier in the decade, the world welcomed the arrival in power of moderate and reform-minded USSR leader Mikhail Gorbachev, who came to power on March 11, 1985, when the Soviet Central Committee named him successor to Konstantin Chernenko immediately after Chernenko's death. Moving quickly to set himself apart from potential rivals, Gorbachev created a platform based on the concepts of glasnost (openness) and perestroika (restructuring of society and economy). The USSR was on the road to reform. Gorbachev signed superpower disarmament treaties. He withdrew Soviet forces from Afghanistan. The Cold War finally ended with a coup; Boris Yeltsin was subsequently elected to power.

But for most people, it was the destruction of the Berlin Wall that signalled the true end of the nuclear race and raging military escalation. General Mohammed Abdul Rahim Al Ali comments: "The end of the Cold War was a seismic shift in the prevailing political landscape. It also caused every military in the world to reassess its capabilities."

In place of two posturing superpowers, the new dangers to humanity came in smaller pockets of trouble. So-called 'rogue states' gained a new notoriety, while civil wars and ethnic cleansing, a cynical name for mass murder and population displacement, came to the fore. Help for the oppressed seemed to come too little, too late. The world community failed miserably in dealing with immediate post-Cold War challenges.

The Balkans were a prime example. Serbian aggression continued unchecked by the international community until 1995, by which time more than three million had been killed, injured or made homeless. Sheikh Maktoum's government placed millions of dollars at the disposal of the Bosnian Muslim government and utilised its own network to pump money into emergency social projects and hospitals in the besieged city of Sarajevo.

At the height of the carnage, UAE Television organised a telethon to raise money for the victims of Serbian evil. Mustering sympathy with television footage of elderly Muslims fleeing Bosnian Serb attacks and images of injured children, the thirteen-and-a-half hour campaign attracted pledges from as far afield as Colombia. Donations included jewellery and pieces of art; one primary schoolgirl gave her teddy bear and another showed up at a donation centre at a shopping mall with a pure-bred Arabian horse. The horse was subsequently sold at auction for $41,000.

As the telethon drew the community together with moving pictures on television screens that served to heighten a sense of frustration, the progress of the appeal was being discreetly observed by Sheikh Mohammed. He kept an eye on the television in his Majlis while continuing with his meetings. Mohammed Mirhashim recalls: "The community spirit shown by the people of the UAE, with stories such as that of the girl who donated her horse for auction, was really quite touching. The strength of feeling was tangible."

Ten hours into the campaign, around $15 million had been raised. Sheikh Mohammed whispered instructions to an aide. The instructions, it transpired, were to match what had been raised to that point. Says Mohammed Mirhashim: "It was Sheikh Mohammed's intention to keep his identity out of the donation, but needless to say, people just don't believe when someone telephones them to offer a $15 million pledge. UAE Television needed full verification of the call before this donation was announced."

UAE Television's desire to confirm the true identity of a donor of $15 million is quite understandable. There are not many people who give such an amount, to any cause, in one go.

But such acts of impromptu philanthropy are not uncommon from a man who, despite his public persona, carries his heart on his sleeve in private. Only those close to Sheikh Mohammed know the extent of his philanthropic nature. Few examples reach the media, as he makes stringent attempts to keep this part of his life private.

In November 1995 Dayton, Ohio marked something of an end to the miseries of the Bosnian people. In the wake of the Dayton Agreement, the UN Security Council passed Resolution 1035, creating the United Nations Mission in Bosnia and Herzegovina (UNMIBH) for an initial one-year period. This mandate has been renewed until the present day. A NATO-led force of 60,000 men moved into Bosnia to police the agreed provisions. With NATO taking charge of military action, the UAE's armed forces assumed humanitarian responsibilities for the urgent delivery of tens of millions of dollars of aid for the Bosnians. Under orders from Sheikh Zayed, Sheikh Mohammed personally directed the Ministry of Defence to airlift wounded Bosnian Muslims to Abu Dhabi and Dubai. The wounded received medical treatment and their families were provided with accommodation and financial allowances. Relief supplies for Bosnia were assembled by the UAE Red Crescent Society and airlifted by the UAE Air Force.

General Mohammed Abdul Rahim Al Ali says: "Organising these and participating in their functions at every stage was Sheikh Mohammed's commitment to the Bosnian Muslims."

In time another bloody Balkan conflict would erupt, one that would require the UAE to take on a peacemaking, as well as a humanitarian role.

After the frustrations of Bosnia, the UAE was able to play a more decisive role in an African crisis during the early 1990s. A famine was raging in Somalia, a tragedy compounded by civil war. By the autumn of 1992, conservative estimates put the death toll at 500,000. Hundreds of thousands more were in danger of dying. Clan violence in Somalia had interfered with international famine relief efforts and the country was in a state of civil war. Public services had broken down.

In September 1992, the UAE Foreign Ministry issued a statement calling upon Arab and international leaders to "take effective action to save Somalia and assist in ending its ordeal. The UAE will not remain a spectator to the destruction and bloodletting in Somalia..."

Unlike the diplomatic quagmire over Bosnia, in Somalia a worsening situation led to the formation of the United Nations Operation in Somalia, UNOSOM. However, UNOSOM quickly proved too weak in the face of opposition to its humanitarian efforts from Somali 'war lords' bent on protecting their fiefdoms from foreign intrusion. Expanded peacekeeping in Somalia began after the failure of UNOSOM. With more Somali civilians starving to death, on December 3, 1992, the UN Security Council Resolution 794 authorised a US-led intervention "to use all necessary means to establish a secure environment for humanitarian relief operations in Somalia as soon as possible." This was a firm mandate that intended to lead from a short term humanitarian mission to political reconstitution of the embattled country. A multinational operation, Restore Hope, was to be protected by UNOSOM II, with UNITAF (unified task force) handling the civil needs of the Somali population.

This was the solution that the UAE had urged for many international problems. Both UNOSOM II and UNITAF received the full cooperation of the UAE's armed forces. The UAE government was one of the first

Active duty: The UAE sent its armed forces to Somalia as part of international peace keeping efforts.

512

to commit men to UNOSOM II. On December 6, Sheikh Zayed ordered Sheikh Mohammed to dispatch a battalion to Somalia to participate in the multinational force that was being created.

"Mogadishu was a dangerous place, as subsequent events would show," says General Al Ali. "The UAE battalion was part of a contingent of 40,000 foreign troops, sent to the country for the good of its people."

Military engineers from the UAE joined those from other nations to clear land mines and unexploded ordnance, build base camps for coalition forces, and drill water wells for Somali citizens. They constructed and improved over 2,000 kilometres of roads, built and repaired several bridges, upgraded and maintained airfields and participated in local civic action projects that helped to open schools, orphanages, hospitals and provide water supplies. During all these operations engineers were guarded by the multinational military force.

The project was so successful that by March 1993 mass starvation had been prevented. The streets were secure. A sense of normal life was beginning to emerge. Ordinary Somalis, terrorised by armed militias, welcomed the stability that UNOSOM II had brought to their lives.

On April 20, Sheikh Mohammed ordered a second battalion of Emirati soldiers to join their countrymen in Somalia. The Emirati armed forces in Somalia later withdrew at the end of the humanitarian action there, without suffering any casualties.

The UAE is estimated by some international institutions to have spent more than $17.4 billion between 1971 and 1996 on foreign aid; more than 40 countries on three continents have been beneficiaries. This is equivalent to 3.5% of GNP during that 25 year period. By comparison, over the same time frame, the United States spent less than 1% of its federal budget on foreign aid.

The UAE government channelled these funds through emergency aid and ongoing aid programmes, often organised and executed through the Emirates' armed forces. States such as Iran, Afghanistan, Egypt, Kuwait and India have all received emergency aid at times of crisis as a result of the UAE's unwavering commitment to its neighbours and the international community at large.

As the UAE had proven in Lebanon, Kuwait, Somalia and Bosnia, in times of international crisis the Emirates were also willing to utilise their armed forces abroad in order to support humanitarian efforts. This was a commitment to the international community that remains a cornerstone of government policy. All too often this is a commitment that the international community has tested.

Kosovo was to be another. In the aftermath of hostilities that tore apart the former Yugoslavia, conflict erupted in the Balkans again in 1997 and 1998. The source of the struggle was the Serbian province of Kosovo, which sought independence. Ironically, the 1995 Dayton Peace Accord, which brought an unsatisfactory end to the war in Bosnia and rewarded the Serbs for their aggression, may have contributed to the frustration and growing violence in Kosovo.

Ethnic Albanians comprised 90% of the approximately 2.2 million people living in Kosovo. After the Bosnian war, the conflict between Albanian Muslims and Orthodox Christian Serbs deepened. Kosovo's bid for autonomy met with brutal resistance from the Serbs, for whom Kosovo is a centre of religious and political significance. In response, Kosovans withdrew from Serbian state institutions and held elections for a shadow government. The international community implemented various political and economic sanctions against Serbia in the hope of prompting its leader, Slobodan Milosevic, to compromise with Kosovo. In June 1998, Western nations issued Serbia with an ultimatum: End the military offensive in Kosovo and return to the negotiating table or face NATO military intervention.

Meanwhile, the UAE began supplying humanitarian assistance to the Kosovan Muslims, who were in a desperate situation. When NATO air forces started a bombing campaign in 1999 to force the Serbs to stop their offensive against the Kosovar population, the UAE was the first non-NATO state to express support for the operation.

After the Serbian forces had withdrawn, the UN assumed responsibility for Kosovo and peace keeping operations were undertaken by a special international force, KFOR. The UAE was the only Muslim state to participate in KFOR, as well as being the only non-NATO participating country, apart from Russia. This was the first operational deployment of UAE forces outside the Middle East, as their earlier foray into Somalia had been graded a humanitarian policing operation.

Kosovo was to provide the UAE armed forces – and Sheikh Mohammed – with one of their sternest tests. One battalion was initially sent to the beleaguered province as part of KFOR. Political tensions still ran high, with active fighting among ethnic groups in the zones where the UAE troops were deployed. It was probably the troops' most demanding task since the Gulf War. They arrived in the province to find devastation on a massive scale. Hundreds of thousands of Kosovans were refugees without shelter. Most had no food other than what they could gather in the fields, no water other than what they could drink from streams. In the course of a Balkan summer laced with cold spells and heavy rain, a humanitarian disaster was in the offing.

Within days of the establishment of the KFOR bridgehead in Kosovo, the UAE air force began aid flights. Giant transporters, filled with food, tents, shoes, blankets, and educational and training facilities for young children flew daily into the province from the UAE.

Under Sheikh Mohammed's orders, the UAE military quickly set up a number of tented villages for 10,000 refugees. Each was a complete town and contained everything the refugees needed - electricity, water, food and health care were available round the clock. Each boasted a modern school for up to 2,000 children and provisions for the elderly and physically handicapped. Telephone exchanges were quickly installed and the UAE purchased luxury coaches to take refugees on outings away from the misery of everyday life. A helicopter was also on standby for anyone who needed urgent medical treatment at a specialist facility elsewhere. All such villages were also equipped with a 200-bed hospital, one of which had an operating theatre, emergency room and a number of in-patient wards.

In the West, some questioned the value of such aid. One writer from the *Economist Intelligence Unit* in London wrote: "I think what is important is that the international community develops some sort of exit strategy because there is a real danger that we are going to create a dependency culture here... [this situation] raises a great danger that we're going to create another Cyprus, another situation where the international community will have to be here for 20, 30 or 40 years."

Sheikh Mohammed rejected long-term worries in favour of the short-term needs of the hundreds of thousands of refugees, telling the Kosovan media: "The forces of the United Arab Emirates will stay in Kosovo for as long as they are needed. We are committed to creating security and serving the needs of the displaced. We are also committed to KFOR operations."

The UAE's participation in Kosovo as part of KFOR continues to the present day. The UAE's humanitarian commitment to the people of the province is also ongoing. The destruction of infrastructure by the Serbs took a matter of months, but rebuilding will take a generation.

Sheikh Mohammed's professional commitment to this process, through the UAE military, is complemented by his private commitment. His charity, the Mohammed bin Rashid Al Maktoum Charitable and Humanitarian Foundation, has worked in Kosovo since 1998. During a visit to the province, Sheikh Mohammed was alerted to the Serbs' systematic destruction of mosques. In August 2000, the Foundation announced that its patron had ordered the building of 50 mosques around the province at his expense. He also commissioned programmes to repair schools and provide housing for communities targeted by the Serbs.

The UAE's foreign policy priority remains the security of the Gulf and so its military has always concentrated on affairs close to home. It has done so within the framework of the country's second policy objective, promoting ties with fellow GCC members.

The UAE's Arab identity is also important and is reflected in the country's approach toward the rest of the Arab world. The promotion of good relations within the Arab world represents a third foreign policy objective.

A fourth foreign policy strand derives from identification with fellow Muslims around the world and development of relations with the countries where they live, including Western nations. Finally, UAE foreign policy reflects the fact that the country's size requires it to collaborate, wherever possible, with other like-minded states. A major component is the belief in supporting and working with, and through, international organisations and at the centre of the international community. The UAE has diplomatic relations with 143 countries and hosts 62 embassies, compared to just three in 1971, in addition to 29 non-resident embassies and 37 consulates in Dubai. The UAE has 40 embassies abroad, five consulates and two Permanent Missions.

"Sheikh Maktoum was ardent in his support of the United Nations and its aims," says Abdulaziz Nasser R. Al Shamsi, UAE Ambassador Extraordinary and Plenipotentiary in New York. "Sheikh Maktoum had consistently reaffirmed the UAE's intention to play a strong role within the UN and, as the UAE government has shown repeatedly, this nation is consistent in its willingness to play an active role in promoting a peaceful, increasingly prosperous world."

In addition to the UN and the Arab League, the UAE is a member of the International Monetary Fund, World Trade Organisation and International Labour Organisation.

From the Balkans to Somalia, the UAE has proven itself willing and adept at playing an active role in international politics. Led first by Sheikh Zayed bin Sultan Al Nahyan and, more recently by Sheikh Khalifa bin Zayed Al Nahyan, Sheikh Maktoum and then Sheikh Mohammed's government set itself on a path of internationalism.

Finally the UAE had cause for celebration at the end of 1991: In December it marked its first two decades as a federation. On December 2, Sheikh Maktoum, Sheikh Hamdan and Sheikh Mohammed – Vice President and Prime Minister, Minister of Finance and Industry and Minister of Defence — joined the Rulers of the seven emirates to review a large military parade in Abu Dhabi. It was a grand day, full of pomp and ceremony that gave nationals and expatriates the chance to revel in the achievements of the previous 20 years. The UAE's people stood back for a moment to savour their achievements.

It was also an opportunity for reflection. In Dubai, Sheikh Maktoum and his brothers could look out at a landscape far removed from that which greeted them exactly two decades earlier when they witnessed their father signing the UAE's constitution at Union House. The city was now well developed and booming. High-rise office and apartment blocks now towered over pre-1971 buildings. Dubai teemed with life and was, in every way, evolving in the direction that Sheikh Rashid had envisioned decades earlier.

The people now had schools and hospitals, a modern road network linked the remotest parts of the country with the major cities. Homes had clean, running water and electricity. The deprivation and suffering of the recent past had been all but eliminated, replaced with tremendous new, world class infrastructure.

It was the kind of world class infrastructure that Dubai needed if it was to meet ambitious development targets. With its limited oil reserves, Dubai government plans called for the economy to be virtually non-oil reliant by 2010. This left a remarkably small window during which Dubai had to secure and guarantee its future.

That future, if not exactly in the balance, was nevertheless at a cross-roads. Dubai's hydrocarbon reserves would not last forever. Time was running out.

Chapter Thirty-Two

New Direction

You may delay, but time will not.
— *Benjamin Franklin, statesman*

On January 4, 1995, Dubai and the UAE awoke to ground breaking news. The previous day, Dubai Ruler Sheikh Maktoum, had signed two decrees that were to have a dramatic effect on the future of the emirate. One appointed Sheikh Mohammed as Crown Prince of Dubai; the second recognised Sheikh Hamdan as Deputy Ruler of the emirate.

To those unacquainted with the workings of the Maktoum family it was a breathtaking and unexpected move. To those on the inside, however, Sheikh Maktoum's decision was seen as a firm step in the right direction, done after months of deliberations within the Ruling family and many discussions between the four brothers.

Sheikh Mohammed bin Khalifa Al Maktoum spoke for many when he said: "Sheikh Maktoum was very, very clever to appoint Sheikh Mohammed as Crown Prince and Sheikh Hamdan as Deputy Ruler. Although both were already playing integral roles in securing the future of Dubai, their efforts had to be recognised and their powers enhanced. Sheikh Mohammed reminded many people of his father, Sheikh Rashid, for his vision. It was clear that Dubai needed to harness this, and to bring his tremendous energy to bear at all levels. Sheikh Hamdan continued to achieve a great deal for Dubai through his role as head of Dubai Municipality and in so many of the emirate's most vital economic projects."

Much later Sheikh Mohammed shed some light on his skills and where they came from when he stated: "I do not know if I am a good leader, but I am a leader. And I have a vision. I look to the future, 20, 30 years. I learned that from my father, Sheikh Rashid. He was the true

An explosion of fireworks over Dubai Creek Golf and Yacht Club. The emirate has been transformed over one generation and — in January 1995 — its leadership received fresh impetus.

519

Father of Dubai. I follow his example. He would rise early and go alone to watch what was happening on each of his projects. I do the same. I watch. I read faces. I take decisions and I move fast. Full throttle."

It was this "full throttle" approach that Sheikh Maktoum hoped to harness on behalf of Dubai. Sheikh Mohammed and Sheikh Hamdan had succeeded in surrounding themselves with some of the most able and highly motivated young nationals in Dubai. Like their mentors, these young men were intent on pursuing a vision of a new Dubai. Their talents were being nurtured with as much attention to detail as the many grand plans for Dubai that, even just 10 years ago, were still on the drawing board and being kept highly secret.

By the mid-1980s the nation was also on the verge of reaping the harvest of its massive investment in education, the emergence of talented and ambitious young graduates. These young men and women were being eagerly welcomed back from higher studies abroad and the majority placed on a promotional fast track within government. Sheikh Mohammed bin Khalifa remarks: "Around Sheikh Hamdan, Sheikh Mohammed and Sheikh Ahmed you see them. Educated and talented young men are spotted, groomed and then placed in positions of responsibility. They are watched. If they succeed they will jump up the promotional ladder.

"Many times, especially in the last decade, what looks like a new face has appeared at the helm of one of Dubai's big visionary projects. But when you look at the background of this man who suddenly has so much power, you discover that one of the sheikhs has nurtured his career. Many, many of those who you see in senior positions in Dubai today were brought through in the same way."

By the mid-1990s, many from this pool of talent were already prominent figures in Dubai, the high achievers of the Dubai government. Names such as Sultan bin Sulayem, chairman of JAFZA; Khalid Ahmed bin Sulayem, director general of the Department of Tourism and Commerce Marketing, Mohammed Al Gergawi, chairman of the board of Dubai Development and Investment Authority; and Mohammed Alabbar, chairman of Dubai Economic Department, are just a few of the people on a list that numbers in the dozens today.

Others still "in training" at this point and set for high office includes

Four of the new Camelot generation (clockwise) Mohammed Al Gergawi, Mohammed Ali Alabbar, Saeed Al Muntafiq and Sultan bin Sulayem

the likes of Ibrahim Belselah, Saeed Al Muntafiq and Ahmed Al Banna.

These men and others like them are well educated, in some cases having completed their studies abroad in Ivy League universities in the US or Oxbridge in Britain. They returned to Dubai with big ideas and full of fervour for modernisation, and would become the backbone of the Dubai government. All were part of an administrative elite who would help bring life to the Maktoums' grand plan.

"Sheikh Maktoum was surrounded by young, talented and highly educated individuals. He was a very trusting leader and offered many their first opportunity in senior positions," says Sheikh Mohammed bin Khalifa. "If they proved themselves, Sheikh Maktoum was very nurturing and would ensure that their skills were fully utilised."

Sheikh Mohammed's Majlis was a good example of what this process was doing. He needed people on whom he could rely, and his Majlis needed dynamic young minds. If Sheikh Mohammed was to become the engine that powered the drive to build and modernise Dubai, his Majlis was his energy source, fueling him with the ideas and concepts that, over time, would infuse new life into the emirate.

Another of the UAE's proud claims is that men and women have equal opportunities in education. Statistics bear this out: Roughly equal numbers of boys and girls attend the nation's schools. Indeed, at university level around 75% to 80% of pupils are female.

Late UAE President Sheikh Zayed's philosophy on the subject, which had been incorporated into the laws of his country, was that "Islam gives women their rightful status, and encourages them to work in all sectors as long as they are afforded the appropriate respect. The basic role of women is the upbringing of children but, over and above that, we have to support a woman who chooses to perform other functions."

This does not just stand in the normal work place. This attitude towards women's place in society has even extended to the UAE armed forces. The roots of this are Sheikh Mohammed's experiences at times of national crisis such as the Arab-Israeli conflicts of 1967 and 1973, the Gulf War and the Iraqi invasion of Kuwait, when the Ministry of Defence and other government institutions were inundated with pleas from ordinary citizens volunteering to undertake emergency military training.

During the Kuwait conflict, Sheikh Mohammed headed a number of

Sheikh Ahmed with the deputy director general of his office, Shareef Al Halawani

meetings with senior government and defence ministry officials to form an official position. What emerged, with the minister's whole-hearted support, was a women only unit in the UAE army. This required extra expenditure, as separate facilities are needed to ensure female modesty is protected as required in Islam. Sheikh Mohammed ordered his army to proceed at speed in forming an all female unit.

It was a decision that he has not regretted. In the wake of the Gulf War, the UAE army has continued to strengthen and develop its women only units. In so doing, it reinforces a widely-held belief that introducing more women into the national workforce is the only way to lessen the impact of foreign workers on the UAE's culture and economy.

That said, the Dubai government has understood that the emirate cannot develop with just the talents of its own limited national workforce. Accordingly, Dubai has worked hard to provide easy access into the employment market for workers and business people from around the world. Today, nationals make up just 10% of the total workforce and a mere 1% to 2% of private-sector workers.

While recognising the benefits of importing talent and skills, to offset this reliance on expatriates the Dubai government is working to find more jobs for young nationals, especially women. In an interview Sheikh Mohammed observed: "Now we are educating the ladies. Every single girl now coming out of university will have a job. We are pushing women. Yes, it is late, but we have ladies in the police, in the army. You will find women employed at immigration and at the new stock market."

This initiative brought women into the UAE army, Dubai Police and

Dubai government departments, an initiative that has been applauded and copied throughout the Emirates. The most famed example of the personal nurturing of talent within the Dubai government is female. One such personality who fits into this mould is one of the most remarkable women in the Arab world, Sheikha Lubna Khalid Sultan Al Qassimi

A niece of Dr Sheikh Sultan bin Mohammed Al Qassimi, Ruler of Sharjah, she graduated from California State University with a Bachelor's Degree in Computer Science, and has an Executive MBA from the American University of Sharjah.

Returning to the Emirates following a stellar education, she acted as the Dubai branch manager for the General Information Authority, an organisation responsible for automating the UAE government, later moving to Dubai Ports Authority. It was at DPA that she was 'spotted' by Sheikh Mohammed. In 1999 he awarded her with the 'Distinguished Government Employee Award' and appointed her as Chief Executive of Tejari, the first Middle Eastern Business-to-Business online Marketplace. She later joined Dubai Chamber of Commerce and Industry on the Board of Directors and the Board of Trustees for Dubai University College.

Sheikh Mohammed took a keen interest in her talents and was proven entirely correct when, in November 2004, she was appointed UAE Minister for Economy and Planning, the first woman to hold a ministerial post in the Emirates.

The glass ceiling was well and truly broken.

Major General Dhahi Khalfan Tamim, head of the Dubai Police, grew up around the Maktoum family. He says: "These are dynamic times. Sheikh Mohammed has evolved a team made up of the best and brightest. He also has a firm vision of the direction in which he wants to take Dubai. It is extraordinary to feel the energy surrounding him."

There was already an overall plan for Dubai's future. Sheikh Maktoum, Sheikh Hamdan, Sheikh Mohammed and Sheikh Ahmed had formulated an outline for development based upon the original blueprint laid down by Sheikh Rashid a generation before. The brothers' vision centred around a three-pronged strategy: The Three Dubais.

First was 'Destination Dubai', the tourism industry. Over the five years until 1995, the number of visitors staying at hotels in the emirate jumped by nearly a million to 1.6 million. A long-term plan was based

The incomparable Sheikha Lubna Khalid Sultan Al Qassimi.

on forecasts that this figure would increase substantially over subsequent years, until tourism represented a major portion of Gross National Product (GNP).

Second, was 'Hub Dubai', the development of the emirate as a centre for global trade and transhipment. Taking advantage of its geographical location, Dubai has developed its economy and facilities to provide the world's commercial sector with direct access to a wider regional market estimated at more than two billion consumers. In many ways, Hub Dubai was a continuation of the vision of the far-sighted Sheikh Maktoum bin Hasher Al Maktoum in the 1890s, who had set his sights on establishing his small town as the region's trade capital. Hardly a century on, Dubai was there. According to statistics released by the Dubai Chamber of Commerce and Industry, in 1995 non-oil trade in Dubai amounted to approximately $19.7 billion, well above oil related activities.

Third, and perhaps boldest of all, was 'e-Dubai'. In 1995, this third vision for the emirate was still largely unknown to anyone other than the higher echelons of the Maktoum family and a handful of people close to Sheikh Mohammed. Always one with an eye for a new and better way of doing things, Sheikh Mohammed believed that Dubai should become the regional information technology capital, perhaps even a global centre for e-commerce.

Information technology fascinated him. Computer-literate himself, he observed that the much-vaunted IT revolution was going nowhere fast in the Middle East. So he set in motion studies that would later take the emirate in a strikingly new direction.

Sheikh Mohammed later said:

> *...at a relatively early stage, [Dubai had] drawn up necessary plans to have in place the requirements for positive interaction with the new economy. We [aimed] to move in several directions at the same time, namely promoting awareness of the information culture, improving education and rethinking its programmes and tools, initiating infrastructure projects for the new digital economy and launching the Electronic government initiative, which renders the Web a major tool in the management of services and completion of tasks within government departments and with the business sector.*

With his new mandate as Crown Prince, one of Sheikh Mohammed's first tasks was to take a long, hard look at the Dubai government. For the most part, it was functioning well but, since the days of Sheikh Rashid, the Maktoum family had considered bureaucracy as a trade inhibitor. Dubai needed strong state apparatus if it was to grow, but the layers of administration were tolerated rather than welcomed. Keeping Dubai's bureaucracy in shape was something for which Sheikh Mohammed quickly became known. A firm believer in the approach of US President Theodore Roosevelt who said: "Speak softly and carry a big stick," he encouraged Dubai's administrators to be diligent, and was not averse to coming down hard if his encouragement was ignored. Termination of employment – practically unheard of in Gulf civil services – was within his remit, and he used it.

Corruption of any sort is a ticket to jail. "In Dubai there is no corruption," he told one interviewer. "Whenever we hear about a case of corruption, somebody must bear the consequences. Openness? Of course, openness applies not only to the government, but also to companies and all sectors."

He began his campaign by striking fear into the hearts of tardy government employees with a series of unannounced, early-morning visits to a variety of different departments. *Reuters* reported one visit to the Dubai Courts:

> *When Sheikh Mohammed turned up unannounced at a number of departments on Saturday he did not like what he found. All managerial staff – including the director, chairman and deputy chairman – are to be replaced at the Dubai Courts...*
>
> *Sheikh Mohammed found empty offices, absent managers and too much red tape. Judges and legal staff turned up late and too many police officers roamed the courts annoying the public... 'Any negligence or delay in rendering public services will not be tolerated,' Sheikh Mohammed said.*

Such spontaneous inspection tours remain in Sheikh Mohammed's diary. The majority are not reported: He wants to encourage a culture of responsibility, not one of fear.

During this period national responsibility was also an issue in the news, Dubai was playing a full part of an extraordinary nationwide

The UAE now boasted one of the most comprehensive and modern education systems in Asia and the Middle East.

campaign launched by late UAE President Sheikh Zayed. One of the social problems that can afflict wealthy nations is voluntary unemployment among the children of rich families. Many youths, because of their social status or education, were reluctant to start at the bottom either in public or private sector employment. During the mid-1990s, this phenomenon threatened to get out of hand.

In a series of major speeches throughout 1995, Sheikh Zayed stressed the importance of the work ethic, and its vital role in the development of society. "I cannot understand," Sheikh Zayed said pointedly, "how a physically fit young man can sit idle and accept the humiliation of depending on others for his livelihood."

The government had clearly done its part and Sheikh Hamdan's Ministry of Finance and Industry had continued to allocate a greater figure from the Federal budget to education. During the scholastic year 1993/4, the Ministry of Education spent $870 million. The UAE's population had grown from 180,000 in 1971 to over two million residents in less than a quarter of a century. While there were fewer than 30,000 students in the UAE's schools in 1971, by the mid-1990s there were 400,000 in primary and secondary schools. There were also around 15,000 students in institutions of higher education, the largest of which remains the prestigious UAE University in Al Ain.

With the country still relying heavily on expatriate labour, education spending was tantamount to wasting vast amounts of money if those completing education chose unemployment ahead of working for a living. This phenomenon was also a woeful waste of human talent.

Sheikh Zayed's rallying call was taken up by many of his colleagues in the UAE Supreme Council and government during June 1995. In public statements, Sheikh Mohammed dubbed unemployment among young nationals "a waste of the UAE's natural resources" and said it was "wrong when the UAE is providing all its sons and daughters with opportunities that were unattainable a generation ago..."

Throughout the Emirates, registration centres were opened and nationals were encouraged to make themselves available for work. All were promised worthwhile jobs with a genuine opportunity for advancement. By the end of this campaign, 15,594 youngsters had registered. Those living in Dubai became the responsibility of the local government. Jobs were found for all in both the public and private sectors, with all four brothers finding space within organisations that were part of their remit, or seeking support from the private sector

Quite often the diversity of key projects shared between the brothers underlined the fact that they are linked as part of a grand design. Perhaps the most notable example of this was provided in 1996 when a handful of projects came together with the stated aim of establishing Dubai as an internationally recognised brand and as a tourist destination.

During the first half of the 1990s Dubai had opened numerous hotels and facilities. In Dubai's search for an upmarket niche, developments had been headlined by the creation of Emirates Golf Club and the Dubai Creek Golf and Yacht Club. The Dubai Desert Classic golf tournament, a prestigious event on the European PGA Tour, and the Dubai Open tennis tournament were now established, branding opportunities that heightened awareness of Dubai and also reached out to the upmarket demographic Dubai sought for its tourism sector.

Dubai International Airport was expanding to deal with the increase in traffic. Dubai's Emirates airline had firmly established itself since its launch in 1985.

Sheikh Ahmed bin Saeed Al Maktoum, chairman of Emirates, described the airline's success in a nutshell. "At the end of the day, most airlines operate the same, or similar, aircraft, of the same size, speed and passenger capacity. To have an airline that stays competitive and still makes money, you have to differentiate it from others. This has to be done by providing a consistently good service and by employing the best staff and quality professionals – and that is, I believe, what we have with the Emirates team.

"Decisions have to be commercial and not political. It is important for an airline to have bilateral agreements. You cannot work in isolation and must have firm arrangements with other airlines to carry your passengers to destinations to which you do not travel."

Among its innovations, in 1992, Emirates was credited as the first airline to install personal video systems in all seats, in all classes, with video cassette players in all first-class seats. In 1995, Emirates was the first to install phones and fax machines throughout its fleet. In 1996, it took delivery of the first of the nine Boeing 777s fitted with features such as 17 video channels, 22 audio channels, and cameras relaying the view of takeoff and landing to passengers. The company's dedication to staying at the forefront extends to its aircraft replacement policy. Emirates will not fly any aircraft more than five years old; it has the youngest fleet of any airline in the world.

With tourism to Dubai on the rise and the necessary infrastructure

The Emirates Boeing 777 revolutionised civil aviation (inset) Sheikh Mohammed tests the PVS, watched by Sheikh Ahmed bin Saeed Al Maktoum.

and services in place, the time was ripe in 1996 to introduce another of the family's passions, horse racing, into the heady mix being created. Racing would be the focal point of a project to bring the world to Dubai.

Late in 1995 saw the creation of the Dubai Shopping Festival (DSF). A concept developed over a number of years, it was conceived as a focal point for the peak winter season for trade and tourism, an annual festival and part promotion that would be promoted worldwide.

The DSF was an ambitious undertaking. The inaugural event was a 43 day extravaganza, staged between February 15 and March 28, 1996, with organisers set a goal of attracting one million visitors to the emirate, from all over the region. The DSF programme was a mixture of cultural, sports and entertainment events – more than 500 in all – with 15 tonnes of fireworks lighting the sky every night in a spectacular display.

Hussain Ali Lootah, now executive chairman of DSF, recalls: "Organising the Dubai Shopping Festival is a phenomenal undertaking, embracing as it does dozens of Dubai government departments and institutions, along with thousands of private companies based in Dubai and multinational hotel chains and airlines. This is just an example to illustrate the breadth of the task. There are thousands of elements."

The inaugural Dubai Shopping Festival, ended up being the largest 'event' ever staged in the UAE. Thousands of people from dozens of departments and companies were involved in its organisation. Over 2,500 retail outlets, department stores and shopping malls participated through sales and special offers. Hotels dropped their rates by 40% and airlines were encouraged to offer special discounts and excess baggage allowances.

The event was a master success. An estimated $1 billion in revenue was generated by participating retail outlets during that first event.

The DSF needed a centrepiece – a memorable focal point – and that involved horse racing. The sport had been transformed under the Emirates Racing Association (ERA), headed at the time by internationally renowned racing administrator Dr Michael Osborne. Thoroughbred ownership had grown more widespread since the early years of professional racing when it was almost an exclusive privilege of members of the ruling families. The sport now belonged to the people and hundreds of people owned horses in training, including members of the expatriate community.

With more horses available to compete, the ERA could manage an expanded programme of meetings each winter. The sport became more competitive and professional. More racing and one of the highest ratios of prize money to training fees in the world meant more opportunities for owners. As the standard of the horses improved, the ERA made its biggest breakthrough in December 1995 when the International Cataloguing Standards Committee bestowed 'Listed' status on nine races in the Emirates. The first so-called 'Black Type' race in the UAE, the National Day Cup at Abu Dhabi Racing Club, was staged on December 2, 1995

With the ERA establishing an international reputation for Dubai's domestic racing programme and Godolphin carrying the flag abroad, it was down to the UAE Ministry of Agriculture and Fisheries to deliver the final element. A series of serological surveys had showed the

Emirates' equine population to be free of prohibited diseases, particularly African Horse Sickness. With strict controls in place on equine movements into and out of the UAE to prevent the import of infection, the European Union removed the Emirates from its black list and eased quarantine requirements. The Unites States followed soon after. Godolphin immediately capitalised on this by flying Red Bishop to America where he won the San Juan Capistrano Handicap.

For three years, the highlight of the UAE racing season had been the Dubai International Jockeys' Challenge. Following the 1995 event, won by Richard Hills and Johnny Murtagh representing the UAE, Dubai was finally ready to take the next step in its development as a major world racing nation.

On April 10, 1995, it was announced that the inaugural Dubai World Cup would be staged the following March, at the end of the new Dubai Shopping Festival. It would be the world's richest horse race with a purse of $4 million, $2.4 million of which would go to the winner.

"It was more than a simple race. It was a rallying call for the globalisation and modernisation of the sport the Maktoums' love," said Dhruba Selvaratnam, trainer for Sheikh Ahmed bin Rashid. "Sheikh Ahmed has been one of the biggest supporters of racing in this country and has been very supportive of the Dubai World Cup."

"Sheikh Mohammed had planned the road to the Dubai World Cup, step by step, for five years or more. Developments such as the Dubai Shopping Festival, which had the Dubai World Cup at its heart, and his work in promoting Dubai as a tourist destination, were all seemingly unassociated projects that were neatly tied together in 1996. The Dubai World Cup was a masterstroke," says Ali Khamis Al Jafleh, former chairman of the Dubai Racing Club

That first event was won by 'Cigar', one of the greatest horses of the 20th Century, and has since have been claimed by some of the planet's greatest thoroughbreds, a roll call including 'Silver Charm', Sheikh Hamdan's 'Almutawakel', 'Captain Steve' and 'Pleasantly Perfect', and of course Godolphin's incomparable 'Dubai Millennium'.

A decade ago, the 1996 running of the race attracted a glittering array of celebrities. Dubai was alight with a new international flavour; the rich and famous came from far-flung corners of the Earth. Around the globe, newspaper column-inches and television footage were dedicated to the race – and to the Dubai experience that was wrapped around it.

Sheikh Mohammed oversees a gallop at Godolphin's stables in Dubai. The sport of thoroughbred racing and the family's passion for development came together in spectacular style when the new world's richest race - the Dubai World Cup - was rolled out as the highlight of the new Dubai Shopping Festival.

The organisation and execution of the event cost many times the $2.4 million that Cigar's owner, Allen Paulson, took home in winnings, but in terms of exposure – and branding – tens of millions of dollars worth of publicity had been generated for Dubai.

One year later, the Dubai Shopping Festival 1997 would deliver more visitors and greater revenue to the emirate – as DSF would every year.

By the mid-1990s the Gulf region remained at its most stable politically since the beginning of the Iran-Iraq war in 1982. The resolution of the Iran-Iraq conflict and the swift end to the invasion of Kuwait brought to an end a decade of strife. With rising confidence, regional prosperity returned. Dubai's trade-based economy boomed while the Maktoum family made efforts to consolidate the emirate's position as Hub Dubai. The best way to reach out to global commerce quickly is through trade exhibitions. With Dubai promoting itself as a gateway to the region, its exhibition business grew steadily.

While the UAE's principal exhibition venue, the Dubai World Trade Centre (DWTC), comes under the auspices of Sheikh Hamdan, Hub Dubai is a family affair and the emirate's exhibition-hosting business is taken very seriously. The involvement of Sheikh Hamdan and Sheikh Mohammed, along with other senior members of the family, is viewed as crucial to the success of the project.

One exhibition hall had been built in 1979 next to Sheikh Rashid's original Dubai World Trade Centre. Three more had been added in the early 1980s. Ever since, the DWTC had been the location for more than 90 exhibitions staged each year. Because of this success, the exhibition halls were expanded in 1996, with an additional three halls raising total exhibition space to 33,000 square metres in seven halls. Mohammed Alabbar, then chairman of the DWTC, said: "The DWTC management has invested $400 million on projects since its inception in 1979, and it will not hesitate to invest further if demand warrants."

The exhibitions held at the DWTC over the course of a year vary from travel and tourism, industrial and trade, retail and commercial. There is a toy fair, an exhibition of furniture, a show exclusively for women, exhibitions which feature the latest technology in television, oil and gas, security, health and household appliances, among others. One showpiece event, GITEX, is the third biggest computer and IT exhibition in the world. In 1998, around 750,000 visitors were attracted to the 45 exhibitions – just less than one a week – at the DWTC.

Sheikh Hamdan and the family as a whole also supports exhibitions staged at the new Dubai Airport Expo Centre, at various hotels in the emirate, including many at Jumeirah properties, and at the Dubai Chamber of Commerce and Industry headquarters.

"Sheikh Hamdan patronises many exhibitions and will always make room in his diary to support exibitions and tour the halls, meeting exhibitors," says Wahid Attala, DWTC's former general manager. "Obviously Sheikh Hamdan is very personable and his personal interest in these events and also in the exhibitors themselves helps a great deal. His name and participation have helped both fill the halls with exhibitors, and then to publicise these events regionally, attracting more industry buyers."

"This sort of support has also become a hallmark of Sheikh Mohammed's involvement. Like Sheikh Hamdan, he is much more than a figurehead and shows a genuine interest in our exhibitors, always looking for new ideas."

One friend of Sheikh Mohammed's says: "Many times he will suddenly ask you to get in the car with him and he spontaneously goes to an exhibition. Once I went with him to GITEX. We arrived at 3pm. He toured the stands, stopping occasionally to see something that pricked his interest. We left at 7pm.

"During this visit, I mentioned that GITEX was so big but that there was not enough exhibition space available. Without comment, he took us to the West Marina and showed us drawings that he had already approved for a new hall, Hall 8."

Mention of GITEX leads to the third of Dubai's troika of developments.

Sheikh Mohammed's role as Crown Prince brought him closer to some aspects of Dubai and UAE life that had previously not been his responsibility. One of these was education. Visiting schools in the emirate, and meeting teachers and lecturers in his Majlis, the moderniser in Sheikh Mohammed was drawn to a startling conclusion. As former UAE President Sheikh Zayed had once said, the UAE's people, not its mineral reserves, were its greatest natural asset.

In the past too many youngsters had been lost as productive members of society through a lack of education. In recognition of this, the federal government had spent billions on building a comprehensive education system that produced young men and women able to provide

for their families, and to be productive members of a wider society.

Sheikh Mohammed recognised that progress had been made, but now had the opportunity to take a long, hard look at the education system. One major point of concern hit him. In an interview, he concluded:

We have an outdated education system. There are some subjects that are no longer relevant to the syllabus. We must teach the students new subjects. I don't think one should graduate as an engineer, for example, without first learning about computers and electronics. Otherwise one will be left behind, uncertain of one's duties and of the future. I think those equipped with knowledge of IT can get suitable jobs, or set up their own business. The government and private sector will help them and guide them to the right path... we have to change the syllabus and invest more in it.

It was a changing world, one dominated by I.T. But when visiting schools, colleges and universities, it was clear that many had only basic computer systems. What was more, around the Middle East this pattern was repeated everywhere. The Middle East, in sharp contrast to the economic powerhouses of Europe and North America, was lagging behind.

Something had to change. At home, bricks and mortar could modernize the city but, if the people were unable to grow with the technology that was shaping the larger world, Dubai and the UAE – indeed the entire Middle East and Arab world – would always lag behind in terms of social opportunity and economic development.

The concept of 'e-Dubai' had begun to take shape.

Dubai had its feet firmly in the old economy, but was preparing to supplant itself at the forefront of the new.

Chapter Thirty-Three

e-Dubai

The foundation of every state is the education of its youth.
— *Philosopher Diogenes of Sinope*

Some experts say the Internet is more of a historical accident than an invention. In 1962, the RAND Corporation was commissioned by the United States to devise a communications system that could continue to function even if a substantial portion of it was destroyed. RAND's subsequent report - Distributed Communications - outlined a network with no central hub to destroy. The Internet of today is derived from a Cold War dilemma - How to keep communications in America operating in the event of Soviet attack?

The system, named ARPANET, appeared in 1969. It had just four computers. By 1972 there were 37 subscribers, mainly scientists and researchers involved in developing this emerging network. During the 1970s slow but sustained progress saw the number of ARPANET subscribers grow. Newsgroups and mailing lists - email forerunners - were introduced to allow direct and instant communications between users.

But it was 1986 before the Internet as we know it began to take shape. Britain's Joint Academic Network (JANET) was established in 1984. In the US, the National Science Foundation Network (NSFNET) became operational in 1986. When these systems and others could be linked through gateways, which allowed communication between different systems, this new network suddenly encompassed thousands of users.

While many claim parentage, the father of the World Wide Web could perhaps be considered to be Tim Berners-Lee, a communications specialist with Geneva's European Particle Physics Laboratory. His system, devised in 1989, was faster and far more accessible. In 1990 the

Sheikh Mohammed's regional leadership in the area of Internet and e-commerce led some publications to dub him the e-sheikh.

World Wide Web began operating, centrally for the exchange of text-based information between scientists and researchers. The Web metamorphasised into its modern form several years later when browsers such as Mosaic and Netscape, which became widely available around 1993, made it easier to use, allowed the use of photographs and introduced graphics.

The Internet had come of age and was now accessible to the general public. And as 'The Net' became more popular, so did its value in a number of contexts. In 1989, only the Internet – not telephone services – survived the San Francisco earthquake. In 1991, the Net provided the world with valuable information on the coup in the former USSR and demonstrations in China's Tiananmen Square when traditional news broadcasting faced obstacles. In the Middle East, websites allow the disenfranchised to disseminate around the world information on the Palestinian struggle.

But the meteoric growth of the Internet was loaded in favour of the developed 'First World'. The Internet needed computers and telephone connections to expand. While these were prevalent in Europe and especially North America, the rest of the world lagged far behind. In 1990, the *Computer Industry Almanac* estimated that 349 million people would be on line by the year 2000. By 2005, this would grow to 765 million.

But by the late 1990s, the disparity between regions was already huge. Africa had only two million users and Latin America had only eight million. Of most concern to modernisers in the Middle East, was the fact that figures suggested just below two million people would be on line in the region by 2000 - less than some individual European countries.

Statistics suggested that only half of one per cent of Internet users worldwide were Arabs. If this remained the case, the opportunities presented by access to information, greater global communications and even e-commerce would bypass the Middle East almost completely.

During one speech Sheikh Mohammed commented:

The greatest challenge... is the technological gap between the industrialised and developing countries. It is most unfortunate that this gap is growing bigger and bigger. During the 20th century, we have seen the image of the world split, at one time, between advanced countries and developing countries, and at

Sheikh Rashid bin Mohammed Al Maktoum. For his and future generations, Sheikh Mohammed was preparing to place Dubai at the heart of the new economy.

another, between rich countries of the North and poor countries of the South. It appears that the 21st Century split will be based on information between communities that know and others that do not know.

We all have to wonder about the potential impact of such a gap – not only on the stability of the global economy – but on the security and tranquillity of the whole world. We also wonder about a world singing the praises of globalisation and the Global Village while its basic wealth, which is information, is concentrated in the hands of a few countries. Such concentration is further deepened by a growing tendency towards monopoly of information through extension of intellectual property rights by industrialised countries to include even applied aspects of knowledge, such as medical processes and genetic engineering achievements...

In many ways, this brought Sheikh Mohammed to the same difficult decision that his father and the former UAE President Sheikh Zayed had confronted a generation earlier. They were faced with a nation that was backward and had been isolated from the rest of the world for more than a century. Bringing development to the Emirates meant opening up the country to a vast foreign influence that inevitably threatened the Emirati culture. Only by striking a careful balance did they guide their people and succeed in preserving a national identity while the people enjoyed the fruits of a massive social and economic boom.

A generation on, the Dubai government was forced to consider whether the booming information superhighway was everything it was supposed to be. The Web offered the golden promise of a colossal library containing much of humanity's knowledge accessible to anyone with a computer, regardless of the person's age, culture and maturity or the quality of the information. It is also a Pandora's Box for all manner of subversive and depraved material. As leaders in a society that has always expressed a desire to preserve its culture, heritage and family values, the Maktoums had difficult issues to grapple with before pressing ahead on a remarkable new project that was being mooted at the highest levels of government.

"All countries of the world are undoubtedly eager to adjust to these transformations, as smoothly and as safely as possible," said Sheikh Mohammed. "Yet a host of constraints and challenges appear to stand between the majority of developing countries and the fulfillment of their aspirations."

Recognising that if Dubai missed the e-revolution, there would be long-term repercussions on the emirate's push to become a world leader, Sheikh Mohammed drew around him several Dubai nationals who shared his point of view and were I.T. savvy. The Dubai government considered the options and attempted to build a development model for Dubai. Several ideas were selected and quietly studied in depth. The world was moving on I.T. at breakneck speed. Decisive action needed to be taken quickly. Sheikh Mohammed believed that the emirate needed to start establishing its niche before the end of 2000 if it was to be successful in the long term. Within a year, he was to announce a brace of remarkable new initiatives.

On October 29, 1999, Sheikh Mohammed called a press conference in Dubai. To the assembled newsmen, Sheikh Mohammed announced: "One year from today, we will inaugurate... a new initiative, not only for Dubai but for the rest of the world. We call it Dubai Internet City."

He went on to describe his vision. The Internet City zone would cover 25 square kilometres and would encompass the infrastructure, environment and attitude to enable 'new economy' enterprises to operate worldwide, out of Dubai, with significant competitive advantages.

Just as Sheikh Rashid's Creek dredging scheme had transformed the emirate a generation earlier, Sheikh Mohammed believed that this new initiative would open Dubai to a new era of opportunity.

Sheikh Mohammed views plans with Mohammed Al Gergawi. Dubai Internet City was Al Gergawi's first major appointment.

He said: "Dubai will position itself at the heart of the information technology industry, through the provision of world-class facilities, also relying on the emirate's geographical location which places us perfectly as a gateway to markets with billions of consumers, including the Middle East, North Africa, Indian subcontinent and CIS."

The Dubai government planned to invest $272 million in setting up the zone and providing technical infrastructure. The I.T. division of Siemens would handle design and installation of the structure; Cisco Systems' 'New World' networking solutions, combining data and voice communication would be installed; while Sun Microsystems would provide computing platform and software applications.

The parameters set were that DIC should provide the best in terms of a working environment, plus state-of-the-art urban infrastructure facilities for employees. In addition, there was to be minimum red tape, especially for company registration and immigration processes. Investors would have 50-year renewable land leases, the right of total foreign ownership of the company, and a single window for all government clearances. By any standard the move was bold. At a stroke, Dubai's colours had been raised high in the hope of establishing the emirate's name within the world's fastest-growing industry. To spearhead this new initiative Mohammed Al Gergawi was named chief executive of DIC. Al Gergawi was a noted member of Sheikh Mohammed's Majlis where his energy and enthusiasm had drawn him into the inner circle. With an I.T. education and background, he had been heavily involved in the process that led to the DIC concept. Who better to run the most important new initiative in Dubai?

Says Al Gergawi: "Sheikh Mohammed's influence is everywhere in Dubai Internet City. One cannot underestimate his impact and his continuing involvement in steering this massive project. It is important to recognise that he does not just initiate a project and leave it to experts to handle. He is an expert in his own right. He studied the I.T. industry at length and only moved when he knew the exact parameters of the entity he wished to create."

Four months later, in February 2000, an Emiri decree was issued by Sheikh Maktoum. It was the Dubai Technology, Electronic Commerce and Media Free Zone Law No. (1) of 2000 covering the set-up of a free-trade zone for electronic commerce and technology. The decree established an independent body, a free zone authority which would operate under the Dubai government to spearhead the emirate's drive to become a regional centre for electronic commerce, technology and information. This would offer foreign companies a host of benefits including 100% tax-free ownership, 100% repatriation of capital and profits, and no currency restrictions. Companies joining the community have complete exemption from taxes on sales, profits and private income. Fully supported by the government, Dubai Internet City has established Free Zone specific corporate laws that empower the companies in the community and help them grow.

By September 2000, DIC had attracted more than 100 information technology companies, including industry giants Microsoft, Oracle and Compaq. Another 350 firms were awaiting approval. The total investment planned by those already holding licences was estimated at around $700 million.

Sheikh Mohammed said: "The response on an international, regional and local level has been extremely encouraging, with many of the big players listed on the NASDAQ exchange expressing interest in the project. We are very pleased with the overall response to our initiative.

"Dubai Internet City is multi-faceted and is not just aimed at e-commerce companies. It will encompass all I.T.-related sector companies that are venturing into the field of electronic business. These will include such areas as e-finance, e-marketing, e-design and multimedia. Our marketing strategy is both broad-based and extensive and we have developed a critical path to meet our timeframes."

Looking back on the experience today, Al Gergawi recalls: "We were given 365 days and told to go and make it happen. It was an exhilarating time filled with possibility. I did not sleep for a week."

During the second quarter of 2001, Microsoft (Gulf and Eastern Mediterranean) began operating from its new regional headquarters at DIC, the first of the big industry names to complete its move.

Today, Dubai is the most wired city in Arabia and is among the world's top I.T. users. Dubai Internet City is well equipped to play a key role in supporting and promoting regional I.T.-related activities. It is the biggest I.T. infrastructure in the entire Middle East with the world's largest commercial Internet Protocol Telephony system. Designed to support the business development of Information and Communications Technology (ICT) companies around the world, Dubai Internet City is a strategic base for firms that are targeting emerging markets in a vast region extending from the Middle East to the Indian subcontinent, from Africa to the CIS, covering two billion people with a combined GDP of $6.7 trillion.

Featuring four massive buildings clustered around a shimmering lake, it is a perfect setup for an entire range of ICT industries. Established ICT companies, multi-media companies, remote service providers, service companies, consultants, venture capitalists, incubator companies and educators have become part of this community.

In a short span of time, a dynamic community of international ICT companies has established itself inside this city-within-a-city. DIC's burgeoning ICT cluster includes global giants such as Microsoft, Oracle, HP, IBM, Compaq, Dell, Siemens, Canon, Logica, Sony Ericsson and Cisco, to name a few, representing a formidable community of over 5,500 knowledge workers. The latest entrant to set up in DIC is the New Zealand Technology Oasis Beachhead, which is sponsored by New Zealand Trade & Enterprise (NZTE), the New Zealand government's national economic development agency.

The large concentration of ICT companies all working from a single location offers tremendous networking, business interaction and knowledge sharing opportunities. DIC has an excellent business environment that fosters a climate for growth and innovation. Its wide tenant breadth creates a large pool of knowledge, resources, talent, and expertise that member organisations can tap for solutions, ideas, and mutually beneficial partnerships.

Dubai Internet City attracted a plethora of multinationals and helped establish Dubai at the forefront of the new economy.

Naturally, integrity was also a major issue for potential investors, so DIC made it clear that it intended to implement stringent and sophisticated intellectual property and cyber regulations to protect e-business. There is a dedicated government agency on the premises to ensure enforcement.

Widely acknowledged as the Middle East's information and communications technology (ICT) industry hub, DIC offers a business-friendly environment, superior infrastructure, high bandwidth Internet services, low-cost telecommunications, strong copyright laws and a high-quality lifestyle - making it one of the world's most productive bases for ICT businesses.

"Dubai Internet City was a smart move that transformed the prospects of the Middle East in the information age by not only establishing Dubai as a regional centre, but also pushing the region as a whole forward," says Microsoft founder, Bill Gates.

While DIC would attract the cream of I.T. talent in the short and medium term, for the industry to put down permanent roots in the UAE, it had to offer something of value to the people of the country itself. Hand-in-hand with a major schools I.T. education initiative, a higher seat of I.T. learning was created. Says Sheikh Mohammed: "We have a lot of enthusiasm and conviction for the establishment of an Information Technology University. We believe it is as important as the Dubai Internet City itself because it will train and graduate a workforce that is highly skilled in using and carrying out research in information technology.

"We are evaluating various options for setting up the university, and our strategy is to bring together a programme that goes beyond offering quality training courses to granting accredited university level degrees in areas such as e-business, e-finance, e-marketing, multimedia, e-design and e-management.

"The Dubai government will have responsibility for establishing the university in co-operation with private institutions and top universities and colleges. The aim is to constantly upgrade the skills pool and to give companies access to highly trained I.T. specialists."

It would, however, take time before the UAE's schools – boasting one of the world's most advanced I.T, syllabuses – could supply graduates into what the international media dubbed the 'silicon desert'. If the DIC project was to succeed, it needed expertise.

While much of Dubai's new I.T. industry was to be based in the out-of-town zone that was being hurriedly prepared, the Maktoums also recognised that the city itself needed to embrace 21st century technology. To bring about modernisation, the Dubai government would have to take the lead and then encourage the private sector to follow. On May 11, 1999 – at a gathering of senior officials for the Dubai Quality Awards, a public and private sector orientated scheme to promote higher standards at all levels – a new initiative was announced.

"Within 18 months," said Sheikh Mohammed, "the Dubai Government as a whole will be online, a factor that will increase efficiency and make the process of government faster and smoother. Among other things, I want to see visa applications and other transactions carried out online and government departments communicating with each other electronically."

Department heads were given just three weeks to show that they were actively pursuing this order.

"Our e-government initiative is imperative for Dubai to continue to thrive economically. I am personally committed to this initiative and prepared to take hard decisions," he said, adding in the direction of government officials in his audience: "This project is a must if you want to continue with me in government."

In April 2000, the Dubai e-Government Group was formed, an eight member committee with representatives of several major government departments. The committee was charged with exploring the possibilities of what lay ahead. Several consultant firms advised on the process. Salem Khamis Al-Shair, e-services director of the Dubai e-Government Group, said at the time: "The challenge is to fix our own house internally and deliver a better service to our customers."

The task and timescale were monumental considering the brief applied to some 27 government departments. Three issues needed to be addressed: The building of an infrastructure that would bind these departments together, the development of shared applications for internal use and creation of a single portal, allowing users to deal with the government through one interface. Achieving the latter could conceivably lead to government services eventually being offered by telephone and via WAP, in addition to the Internet.

The e-government era was set to arrive in Dubai, placing the emirate ahead of any developed world nation and, more importantly, introducing a superbly streamlined government that would have made the anti-bureaucratic Sheikh Rashid proud.

By 2004, DIC had already reached its 2007 objectives and began exploring globalisation options by building, operating, or advising on similar projects abroad, or capturing other parts of the value chain.

Having developed considerable expertise in business campuses that provide infrastructure and support services for I.T. companies, DIC signed Memoranda of Understanding with several international ICT industry bodies in India, Pakistan, Malaysia, Australia etc to promote and facilitate investments in remote services and technology. DIC has recently signed an MOU with the government of the south Indian state of Kerala to develop 'Smart City', which is going to be one of India's largest I.T. parks and is expected to generate at least 33,000 jobs in seven years.

And while DIC was transforming the emirate, Dubai's drawing board was piled high with plans for projects in each sphere that concerned Dubai's future. Destination Dubai, in particular, was evolving rapidly with projects underway that would transform Dubai International Airport and see breathtaking new hotels and tourist facilities opening. Already, the emirate had seen the inauguration of the Jumeirah Beach Hotel, which was quickly voted by travel industry polls as one of the world's top five-star hotels. This 26-storey building, designed in the shape of a breaking wave, has 618 generously-proportioned oceanfront rooms and suites. Inaugurated by Sheikh Mohammed in 1997, Jumeirah Beach Hotel runs consistently at 100% occupancy during the peak winter season.

Elsewhere, work was under way on an imposing dual tower structure along Sheikh Zayed Road, the main artery into Dubai from Abu Dhabi, which encompassed a major hotel. A stone's throw from Jumeirah Beach Hotel, an artificial island was being created some 100 metres offshore as the base for one of Dubai's boldest projects: A hotel that would be only 60 metres shorter than New York's Empire State Building.

But undoubtedly the most visible development at the time was the 1998 opening of a new terminal at Dubai International Airport, appropriately named the Sheikh Rashid Terminal in honour of the late Dubai Ruler. This marked the completion of the $540 million first phase of the Dubai government's airport expansion plan that will ultimately provide facilities to handle the 60 million passengers expected to pass through Dubai each year by 2013. Headlining the expansion programme

Dubai Duty Free is the third biggest duty free business in the world.
(below) Sheikh Mohammed presents a Dubai Quality Award to Colm McLoughlin.

was the construction of the new, futuristic concourse, 800 metres in length and comprising five levels. In addition there was a new runway and state-of-the-art landing systems.

"…We want people who come to Dubai to take away a lasting impression of the new airport," said Sheikh Ahmed bin Saeed Al Maktoum. "We have spent a great deal of time considering the design of the airport and studying other international airports, including Singapore, Denver, Hong Kong, Heathrow and Chicago, to come up with the most suitable design for Dubai."

Architecturally, the final design was unique. Elegant and aerodynamic, the steel structure, with blue-green tinted glass panels, mirrors the colours of the sky. The plan is intended to cement Dubai's position as the regional hub for the Gulf while the airport's new passenger, freight and fuelling facilities combine to create a model for 21st century air travel. In a bid to position Dubai International Airport as one of the world's top 20 international airports, the development of the Dubai Airport Free Zone and Business Village is an integral part of the expansion plan, and 2.2 million square metres on the north side of the airport have been allocated to the project. The Free Zone, the first one million square metre phase having been opened in 2000, supports a wide variety of technology driven industries, including retail and light industrial companies as well as commercial and distribution services.

Dubai International Airport is the busiest airport in the Middle East, having surpassed Jeddah in 1999. During 2005, 27.7 million passengers passed through the airport – an increase of 14.7% over the previous year. The number of airlines operating out of Dubai International Airport has gone up to 110, serving 145 destinations.

Dubai Duty Free is a fascinating case study, not only in how to capitalise on an opportunity but, on a wider scale, as to the business orientated mind-set that has made the emirate itself a success. In 1983, DDF was 16 shops on two levels, all privately owned concessions. In July that year Irishman Colm McLoughlin arrived in the emirate on a three-day visit at the behest of the Dubai Civil Aviation Department.

"DDF was like a souk. Our brief was to turn it around and create something that was run along European duty free lines," says McLoughlin, whose initial six month secondment from Shannon Airport has now stretched to well over two decades. "Yet the potential was clear and we convinced the government that it should abandon the was clear and we convinced the government that it should abandon the concessions system and operate the duty free itself."

On December 20, 1983 the new DDF opened and did a reasonable Dhs. 160,000 turnover. In 1987 the facility achieved Dhs 1 million in a day for the first time. Within the industry, it is considered the norm if one in five departing passengengers buys at a duty free. DDF boasts over 40% and today, McLoughlin brands it "disappointing" if Dhs 5 million in turnover is not achieved every day. At the beginning, he recalls suppliers were unsure about supplying Dubai as they were unsure as to its location, or viability as a customer.

"I remember we were buying a price ticket machine in the early days. I asked the supplier where the nearest service agent was. He told me Louisiana! Perception has now changed considerably and now everyone knows exactly where Dubai is," says McLoughlin.

"When we started we were in no doubt that DDF would become one of the best in the world. In no small measure the fact that we are today the third biggest duty free in the world, serving an airport that is twelvth biggest in the world in terms of traffic, is thanks to the vision of the government, and especially Sheikh Ahmed bin Saeed Al Maktoum, in allowing us a free hand. Because of this business-like attitude, and the extraordinary expansion of Dubai International Airport, we expect to achieve annual turnover of $1 billion in 2008 or 2009."

"The airport is one of the most important developments for the economy of Dubai," says Sheikh Ahmed. "It is the emirate's heartbeat and, as Dubai has expanded, we have worked to ensure that we can support the ambitious future being mapped out by our government."

Dubai International Airport handled 24.7 million passengers in 2005 and with massive expansion underway this figure is set to increase sharply.

Chapter Thirty-Four

The Jigsaw Puzzle

"Waiting was never our choice. Not in the past, nor the present.
We have always anticipated the future in the UAE."
— *Sheikh Mohammed bin Rashid Al Maktoum, statesman*

"Dubai has always been a haven of tranquillity, and of tolerance,"
says Abdullah Saleh, chairman of the National Bank of Dubai.
"Generations of Maktoum Rulers have dictated this policy and it has
become imbibed in our culture."

In the early 1900s Dubai's unique brand of open society had
succeeded in attracting to the sheikhdom a new generation of
businessmen, merchants and their families. They were lured by an open
trading environment, but the town became a permanent home for many
due to its acceptance of religions, nationalities, creeds and colours.
Successive Rulers believed that an individual could believe, worship
and witness as they wished and were watchful for hate and intolerance.

For nearly a century this was the basis upon which Dubai was
constructed. The emirate was a place to do business.

But towards the end of the century Dubai was emerging with a new
string to its bow. The same acceptance of foreign cultures, coupled with
traditional Arab warmth and hospitality, would set Dubai at the heart of
one of the world's fastest growing industries.

At the turn of the millennium, through public investment and private
initiative, Dubai had succeeded in developing the infrastructure that
would sustain a major tourism industry. Dubai's branding and long-term
growth in tourism continues to be spearheaded by the Emirates Group,
through projects such as the Al Maha Desert Resort, a former Maktoum
winter camping ground selected for its natural beauty, and subsidiaries,
such as Emirates Holidays and Arabian Adventures.

But it is Emirates, the airline, that remains the most visible, tangible

Sheikh Hamdan spoke out on tolerance and understanding between cultures.

example of modern Dubai. It cemented its place in both international aviation and tourism in November 2001, during the Dubai 2001 air show - the seventh international aerospace exhibition - with the news that it planned to buy up to 60 new wide-body aircraft worth $15 billion and was negotiating with both Airbus and Boeing. Sheikh Ahmed bin Saeed Al Maktoum confirmed that Emirates planned to increase its fleet, which at the time stood at 35 aircraft, to 100 by 2010.

At the time, Emirates already had on order seven Airbus A380s, making it the first airline to sign a firm deal for the controversial giant 555-seat aircraft that are scheduled to enter service in 2007. Emirates executive vice chairman Maurice Flanagan says: "The case for the A380 is absolute. With a shortage of landing slots worldwide, and a growing market, bigger aircraft allow each seat to be carried for less cost, allowing lower fares."

Emirates already had plans to add six Airbus A340-500s to its fleet during 2002 and 2003, giving the airline full ultra long-haul capability and the possibility of flying regular non-stop services from Dubai to the United States and Australia. New York, Chicago, Los Angeles and Sydney were the most likely destinations, with the first being Sydney in 2003 and New York in 2005. A non-stop service from Los Angeles to Dubai – 17 hours in the air – would establish another marker: The longest non-stop flight in the world. At the time Emirates had $26 billion of aircraft on order, including 45 A380 double-decker, four-engined jetliners, the largest order for A380s of any airline in the world.

Said Sheikh Ahmed: "We are committed to the long-haul market and confident the interest will be there when we are ready." But he admitted that the US market is price-driven, and a route from America would be costly to maintain. Sheikh Ahmed was also acutely aware of the need to maintain a reputation for excellence. "An airline that cuts its costs to the bare minimum to attract passengers cannot survive," he said. "There are fixed costs, operating costs, fuel costs and landing fees to take into account. You have to manage your resources well. You must examine the suitability of aircraft, and carry out proper feasibility studies and market research. At the end of the day, however, what is most important is that you are running a safe operation and not putting passengers or planes at risk."

At the time the Dubai government was also planning how it would house the increasing millions of visitors forecast to be arriving in the emirate. Another project that prompted much press speculation and many raised eyebrows was Burj Al Arab. Its name translates as 'Arabian Tower.' It was inaugurated on December 1, 1999. Arguably the most ambitious – and certainly the most visible – project in Dubai, the hotel's designers had one primary goal - to create a landmark that symbolised Dubai, not unlike the Eiffel Tower in Paris, or Sydney and its Opera House.

The result was the world's tallest hotel, all 320 metres of it, standing sentry-like, overlooking the city from its tiny man-made island. Burj Al Arab was a constant reminder of the bold thinking behind the emirate's future.

The Burj Al Arab story began in 1995, when specialist contractors flew into Dubai. Their task was to lay the foundations for the hotel or, more precisely, to create the man-made island on which it would sit.

The plan called for a concrete island with foundation piles penetrating some 40 metres beneath the seabed. These are held in place not by bedrock, but by friction. The load is not focused at the base of each pile but absorbed along its length by the loosely cemented sand and silt around it.

The foundations and island were completed in March 1996, and handed over to building contractors. Over the next three years, the sea off the Jumeirah Beach Hotel was dominated by building work as the colossal form took shape. A massive steel exoskeleton steadies the tower against seismic loads and the wind. This V-shaped, teflon frame wraps around a second V, the reinforced concrete tower containing the hotel rooms and lobbies. The two structures connect along a shored, reinforced concrete spine at the base of the V, and at two points along the curving atrium wall.

The superstructure rises 260 metres from the ground, on top of which a mast extends another 60 metres. The central atrium is more than 180 metres high, and takes up a good third of the interior space. Around 3,500 designers were involved in the project; 360,000 cubic metres of concrete and 9,000 tonnes of steel were used.

The outside of the structure was a tourist attraction well before the Burj Al Arab opened, while behind the scenes work was under way to ensure that the interior matched the somewhat extraordinary exterior. Gerald Lawless, CEO of Jumeirah Group, recalls: "Sheikh Mohammed insisted that this project set out, from the start, with a single overriding motive, to create a hotel of renowned opulence. The industry had never seen anything like it. If the hotel was to be a symbol of Dubai, Sheikh Mohammed believed it should epitomise luxury and class."

The 202 suites, as well as the public areas, were fitted with marble from Brazil, leathers from Scotland and linen from Ireland. Around 21,000 square feet of 22-carat gold leaf was used around the complex. Sheikh Mohammed approved the interiors personally – and also approved the world's largest fleet of Rolls-Royce Silver Seraphs to transfer guests in luxurious style from Dubai International Airport to the hotel.

Burj Al Arab officially opened its doors on December 1, 1999, to a fanfare of media attention. The exact project cost is, understandably, a secret and those attached to the hotel admit that the investment could take decades to recoup. This fact, however, is of less significance in the larger picture.

Says Lawless: "Features on Burj Al Arab appear on national network television in the US and many European countries every week. It would be impossible to purchase such a volume of coverage for the hotel and Dubai. Every month, Burj Al Arab attracts millions of dollars of media coverage."

Such publicity is highly effective in terms of establishing not only the hotel but also Dubai as a destination in the minds of a public bombarded with information, through the media and advertising, about potential holiday destinations. Just weeks after a particularly notable broadcast in Italy, for example, Burj Al Arab reported a surge of bookings from the country, 25 suites over one Easter period alone. Lawless believes that around 50 per cent of Burj Al Arab guests have learned about the hotel through television.

Likening Burj Al Arab to a locomotive pulling Dubai's tourism forward, Lawless adds that Sheikh Mohammed visits the hotel regularly when he has various delegations and dignitaries visiting Dubai.

"We believe that we are the best. Burj Al Arab is the world's most luxurious hotel. If something breaks, or is not just so, it is fixed immediately," says Lawless.

"Sheikh Mohammed has set a new standard in the industry. In doing so, he has created a giant. The cost of developing Burj Al Arab is enormous, and it may indeed be a generation before the investment is

Burj Al Arab - the world's first seven star hotel.

560

Mina A'Salam and (opposite page) the Jumeirah Beach Hotel, two landmarks in Dubai from the Jumeirah portfolio.

repaid. But in creating real awareness worldwide of Dubai the destination, this hotel has placed us on the map."

Overall management responsibility for Burj Al Arab comes under Jumeirah. Jumeirah Group was founded in 1997 with a bold vision to become a hospitality industry leader through establishing an excellent portfolio of hotels that redefine the hospitality benchmarks set by the world's top-class hotels. In an endeavour to create a strong brand platform for local, regional and international expansion, and to strengthen Jumeirah's position as the world's leading luxury hospitality group, Jumeirah International changed its name to Jumeirah on 21 June 2005. All of the hospitality group's hotels now feature the Jumeirah identity, yet each will retain its distinctive style and uniqueness. The group's existing portfolio of hotels was renamed, with the brand 'Jumeirah' featuring in the name, for instance, Emirates Towers Hotel will now be called Jumeirah Emirates Towers.

The Jumeirah Group manages some of the finest deluxe hotels in Dubai, New York and London. In addition to Burj Al Arab, the award-winning Jumeirah Beach Hotel, Jumeirah Emirates Towers Hotel, Jumeirah Beach Club Resort and Spa and Jumeirah Bab Al Shams Desert Resort and Spa. In London Jumeirah Carlton Tower Hotel and Jumeirah Lowndes Hotel and, in New York, the Jumeirah Essex Hotel. Jumeirah also operates associated ventures such as Jumeirah Hospitality, and The Emirates Academy of Hospitality Management. Madinat Jumeirah, the Arabian Resort in Dubai, takes visitors back in time to give offer an authentic expression of rich Arabian heritage.

Styled to resemble an ancient Arabian citadel, this luxurious and ornate property is a unique combination of modern opulence and rich tradition. Enhancing Dubai's reputation as one of the world's most idyllic destinations, the 40-acre resort offers the ultimate Arabian experience against the setting of a highly luxurious, world-class, multi-facility resort. Meandering waterways transport guests to all parts of this resort featuring two boutique hotels, courtyard summer houses, a traditional souq, an amphitheatre, Six Senses Spa and unlimited recreational facilities.

The first completed phase of Madinat Jumeirah opened its doors in 2003, with the very successful debut of the grand boutique hotel, Mina A'Salam – the 'Harbour of Peace', so named because this 292-room hotel is built around a beachside harbour, adjoining 3.7 kilometres of waterways. A tribute to Dubai's sea-faring heritage, the hotel reflects the city's historic roots as a trading hub from which ships and dhows sailed to distant shores. With its unique shape and omnipresent wind-towers, this graceful, sand-coloured property heralds a step back in time - yet modern facilities and luxurious interiors make it a matchless destination offering style, luxury and heritage. Since its launch, the hotel has witnessed an overwhelming response from the regional and international market.

Dubai's expansion was more than mere tourism however. A plethora of economic projects was boosting the population. Expatriate expertise was flooding into the emirate.

For example, around 40% of the talent in California's Silicon Valley was Indian. The Dubai government believed that many Indians would

prefer to live in Dubai, little more than an hour away from their homeland, rather than on the West Coast of the US. But if Dubai was to achieve its stated aim and become a 'Capital of Talent,' it also needed to be an attractive place to live.

One of the key elements in attracting the cream of the I.T. world's workforce, was a new town for up to 40,000 people, around 20 kilometres from the ever-spreading outskirts of Dubai city. Typically for the technology-minded Crown Prince, his new town – Dubai Marina – is billed as the world's first "intelligent city". The project was handled by Emaar, one of the UAE's largest property development companies, 33% owned by the government of Dubai and 67% by private investors, which also handled the up-market Emirates Hills and Emirates Lakes estates.

The $10 billion Dubai Marina, just minutes away from DIC, features a three-kilometre beach, 100 low, medium and high-rise office and apartment towers, landscaped parks, schools, shopping centres, luxury

Sheikh Mohammed and the Sultan of Brunei are briefed on the Dubai Marina project by Emaar chairman Mohammed Ali Alabbar.

hotels, medical facilities and a full range of recreation and entertainment facilities. The project is divided into eight stages, planned over a 20-year period. The first development stage included the construction of six residential towers - each created by world-class architects, while international designers drew upon Arabic culture to create a look that is individual and unique to each.

Between them, the Emirates Hills, Emirates Lakes and Dubai Marina developments will provide a total of 4,000 homes in their initial stages alone.

Sheikh Mohammed said: "We have given ourselves the challenge of ensuring that the UAE will always go for the best. Development has driven Dubai to a new level of sophistication, which you can now see... Now this new 'intelligent city' brings us into a new era of lifestyle, which will integrate every aspect of living and working in Dubai.

"Until now, it has been difficult for most communities to turn the concept into reality, because of the limitations of existing technologies, such as low bandwidth networks and ageing access equipment. The idea of a large on-line community has remained a dream."

As Sheikh Mohammed suggested, the most remarkable facet of Dubai Marina was not in its bricks and mortar, but its technology. Emaar appointed Marconi as technology partner with a brief to design, build and operate a totally new communications network for Dubai Marina using the most advanced technologies and applications available, including regular upgrades so that the network remains at the cutting edge of global communications. All residents will have access to video on demand, video telephony, video camera security and access control. They will be able to use the network to control their living environment and appliances. For example, householders may turn on cookers or air conditioners from their offices before they leave for home.

John Marshall, Marconi Middle East's regional director, says: "Building an entirely new city will enable us to show the full potential of convergence in communications technology for the first time on such a large scale. The facilities provided for the people who live and work in Dubai Marina will be a template for developments across the world. At Dubai Marina we have the unique opportunity to create a communications environment which is totally state-of-the-art and all-embracing."

Dubai was set to embark upon an unprecedented property boom and this was led by Nakheel. With over $30 billion worth of properties currently under various stages of development, Nakheel provides direction to the sector's growth in the Middle East. Nakheel's unique properties, such as The Palm Islands and The World, reflect the vibrancy that has driven Dubai into an emerging international commercial and economic hub and leading tourist destination.

Nakheel is where the vision of Dubai gets built, Sultan bin Sulayem, executive chairman of Nakheel says, "In an effort to redefine the concept of property development in Dubai whether residential, tourist, commercial or retail, Nakheel has placed great importance on examining the requirements of the different sectors of the community and is developing its visionary projects around these findings."

Nakheel's ambitious Palms project will change the face of Dubai completely... and its geography.

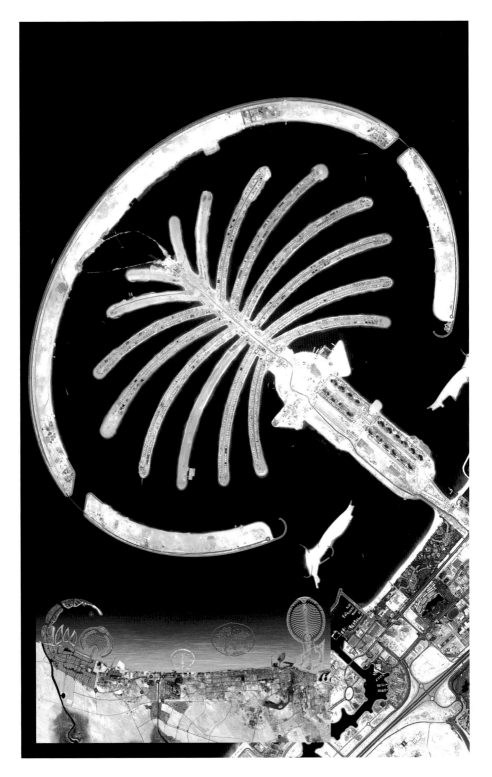

From projects that will go down in history for sheer magnitude and grandeur like The Palm, to dream-like residences that redefine community living, Nakheel's developments all bear a common stamp – innovative yet practical, exclusive yet affordable, always unique and iconic.

Nakheel's signature development, The Palm, involves the creation of the world's largest three man-made islands known as The Palm, Jumeirah, The Palm, Jebel Ali, and The Palm, Deira. The first Palm to be finished will be The Palm, Jumeirah. Reclamation is complete, and highlights of The Palm include a 500,000 square metre Atlantis water park themed hotel at the head of the Crescent, and 2,500 villas and 2,700 shoreline apartments offering luxury beachfront living.

Lying just off Dubai's coastline, the three palm tree-shaped islands will increase Dubai's shoreline by a total of 520 kilometres and create a large number of residential, leisure and entertainment opportunities, all within a unique and inspiring setting. While the first two islands will comprise approximately 100 million cubic metres of rock and sand, Palm Deira will take in one billion cubic metres of rock and sand – all of which will be quarried in the UAE. Between the three islands there will be over 100 luxury hotels, 10,000 exclusive residential beachside villas, 5,000 shoreline apartments, marinas, water theme parks, restaurants, shopping malls, sports facilities, health spas, cinemas and extensive dive sites.

Each island will be built in the shape of a palm tree and consist of a trunk; a crown with 17 fronds on the Palms Jumeirah and Jebel Ali and 41 fronds on The Palm Deira.

In his first foray into the Middle East, American real estate king Donald Trump is building a tulip-shaped hotel on Palm Jumeirah. Trump is behind the construction of Manhattan skyscrapers and casinos in Las Vegas and Atlantic City, New Jersey.

"We're tapping into his (Trump's) knowledge and ability in the high-end sector," says bin Sulayem.

A second project, The Trump Plaza and Marina Residences, will also be built on The Palm Jumeirah.

"Dubai has proven to be an economic anchor, an engine for growth and tourism in the Middle East," said Trump in the statement. "We anticipate a long-term relationship between The Trump Organisation and Nakheel that will involve direct investment, sales and marketing, and management."

Property mogul Donald Trump entered the Dubai market with The Palm Trump International Hotel and Tower.

With The Palm having placed Dubai firmly on the world map, Nakheel decided to take the next step and put the world map on Dubai. Nakheel's iconic development – The World – consists of a series of 300 man-made islands, positioned strategically to form the planet's most visually stunning development: the shape of the world map on the sea.

Almost two years of extensive planning, research development and design took place before The World was announced to an astonished real estate industry. Measuring approximately nine kilometres in width by seven kilometres in length, the development will cover approximately 9,340,000 square metres, will be visible to the naked eye from space and will add an additional 232 kilometres of beachfront to Dubai's coastline. For The World to take shape, Nakheel is moving over 326 million cubic metres of sand to form the islands as well as building a 26 kilometre-long oval shape breakwater.

The announcement of Jumeirah Islands followed, comprising 50 man-made islands with villas set amongst cascading waterfalls and winding promenades. Nearby Jumeirah Lake Towers is similarly ambitious; set amidst man-made lakes and landscaped grounds, the 79 towers will be a mix of ultra-modern residential and commercial developments.

Officially launched in September 2005, Jumeirah Golf Estates will create four of the best courses in the world, including two designed by the legendary Greg Norman. Completing the Jumeirah portfolio of brands, Jumeirah Village, inspired by a rural setting, consists of more than 7,000 villas and townhouses designed in classic Arabic

Sultan bin Sulayem and golfing legend Greg Norman discuss plans for Jumeirah Golf Estates.

Mediterranean architectural style.

Other Nakheel developments include International City – which will feature ten internationally themed residential districts accommodating 70,000 to 80,000 residents, while, inspired by the success of The Gardens, Nakheel's Discovery Gardens is a 2.4 million square metre development of six themed communities. Located some 35 kilometres south west of Dubai, sheltering The Palm, Jebel Ali, Nakheel's most recently launched project is the Dubai Waterfront – the world's largest waterfront development. It will be a balanced mix of residential, retail, commercial and industrial offerings across 81 million square metres of beachfront. Carefully crafted and developed by an international consortium of the world's best architects, planners and urban developers assembled by Nakheel in 2004, when complete Dubai Waterfront will be a city in itself with more than 500,000 residents. Also planned is the 75 kilometre Arabian Canal winding through the desert sands around the Jebel Ali area.

All this falls under one of the most low-key, yet most influential figures in Dubai. Sultan bin Sulayem is the son of Ahmed bin Sulayem, one of Sheikh Rashid's most trusted lieutenants. And Sheikh Rashid's sons have embraced the son of their father's leading Majlis advisor. A keen endurance rider, he cut his managerial teeth when appointed chairman of Jebel Ali Free Zone on its formation in 1985. The zone grew apace and today boasts some 2,200 companies from over 100 countries. As chairman of Dubai Ports Authority (DPA), formed in 1991, he oversaw stunning growth that reached a record throughput of over 3.5 million TEUs in just 10 years.

Sultan bin Sulayem embodies the Dubai spirit that is so evident in the 21st century. He's a tough businessman, embraces opportunity and goes for it. Today he holds a plethora of top posts including chairman of Tejari.com and executive chairman of Nakheel and was elected as a Global Leader for Tomorrow by the World Economic Forum.

Dubai's Ports, Customs and Free Zone Corporation has been under bin Sulayem since 2001 when Dubai Customs merged with Jebel Ali and Dubai Ports Authority to create a billion-dollar organisation.

While his influence has been felt in these roles, it is in his position as chairman of Nakheel that it is most publicly visible. The Palm, heralded as "the eighth wonder of the world," is perhaps the grandest of its projects stable, but is just one of a series that are transforming the emirate.

"The Dubai government is full of encouragement and strategically supports the efforts of Nakheel, and indeed this sector as a whole, in our determination to shape the future," says bin Sulayem. "Sheikh Maktoum personally encouraged us in every endeavour.

"The energy surrounding Dubai is just so incredible. So many elements have been put in place by the Maktoum family and the Dubai government. I liken it to a massive jigsaw puzzle. Everything has been put into place and the result has been this explosion of the economy, a boom in construction and development and an overall picture of Dubai as one of the world's most vibrant cities. Sheikh Rashid laid the foundations. His sons have fulfilled the dream."

Chapter Thirty-Five

Ur

What is the city but the people?
—*William Shakespeare, playwright*

Early humans led a nomadic existence, relying on hunting and gathering for sustenance. Between 8,000 and 10,000 years ago, systematic cultivation of plants and the domestication of animals allowed for more permanent settlements. During the fourth millennium BC, the requirements for the 'urban revolution' were finally met: the production of a surplus of storable food, a writing system, a more complex social organisation, and technological advances such as the plough, potter's wheel, loom, and metallurgy.

Although historians have varying theories, it seems most likely that the first 'city' was Ur - an ancient settlement in southern Mesopotamia, near the original mouth of the Euphrates and Tigris rivers. Because of marine regression, the remains are now well inland in present-day Iraq, south of the Euphrates. Ur was inhabited during the Ubaid period when in the early third millennium BC, the small farming villages of the Ubaid culture consolidated into larger settlements, Ur's location was beneficial for sea trade and also by land routes into Arabia.

Ur had three defined social strata. The rich, like government officials, priests and soldiers, a middle class of merchants, teachers, labourers, farmers and craftsmen, and a working class made up of slaves captured in battle. Buildings, named, ziggurats, stood like modern skyscrapers over the city - some stood 70 feet tall.

Towns and cities have a long history, although opinions vary on whether any particular ancient settlement can be considered a city, but the first towns we know of were located in Mesopotamia. In addition to Ur, there was Akkrad and Lagash. The growth of ancient and medieval

A restored ziggurat at Ur, in modern day Iraq. Ur is widely recognised as being the world's first city and its ziggurat's were considered the equivalent of skyscrapers.

573

empires led to ever greater capital cities and seats of provincial administration, with ancient Rome, Constantinople and successive Chinese and later Indian capitals approaching, or exceeding, the half-million population level. Until the rise of the Roman Empire, the town or city was largely an eastern concept, with Mesopotamia (Iraq) and Egypt dominating lists of early cities. Around 612 BC, Babylon was the first 'city' in the known world to boast a population in excess of 200,000.

More than a millennium later, the modern world is dominated by major conurbations – New York, London - the first city with a population over five million - Tokyo, Paris, Moscow and Rio, to name a few. Many cities have pretensions to be at the forefront of the world's 21st century cities.

Urban settlements the world over are confronted with pressing issues at local, regional and international levels. While the challenges facing cities in the developed and developing world may be different, there are also many common concerns, such as globalisation and information technology.

Many cities are plagued by common woes of overpopulation, a housing crisis, pollution, environmental damage and ageing infrastructure that requires massive investment to cope with the needs of a burgeoning population. At the same time, others are investing in the promise of new technologies, the emergence of new design paradigms and the possibilities offered by economic growth.

Attempting to meet these challenges cities such as Athens, Barcelona, Berlin, Johannesburg, Moscow, Rome, São Paulo and Sydney are desperately attempting to reinvent themselves, while others, such as Las Vegas, Melbourne, London and the unlikely Scottish city of Inverness all have run campaigns billing themselves as cities of the new millennium, promising to make the transition from old to new.

Most experts agree that the world's next iconic city – a New York or a London — may well come from Asia. Cities such as Bangkok, Delhi, Seoul, Jakarta, Osaka-Kobe, Manila, Beijing and Shanghai are all undergoing major change.

Even a decade ago, it would have seemed unlikely that the emirate of Dubai would be on the same list. But the emirate is already on its way. Dubai has already claimed the title of 'Middle Eastern City of the Future,' from London's *Financial Times*. More than 20 cities from 15 countries were under consideration for the prestigious title by *FDi Magazine*'s panel of judges.

"We are obviously delighted," said Mohammed Al Gergawi, Chairman of the Board of Dubai Development and Investment Authority (DDIA), at the time. "The title of 'The Middle Eastern City of the Future' is a global acceptance of Dubai's stature as an emerging world city.

"The title is also a motivation for us to strive further. Under the leadership, guidance and direction of Their Highnesses, the Rulers of Dubai, we affirm our resolve to make real their far-reaching vision of a Dubai that stands shoulder-to-shoulder with the major cities of the world."

The *Financial Times* publication pointed out that: "Time and time again, it (Dubai) has shown what can be achieved when oil resources are invested wisely. Although Dubai's rapid economic growth began in the 1960s with the first production of oil, the city's wealth is no longer dependent on natural resources. In 2003, tourism overtook oil revenues as the prime source of income. Dubai's annual gross domestic product (GDP) is now approaching $20 billion, with annual foreign direct investment (FDI) inflows of more than $2 billion."

The same publication pointed out that; "Dubai's increasingly sophisticated population has access to an excellent range of services. For example, 39% of households have Internet connection and more than 98% of the adult population has a mobile phone." It also referred to the fact that Dubai's GDP growth was of more than 6.5% in both 2002 and 2003, and with its FDI inflows, the emirate shows a "strong" economic performance."

Dubai also won the 'Best Transport Infrastructure' and 'Best IT and Telecommunications' category.

This accolade from the *Financial Times* was built upon a collective vision that transcended from the days of Sheikh Rashid. In its 21st century setting, the same sense of desire for rapid progress remained with Sheikh Maktoum and his brothers and, was passed down through government and was also imbibed in the can-do culture of the private sector.

The first years of the 21st century were marked by a number of vast new projects that would turn areas of the emirate into construction sites and lay the foundations for the future. Nakheel was foremost in the development sector, but by no means dominated it, despite the size of its stable of projects. Dubai Internet City was really something, but began to be dwarfed, mundane even, as it was forced to compete for headlines with the many new initiatives emanating from the brothers' Majlis'. A raft of initiatives regarding Dubai's infrastructure programme, was announced.

On November 4, 2000 Sheikh Mohammed launched Dubai Media City, a unique initiative intended to establish the emirate as a regional media centre. He appointed another of his national protégés, Saeed Hussain Al Muntafiq, to the project.

Spread over 200 hectares of land, Dubai Media City (DMC) would set a benchmark. At the launch, Sheikh Mohammed said:

> *Dubai Media City is yet another giant step that Dubai is taking to establish its growing reputation as a multi-dimensional regional hub, and also to provide a comprehensive base from where media businesses will be able to face and overcome the tough challenges and choices of the future. Dubai Media City will be the vehicle that will place Dubai on the global map of information and content. Dubai Media City will help turn media companies into major success stories by giving them the infrastructure, environment and the 'Freedom To Create'.*
>
> *I guarantee freedom of expression to all of you in the media. I give you the right to speak your minds, be completely objective in your views and reporting. I instruct you, the media, to be the eyes, ears and conscience of collective interest and vigilance.*
>
> *Let us embrace freedom of expression for all. But I will hold the media accountable for its use of this freedom. You must thoroughly research and gather facts well and make no accusations without evidence and cast no slurs without proof.*

This was an extraordinary statement for a Gulf statesman, the most forthright expression yet in defence of freedom of the press. The most media savvy Arab leader understood more than anyone the benefits of a well-established press. Through Dubai Media City (DMC) he rejected state-run media and boldly ushered in a new era of openness, unlike anything ever seen in the Arab world. Strategically located at the crossroads of the Middle East, Africa and South Asia, DMC is the

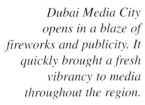

Dubai Media City opens in a blaze of fireworks and publicity. It quickly brought a fresh vibrancy to media throughout the region.

region's media hub. DMC has been established by the Dubai Technology, e-Commerce and Media Free Zone Authority (TECOM) to provide the infrastructure and environment that will enable media-related enterprises to operate globally out of Dubai. DMC provides the infrastructure and environment for enterprises like CNN, BBC, MBC, CNBC, EMI and Reuters, and publishing houses like *Time*. They receive commercial benefits such as 100% foreign ownership and a 50-year corporate and personal tax exemption. Since its launch, the zone has become home to more than 800 companies.

DMC encourages every facet of media business - Broadcasting, Publishing, Advertising, Public Relations, Research, Music and Post Production - to thrive and have the freedom to create. It is a community for media talent to share best practices and build interdependent productive relationships.

"We have partnered with investors who understand the business of the Free Zone and have a long-term track record in the market. These are businesses who understand infrastructural support for knowledge based companies," said Dr. Amina Al Rustamani, Executive Director of Media, Dubai Technology and Media Free Zone. "Once they develop new properties, we will take on all the management and maintenance responsibilities to ensure a productive and profitable experience for the companies accommodated by the new infrastructure."

TECOM is responsible for all aspects of sales and marketing of value-added property services, as well as facilities maintenance and management.

DMC later announced Dubai Studio City, an initiative that seeks to foster the growth of the regional broadcast and film production industry. To be built within the Dubailand complex, Dubai Studio City will offer a complete technical and community infrastructure for the film, television and music production industry to flourish, including production and post-production facilities, animation studios and services like dubbing, makeup, costume designing, stage designing and building, casting, telnet agencies as well as telecine and labratory facilities. It will also have a Production Studio Complex that will accommodate pre-built studios, sound stages, workshops, backlots and stage areas. The infrastructure for the first phase will be complete by the first quarter of 2006. The cluster will also house film and television schools and academies and companies providing location shooting and management services, as well as music recording services.

Soon after DMC another global project was announced. The Dubai Financial District is unparalleled in the region and is currently one of the biggest projects in the world. The vision of creating a world-class Financial District, has meant that Dubai is all set to take its place among leading cities such as London, New York, Tokyo, Singapore and Hong Kong as a major financial centre — an onshore capital market designated as a financial free zone designed to create a unique financial services cluster economy for wealth creation initiatives.

Dubai International Financial Centre (DIFC) is primed to become a regional gateway for capital and investment to the Middle East, and to propel the emirate to the forefront of the international financial world. Banking Services, Capital Markets, Asset Management and Fund Registration, Reinsurance, Islamic Finance and Back Office Operations are the six focus areas. DIFC offers commercial activities in a landscaped environment with residential towers. The DIFC offices will employ the highest standards of communication technology, with a functional, integrated infrastructure, in addition to a fully electronic multi-class trading exchange.

Bearing witness to the progress of Dubai, The Gate is DIFC's 15-storey architectural signature. Comparable to centres in Singapore and London, DIFC will feature a unique integration of buildings in one strategic location. Some of the leading institutions that have been

The Gate is the centrepiece of Dubai International Financial Centre.

awarded licences include Swiss Private Bank, Julius Baer, Standard Chartered Bank, Barclays Capital, KPMG, Swiss International Legal Consultants Limited and Permal.

Dr Omar Bin Sulaiman, Director General of the Dubai International Financial Centre Authority (DIFCA), said, "Since the award of the first licences, we have been overwhelmed by demand from many of the world's most respected financial services businesses, and I am delighted to confirm that as last year ended, the total number of firms registered with DIFC exceeded our entire target for 2004. We look forward to achieving new levels of success and will continue to drive our value proposition forward. We are here to meet the needs of the industry and we are proactively using feedback to strengthen DIFC's position as a catalyst for regional economic growth, development and diversification."

Sheikh Maktoum had enacted a law establishing the Judicial Authority at the DIFC which creates and sets out the jurisdiction of the court, allowing for the independent administration of justice in DIFC. In addition to the creation of DIFC itself, institutions such as the Dubai Financial Services Authority (DFSA) that will issue all the laws and regulations for the non-financial entities operating in the DIFC, DIFC Judicial Establishments and the DIFC Registry of Companies have also been formed to allow the centre to operate under the umbrella, but independent of, UAE federal law.

DFSA has been created using principle-based primary legislation modelled closely on that used in London and New York, and the DIFC regulatory regime operates to standards that meet, or exceed, those in the world's major financial centres.

The Dubai Financial Exchange (DIFX), which opened in September, 2005, is also in DIFC. DIFX supplys liquid capital market on an international scale and complements existing regional stock exchanges. Designed to international standards, DIFX is fast becoming one of the leading international stock exchanges between Western Europe and East Asia for equities, bonds, funds, Islamic products and other securities. It will be a gateway for international and regional investment.

Dr bin Sulaiman, says: "The exchange will be a catalyst for economic growth and prosperity. It will strengthen the ties between the countries of the DIFX region, as well as between the region and the rest of the world."

The DIFX market opened with the listing of five Deutsche Bank securities. These are index-tracking certificates, which will cover the US S&P 500, the German DAX 30, the Japanese Nikkei 225, the EuroStoxx 50 and the Stoxx 50.

By the end of 2006, it also expects its issuer base to be the most international in the world, drawn from many countries and with no single country predominating.

Commented one writer; "No nation in our times has been transformed in such a short period of time. Aircraft and some of the best superhighways in the world have replaced dhows and camel trails as means of transportation. Skyscrapers and other mega structures have erased the once mud huts and nomad tents. It is a fantasyland come true - a spic and span metropolis luring tourists and businesspeople…"

Then came Dubai Healthcare City (DHCC), through which Dubai has taken a giant step towards creating a global hub for world-class healthcare, medical education, life science research, and technology leveraged healthcare services. Slated to be fully operational by 2010, this mammoth $6 billion project is set to transform the UAE into a top-notch healthcare destination, where patients, students, healthcare professionals and service providers from all parts of the world will come seeking treatment, higher education, research, and business opportunities. Uniquely, DHCC will be a healthcare community based on a comprehensive partnership between the private and public sector joining hands to deliver services of the highest quality. Harvard Medical International (HMI - the international division of Harvard Medical School) is the key strategic collaborator of DHCC.

While Nakheel headlines much of the high profile work going on around Dubai, it is far from a one-horse race. Established in 1982 as a local catering company, the DAMAC Group has transcended traditional business models with an aggressive evolution into a global conglomerate, with projects in Dubai such as Ocean Heights, Palm Springs, Park Towers at DIFC and The Crescent. Al Futtaim Private Company, ARY Group, Dubai Holding, ETA STAR Properties, Falak Properties, KM Properties are just a few other names amid a market awash with projects and inward investment and it would be impossible to ignore Emaar Properties, a name synonymous with Dubai's increasingly important real estate industry. Emaar's signature developments have been at the heart of the Dubai 'economic miracle'. The residential developments alone – Emirates Hills, Dubai Marina, The Meadows, The Greens, The Springs, Arabian Ranches, The Lakes and Emaar Towers, have effectively changed the face of Dubai within the past five years and redefined lifestyles in the emirate.

Emaar Properties is a Public Joint Stock Company listed on the Dubai Financial Market. Emaar reported record annual profits of Dhs. 1.691 billion for the year ended December 31, 2004. This corresponded to a net profit increase of Dhs. 1.015 billion or 150%. Net profit for fiscal 2003 was Dhs. 676 million. Its property revenues increased by Dhs. 1.527 billion or 41% to Dhs. 5.248 billion for the year ended 31 December 2004, as compared to Dhs. 3.721 billion for 2003.

Mohamed Alabbar, Chairman of Emaar Properties, said: "Emaar has delivered on its promises and on its projects and in the process boosted value for our shareholders. Today, Emaar is not only one of the biggest real estate companies in the world it is also one of the most profitable."

Social responsibility is also an issue when the nation and its expanding population are so expatriate driven. A National Housing Programme has been launched to provide 10,000 residential homes to UAE nationals to be developed by Emaar.

While Emaar continues to actively pursue expansion it has diversified into related business lines to further build value for its 41,000 shareholders. It recently announced the setting up of Emaar Middle East, which will develop mixed-use properties in the Middle East and North Africa.

Emaar International Development, the global arm of Emaar Properties launched in 2004, will be behind over 40 projects in seven countries, with joint ventures in Egypt, Jordan, Morocco, Syria, Saudi Arabia, India and Pakistan. A new venture Emaar Malls, will aggressively expand the company's business with a US$ 3.5 billion investment in 100 shopping malls across the emerging markets of the Middle East, North Africa and the Indian subcontinent. The group is currently developing the 12 million square feet Dubai Mall in the Burj Dubai Development.

And, of course, reference to Emaar would be impossible without reference to the company's showpiece development – indeed what may be Dubai's signature development – Burj Dubai and its surrounds.

This 164-storey development comprises 80% residential area and 20% office space. The world-class urban development centres around the

582

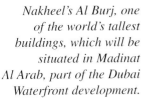

Nakheel's Al Burj, one of the world's tallest buildings, which will be situated in Madinat Al Arab, part of the Dubai Waterfront development.

world's tallest tower - Burj Dubai. Also featuring the award-winning Dubai Mall, the world's largest shopping and entertainment mall, The Old Town, a recreation of old Arabia, residential, commercial, hotel, entertainment and leisure outlets with open green spaces, water features, and a 3.5 kilometre pedestrian boulevard. The Burj Dubai development is set to bring a whole new concept of urban engineering to the construction sector and provide an unprecedented architectural benchmark for global property developers.

"It is a remarkable statistic, but it is a fact that nearly 16% of all the building cranes in the world are in Dubai right now," says Andy Kay, general manager of Dubai Cranes and Technical Services. "It is astonishing for a city to have that kind of economic development and a fair indicator as to the sheer scope of development. What is more that figure is growing."

Almost overnight Dubai has become a surreal juxtaposition of barren desert, 21st-century skyscrapers and building projects that extend as far as the eye can see. The world has come a long way since Ur, in what is modern day Iraq, changed the way mankind lived and worked - the wheel has turned full circle. The second millennium BC was about the West, of Paris and London and New York. It is easy to become caught up in the hubris surrounding the modern miracle of Dubai, but even from a neutral perspective it is possible to see this city-state being the beacon of modernity, in every way the iconic global metropolis of modern times.

Chapter Thirty-Six

A Capital City of the World

Fashion can be fickle, but class never goes out of style.
– Yves Saint Laurent, designer

"It's the latest hot spot for the rich and famous, and it doesn't have a Park Avenue address or a Los Angeles ZIP code. In fact, it's a place many Americans can't find on a map. Dubai … has gone from being a sleepy desert town to the destination of some of the highest-profile names in the United States and Europe, and the fastest-growing city in the world," reports Fox News.

Dubai's hotel lobbies have become venues for celebrity spotting. The city now has several gossip columnists from Western newspapers among its residents. But while New York, Cannes and St Barts may have lost some of their lustre, it is clear that the glamour of Dubai is not set to be short lived.

The date ringed large in the official Dubai government calendar is 2010. Dubai currently attracts 4.8 million visitors a year, a 31% upsurge since 2001, but 2010 is when all the current plethora of developments are scheduled to be ready for the annual number of tourists to Dubai to have risen from its current 4.8 million to 10 million. Tourism is the fastest growing sector within Dubai's economy and with 11.6% of Dubai's GDP invested in tourism ($1.9 billion of economic activity), Dubai has made a huge commitment to this sector of the economy.

"Anyone who looks at these projects as separate ventures," says Sheikh Mohammed, "will not realise that they form a chain of interlinked elements that are part of a clear strategic vision."

Celebrities are one thing, but Dubai has a lot to offer just about anyone. The government emphasised the city's safety record, only second to

In one generation Dubai had gone from backwater to one of the world's fastest developing cities. The National Bank of Dubai headquarters stands as a sentry over the Creek, for so long the central artery of the city.

sterile Singapore and even more remarkable given the multi-cultural society residing in the UAE drawn from 140 nationalities. These issues and more have attracted more than holiday makers. The celebrity set are becoming residents. So are ordinary folk.

Celebrity England Football Team captain David Beckham and his wife, former Spice Girl Victoria Beckham vacation in Dubai frequently and have bought property. Fellow England star Michael Owen is his neighbour. Indeed, Dubai is becoming home to more football internationals than Stamford Bridge. At least one of the Neville brothers has also invested in Dubai. Paul Gascoigne is said to has bought two properties. AS Roma defender Christian Panucci will be seen on The Palm, while Scotland captain Barry Ferguson also has two homes on Dubai's seafront. Away from football, Rod Stewart has been tempted by property in The World. So has Michael Schumacher. Swedish golf aces Thomas Bjorn and Heinrik Stenson are based in the emirate, as is rally driving star Andy Schulz. Spanish crooner Julio Iglesias bought a place in The Villa, Shah Rukh Khan on The Palm and even Mariah Carey went property hunting during a recent visit.

Indeed, the client list of Nakheel and Emaar on some of their most explosive developments is like a who's who of Hollywood, Bollywood, the world of sports and media. This is no accident. Dubai's cache has grown through a mixture of glamourous projects and excellent public relations, spearheaded by Emirates airline

"(The) ultimate goal is to put Dubai in the ranks of the greatest cities of the world and it's quickly becoming a New York, Paris, Tokyo or Chicago," says Franko Vatterott of Human Interest Group. "But whereas those cities took hundreds of years, this city took 25 years. It's got a New York business atmosphere and Caribbean tourism."

Around the city, many of the monuments of Dubai's moderninity are still under construction. Burj Dubai, the world's largest habitable tower with its motto 'History Rising', will rise 350 metres into the air. Even more grand is the $4 billion Dubai Marina, a complex of apartments and hotels that will house a community of 75,000.

"The biggest war that any country can engage in is that of development," says Sheikh Mohammed. "Although it is a long and costly war, the number of soldiers increases instead of decreases. So let's take part in the war of development together, and let our victims be poverty, ignorance and backwardness."

The war on poverty, ignorance and backwardness was set to take on a giant feel... Also underway a two billion square foot project that equals almost the entire the size of developed land thus far in Dubai). Dubailand, Dubai's answer to Disneyland, is a massive $5 billion complex with 50 hotels and a theme park as well as an artificial rain forest under an enormous glass dome. This 180 million square foot project is separated into six lands (Downtown, Eco-Tourism World, Retail World, Attractions World, Sports World and Leisure World), with sub-subsections of the park including an Arabian Theme Park, Aviation World, Dinosaur World, Motor Racing World, and the Pharaoh's Theme Park. London's Natural History Museum is being contracted to design displays and attractions for Dinosaur World. Most projects planned on the site will be opened during 2008.

Dubailand is typical of the sort of public-private partnership that has investors so in love with the emirate. The Dubai government will, according to early figures released, invest around $700 million in Dubailand's infrastructure. Most of the project's capital will come from the private sector. It is an opportunity to which the private secor has responded. The Dubai Development and Investment Authority, which is managing the Dubailand project, has already made major gains. Three prominent UAE investors - Abdul Rahim Al-Zarooni, Abdul Rahman Falaknaz and Abdul Rahman Bukhatir - quickly formed a consortium to develop the $735 million Dubai Sports City.

This will encompass a 25,000 capacity dedicated cricket stadium, an indoor arena for extreme and leisure sports which will accommodate 10,000 spectators, a 10,000 seat multipurpose indoor stadium for all hard court games, ice hockey, concerts and events, a 25,000 capacity multipurpose outdoor stadium for rugby/soccer and track and field events and an outdoor hockey field.

In addition, the project calls for sports academies, Victory Heights golf residential development, international schools and a shopping mall, all set for completion by the end of 2007. Recently opened was the Manchester United Soccer School, while the International Cricket Council (ICC) has moved its headquarters there from Lords in Britain.

The 55-million square metre Dubai Golf City will contain six world class themed signature golf courses, a six-star luxury resort and spa inspired by Arabian architecture, 700 architecturally rich luxury mansions and villas, and 18 themed golf villages containing 2,750 townhouses and chalets. Construction of the £1 billion development is scheduled to start in 2006, with completion expected in 2009.

Elsewhere under development are the $1.6 billion Dubai Festival City, the Middle East's largest privately-funded, mixed-use development, and the Lost City, a re-recreation of a series of old lost cities from different parts of the ancient world

"Dubai is not just about the best development, we have not lost our focus on lifestyle," says Sheikh Ahmed bin Rashid Al Maktoum. "The Dubai and UAE governments were always at the forefront of doing what is best for mankind. As recently as this year, we were proud that the UAE government donated $100 million to earthquake relief in Pakistan for example.

"Dubai has been focused on the future, but we have not lost sight of what is important."

Sheikh Ahmed was referring to Dubai Healthcare City aimed at turning Dubai into a global hub for specialised healthcare where patients will recover in an atmosphere of a five star hotel, and also to Dubai Humanitarian City. The latter, launched on September 8, 2003, focuses on providing a much-needed non-political global platform in the region for facilitating humanitarian efforts. This will establish Dubai as a regional hub for global humanitarian assistance, an operational and logistical hub for aid agencies in the region.

Spread over a vast area of 3.6 million square feet, Dubai Humanitarian City is a station for more than 35 different regional and international aid agencies as well as non-government organisations involved with providing humanitarian services throughout the world. These organisations operating from the city work in fields such as food, agriculture, health, children, education, women and humanitarian services. Dubai Humanitarian City provides all such aid organisations with a unique logistical location from where to store, stockpile and distribute aid cargo via sea, land or air to locations around the world.

A stamp of global approval was received when the United Nations Joint Logistics Centre (UNJLC) was also one of the first UN organisations to set up operations in DHC. UNJLC is a UN inter-agency emergency response mechanism for major humanitarian disasters. The role of the UNJLC is to optimise and complement the logistics capabilities of UN agencies and NGOs within a well-defined crisis area for the benefit of the ongoing humanitarian operation.

"Until his passing, Sheikh Maktoum remained at the heart of efforts to play a role within the international community as best that we can, given our relatively small size both geographically and in terms of population," says Sheikh Ahmed. "I believe that Dubai Humanitarian City, which was an initiative born out of a commitment to that vision, offers a prime example of Dubai and the UAE's commitment to mankind."

While these innovations — particularly Dubai Humanitarian City — are putting Dubai on the map, at home the city and its government must now keep their eyes on the drive for modernisation and ensure that the Emirates can compete in the increasingly competitive international environment.

If one project alone can be seen to sum up this vision it is, arguably, not one of the astonishing construction projects that is transforming the city, but in the less glamorous area of public services.

Coping with this influx of population, especially when one considers that one project alone will double the developed area of Dubai, is a remarkable feat. Failure in providing roads, water, electricity, sewerage collection and the entire spectrum of social services would lead a failure of the Dubai project as a whole. This less visible and certainly less recognised facet of development, in no short measure, falls to Dubai Municipality. Formed half a century ago to cope with the burgeoning demands of a sheikhdom with 30,000 residents, today the organisation cares for an emirate of over one million.

"Dubai's population is increasing at an average of 6% a year, a figure that is due to increase," says Dr Abdul Qader Al Shaibani of Dubai Municipality.

The population explosion in Dubai has not come without its challenges. Under Sheikh Hamdan, Dubai Municipality's budget has grown to exceed $650 million per year, from which around 90% is allocated for infrastructure development. This is headlined by a five-year development plan that allots some $2 billion for roads and bridges, $3.4 billion for the Light Rail Transport project, $300 million for Drainage and Irrigation projects and $700 million for public projects.

"The five year plan aims to keep Dubai ahead of the massive development that we see today," says Dr Al Shaibani. "It is quite a responsibility."

Dubai's road network is among the most modern in the world with a total length nearing 10,000 lane kilometres and an investment, to date, of $2.5 billion. Between 2007 to 2010 this figure will be almost doubled as Dubai Municipality plans to introduce an intelligent transportation system (ITS) that includes a dynamic navigation system and variable sign messages. Dubai's ITS will be the most advanced in any city around the world.

"A generation ago the demands on Dubai Municipality were relatively minor compared to today," says Sheikh Hamdan. "The city must be prepared correctly for this current wave of expansion and, overall, I am pleased with the way Dubai Municipality has coped with the strains of a rapidly expanding population and the base of services and infrastructure that must be in place."

While people can point to Burj Dubai or The Palm and see radical evidence of Dubai's progress, Dubai Municipality and its employees are the unsung heroes, behind the scenes, ensuring that such enormous developments are backed up by world class infrastructure. Who, for example, is aware that expenditure on irrigation and drainage projects had exceeded $1.5 billion?

However that low-key image somewhat changed when Dubai Municipality recently awarded the contract for one of the most biggest projects that will ever transform the emirate. In order to improve transportation efficiency Dubai Municipality recently signed contracts on a $3.4 billion Light Rail Transit System, a fully automated and driverless system that will run over 67 kilometres, with two lines serving 45 stations. It will be operational in the beginning of 2010.

The Red Line will run from Rashidiya to Jebel Ali, and the Green Line, between Dubai Airport Free Zone and Dubai Healthcare City. Around 32,000 passengers will travel on the Red Line hourly, while 22,000 passengers will travel on the Green Line each hour. It is projected that Dubai Metro will eventually handle 1.85 million travellers per day by 2020.

"The emirate would have faced complete gridlock in the future if solutions to its transport challenges, such as a Metro, had not been addressed quickly," says Dr Al Shaibani.

It is strategic thinking, grand (but plausible) ideas and a willingness to invest in the absolute best in infrastructure, which has transformed Dubai, not only in the new Millennium, but a generation ago. There may be a difference in scale, but the parallels in thinking are clear. Around be a difference in scale, but the parallels in thinking are clear. Around the region and in the financial capitals of the world the doubters remain. How can this be possible? Can the boom last? Can the government of Dubai sustain this extraordinary level of development?

"They should not look at what we have achieved," says Sheikh Mohammed, "but what we will achieve."

593

Epilogue

The Quiet Statesman

The essence of statesmanship is not a rigid adherence to the past,
but a prudent and probing concern for the future.
— Hubert H. Humphrey, statesman

Sheikh Maktoum bin Rashid Al Maktoum could perhaps be described as the quiet man of UAE politics. Despite being Vice President and Prime Minister of the UAE and Ruler of Dubai, he shunned the spotlight and preferred to make his contribution to his nation in a quiet, diplomatic way. Yet his presence was always felt.

It had always been so. In the summer of 1958 the inauguration of Sheikh Rashid had seen his eldest son and heir apparent forced into the spotlight for the first time aged 15, when he made his first public speech at an event to mark the accession of the new Ruler of Dubai. During this speech Sheikh Maktoum is recalled as being faltering and less than comfortable. In the near half century since then, Sheikh Maktoum grew into a statesman whose style was to discharge his duties in private. The parallels between two generations of leadership are quite apparent.

"Sheikh Rashid instilled in his sons - and indeed the Maktoum family as a whole - his guiding principals. I think we have seen abundant evidence of that in the modern leadership of Dubai," says Sheikh Mohammed bin Khalifa Al Maktoum. Anita Mehra Homayoun adds: "Sheikh Rashid was old school, a role model, and the secret of Dubai's success is its Ruling family. Sheikh Rashid passed on his compassionate, progressive leadership style. Sheikh Maktoum was, in so many ways, like his father, and one can see so much of Sheikh Rashid in Sheikh Mohammed."

Colm McLoughlin says; "Under Sheikh Rashid and Sheikh Maktoum, and under Sheikh Mohammed, there has never been heavy handed political interference. The business is totally independent and there is absolute freedom. That has always been Dubai's success, its

Sheikh Maktoum bin Rashid Al Maktoum.

Rulers are concerned only with what is good for the nation."

On January 3, 2006, Sheikh Maktoum died, aged 62. His funeral became a state occasion as international leaders poured into Dubai to pay their respects. Of all the public tributes paid, and amid a plethora of statements and newspaper profiles, arguably the keenest assessment of what had made Sheikh Maktoum such a success in power came from former British ambassador Anthony Harris, who stated; "In his quiet way, Sheikh Maktoum was a pillar of the federation. He...was remarkable for an Arab leader because he allowed his younger brothers to have a higher profile."

As his father a generation earlier, Sheikh Maktoum had ruled by consensus, allowing the talents of his brothers to shine. Indeed, where the Sheikh Rashid era had been dominated by one Camelot, modern Dubai had the benefit of several, as each of the brothers drew around them the best and the brightest that they encountered. Sheikh

The passing of Sheikh Maktoum was a state occassion that brought to Dubai many national and international leaders. Among those pictured are UAE President Sheikh Khalifa bin Zayed Al Nahayn, King Abdullah bin Hussain Al Hashemi of Jordan, King Mohammed of Morocco, Sheikh Sultan bin Mohammed Al Qassimi, Ruler of Sharjah, Sheikh Hamad bin Mohammed Al Sharqi, Ruler of Fujairah, Sheikh Hamdan, Sheikh Mohammed bin Khalifa Al Maktoum and Sheikh Mansoor bin Zayed Al Nahyan.

Maktoum's success was not only his quiet and effective statesmanship on a national and international level, but the inclusive nature of his era in power.

As it had a generation earlier, the burden of leadership of Dubai passed smoothly to another member of the Maktoum family. Sheikh Mohammed bin Rashid Al Maktoum had already established his credentials as a leader and a man with a decisive vision of the future. Dubai is set to enter the most remarkable period of its history.

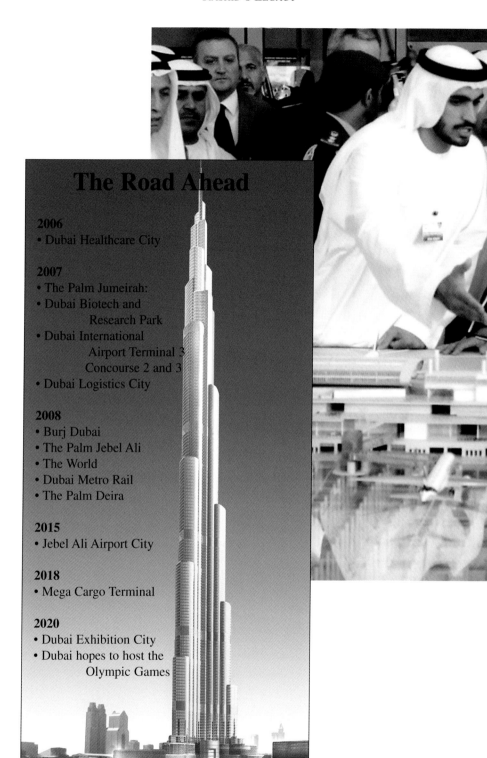

The Road Ahead

2006
• Dubai Healthcare City

2007
• The Palm Jumeirah:
• Dubai Biotech and
       Research Park
• Dubai International
       Airport Terminal 3
       Concourse 2 and 3
• Dubai Logistics City

2008
• Burj Dubai
• The Palm Jebel Ali
• The World
• Dubai Metro Rail
• The Palm Deira

2015
• Jebel Ali Airport City

2018
• Mega Cargo Terminal

2020
• Dubai Exhibition City
• Dubai hopes to host the
       Olympic Games

The new UAE Vice President and Prime Minister and Ruler of Dubai, Sheikh Mohammed has a reputation as an arch-moderniser. He is pictured here reviewing plans for expansion at Dubai International Airport, along with Sheikh Ahmed bin Saeed Al Maktoum, Anita Mehra Homayoun and Khalfan M. Belhoul. (Inset) The new Ruler acceds at a time when the emirate is set to see unprecedented growth. The accompanying image summarises many of the mega-projects that will be completed over the next decade.

Dramatis Persona

Al Ali, Mohammed Abdul Rahim	Ministry of Defence official
Al Assad, Bashar	President of Syria
Al Assad, Hafez	President of Syria, 1971-2000
Al Banna, Ahmed	Dubai government official
Al Bitar, Uday	Legal advisor to Sheikh Rashid
Al Futtaim, Majid	Part of 'Camelot' Majlis, businessman
Al Gergawi, Mohammed	Minister of State for Cabinet Affairs CEO of Dubai Holdings
Al Ghurair, Abdullah	Part of 'Camelot' Majlis, businessman
Al Ghurair, Saif Ahmed	Part of 'Camelot' Majlis, businessman
Al Gurg, Easa Saleh	UAE Ambassador to Great Britain
Al Habtoor, Khalaf	Part of 'Camelot' Majlis, businessman
Al Hashemi, Abdullah bin Hussein	King of Jordan
Al Hashemi, Hussein bin Talal	King of Jordan, 1952-99
Al Khalifa, Isa bin Salman	Emir of Bahrain, 1961-99
Al Khalifa, Hamad bin Isa	King of Bahrain
Al Khalifa, Salman bin Hamad	Emir of Bahrain, 1942-61
Al Khateeb, Zuhdi	Headmaster at Al Saeedia School
Al Majid, Juma	Part of 'Camelot' Majlis, businessman
Al Maktoum, Ahmed bin Obaid	Sheikh Saeed's father-in-law
Al Maktoum, Ahmed bin Rashid	Deputy Chief of Dubai Police and General Security
Al Maktoum, Ahmed bin Saeed	Chairman and Chief Executive, Emirates President, Dubai Department of Civil Aviation
Al Maktoum, Buti bin Suhail	Sixth Ruler of Dubai, 1906-12
Al Maktoum, Hamdan bin Rashid	Minister of Finance and Industry of UAE, Deputy Ruler of Dubai
Al Maktoum, Hasher bin Maktoum	Third Ruler of Dubai, 1859-86
Al Maktoum, Juma bin Maktoum	Senior ruling family member
Al Maktoum, Khalifa bin Saeed	Brother of Sheikh Rashid
Al Maktoum, Maktoum bin Buti	First Ruler of Dubai, 1833-52
Al Maktoum, Maktoum bin Hasher	Fifth Ruler of Dubai, 1894-06
Al Maktoum, Maktoum bin Rashid	Ninth Ruler of Dubai, 1990-2006
Al Maktoum, Mohammed bin Khalifa	Chairman of Dubai Lands Department
Al Maktoum, Mohammed bin Rashid	Vice President and Prime Minister, Tenth Ruler of Dubai
Al Maktoum, Obaid bin Juma	Headman of Henjam island
Al Maktoum, Rashid bin Maktoum	Fourth Ruler of Dubai, 1886-94
Al Maktoum, Rashid bin Saeed	Eighth Ruler of Dubai, 1958-90
Al Maktoum, Saeed bin Buti	Second Ruler of Dubai, 1852-59
Al Maktoum, Saeed bin Maktoum	Seventh Ruler of Dubai, 1912-58
Al Maktoum, Suhayl bin Buti	Cousin of Sheikh Saeed

Al Moalla, Rashid bin Ahmed	Ruler of Umm Al Quwain
Al Moalla, Ahmed bin Rashid	Ruler of Umm Al Quwain, 1929-81
Al Moalla, Hamad bin Ibrahim	Ruler of Umm Al Quwain, 1923-29
Al Muntafiq, Saeed	Dubai government official
Al Nahyan, Abdullah bin Zayed	UAE Foreign Minister
Al Nahyan, Hamdan bin Hamdan	Brother-in-law of Sheikh Rashid
Al Nahyan, Hamdan bin Zayed	Ruler of Abu Dhabi, 1912-22.
Al Nahyan, Hazza bin Sultan	Brother of Sheikh Zayed bin Sultan Al Nahyan
Al Nahyan, Khalifa bin Zayed	UAE President, Ruler of Abu Dhabi
Al Nahyan, Latifa bint Hamdan	Wife of Sheikh Rashid
Al Nahyan, Mohammed bin Zayed	Crown Prince of Abu Dhabi
Al Nahyan, Saqr bin Zayed	Ruler of Abu Dhabi, 1926-28
Al Nahyan, Shakhbut bin Sultan	Ruler of Abu Dhabi, 1928-66
Al Nahyan, Zayed bin Khalifa	Ruler of Abu Dhabi, 1855-1909
Al Nahyan, Zayed bin Sultan	President of UAE, 1971-2004
Al Naboodah, Mohammed	Dubai businessman
Al Naboodah, Khalifa	Part of 'Camelot' Majlis, businessman
Al Nuaimi, Humaid bin Rashid	Ruler of Ajman
Al Qassimi, Lubna Khalid Sultan	UAE Minister for Economy and Planning
Al Qassimi, Khalid bin Mohammed	Ruler of Sharjah, 1965-71
Al Qassimi, Saqr bin Mohammed	Ruler of Ras Al Khaimah
Al Qassimi, Saqr bin Sultan	Ruler of Sharjah, 1951-65
Al Qassimi, Sultan bin Mohammed	Ruler of Sharjah
Al Qassimi, Sultan bin Salim	Ruler of Ras Al Khaimah, 1921-48
Al Qassimi, Sultan bin Saqr	Deputy Ruler of Ras Al Khaimah
Al Ragabani, Saeed Mohammed	Minister of Agriculture and Fisheries
Al Owais, Ali	Part of 'Camelot' Majlis, businessman
Al Owais, Mohammed Ali	Businessman
Al Sabah, Abdullah Al Salim	Emir of Kuwait, 1950-65
Al-Sabah, Jaber Al-Ahmed	Emir of Kuwait, 1977-06
Al Saud, Abdullah ibn Abdul Aziz	King of Saudi Arabia
Al Saud, Fahd ibn Abdul Aziz	King of Saudi Arabia, 1982-2005
Al Saud, Faisal ibn Abdul Aziz	King of Saudi Arabia, 1964-75
Al Saud, Khalid bin Abdul Aziz	King of Saudi Arabia, 1975-82
Al Saud, Saud ibn Abdul Aziz	King of Saudi Arabia, 1953-64
Al Sayegh, Hassan Mirza	Dubai education pioneer
Al Sayegh, Mirza	Deputy Chairman, Oilfields Supply Centre
Al Shamsi, Abdulaziz Nasser R.	UAE Ambassador to the United Nations
Al Sharqi, Hamad bin Mohammed	Ruler of Fujariah
Al Sharqi, Mohammed bin Hamad	Ruler of Fujariah, 1932-74
Al-Thani, Ahmed bin Ali	Emir of Qatar, 1960-72
Al Thani, Hamad bin Khalifa	Emir of Qatar
Al Thani, Khalifa bin Hamad	Emir of Qatar, 1972-95
Abbas-Hoveyda, Amir	Iranian Prime Minister, 1965-77
Abdulatif, Isa bin	Former British Residency Agent
Alabbar, Mohammed	Chairman, Emaar Properties

Alexander the Great	King of Macedon, 336-323 BC
Allen, Neville	Engineer, Sir William Halcrow
Arafat, Yasser	Chairman of Palestinian Authority 1993-04
Baker, James	Former United States Secretary of State
Belselah, Ibrahim	Dubai government official
Benny, Hillary	Non-Commissioned Officer, Mons Officer Cadet School
Bhutto, Zulfikar Ali	Pakistan President, 1971-73
Caligula	Roman Emperor, 37-41 AD
Chernenko, Konstantine	Soviet President, 1984-85
Chetwynd-Stapylton, R G H	Officer, Mons Officer Cadet School
Churchill, Winston	British Prime Minister, 1940-45 and 1951-55
Craig, James	Former British Political Agent
Crawford, Stewart	Former British Political Resident in Bahrain
Codrai, Ronald	Photographer and illustrator
Cox, Percy	Former British Political Agent
Curzon, George Nathaniel	Viceroy of India,1898-1905
Dalmuk, Muhammad bin	Philanthropist and pearl merchant
Drai, Humaid bin	Former Dubai government official
Duff, Bill	Advisor to Sheikh Rashid
Doleh, Zakariah	Property developer
Douglas-Home, Alec	Former British Foreign Secretary
Eden, Anthony	British Prime Minister, 1955-57
Elizabeth II	Queen of Great Britain
Emara, Hashim Abu	Headmaster, Al Saeedia School
Flanagan, Maurice	Emirates Execuitve Vice Chairman
Gorbachev, Mikhail	USSR leader, 1985-91
Hahn, Dr Kurt	Founder, Gordonstoun School
Hamza, Kamal	First head, Dubai Municipality
Hawley, Donald	Former British Political Resident
Hawley, James	Former British Political Agent
Hannus, E.J.	Former British Political Resident in Gulf
Healey, Dennis	Former British Minister of Defence, Chancellor
Heath, Edward	British Prime Minister, 1970-74
Heidenstram, Phillip	Officer, Mons Officer Cadet School
Hindi, Mohidin bin	Former Director General, Dubai Department of Civil Aviation
Hitler, Adolf	Chancellor of Germany, 1934-45
Hurd, Douglas	Former British Foreign Secretary
Hussein, Saddam	President of Iraq, 1979-2003
Lulla, L R	Dubai hotelier
Khalifa, Kraif	Media advisor to Sheikh Rashid
Kharbash, Dr Mohammed bin	Minister of State for Financial and Industrial Affairs
Khomeini, Ayatollah Ruholla	Spiritual leader of Iran, 1979-89
Kier, William Grant	British naval commander

Penhaligon, Arthur	King of the Britons
Lootah, Ali Hussain	Executive Chairman, Dubai Shopping Festival
Luce, William	Former British Political Agent
MacMillan, Harold	British Prime Minister, 1957-63
McCaully, Donald	Former Senior Medical Officer, Trucial States
Mikimoto, Kokichi	Japanese co-inventor of the cultured pearl
Mirhashim, Mohammed	Dubai businessman
Mise, Tatsuhei	Japanese inventor of the cultured pearl
Moosa, Ahmed	Part of 'Camelot' Majlis, businessman
Mubarak, Hosni	President of Egypt
Nasser, Gamal Abdul	President of Egypt, 1954-70
Nishikawa, Tokichi	Japanese co-inventor of the cultured pearl
Nowfal, Dr Sayyid	Former Secretary General of the Arab League
Pahlavi, Mohammed Reza Shah	Shah of Iran, 1941-79
Pahlavi, Riza Shah,	Shah of Iran, 1925-41
Ptolemaeus, Claudius	'Ptolemy', Greek geographer
Roberts, Goronwy	Former British Minister
Sadat, Anwar	President of Egypt, 1970-81
Said, Qaboos bin	Sultan of Oman
Saleh, Abdullah	Part of 'Camelot' Majlis, Chairman, National Bank of Dubai
Seddiqi, Abdulmagied	Dubai businessman
Selwyn, Lloyd	Former British Secretary of State
Sharon, Ariel	Former Israeli Prime Minister
Sukat, Hamad bin	Confidante of Sheikh Rashid
Sulayem, Ahmed bin	Part of 'Camelot' Majlis
Sulayem, Khalid bin	Director General, Dubai Tourism and Commerce Marketing
Sulayem, Sultan bin	Chairman, Nakheel. Execuitve Chairman, Ports Customs and Free Zones Corp
Suf, Zayed bin	Headman of Dubai 1920's
Tamim, Dhahi Khalfan	Chief of Dubai Police
Taryam, Dr Abdullah Omram	Former Minister of Education
Thesiger, Wilfred	British traveller and explorer
Treadwell, James	Former British Political Agent
Tripp, J P	Former British Political Agent
Trump, Donald	American property tycoon
Tullock, Eric	Senior engineer, Dubai government
Ul-Haq, Mohammed Zia	Pakistan President, 1978–88
Wiggin, Charles	Former Grenadier Guards Officer
Wilson, Harold	British Prime Minister, 1964-70 and 1974-76
Yeltsin, Boris	President of Russia, 1991-99

604

Abbreviations

AD	Anno Domini (Latin)
ADDF	Abu Dhabi Defence Force
ADF	Arab Deterrent Force
AHS	African Horse Sickness
AOPEC	Arab Organisation of Petroleum Exporting Countries
ARPANET	Advanced Research Projects Agency Network
ASRY	Arab Ship Repair Yard
ATM	Arabian Travel Market
BAC	British Aircraft Corporation
BBC	British Broadcasting Corporation
BBME	British Bank of the Middle East
BC	Before Christ
BD	Bahraini Dinar
BOAC	British Overseas Airways Corporation
BP	British Petroleum
BPD	Barrels Per Day
BPSNC	Bombay and Persia Steam Navigation Company
CBA	Curragh Bloodstock Agency
CBE	Commander of the Order of the British Empire
CEO	Chief Executive Officer
CERN	European Particle Physics Network
CIS	Commonwealth of Independent States
CNBC	Consumer News and Business Channel
CNN	Cable News Network
CONOCO	American Continental Company
DAX	Deutscher Aktien Index
DC	District of Columbia
DCA	Department of Civil Aviation
DEC	Dubai Electricity Company
DTCM	Department of Tourism and Commerce Marketing
DTCPB	Dubai Tourism and Commerce Promotion Board
DC-3	Douglas DC-3 (aircraft)
DDF	Dubai Defence Force
DDF	Dubai Duty Free
DDIA	Dubai Development and Investment Authority
DIFC	Dubai International Financial Centre
DIFCA	Dubai International Financial Centre Authority
DIFX	Dubai Financial Exchange
DIMC	Dubai International Marine Club
DIC	Dubai Internet City
DHCC	Dubai Healthcare City
DMC	Dubai Media City

DMCC	Dubai Metals and Commodities Centre
DNATA	Dubai National Air Travel Agency
DPA	Dubai Ports Authority
DPC	Dubai Petroleum Company
Dr	Doctor
DSF	Dubai Shopping Festival
DUBAL	Dubai Aluminum Company
DUCAB	Dubai Cable Company
DUGAS	Dubai Gas Company
DWT	Deadweight (Tonnage)
DWTC	Dubai World Trade Centre
EMI	Electric and Musical Industries Ltd
ERA	Emirates Racing Association
EU	European Union
FDI	Foreign Direct Investment
FNC	Federal National Council
GCC	Gulf Cooperation Council
GDP	Gross Domestic Product
GITEX	Gulf Information Technology Exhibition
GNP	Gross National Product
GSA	General Sales Agent
HIV	Human Immuno-deficiency Virus.
HMI	Harvard Medical International
HMS	His/Her Majesty's Ship
HP	Hewlett-Packard
HSBC	Hong Kong and Shanghai Banking Corporation
IBM	International Business Machines
ICC	International Cricket Council
ICT	Information and Communications Technology
IMF	International Monetary Fund
IT	Information Technology
ITC	Imperial Trading Corporation
ITS	Intelligent Transportation System
JAFZ	Jebel Ali Free Zone
JAL	Japan Airlines
JANET	Joint Academic Network
JRA	Japan Red Army
JUO	Junior Under Officer
KFOR	Kosovo Force
LNG	Liquid Natural Gas
MBA	Master of Business Administration
MBC	Middle East Broadcasting Corporation
MBE	Member of the Order of the British Empire
MEA	Middle East Airlines
MoD	Ministry of Defence
MV	Merchant Vessel

NASDAQ	National Association of Securities Dealers Automated Quotation
NATO	North Atlantic Treaty Organisation
NBD	National Bank of Dubai
NGO	Non Governmental Organisation
NSFNET	National Science Foundation Network
NTRA	National Thoroughbred Racing Association
NZTE	New Zealand Trade and Enterprise
NYRA	New York Racing Association
OECD	Organisation for Economic Cooperation and Development
OIC	Organisation of the Islamic Conference
OPEC	Organisation of Petroleum Exporting Countries
PCFZ	Ports, Customs and Free Zone
PCL	Petroleum Concessions Ltd
PFC	Provisional Federal Council
PGA	Professional Golfers' Association
PLO	Palestine Liberation Organisation
PNA	Palestinian National Authority
RAND	Research And Development Corporation
RAF	Royal Air Force
Rs	Rupee
S&P	Standard & Poor's
TEU	Twenty-Foot Equivalent Units
TI	Transparency International
TOL	Trucial Oman Levies
TOS	Trucial Oman Scouts
TSDB	Trucial States Development Board
TSDF	Trucial States Development Fund
UACE	Union of Arab Coastal Emirates
UAE	Union of Arab Emirates
UAE	United Arab Emirates
UAR	United Arab Republic
UDF	Union Defence Force
UN	United Nations
UNICEF	United Nations Children's Fund
UNITAF	Unified Task Force
UNMIBH	United Nations Mission in Bosnia and Herzegovina
UNOSOM	United Nations Operation in Somalia
UNOSOM II	United Nations Operation in Somalia 2
UNSCOM	United Nations Special Commission in Iraq
US	United States
USS	United States Ship
USSR	Union of Soviet Socialist Republics
WAP	Wireless Application Protocol
WHO	World Health Organisation
WTO	World Trade Organisation

Glossary

Abbasid	Family descended from Abbas, uncle of the Prophet Mohammed
Abra	Water taxi
Abu	Father of
Al	The
Al Ardha	War dance
Al Kharabi	Children's game
Al Samaamik	UAE colloquial term for fishermen
Anna	One-fiftieth of one rupee
Aquifer	Underground layer of permeable rock
Ayatollah	Third level Shiia cleric
Baghila	Traditional Arab boat
Barasti	Home constructed of woven palm fronds
Barb	Type of horse breed
Bastikiyya	Wind-towers
Bedouin	Nomadic people of the deserts of Arabia
Bedu	Arabic word from which the name bedouin, means "inhabitant of the desert"
Bin	Son of
Bier	Flat frame, traditionally wooden used to carry a corpse for burial in a funeral procession
Bint	Daughter of
Bisht	Arabic male dress for formal occasion
Black Type	Top class horse races divided into standards
Boom	Type of traditional Arab boat
Broodmare	A female horse used for breeding
Burj	Tower
Cartography	Art or technique of making maps or charts
Charge d'Affaires	Senior diplomatic post
Cholera	Acute, diarrheal illness
Civil List	List of British Royal family members paid by the government
Classic	Elite race for thoroughbreds
Colt	Young male horse
Consort	Spouse of a monarch
Coup d'etat	Sudden overthrow of a government
Creek	Tidal basin
Dalouka	Large Arabic drums
Dhow	Small boat used by fishermen and traders
Dinar	Unit of currency used in Bahrain and Kuwait
Dirham	Unit of currency used in the UAE
Diwali	Hindu festival of lights

Diwan	Office of a state ruler
Dugong	Aquatic mammal also known as 'sea cow'
Durbar	Ceremony acknowledging sovereign as Emperor of India
Eid Al Adha	Islamic festival
Eid Al Fitr	Islamic festival
Emir	King/Prince
Emirate	Land ruled by an Emir or Sheikh
Fajr Salaat	Congregational dawn prayers
Falaj	Form of irrigation
Fateer	Bedouin cookies
Fateh	Conqueror
Fahrenheit	Temperature scale
Filly	Young female horse
First World	Developed, mostly western countries
Foal	Young horse, under the age of one
Frankincense	Fragrance from Boswellia tree
Gaba	Arabic football game
Gazelle	Slender-horned deer found in Asia and Africa
Gallebeyahs	Arabic male garment
Guinea(s)	Old British currency
Guano	Collected droppings of seabird or bats
Guppti	A tiny Arabic pipe
Gutra	Dominant head dress in the Gulf, expressing identity of an area or tribe
Group race	Top class thoroughbred races
Haban	Traditional dance
Hafit period	Period of human development, 2500–2000 BC
Hajj	Pilgrimage, month in the Islamic calendar
Hajji	One having made the pilgrimage
Harbiya	Traditional dance
Harise	Arab meat dish with wheat
Heir Apparent	Crown Prince
Hindi	Common language in India
Holy Quran	Holy book of Islamic faith
Houbara	Indigenous Arabian game bird
House of Saud	Term for the ruling family of Saudi Arabia
Hub	Common connection point
Huwaim	Children's game
Ibn	Son of
Imam	Religious leader
Inshallah	If God wills
Intifada	Popular uprising
Ivy League	Use to connote the academic excellence of top American universities
Iyala	Emirates version of Al Ardha

Jaulbaut	Traditional Arab boat
Jacinth	Red transparent zircon used as a gemstone
Jebel	Hill
Juvenile	Two-year-old thoroughbred horse
Kandoura	Traditional clothing used by men in the Gulf
Karat	Unit of measurement of gold in an alloy
Kerosene	Colourless flammable hydrocarbon liquid
Khamiri	Traditional dance
Khanjar	Traditional Arabian dagger
Khayali	Traditional dance
Knesset	Israeli parliament
Khobz	Bedouin bread
Koran	Islamic holy book
Kuttab	Religious school
Luhol	Children's game
Madinat	City
Majlis	Ruler's court, council
Malayalam	Dravidian language from Kerala, India
Mastigure	Spiney tailed lizard
Man-O-War	Naval vessel
Manumission	Legally protected release of slaves
Mated	Traditional dance
Mauser	German rifle
Mensaf	Traditional Bedouin meal of rice covered with beef or lamb, cooked with yogurt and pine nuts
Mezza	Platter of traditional Arabic foods
Midwakh	Small-bowled Arabic pipe
Mina	Port
Minaret	Tall, graceful spires of mosque
Moong	Indian dish
Mosque	Islamic house of prayer
Muezzins	Islamic crier who calls the faithful to prayer
Mutawwa	Religious man
Naft	To flow
Nafata	To flow
Nobel Laureate	Nobel Prize winner
Old Harrovian	Former pupil of Harrow School
Oleum	Oil
Persia	Historical name of Iran
Pharsis	Followers of the Zorastria religion
Pork Barrel	Politically motivated government funding
Prix	Prize
Prophet	Interpreter through whom God expresses his will
Qahdi	Religious man who enforces Shariah law
Pedigree	Chart of horse's ancestors
Peninsula	A region of land that juts into a body of water

611

Petra	Rock
Prophet	Religious spokesman for a cause, doctrine
Puri	Indian bread
Pushtu	Language spoken by ethnic Afghans
Ramadan	Month of fasting in the Islamic calendar
Red oxide	Mineral mined in the Gulf
Retainer	Servant
Riyal	Currency used in Saudi Arabia, Oman and Qatar
Rogue states	Term for alleged terror supporting countries
Rupee	Unit of currency
Sadaqat	Voluntary charity in Islam
Sambuk	Traditional Arabian boat
Shabab	Young man/men
Shah	Title bestowed upon Iranian leader
Shamal	Storm or strong desert wind
Sharia	Islamic law as prescribed in Holy Koran
Sheikh	Male member of a ruling/noble family
Sheikha	Female member of a ruling/noble family
Sheikhdom	Kingdom ruled by sheikh
Silk Route	Ancient trade route
Sira	Indian dish
Sloop	Naval vessel
Sponges	Aquatic, chiefly marine invertebrate animals
Spudded	Oil industry term
Stallion	Male horse to have produced offspring
Stud	Horse breeding farm
Sultan	King
Souq	Market
Tahtib	Traditional dance
Thobe	Arabic garment
Thoroughbred	Horse breed
Triple Crown	Classic racing series in the United States
Turk	North African breed of horse
Umm	Mother
Umra	Pilgrimage to Mecca outside Hajj
Viceroy	Governs a country as a substitute to monarch
Waber Al Jamal	Customary black robe of rulers
Wadi	Dried river bed
Wahhabi	A conservative form of Islam
Wali	Ruler's representative in a dependency
Whip	Party political enforcer in Parliament
Windtower	Gulf architectural feature for circulation of air
Yearling	One year old horse
Zakat	Religious tax
Ziggurat	Temple tower of the ancient Mesopotamian valley and Persia

Photographic Credits

222/223	Dubai Petroleum Company	352	Reuters
226	Al Bayan	354	Ministry of Health
229	Dubai Petroleum Company	357	Presidential Archives
231	Ahmed Al Dwaiaty	363	Presidential Archives
237	George Chapman	364	Khaleej Times
239	ADNOC	366	Dubai Petroleum Company
241	Simon Nicolas	367	Dubai Petroleum Company
242	Getty Images	369	Dubai Ports Authority
246/247	Dubai Municipality	371	Dubai Dry Docks
249	Khaleej Times	373	Dubai World Trade Centre
250	Dubai Ports Authority	377	Khaleej Times
252	Pakistan Navy	382	Ministry of Education
253	Dubai Municipality	385	Presidential Archives
255	George Chapman	388/389	Khaleej Times
256	Presidential Archives	392	Presidential Archives
259	Downing Street Archives	393	Presidential Archives
261	Dubai Petroleum Company	394	Mohammed Mirhashim
266/267	Presidential Archives	396	Presidential Archives
268	Presidential Archives	397	Matt Howard
270	Saif Ahmed Al Ghurair	399	Racing Post
272	Ruler's Diwan	401	Racing Post
274	Pakistan Navy	404	Keeneland
276	Mons Officer Cadet School	408	David Hastings
280/281	Hillary Benney	409	(top) Shadwell Farm
286	Presidential Archives		(bottom) Derrinstown Stud
288	Presidential Archives	412/413	David Hastings
292/293	Presidential Archives		(inset) Khaleej Times
297	Gordon Zola	417	Satish Seemar
303	Buckingham Palace Archives	419	David Hastings
306	Ministry of Defence	420	Emirates
311	Ministry of Defence	422	Khaleej Times
312	Downing Street Archives	426/427	Emirates
314/315	Presidential Archives	428	Presidential Archives
317	George Chapman	432	Dubai Ports Authority
318	Ministry of Defence	433	Dubai Ports Authority
322	Durham University	435	Buckingham Palace Archives
326/327	Presidential Archives	436	Downing Street Archives
331	Presidential Archives	438	Ramesh Shukla
333	Reuters	440	Khaleej Times
334/335	Presidential Archives	442	Khaleej Times
338	Presidential Archives	444	French Embassy
340/341	Federal National Council	450	Khaleej Times
345	Non-Aligned Movement	452	Dubai Petroleum Company
346	Ministry of Defence	457	Ministry of Defence
347	Sharjah Ruler's Diwan	458	Ministry of Defence
350	Presidential Archives	460	Reuters

462	Khaleej Times	572	Peter Langer -
465	Ministry of Defence		Associated Media Group
467	Khaleej Times	577	Dubai Media City
469	Ruler's Diwan	578	Elie Moukarzel
470	Department of Civil Aviation	583	Nakheel
474	Ministry of Defence	584	National Bank of Dubai
479	Emirates	592/593	Khaleej Times
480	Emirates	594	Khaleej Times
481	Dubai International Airport	596/597	Kassim Al Hammadi
482/483	Dubai International Airport	598/599	Department of Civil Aviation
486	DTCM	598	Gulf News
490	Dubai Police	604	Khaleej Times
492	Khaleej Times	608	Khaleej Times
494	Dubai Cement Company	613	Khaleej Times
495	Khaleej Times	639	Khaleej Times
498	Khaleej Times	640	Dubai Petroleum Company
499	Khaleej Times		
500/501	Khaleej Times		
503	Khaleej Times		
504	Khaleej Times		
508	Ministry of Defence		
509	Ministry of Defence		
512	Ministry of Defence		
518	Dubai Golf		
521	Khaleej Times		
523	Dubai Real Estate Centre		
524	Tejari.com		
528	Zayed University		
530/531	Gabriel Savit		
531	Emirates		
534/535	Trevor Jones		
538	Al Bayan		
540	Khaleej Times		
543	Khaleej Times		
545	Dubai Internet City		
548	Dubai Internet City		
552	Dubai Duty Free		
555	Konstantin von Wedelstaedt		
556	Khaleej Times		
561	Jumeirah		
562	Jumeirah		
563	Jumeirah		
564	Emaar		
567	Nakheel		
569	Trump Organisation		
570	Nakheel		

Bibliography

Newspapers and Periodicals
Australia: Sydney Morning Herald, West Australian **Bahrain**: Al Ayam, Bahrain Tribune, Gulf Daily News **Egypt**: Al-Ahram Weekly, Cairo Times **France**: Le Figaro, Le Monde, International Herald Tribune **Germany**: Der Spiegel **Great Britain**: Cambridge Evening News, The Economist, Financial Times, The Guardian, London Evening Standard, The Observer, The Racing Post, The Sporting Life, The Telegraph, The Times, The Sunday Times **Israel**: Al Quds Daily, Jerusalem Post **India**: Business Standard, Economic Times, Hindustan Times, Statesman, Times of India **Iran**: Al-Vefagh Arabic Daily, Iran Daily News, Iran News **Iraq**: Al-Iraqi, INA (Iraq News Agency), Iraq Daily **Japan**: Kyoto News, Tokyo Shimbun **Jordan**: Jordan Times, The Star **Kuwait**: Al Watan, Gulf Times, Kuwait Times **Lebanon**: An Nahar, Daily Star, L'Orient-Le Jour Líbano **Pakistan**: Dawn **Qatar**: Al Raya Newspaper, Al-Watan **Russia**: Moscow Times, Pravda **Singapore**: The Straits Times, Business Times **Sri Lanka**: Daily News, Ceylon Daily News **Saudi Arabia**: Asharq Al-Awsat, Al Watan, Riyadh Daily **Palestine**: Al-Hayat Al Jadedah, Al Ayyam, Palestine Times **United Arab Emirates**: Al Bayan, Al Ittihad, Gulf News, Khaleej Times **United States**: USA Today, Wall Street Journal, New York Post, New York Press Association, Washington Post **Pan-Middle East**: Al Hayat, Middle East Economic Digest (MEED).

News Agencies
Agence France-Presse, Associated Press, Australian Associated Press, China News Service, Deutsche Presse, Interfax News Agency, Official Jordanian News Agency, Reuters, Xinhua News Agency and Associated Press of Pakistan.

Websites
emirates.com, bbc.com, airteamimages.com, flightinternational.com, AMEinfo.com, cnn.com, wikipedia.org, forbes.com, gulfnews.com, uaeyearbook.com, airbus.com, sky.com, foxnews.com, abcnews.go.com, cbsnews.com, usatoday.com, reuters.com, washingtonpost.com, sciencenews.org, news.com.au, bloomberg.com

Compilations, Papers and Periodicals
The United Arab Emirates Yearbook (UAE Ministry of Information and Culture)
The Middle East (The Royal Institute of International Affairs)
Problems of the Modern Middle East (St Antony's College, Oxford)
Essays on the Economic History of the Middle East (Frank Cass)
The Middle East. A Political and Economic Survey (The Royal Institute)
Foundations of British Policy in the Middle East (Johns Hopkins Press, 1970)
Records from the British Administration in the Gulf:
                    The Office of Public Records and The British Library, London

Books

Abdullah, Muhammad Morsy, **The UAE. A Modern History** (Hurtwood Press, 1994)

Aburish, Said K, **Arafat: From Defender to Dictator** (Bloomsbury, 1998)

Al-Baharna, Hussain, **Legal Status of the Arabian Gulf States** (Manchester University Press, 1968)

Al-Khalil, Samir, **Republic of Fear** (Hutchinson-Radius, 1989)

Allen, Calvin J and Rigsbee, W. Lynn, **Oman Under Qaboos** (Frank Cass, 2000)

Almana, Mohammed, **Arabia Unified: A Portrait of Ibn Saud** (Hutchinson, 1980)

Amirsadeghi, Hossein, **The Security of the Persian Gulf** (Croom Helm, 1981)

Ayubi, Nazih, **Political Islam** (Routledge, 1991)

Blandford, Linda, **Oil Sheikhs** (London, 1976)

Butt, Gerald, **The Lion in the Sand** (Bloomsbury Publishing, 1995)

Cantwell Smith, Wilfred, **Islam in Modern History** (Princeton University, 1957)

Codrai, Ronald, **Dubai: An Arabian Album** (Motivate Publishing, 1992)

Crystal, Jill, **Oil and Politics in the Gulf** (Cambridge University Press, 1990)

Dunlop, D M, **Arab Civilisation to AD1500** (Praeger Publishers, 1971)

Dyck, Gertrude, **The Oasis** (Motivate Publishing, 1995)

Esposito, John L, **Political Islam** (Westview Press, 1997)

Field, Michael, **A Hundred Million Dollars A Day** (Sidgewick & Jackson, 1975)

Gowers, Andrew, **Arafat: The Biography** (Virgin, 1994)

Heard-Bay, Frauke, **From Trucial States to United Arab Emirates** (Longman, 1996)

Henderson, Edward, **This Strange Eventful History** (London, 1988)

Issawi, Charles, **The Economic History of the Middle East**

Kelly, J B, **Britain and the Persian Gulf 1795 - 1880** (Faber and Faber, 1968)

Kelly, J B, **Eastern Arabian Frontiers** (Faber and Faber, 1964)

Lacey, Robert, **The Kingdom: Arabia & The House of Sa'ud** (Avon, 1981)

Makki, Abbas, **Rashid: The Man Behind Dubai** (UAE, 1990)

Mann, Clarence C, **Abu Dhabi: Birth of an Oil Shaikhdom** (Khayats, 1969)

Mehr, Farhang, **A Colonial Legacy** (University Press of America, 1997)

Mostyn, Trevor, **Iran, Iraq and the Iranian Peninsula** (Facts on File, 1991)

Rajab, Jehan S, **Invasion Kuwait** (The Radcliffe Press, 1993)

Raviv, Moche, **Israel at Fifty** (Weidenfeld and Nicholson, 1998)

Rose, Kenneth, **Superior Person. A Portrait of Curzon** (Weybright and Talley, 1969)

Silverfarb, Daniel, **Britain's Informal Empire** (Oxford University Press, 1986)

Slater, Robert, **Rabin of Israel: Warrior for Peace** (Robson Books, 1996)

Tammam, Hamdi, **The Leader and the March** (UAE, 1981)

Taryam, A O, **The Establishment of the UAE 1950-85** (Croom Helm, 1987)

Taylor, Andrew, **Travelling the Sands** (Motivate Publishing, 1995)

Thesiger, Wilfred, **Arabian Sands** (Penguin, 1991)

Tomkinson, Michael, **The United Arab Emirates** (Tomkinson Publishing, 1975)

Wheatcroft, Andrew, **Sheikh Salman** (Kegan Paul International, 1995)

Zahlan, Rosmarie Said, **The Origins of the UAE** (Macmillan Press, 1978)

Zahlan, Rosmarie Said, **The Creation of Qatar** (Routledge, 1989)

Index

Acknowledgements

Rashid's Legacy has been a collaborative effort involving many individuals and the support of many companies. This project began with Sheikh Hamdan bin Rashid Al Maktoum. His trust was appreciated and his openness and candour the key to our being able to engage in a wide-ranging study.

Those who have witnessed or been part of this story offered unique insights and background that enriched the narrative. These include Sheikh Saqr bin Mohammed Al Qassimi, Sheikh Ahmed bin Rashid Al Maktoum, Sheikh Ahmed bin Saeed Al Maktoum, Sheikh Mohammed bin Khalifa Al Maktoum, Sheikh Mansoor bin Zayed Al Nahyan, Sheikh Nahyan bin Mubarak Al Nahyan and the late Sheikh Abdulaziz bin Mohammed Al Qassimi.

A book of the complexity and sensitivity of *Rashid's Legacy* would have been impossible without Mirza Al Sayegh, whose vision carried us forward and this book is in no short measure thanks to his support. Thank you Mr Al Sayegh.

This project evolved over a number of years and two of Europe's greatest statesmen — both of whom graced the international stage — offered their assistance. I speak of former British Prime Minister Sir Edward Heath and former Foreign Secretary Robin Cook. Both had a keen interest in the politics of this region and helped greatly in offering direction and often using their influence to help the author gain access to fresh sources and archives.

Special thanks must also to go to Mohammed Mirhashim, Mohammed Al Gergawi, Mohammed Alabbar, Ali Khalifa, Lt General Dhahi Khalfan Tamim, Saeed bin Mohammed Al Ragabani, Sultan bin Sulayem, Qassim Sultan, Khalid bin Sulayem, Abdulmagied Seddiqi, General Mohammed Abdul Rahim Al Ali, Ali Khamis Al Jafleh, Hussain Khansaheb, Khalaf Al Habtoor, Saeed Khalfan Al Ghaith, Easa Saleh Al Gurg, Mohammed Khalfan bin Kharbash, Abdulaziz Khansaheb, Khalifa Al Naboodah, Mohammed Rafie Al Mulla, Zakariah Doleh, Hamed bin Sukat, Abdullah Darwish, Saeed Hussain Al Muntafiq, Abdullah bin Mohammed Al Othman, Abdulaziz Al Ghurair, Ahmed Al Tayer, Saif Ahmed Al Ghurair, Khalifa Al Naboodah, Mohidin bin Hendi, Dr Abdullah Omran Taryam, Humaid bin Drai, Dr Omar bin Sulaiman, Khalaf Al Habtoor, Abdulaziz Nasser Al Shamsi, Hussain Ali Lootah, and Saeed Al Ghandi. A special word also for Jamal Al Huwairib for his personal interest in the history of the UAE and his gentle guidance.

We also acknowledge the support of Maurice Flanagan, Peter Hill, Sir Archie Lamb, Eric Tullock, Denis Healey, John L Dunlop, John Hawkins, Sergio Magnaldi, Andy Kay and the late Major Dick Hern. My profound admiration and acknowledgement must also go on record for George Chapman MBE. A remarkable man who has served Dubai for more than half a century.

From Mons Officer Cadet School I was privileged to meet Major A D B Brooks,

Major Richard G H Chetwynd Stapylton, Sergeant-Major Hillary Benney and Charles Wiggin. At The Bell School of Languages in Cambridge, Richard Rossner, Jim Kell, Jane Southwell and Issam Al Khayat provided valuable background. At Sheikh Saeed's House in Dubai, I am indepted to Dr Abdullah bin Jassim Al Muthairy and Hamad Saeed Al Mutaiwei. In Colombo, my research efforts were aided by the ever resourceful Ramzi Ali of Luxury Media International.

Generous with their time have been Ian Carless, Caroline Underwood, Ronnie Lazala, Gertrude Dyck, Elaine Emery, Wolfgang Goetz, Dr Ahmed Hassabulla El Haj, Abdullah bin Sukat, Wafa Al Khatib, Tammy Farha, Rashid Al Daouk, Hanif Rahemtullah, Elie Mazzawi, Bron Lancaster, Kevin Morrissey, Robert Nicholas, Gul Nizari, Maureen Rego, Wafa Ibrahim, Sir Anthony Harris and Satish Seemar. Insight was drawn from Dr Hussein Qandil, Dr Abdullah Al Taboor, Isa Humaid, Mohammed Al Ahli, Vahe Hanissian, Mahmood Saleh, Rashid bin Dafous, Neville Allen, Hashim Al Dabal, Rashid Al Daouk, Richard Blandy, Graeme Mac, Dr Sami Al-Sayrafi, Dr Michael Osborne, Ted Bassett, Phil Blizzard, John Ferguson, Wafaa Ibrahim, Rick Nichols, Rony Khalife, Jyotish Roy, Wahid Attala, John Marshall, Ayman Abdel-Wahab, Abdullah Khalifa, Malcolm Corrigan, Dr David Remple and Franko Vatterott.

Long term residents with a passion for the Emirates are always keen observers of the UAE, both from a position as an expatrate and as a personal stake holder in the narrative I am attempting to illustrate. In this category, I was privileged to work with Anita Mehra Homayoun, Tim Clark, Colm McLoughlin, Zakariah Doleh, G B Choithram Jethwani, L R Lulla, Saleem Sharifee and Anthea Grainger.

Many photographs for this book were generously provided by Mohammed Abdul Hammeed and Captain Humaid Al Naimi at the Ministry of Defence and Mohammed Galadari, Madhu Rao and the *incomparable* Aziz Ur Rehman at Khaleej Times, and Khalid bin Zayed at Dubai Municipality. We wish to put on record our sincere thanks to these individuals and organisations.

Additional illustrations were sourced via Mike Simon, David Hastings, CDI, Dona Haycraft, Emirates, Amina Abdullah Mirza Al Ghaffari, Mohammed Saeed Al Danhani, Younis Ali Kozan, Halima Al Qaz, George Geagea, Yukiko Aramaki, Joanna Morrow, Angela Davis, Peter Langer, Matt Barrett, Mohammed Saeed Al Danhani, Halima Al Qaz, Youris Ali Kozan, Vahe O. Hanssian, Dr Ahmed Hassabulla Elhag, Ali Khalifa, Hatta Fort Hotel, Carlton Towers Hotel (Dubai), Jumeriah, and The Presidential Court for Documentation and Research. Our thanks also to the management and staff of The British Library, The Public Records Office and HM The Queen's Archives in London for providing background documentation and many illustrations and photogaphs.

Producing *Rashid's Legacy* was far from a one man effort and needed the input of a great many people. The book was shaped in no small part by the efforts of an elite team of several historians, editors and academics. Primary among those are Dr Fatima Al Sayegh, Mike Simon, Barbara Saunders, Susan Wilson and Roger Thiedeman. I thank them for their patience and hard work.

My publishers Media Prima showed great professionalism. I commend the efforts of Mohammed Musleh, Leslie Cox, Elie Moukarzel, Ahmed Al Dwaiaty and Raju Maliekal at Media Prima (Dubai), and Paul Wilkin, Declan Heinz and Ben Harris at Media Prima (London).

Many organisations provided invaluable cooperation and assistance in the research process. Principal among these are the British Foreign and Commonwealth Office Library, the British Library, Downing Street, Buckingham Palace, Dubai Chamber of Commerce and Industry Library, Khaleej Times Library, the British Public Records Office, Gordonstoun School, Emirates News Agency (WAM), Al Bayan and Al Maktoum Hospital.

Rashid's Legacy would have been impossible to contemplate without our sponsors. Each has proven to be a partner in this project and Dubai Petroleum Company, Emirates, Nakheel, National Bank of Dubai, Jebel Ali Racecourse, Dubai Real Estate Centre, Dubai Duty Free and Damas have committed themselves to recording this remarkable story.

Within these organisations, I would thank William J. Way and Khamis Juma Bu Amim (Dubai Petroleum Company), Colm McLoughlin and Sinead El Sibai (Dubai Duty Free), Maurice Flanagan and Mike Simon (Emirates), Sultan bin Sulayem (Nakheel), Tawhid Abdullah and Samit Bhaita (Damas), Abdullah Saleh and Walid Al Massri (National Bank of Dubai) and Shareef Al Halawani (Dubai Real Estate Centre) for their personal and much valued contribution to making this project a success.

**Sheikh Rashid bin Saeed Al Maktoum
1912-1990**